AUTOMATIC MAIDEN

The Misato Residence's Maid

Art by Bunjuro Nakayama
Story by Bow Ditama

Los Angeles • Tokyo • London

Table of Contents

第1話 The Blooming Hyrdangea Garden

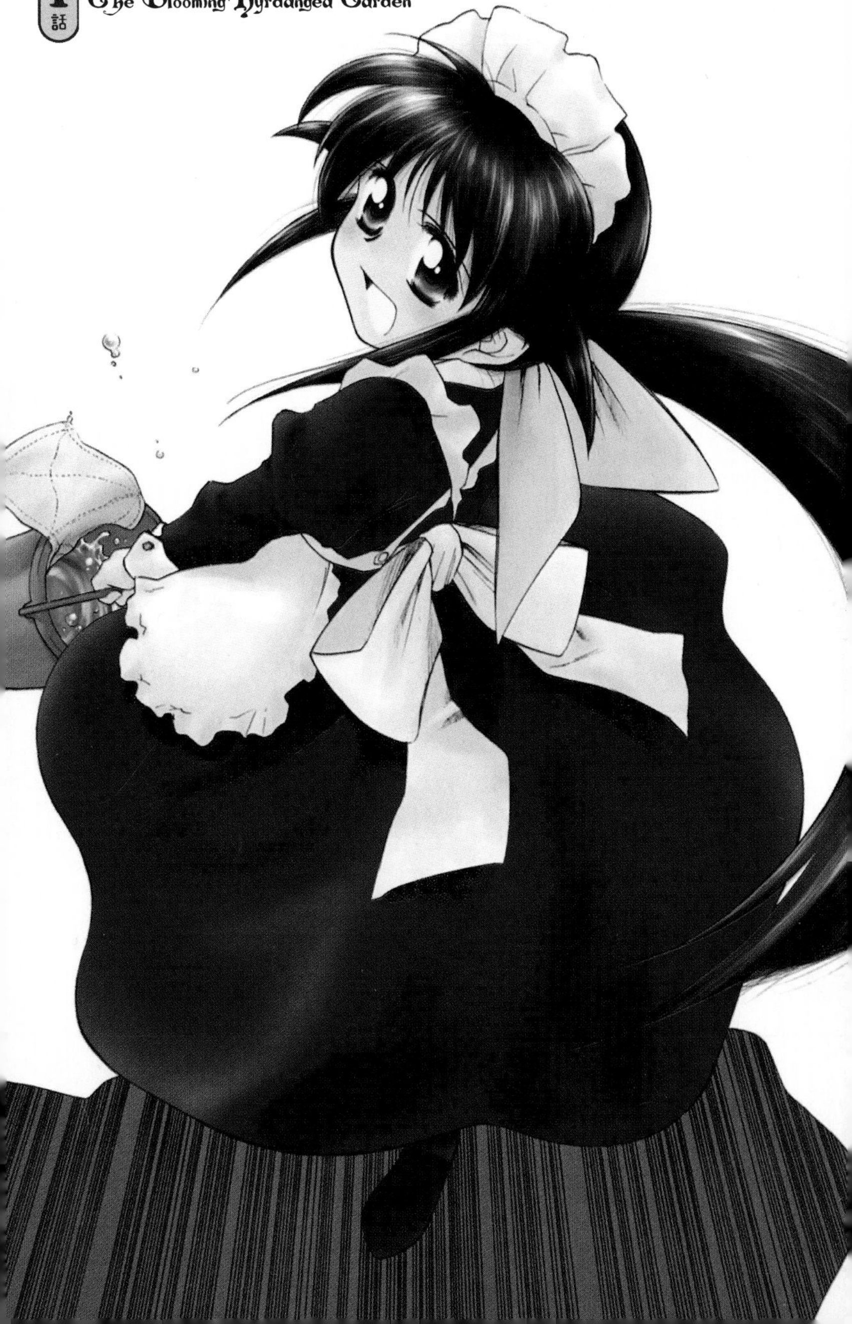

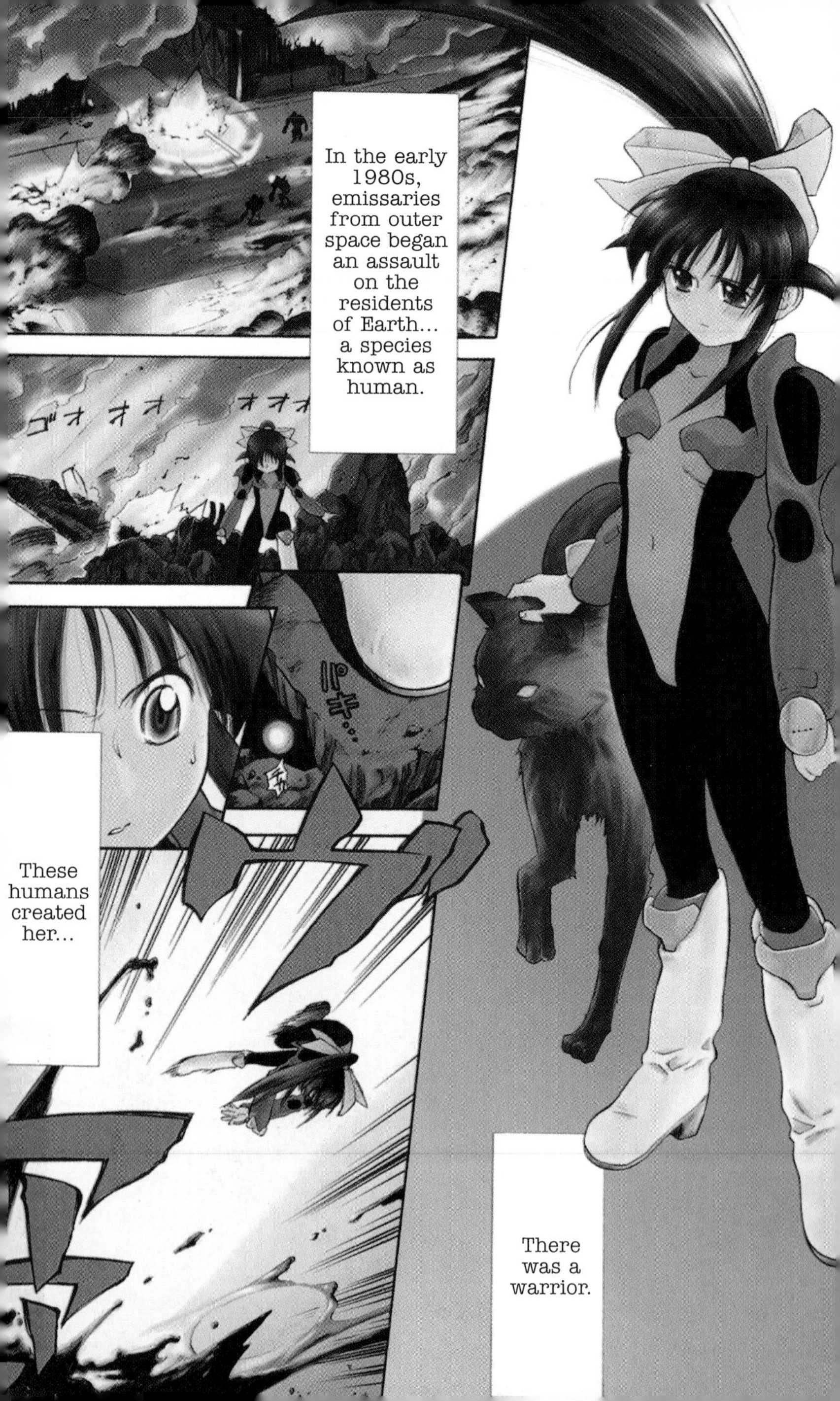
There was a warrior.
In the early 1980s, emissaries from outer space began an assault on the residents of Earth... a species known as human.
パキ…
These humans created her...

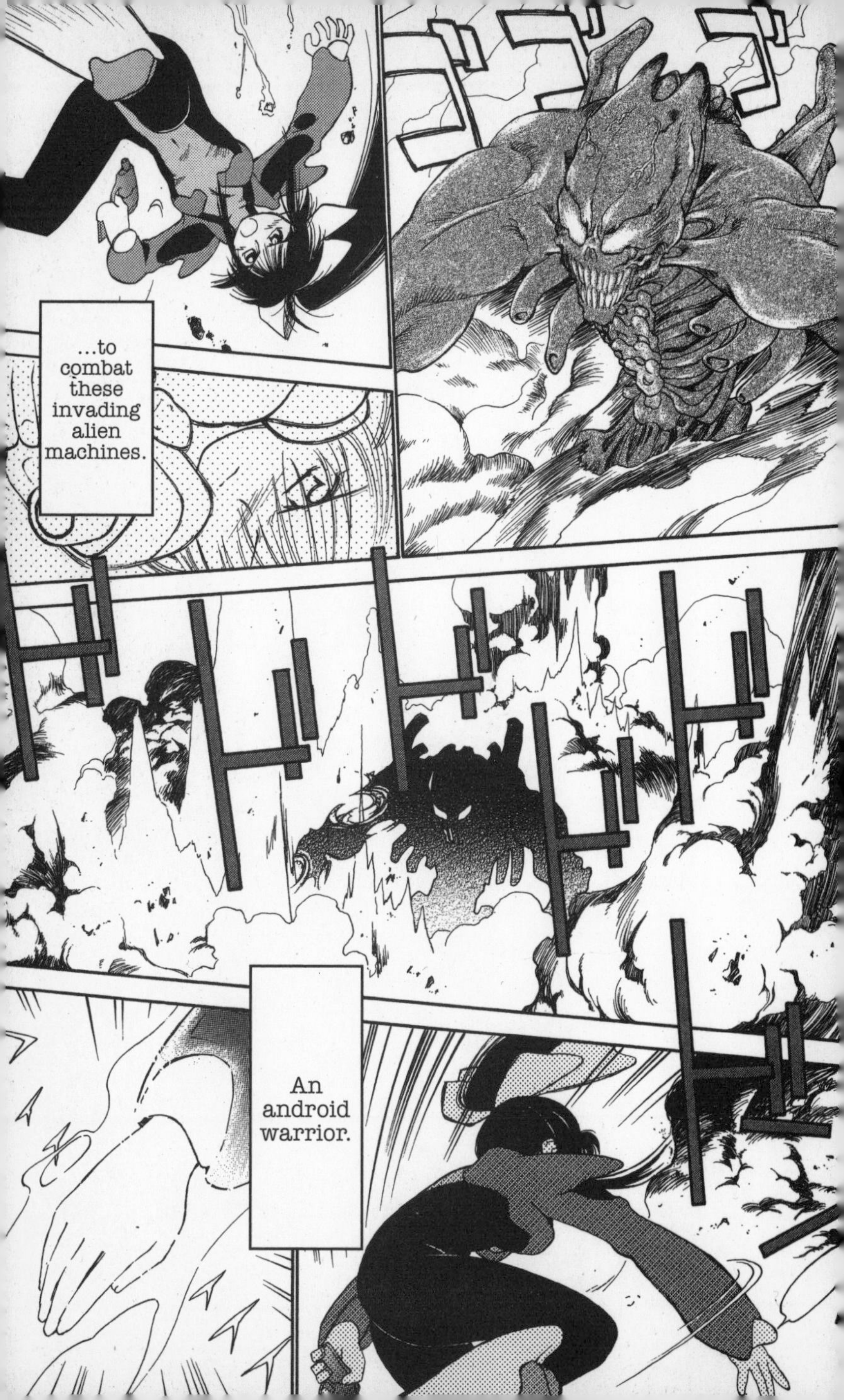
...to combat these invading alien machines.
An android warrior.

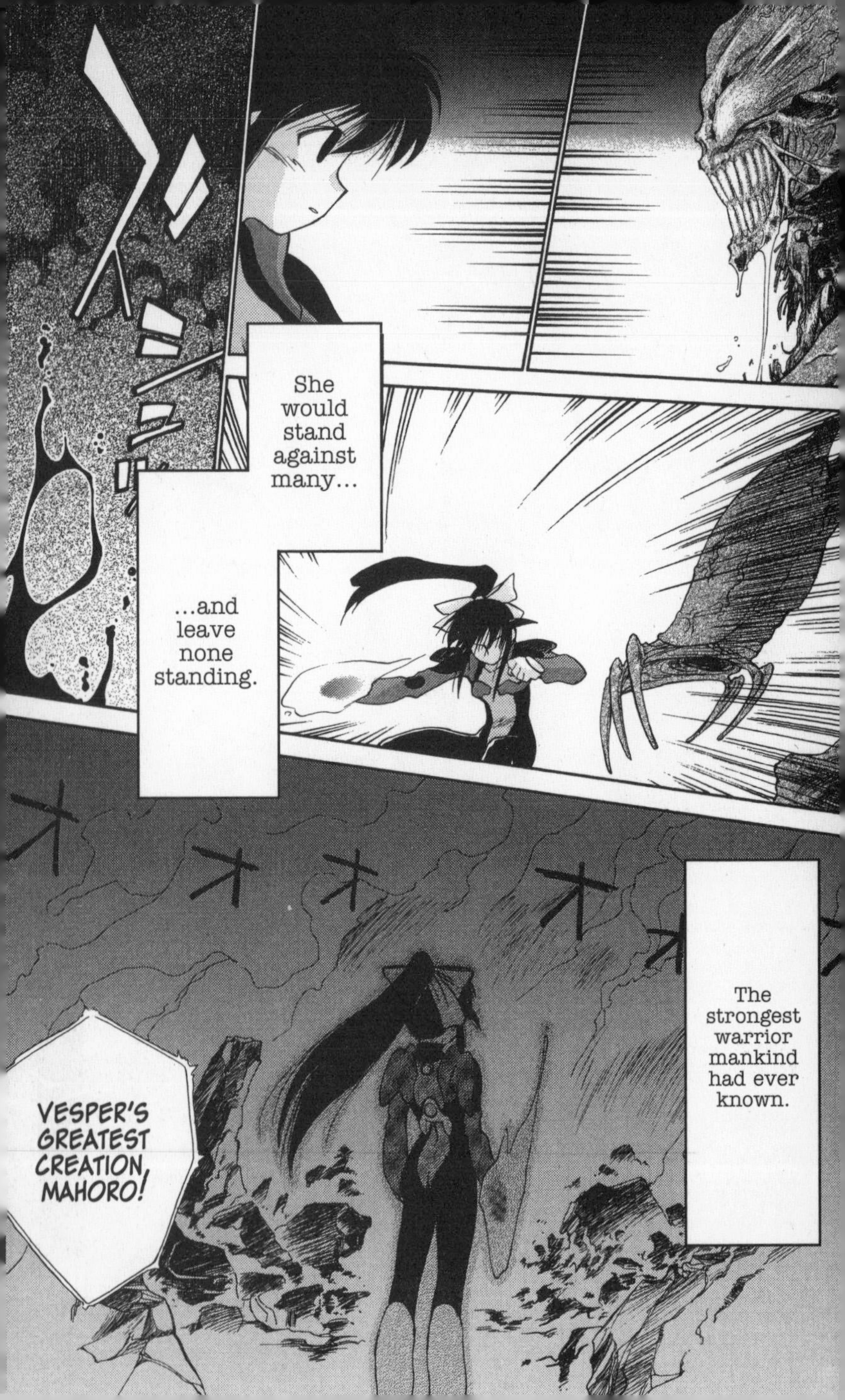
She would stand against many...
...and leave none standing.
The strongest warrior mankind had ever known.
VESPER'S GREATEST CREATION, MAHORO!

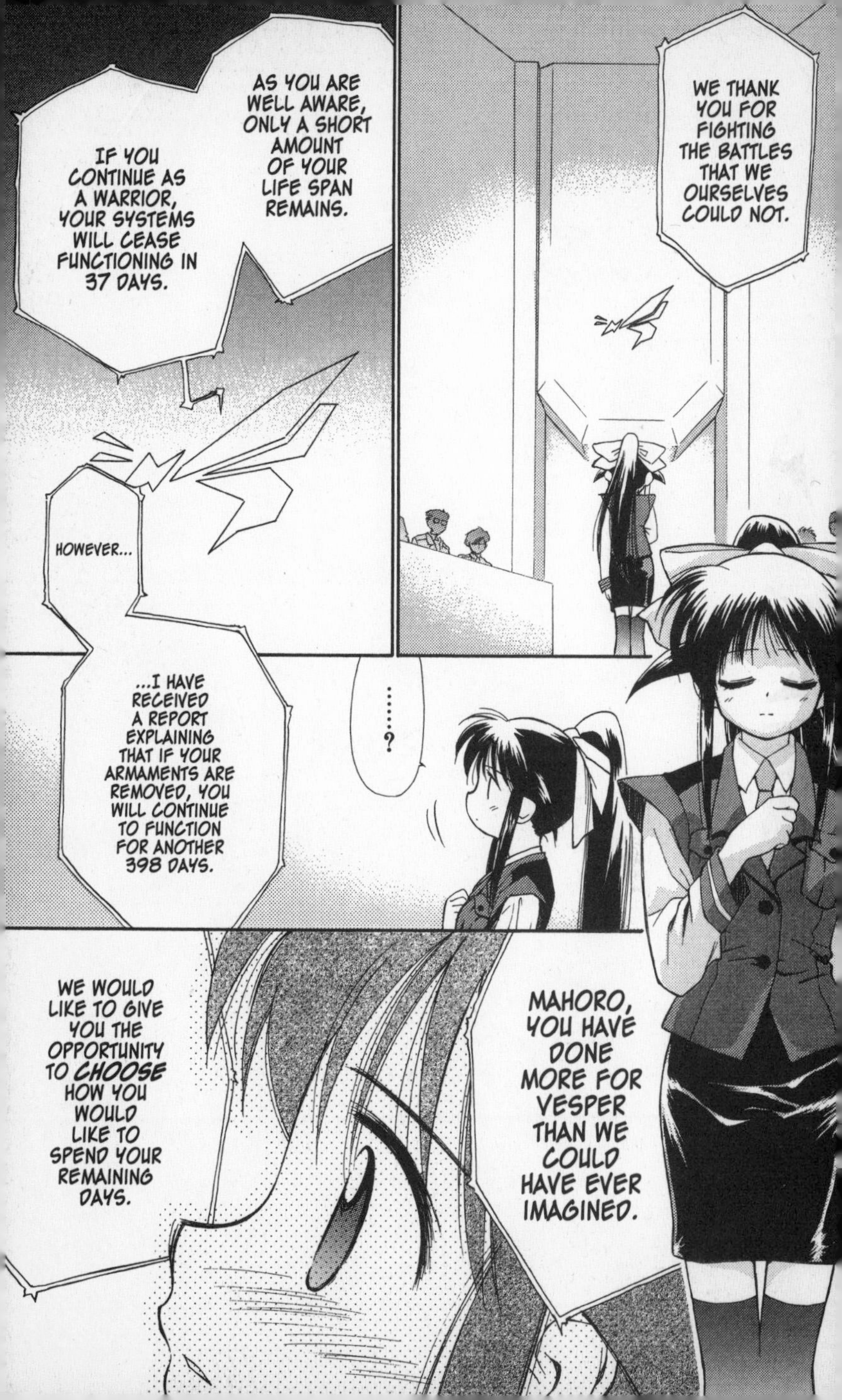

WE THANK YOU FOR FIGHTING THE BATTLES THAT WE OURSELVES COULD NOT.
AS YOU ARE WELL AWARE, ONLY A SHORT AMOUNT OF YOUR LIFE SPAN REMAINS.
IF YOU CONTINUE AS A WARRIOR, YOUR SYSTEMS WILL CEASE FUNCTIONING IN 37 DAYS.
HOWEVER...
...I HAVE RECEIVED A REPORT EXPLAINING THAT IF YOUR ARMAMENTS ARE REMOVED, YOU WILL CONTINUE TO FUNCTION FOR ANOTHER 398 DAYS.
......?
MAHORO, YOU HAVE DONE MORE FOR VESPER THAN WE COULD HAVE EVER IMAGINED.
WE WOULD LIKE TO GIVE YOU THE OPPORTUNITY TO *CHOOSE* HOW YOU WOULD LIKE TO SPEND YOUR REMAINING DAYS.

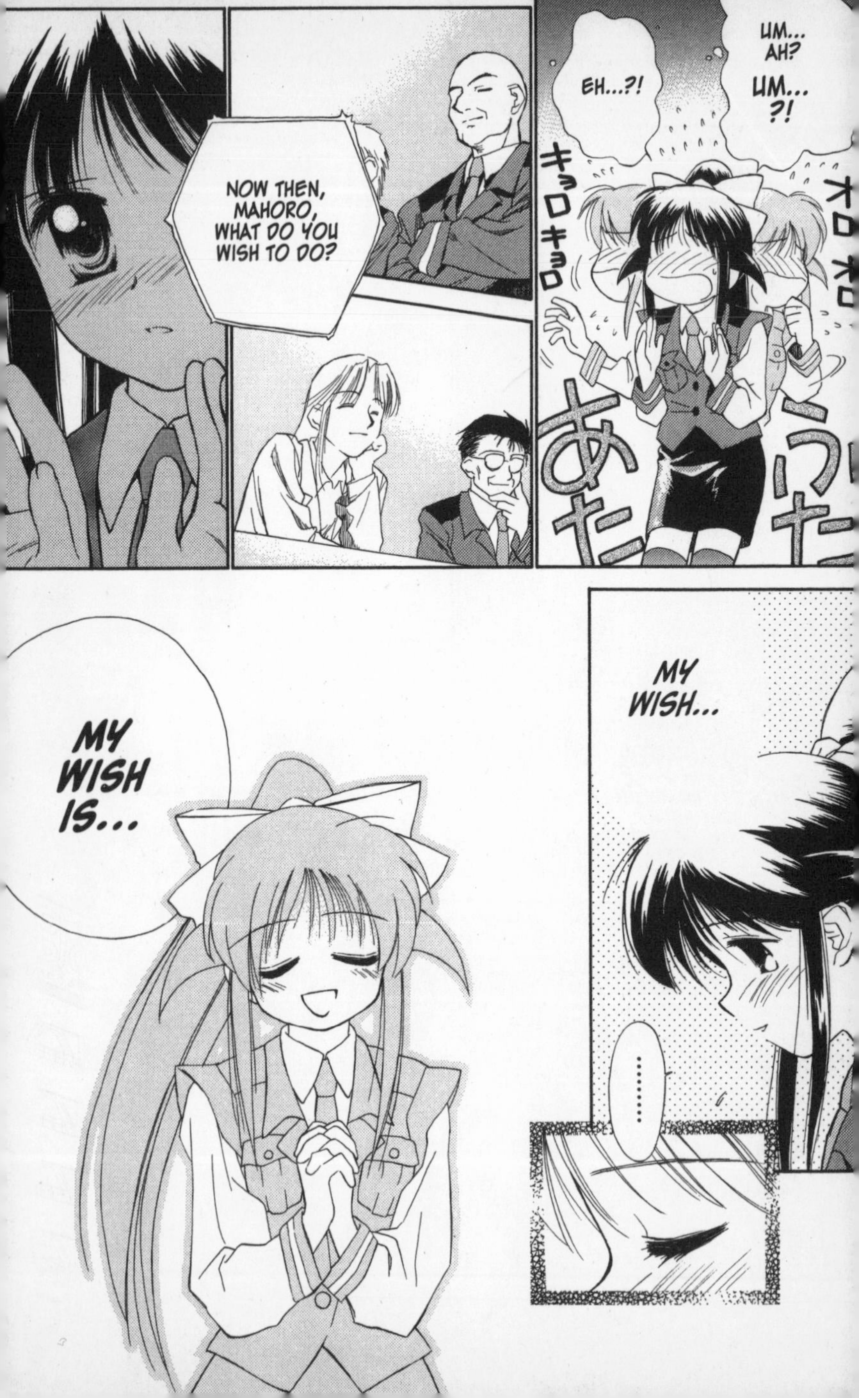
UM... AH? UM...?!
EH...?!
オロオロ
キョロキョロ
NOW THEN, MAHORO, WHAT DO YOU WISH TO DO?
MY WISH...
......
MY WISH IS...

Sign: Hageyoshi Ramen

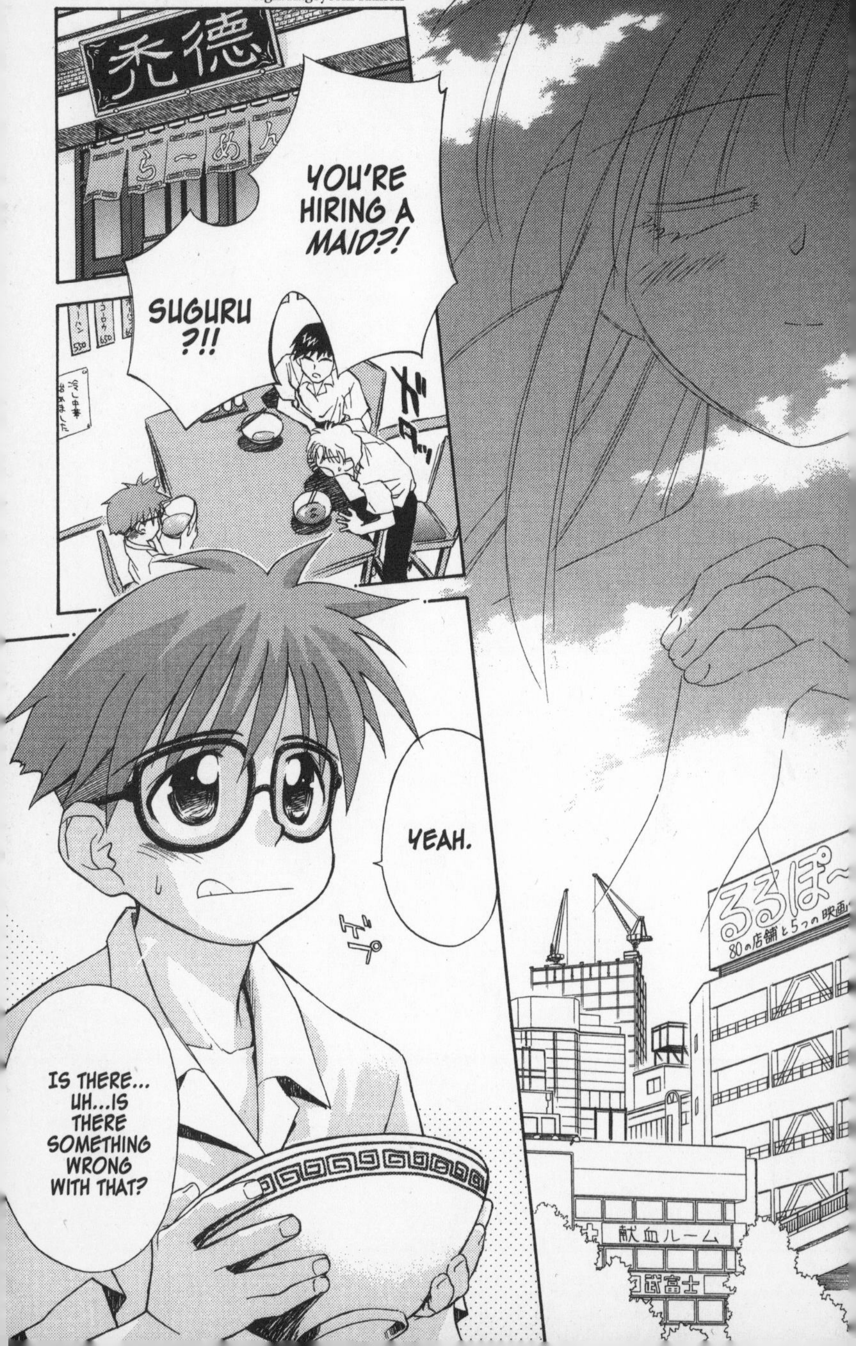

るるぽ〜
80の店舗と5つの映画
献血ルーム
武富士
禿徳
ら〜めん
YOU'RE HIRING A MAID?!
SUGURU ?!!
ガタッ
YEAH.
ゲプ
IS THERE... UH...IS THERE SOMETHING WRONG WITH THAT?

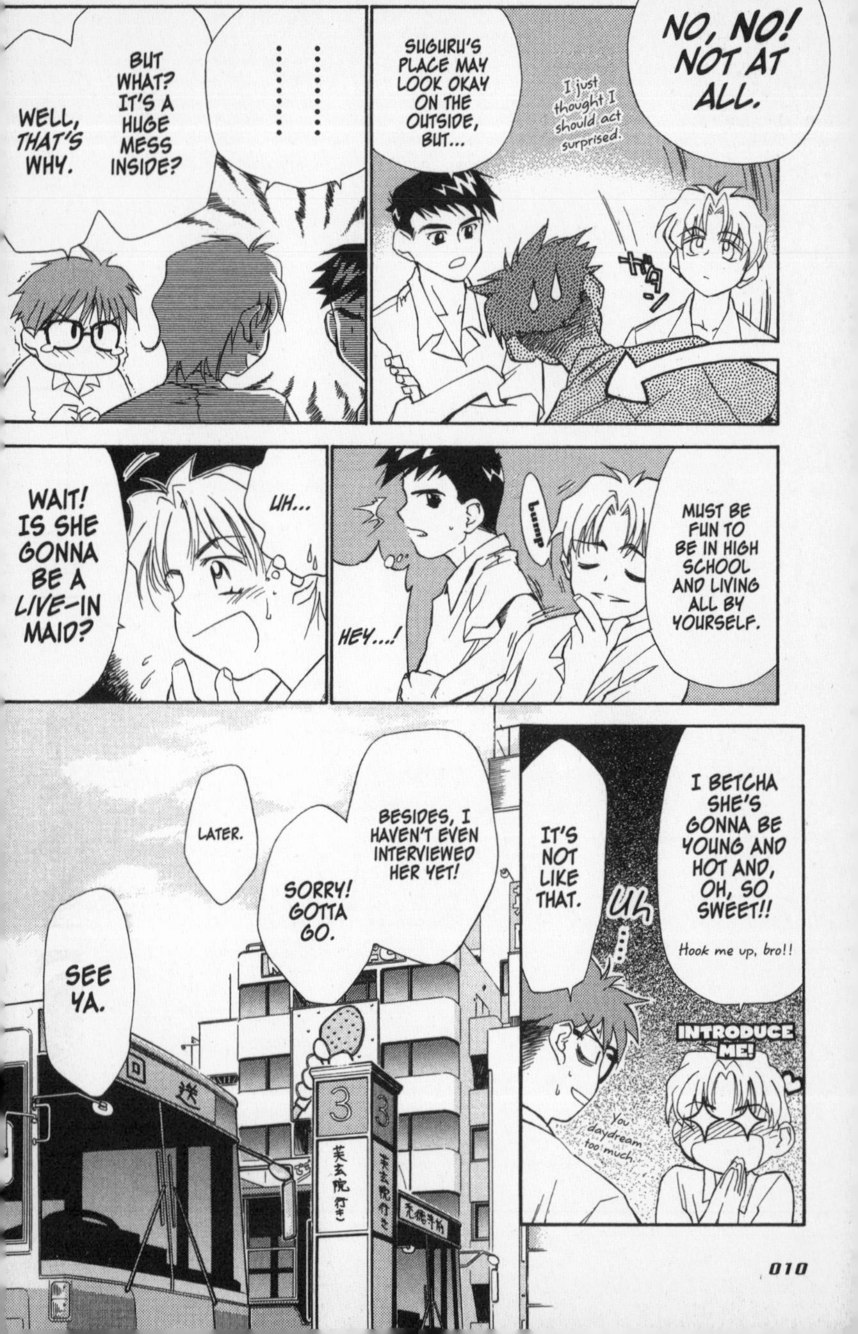
NO, NO! NOT AT ALL.
I just thought I should act surprised.
SUGURU'S PLACE MAY LOOK OKAY ON THE OUTSIDE, BUT...
......
BUT WHAT? IT'S A HUGE MESS INSIDE?
WELL, THAT'S WHY.
MUST BE FUN TO BE IN HIGH SCHOOL AND LIVING ALL BY YOURSELF.
bump
HEY...!
UH...
WAIT! IS SHE GONNA BE A LIVE-IN MAID?
I BETCHA SHE'S GONNA BE YOUNG AND HOT AND, OH, SO SWEET!!
Hook me up, bro!!
INTRODUCE ME!
UH...
IT'S NOT LIKE THAT.
You daydream too much.
BESIDES, I HAVEN'T EVEN INTERVIEWED HER YET!
SORRY! GOTTA GO.
LATER.
SEE YA.

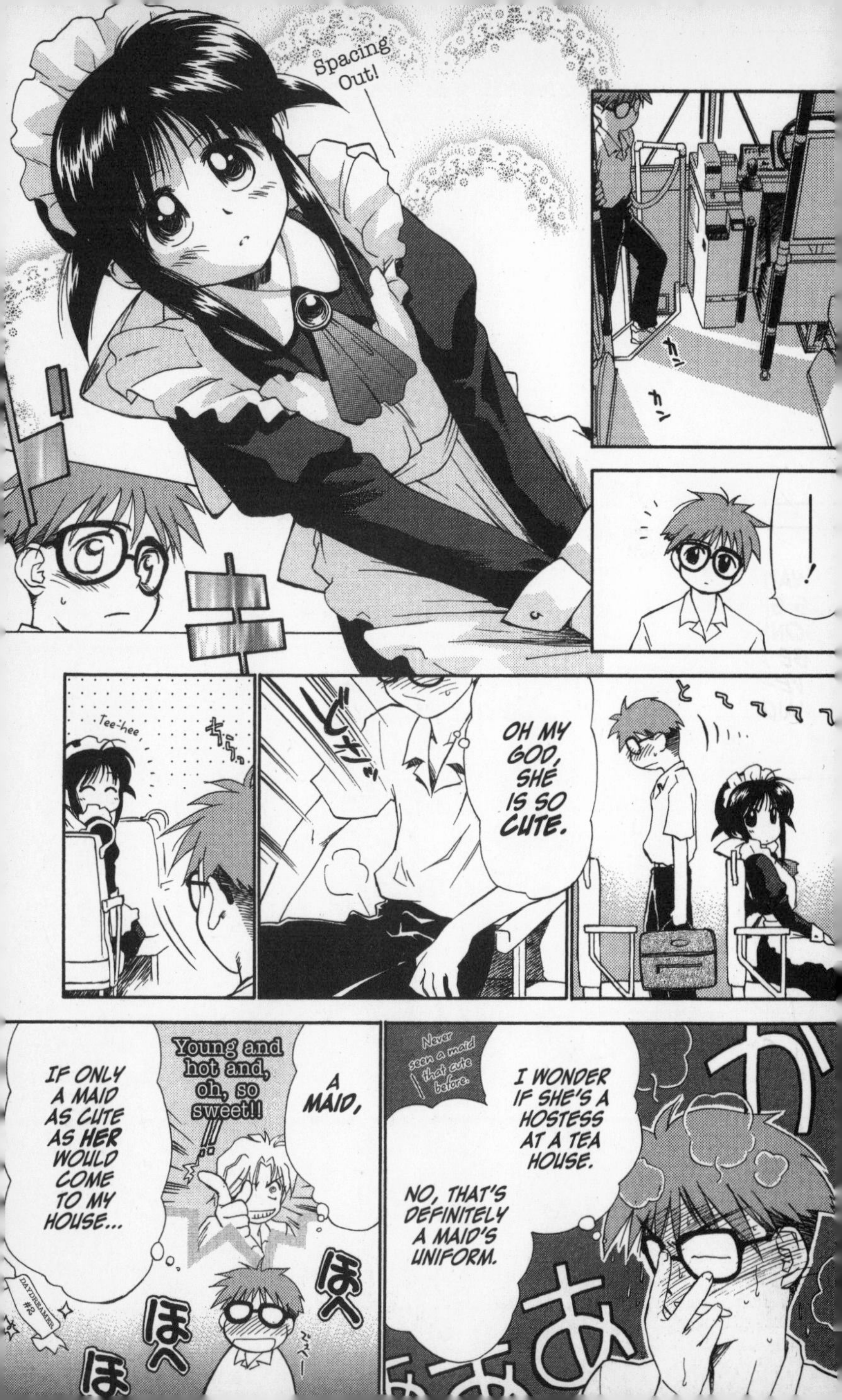

カン
カン
——!
Spacing Out!
OH MY GOD, SHE IS SO CUTE.
Tee-hee
Never seen a maid that cute before.
I WONDER IF SHE'S A HOSTESS AT A TEA HOUSE.
NO, THAT'S DEFINITELY A MAID'S UNIFORM.
A MAID,
Young and hot and, oh, so sweet!!
IF ONLY A MAID AS CUTE AS HER WOULD COME TO MY HOUSE...
DAYDREAMER #2
ほへ
ほへ

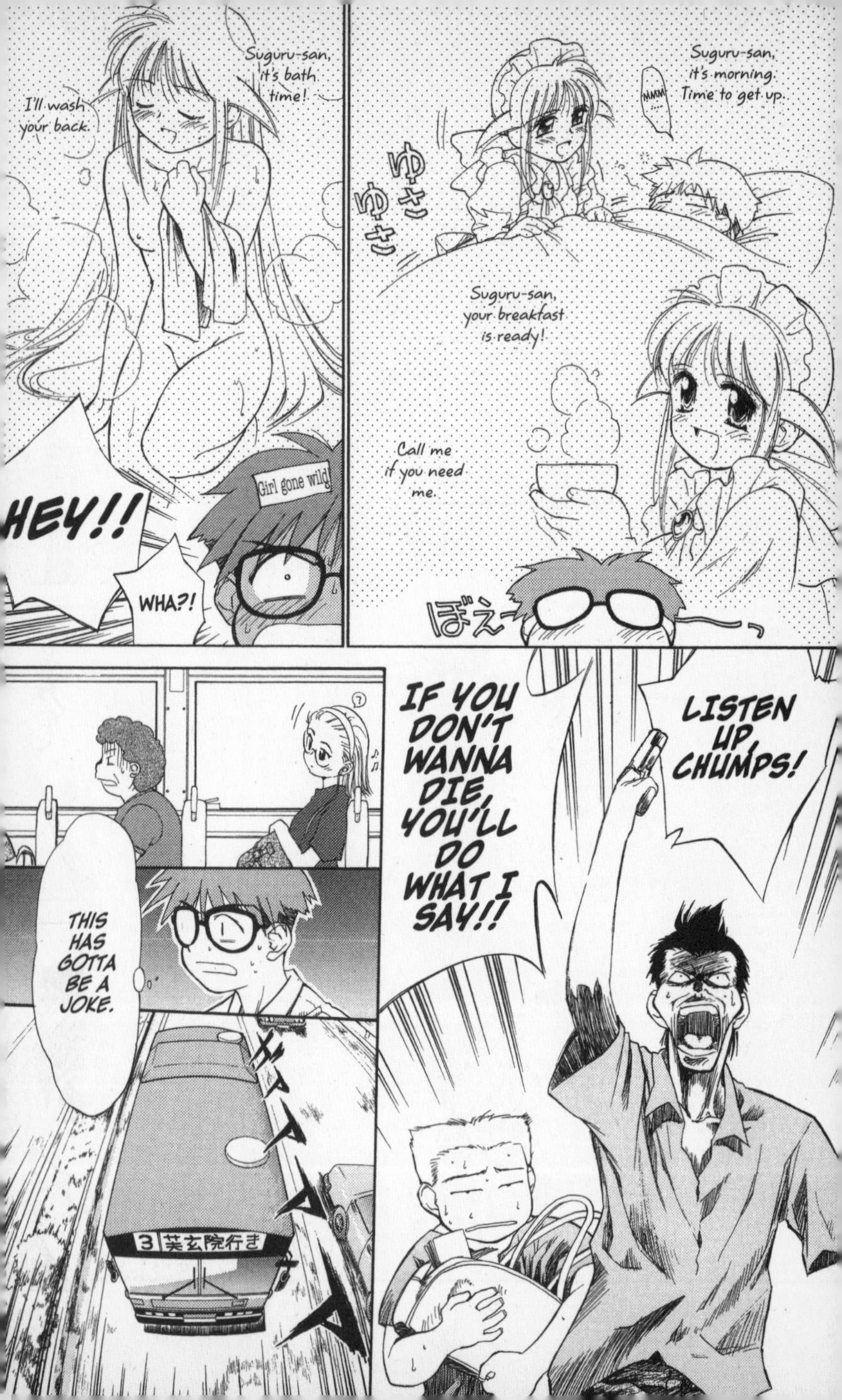
Suguru-san, it's morning. Time to get up.
MMM ....
ゆさゆさ
Suguru-san, your breakfast is ready!
Call me if you need me.
ぼえ〜〜〜っ
Suguru-san, it's bath time!
I'll wash your back.
Girl gone wild
HEY!!
WHA?!
LISTEN UP, CHUMPS!
IF YOU DON'T WANNA DIE, YOU'LL DO WHAT I SAY!!
THIS HAS GOTTA BE A JOKE.

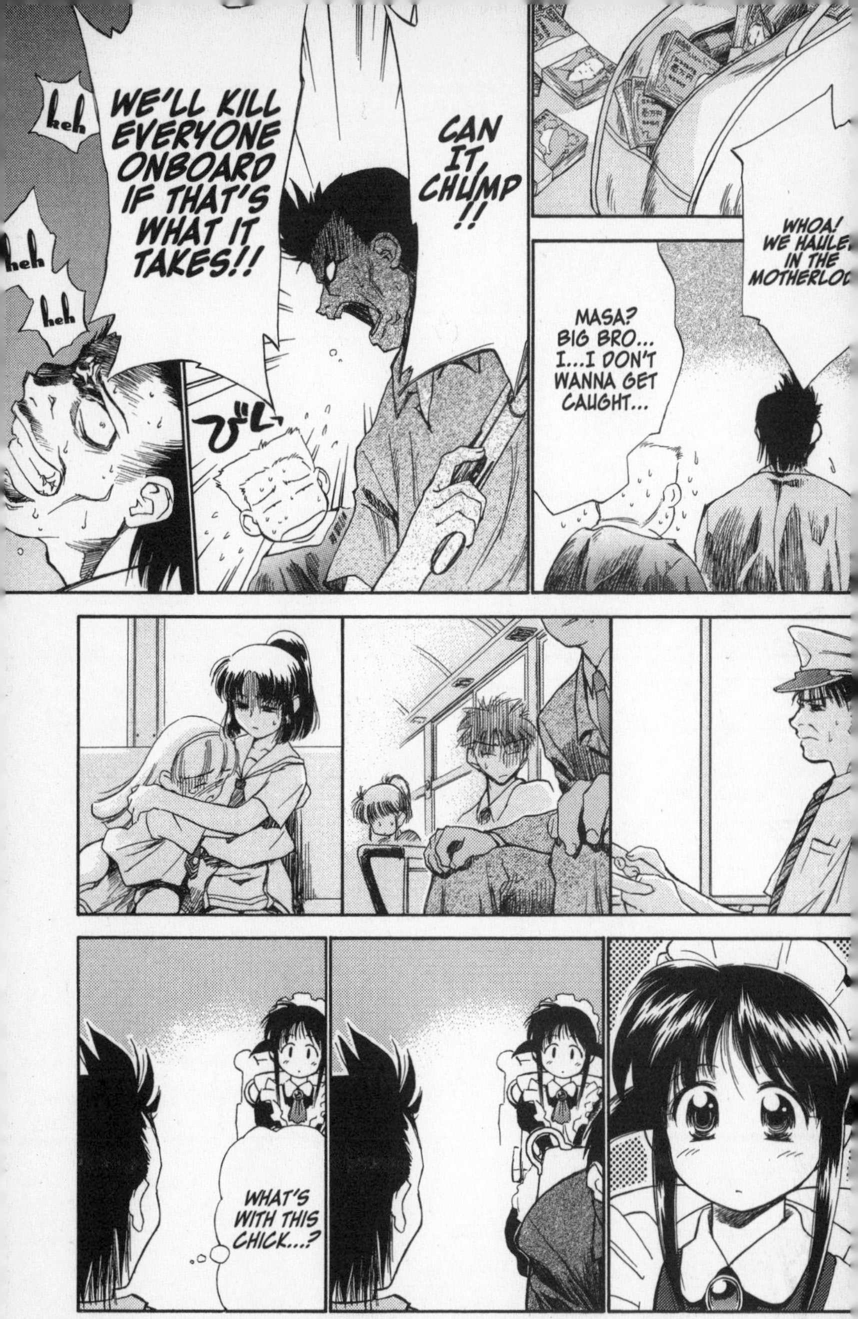
WHOA! WE HAULE IN THE MOTHERLOD
MASA? BIG BRO... I...I DON'T WANNA GET CAUGHT...
CAN IT, CHUMP!!
WE'LL KILL EVERYONE ONBOARD IF THAT'S WHAT IT TAKES!!
びし
keh
heh
heh
WHAT'S WITH THIS CHICK...?

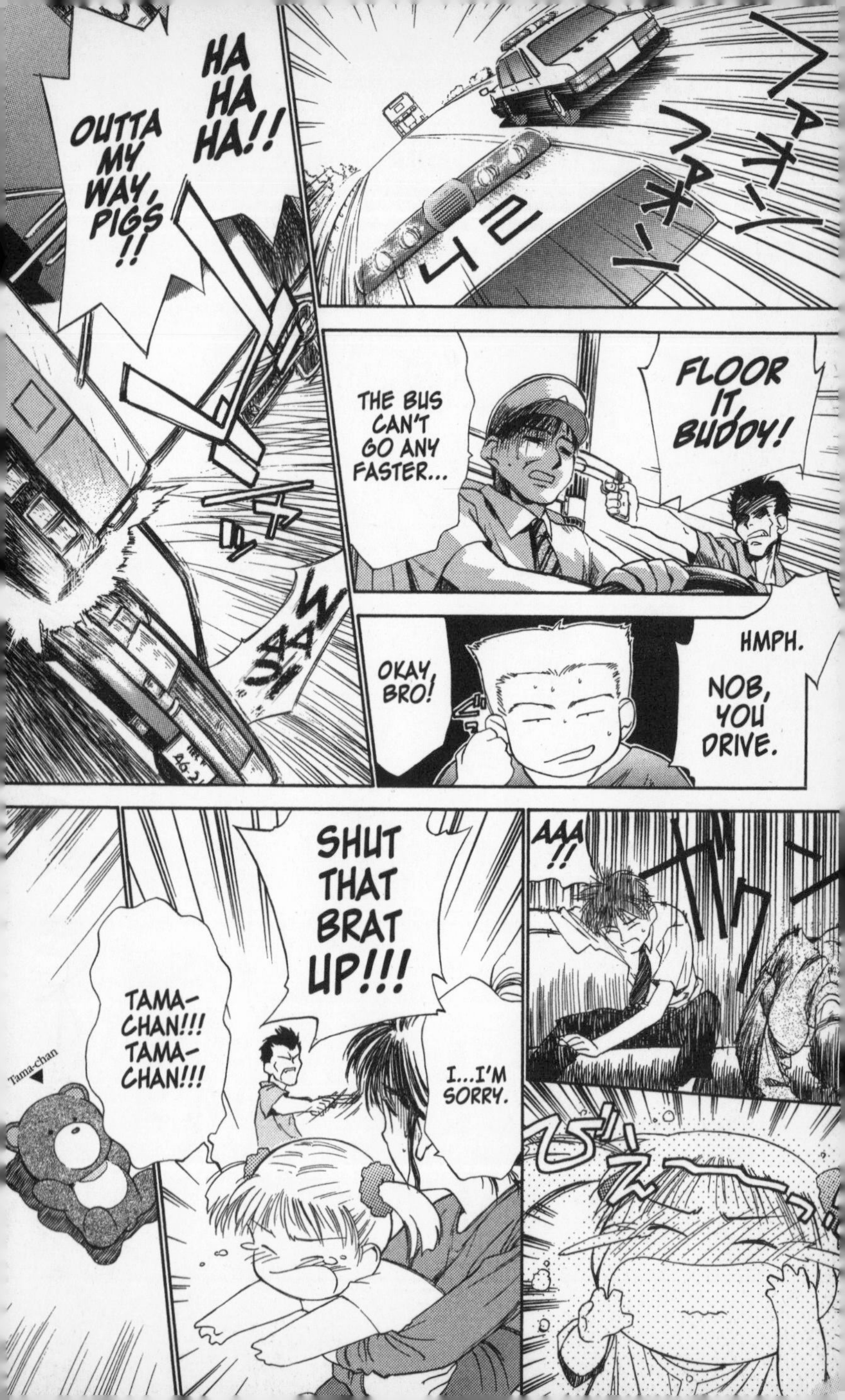
FLOOR IT, BUDDY!
THE BUS CAN'T GO ANY FASTER...
HMPH.
NOB, YOU DRIVE.
OKAY, BRO!
HA HA HA!!
OUTTA MY WAY, PIGS!!
AAA!!
SHUT THAT BRAT UP!!!
TAMA-CHAN!!! TAMA-CHAN!!!
I...I'M SORRY.
Tama-chan

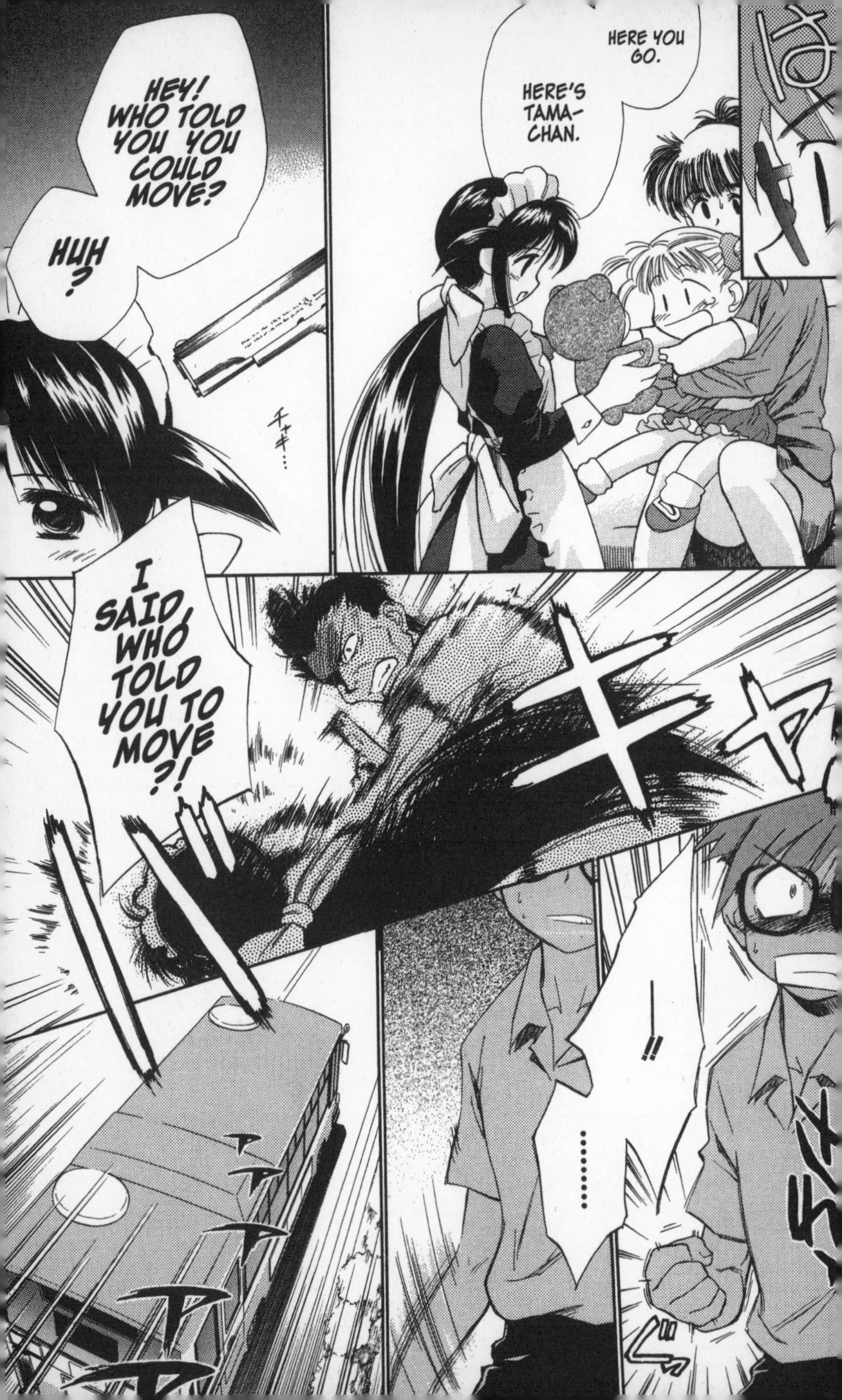
HERE YOU GO.
HERE'S TAMA-CHAN.
HEY! WHO TOLD YOU YOU COULD MOVE?
HUH?
チャキ…
I SAID, WHO TOLD YOU TO MOVE?!
!!
......

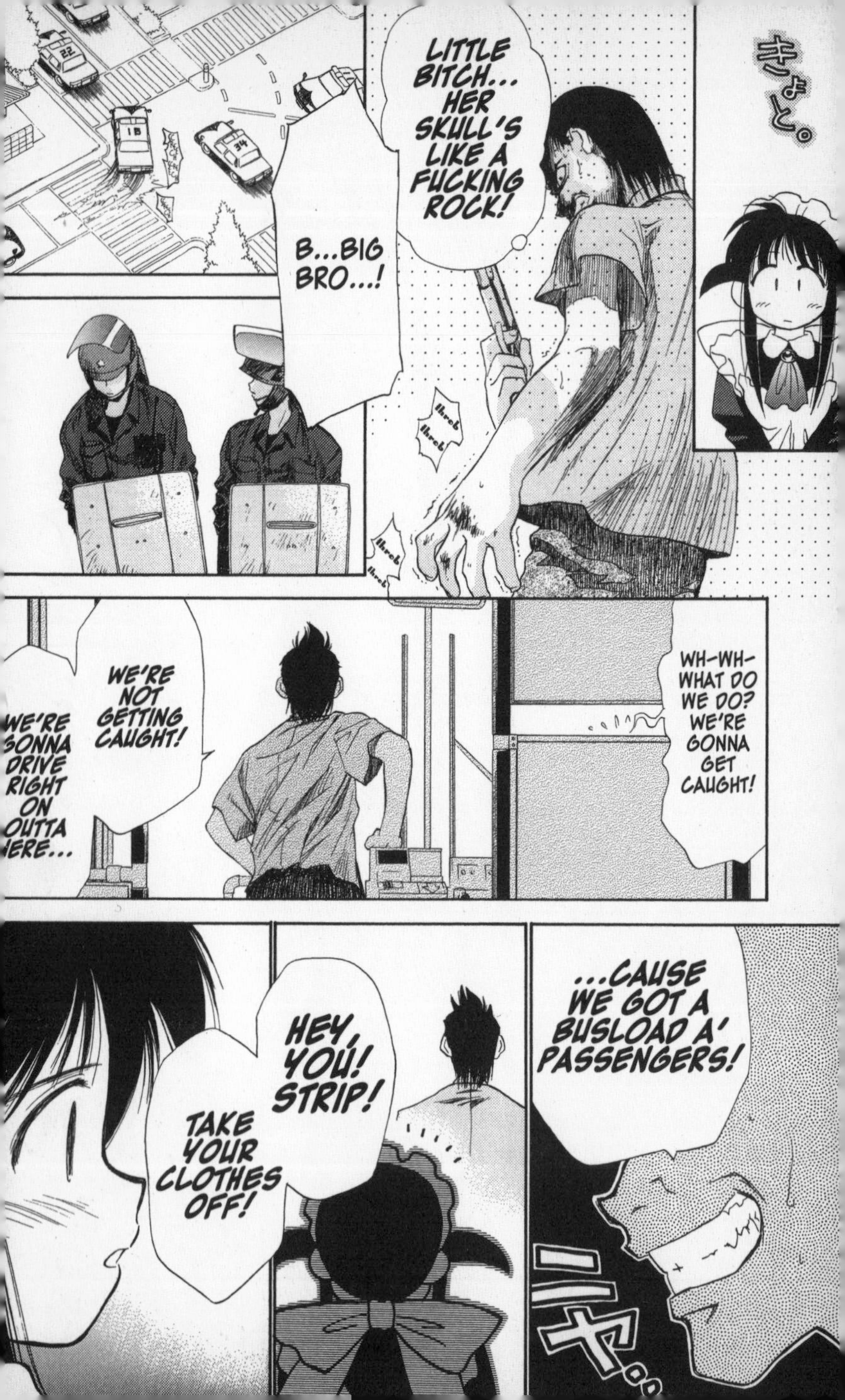

きょと。
LITTLE BITCH... HER SKULL'S LIKE A FUCKING ROCK!
B...BIG BRO...!
throb throb
throb throb
WH-WH-WHAT DO WE DO? WE'RE GONNA GET CAUGHT!
WE'RE NOT GETTING CAUGHT!
WE'RE GONNA DRIVE RIGHT ON OUTTA HERE...
...CAUSE WE GOT A BUSLOAD A' PASSENGERS!
ニヤ。。
HEY, YOU! STRIP!
TAKE YOUR CLOTHES OFF!

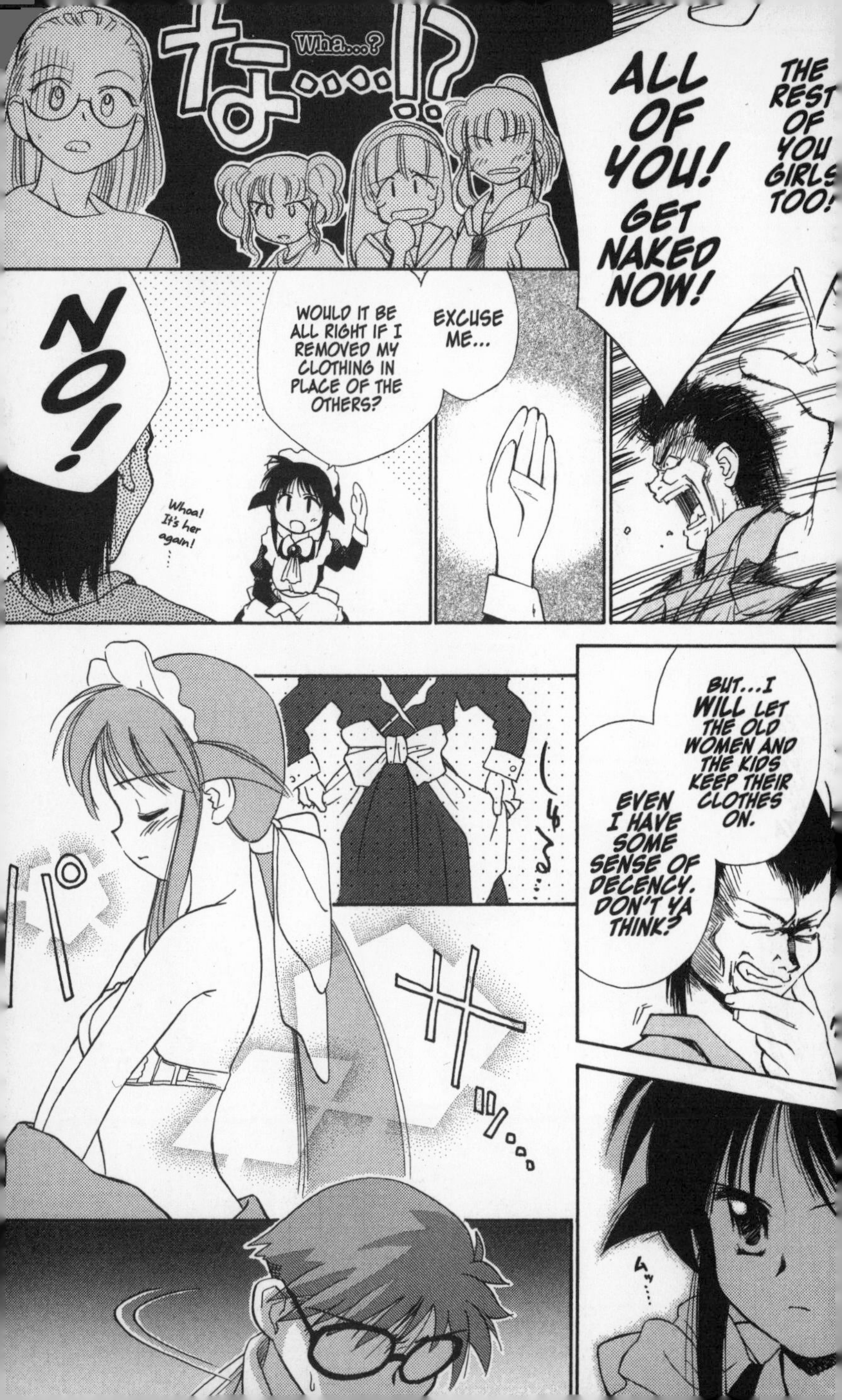

THE REST OF YOU GIRLS TOO!
ALL OF YOU! GET NAKED NOW!
な…!?
Wha…?
EXCUSE ME…
WOULD IT BE ALL RIGHT IF I REMOVED MY CLOTHING IN PLACE OF THE OTHERS?
NO!
Whoa! It's her again! …
BUT…I WILL LET THE OLD WOMEN AND THE KIDS KEEP THEIR CLOTHES ON.
EVEN I HAVE SOME SENSE OF DECENCY, DON'T YA THINK?
ムッ…

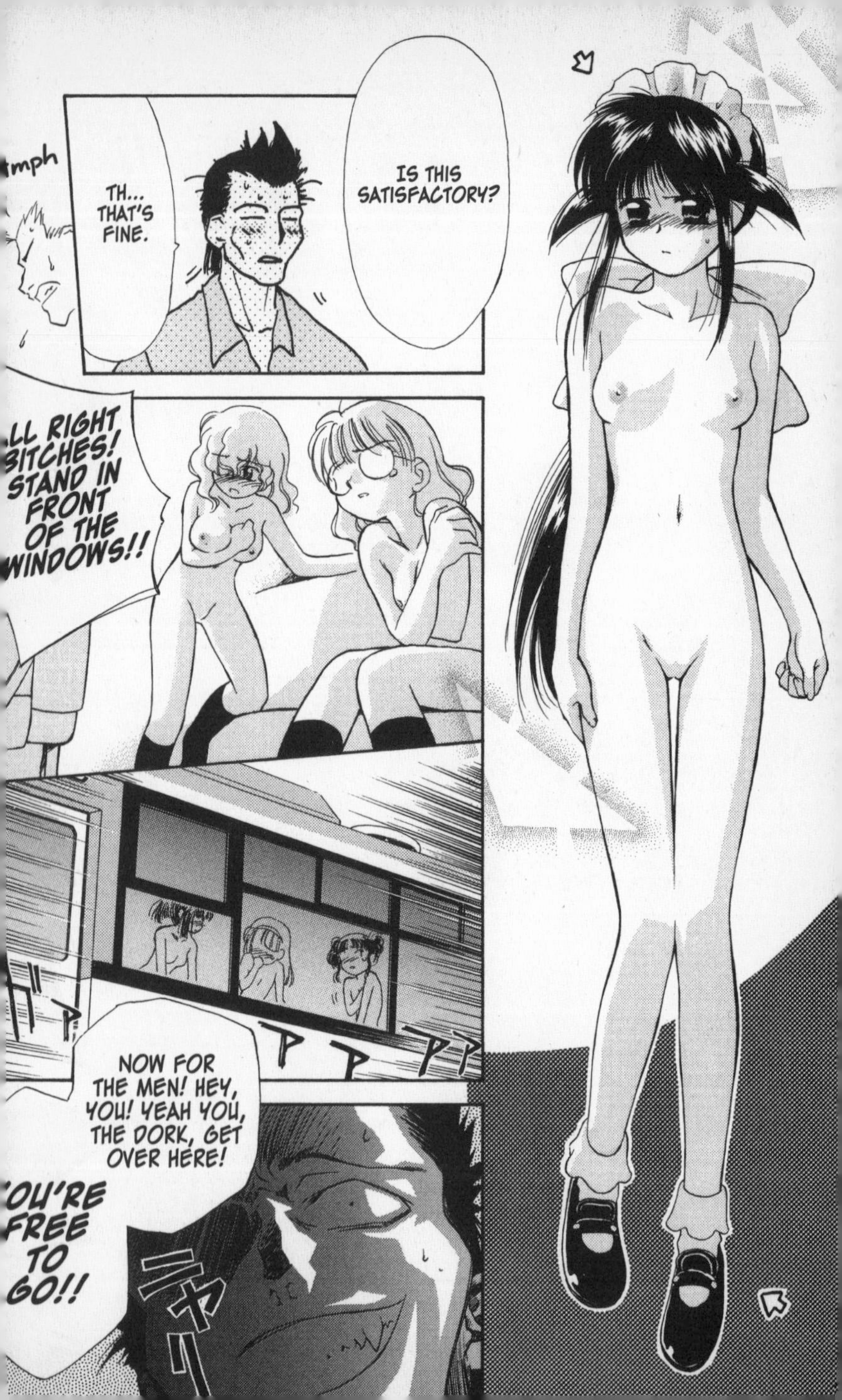
IS THIS SATISFACTORY?
TH... THAT'S FINE.
mph
LL RIGHT BITCHES! STAND IN FRONT OF THE WINDOWS!!
NOW FOR THE MEN! HEY, YOU! YEAH YOU, THE DORK, GET OVER HERE!
OU'RE FREE TO GO!!

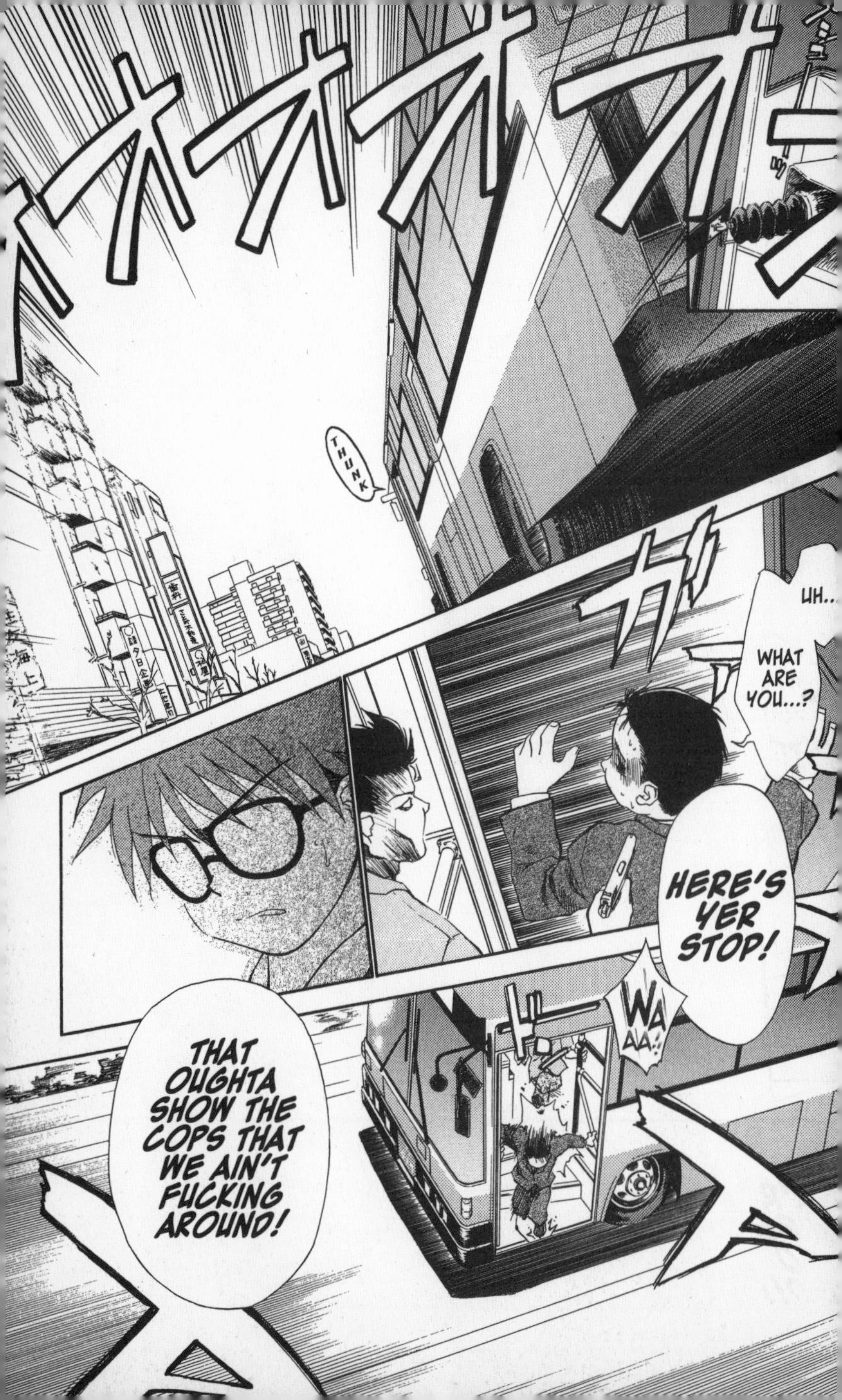
THUNK
UH... WHAT ARE YOU...?
HERE'S YER STOP!
WAAA!!
THAT OUGHTA SHOW THE COPS THAT WE AIN'T FUCKING AROUND!

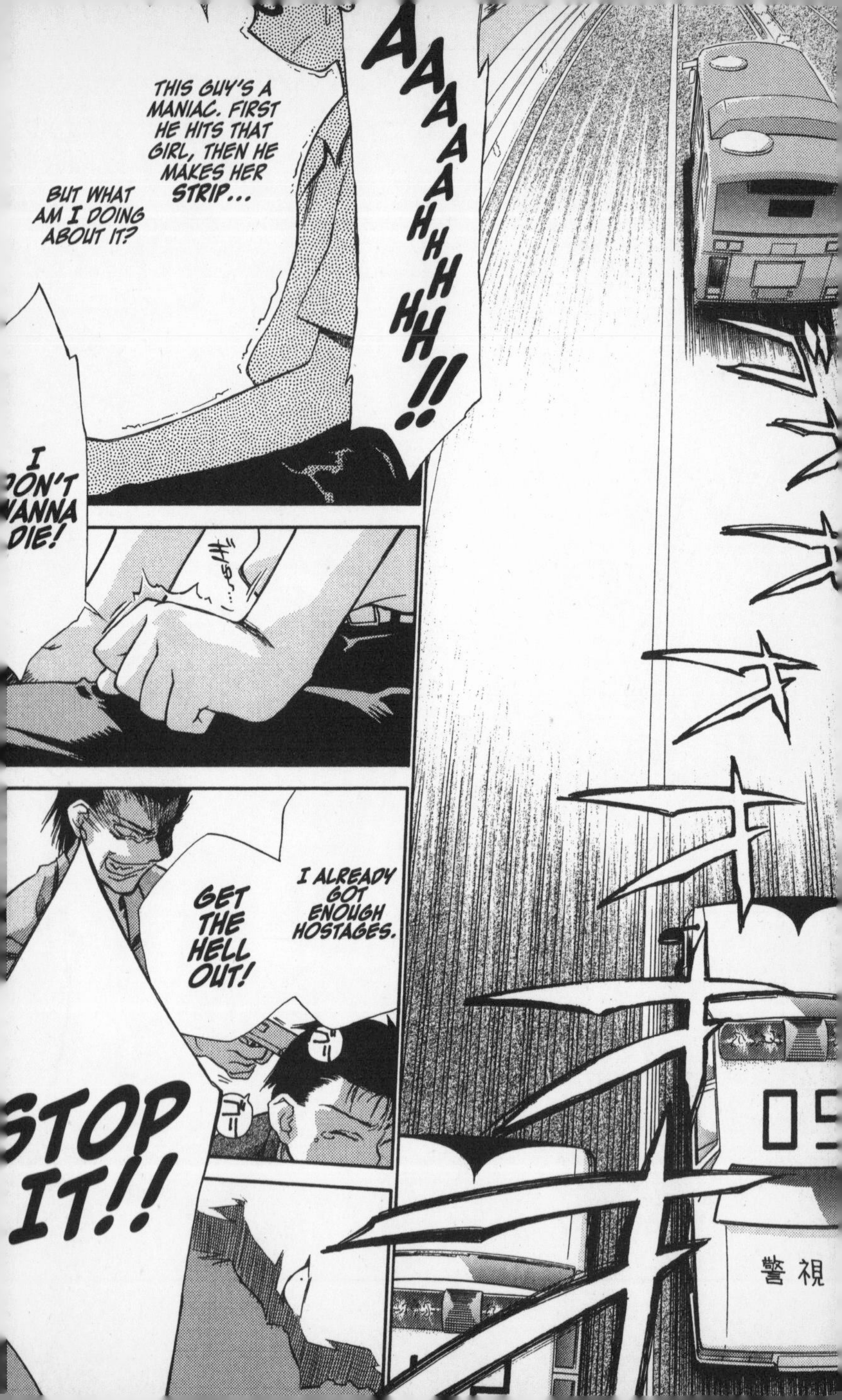

THIS GUY'S A MANIAC. FIRST HE HITS THAT GIRL, THEN HE MAKES HER STRIP...
BUT WHAT AM I DOING ABOUT IT?
AAAAAAHHHHHH!!
I ON'T ANNA DIE!
I ALREADY GOT ENOUGH HOSTAGES.
GET THE HELL OUT!
STOP IT!!

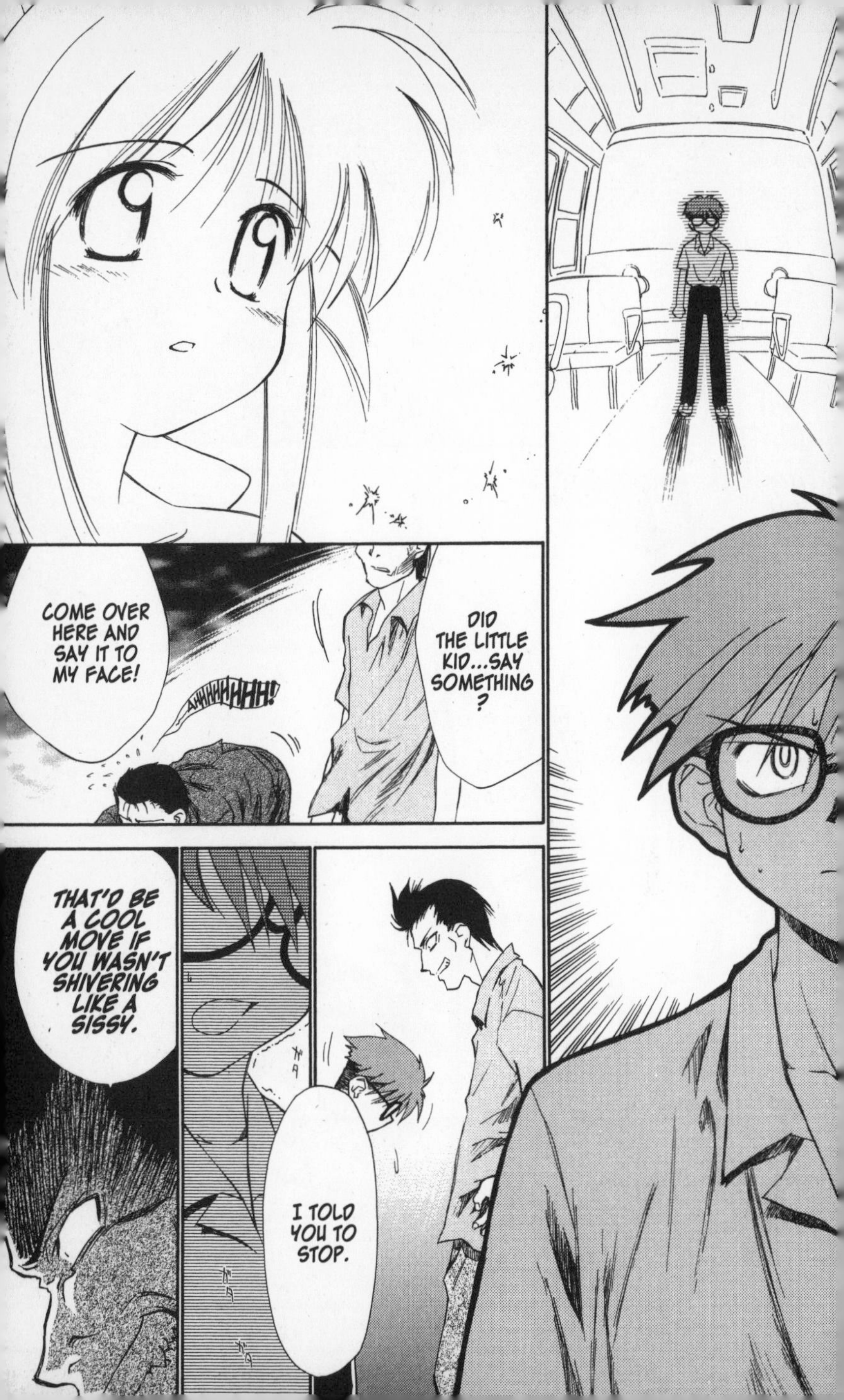
DID THE LITTLE KID...SAY SOMETHING?
AHHHHHHHHH!
COME OVER HERE AND SAY IT TO MY FACE!
I TOLD YOU TO STOP.
THAT'D BE A COOL MOVE IF YOU WASN'T SHIVERING LIKE A SISSY.

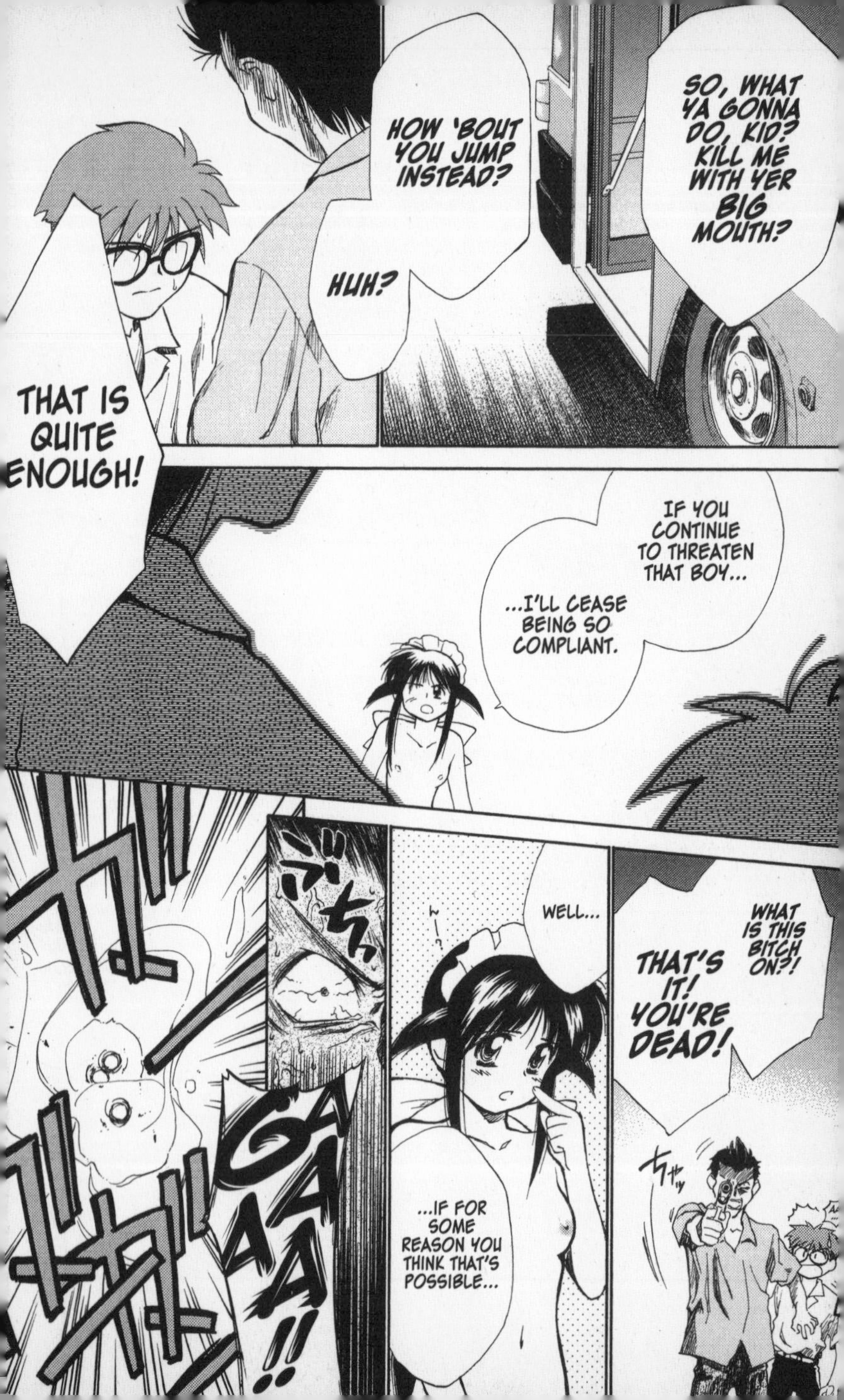
SO, WHAT YA GONNA DO, KID? KILL ME WITH YER BIG MOUTH?
HOW 'BOUT YOU JUMP INSTEAD?
HUH?
THAT IS QUITE ENOUGH!
IF YOU CONTINUE TO THREATEN THAT BOY...
...I'LL CEASE BEING SO COMPLIANT.
WHAT IS THIS BITCH ON?!
THAT'S IT! YOU'RE DEAD!
WELL...
...IF FOR SOME REASON YOU THINK THAT'S POSSIBLE...
GAAAA!!

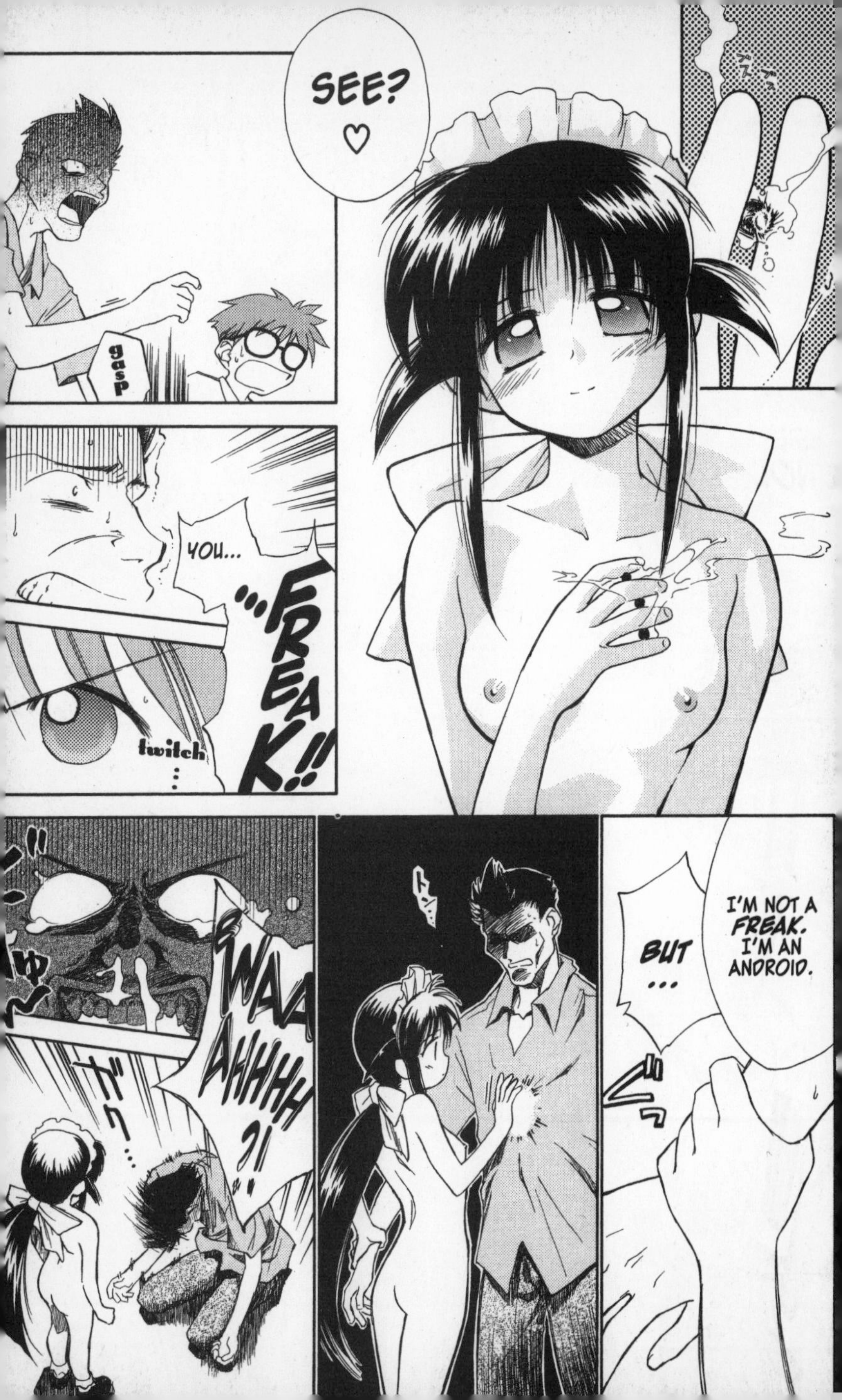
SEE?
♥
gasp
YOU...
...FREAK!!
twitch
...
I'M NOT A FREAK. I'M AN ANDROID.
BUT
...
WAAAAHHHH?!!
ガク…

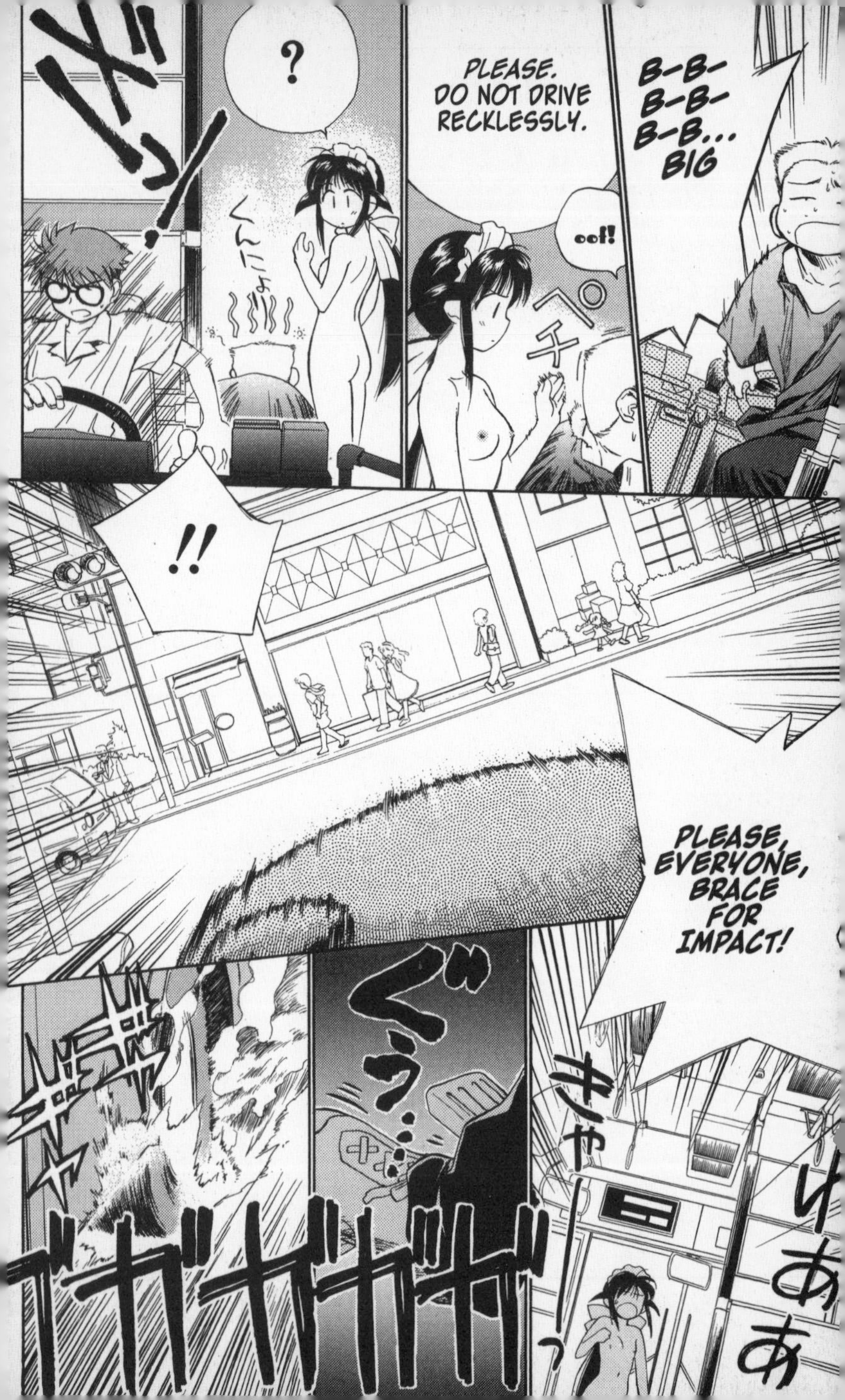
B-B-
B-B-
B-B...
BIG
PLEASE.
DO NOT DRIVE
RECKLESSLY.
oof!
ペチ
?
くんにょ
!!
PLEASE,
EVERYONE,
BRACE
FOR
IMPACT!
きゃー!
ぐう...

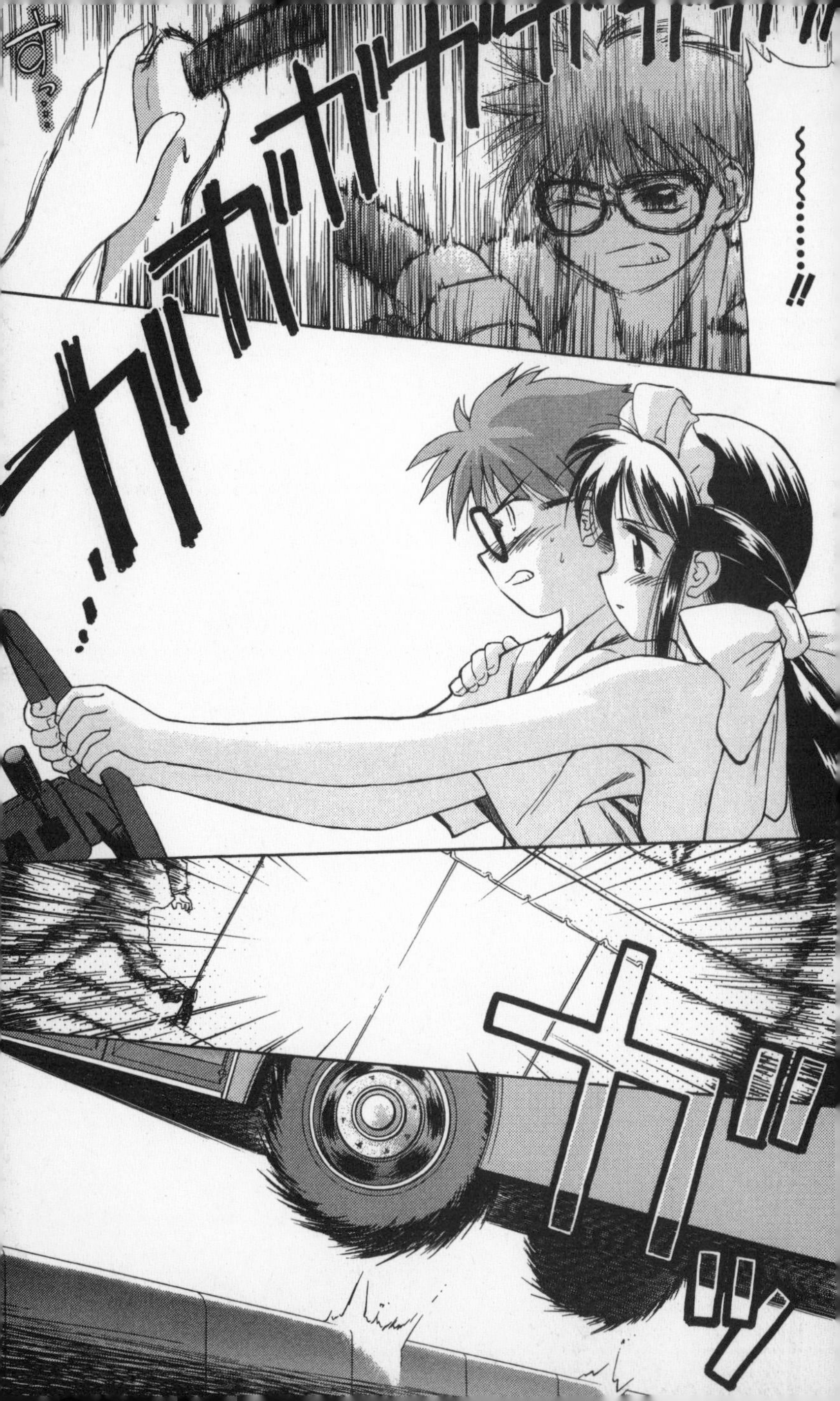
〜〜……!!
すっ…

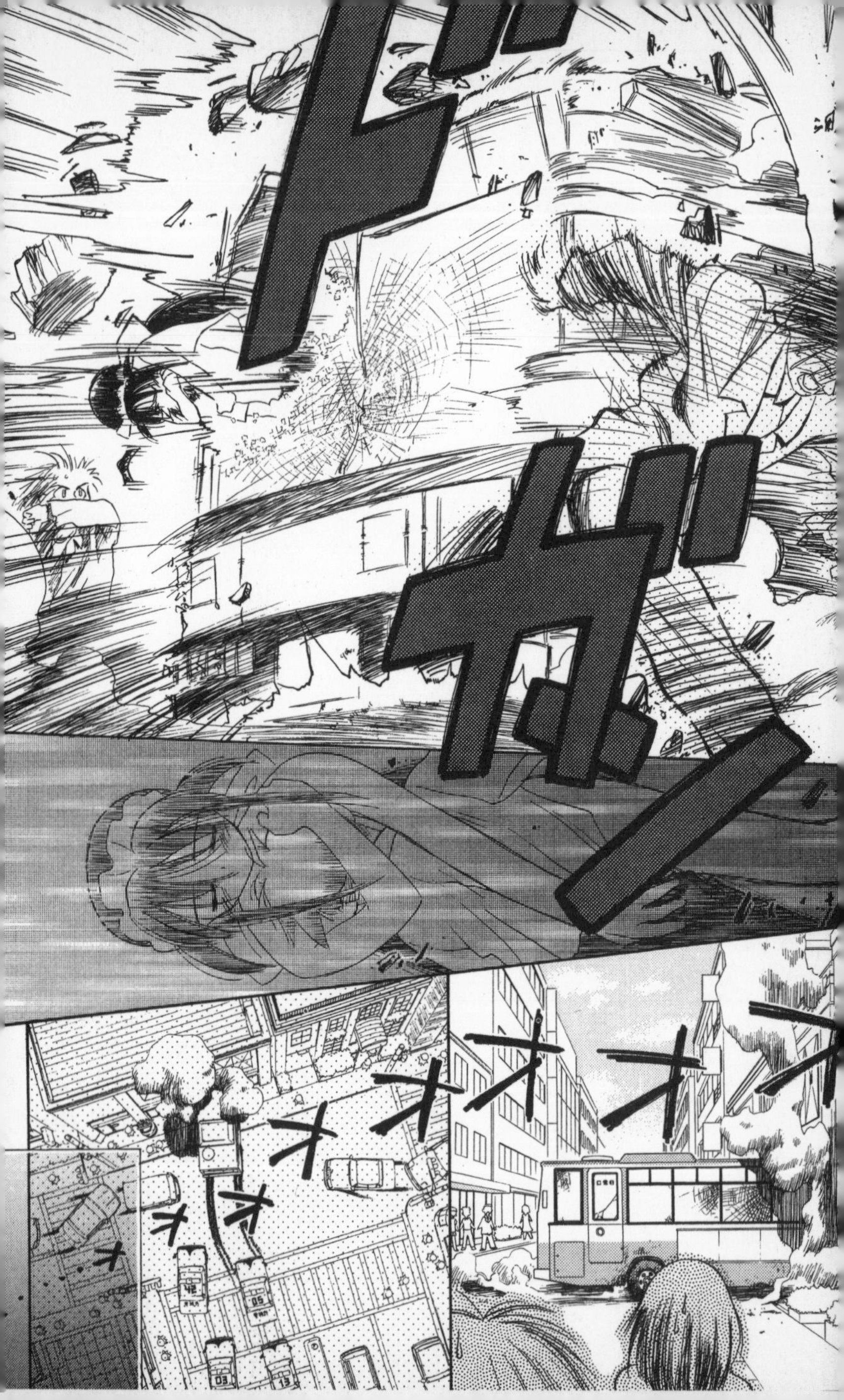
ドガン
オオオ
オオオ

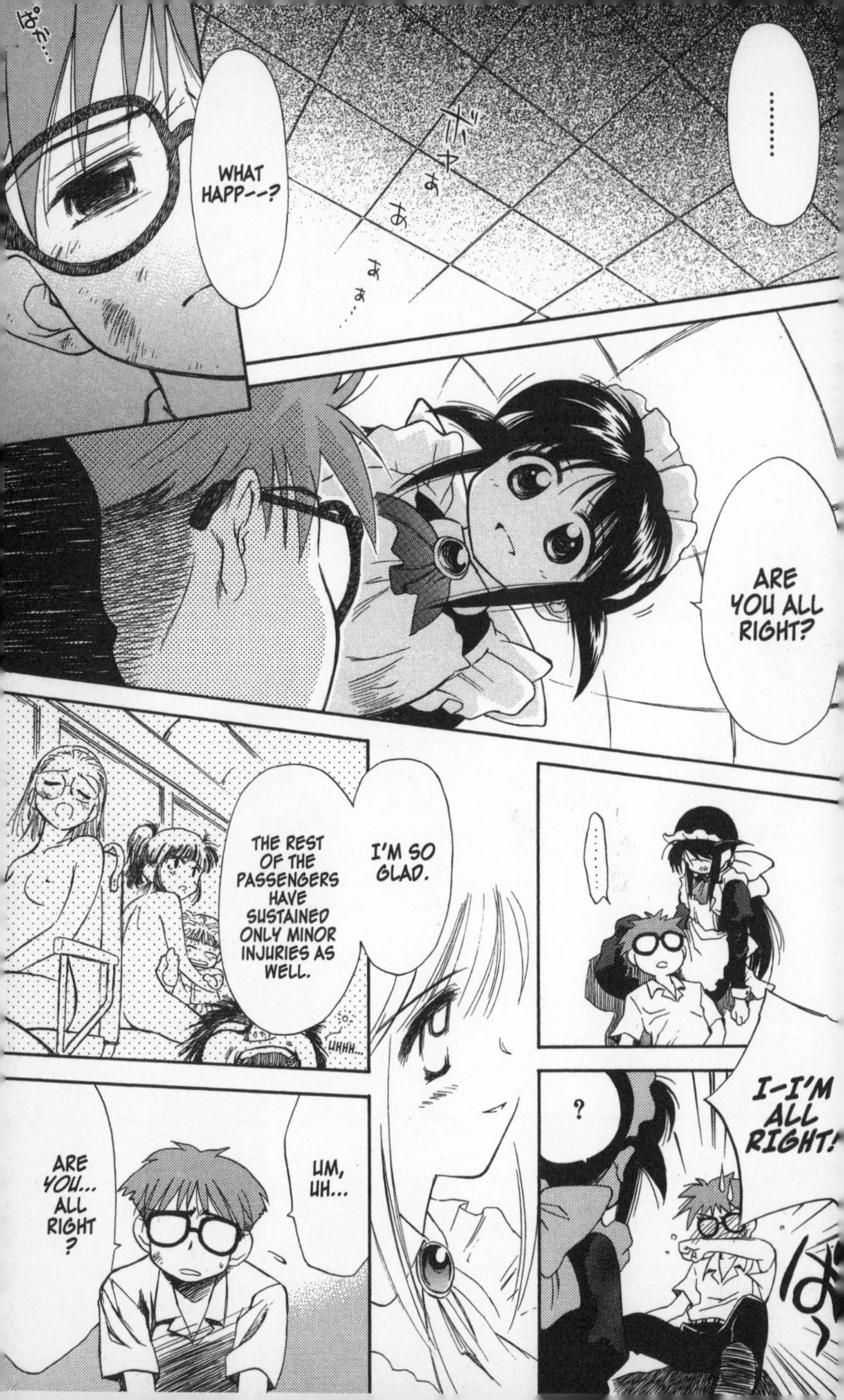
......
WHAT HAPP--?
ボヤぁあぁ…
ぱか…
ARE YOU ALL RIGHT?
......
I'M SO GLAD.
THE REST OF THE PASSENGERS HAVE SUSTAINED ONLY MINOR INJURIES AS WELL.
UHHH...
I-I'M ALL RIGHT!
?
はっ
UM, UH...
ARE YOU... ALL RIGHT?

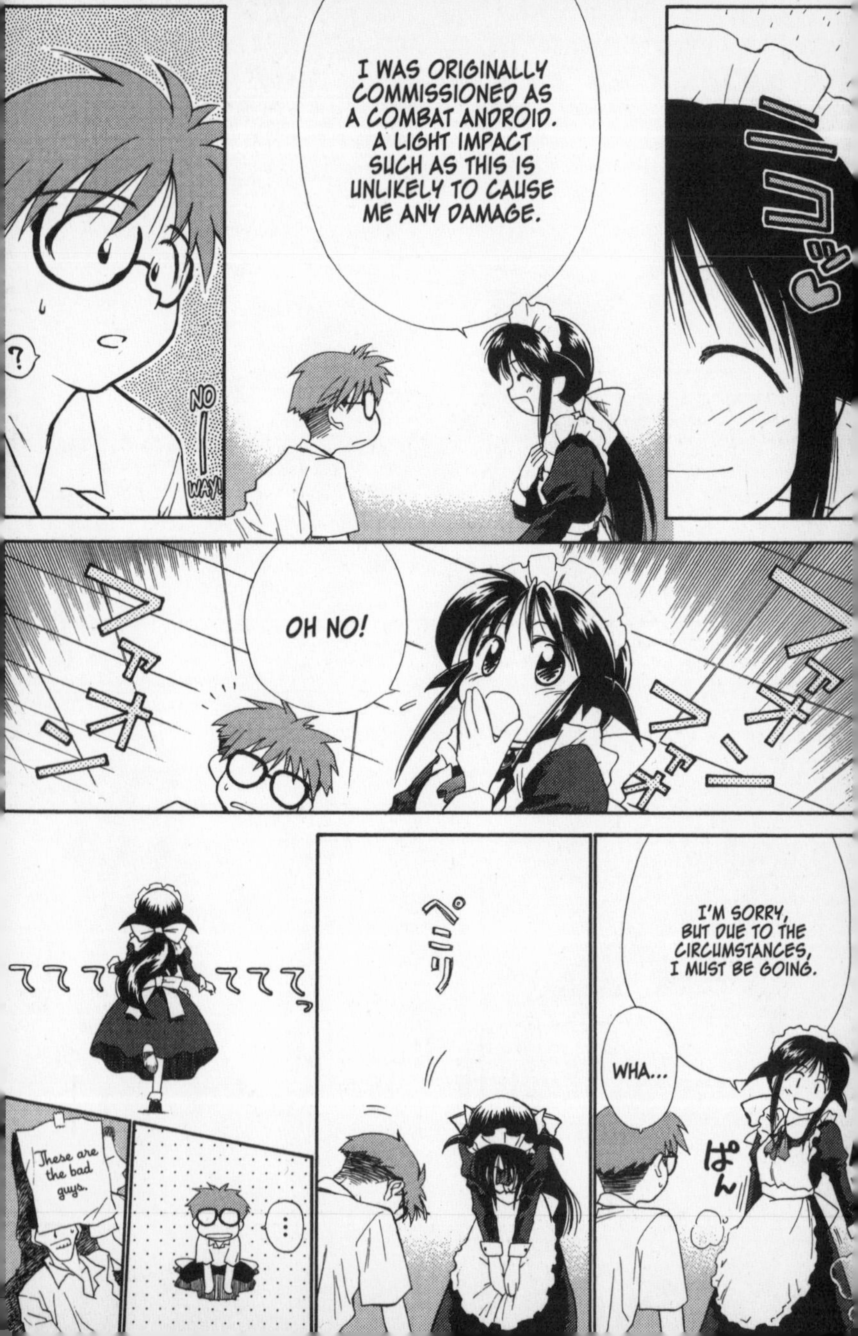
ニコッ♥
I WAS ORIGINALLY COMMISSIONED AS A COMBAT ANDROID. A LIGHT IMPACT SUCH AS THIS IS UNLIKELY TO CAUSE ME ANY DAMAGE.
?
NO—WAY!
ファオーン
OH NO!
ファオーン
I'M SORRY, BUT DUE TO THE CIRCUMSTANCES, I MUST BE GOING.
WHA...
ぱん
ぺこり
ててて ててて
These are the bad guys.
...

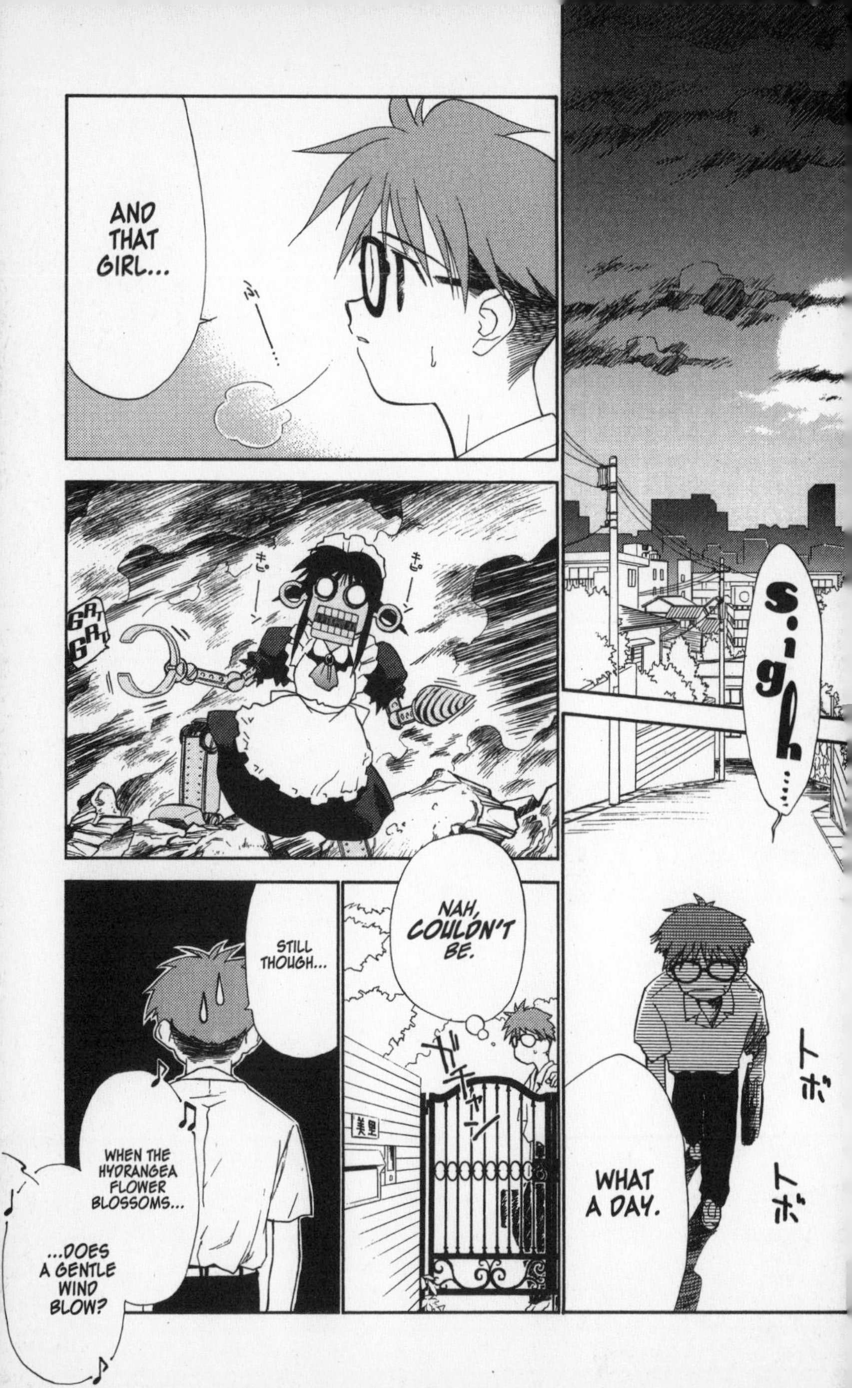
Sigh....
トボ トボ
WHAT A DAY.
AND THAT GIRL...
ふー...
キピーン
キピーン
GR GR GR
NAH, COULDN'T BE.
ガチャン
美里
STILL THOUGH...
WHEN THE HYDRANGEA FLOWER BLOSSOMS...
...DOES A GENTLE WIND BLOW?

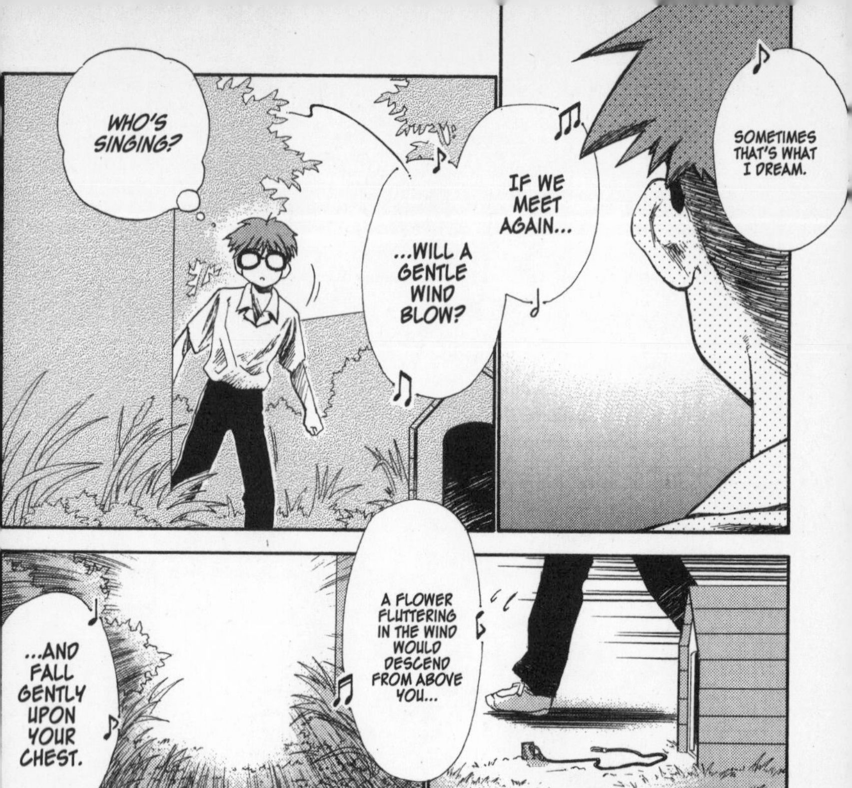
SOMETIMES THAT'S WHAT I DREAM.
IF WE MEET AGAIN...
...WILL A GENTLE WIND BLOW?
WHO'S SINGING?
A FLOWER FLUTTERING IN THE WIND WOULD DESCEND FROM ABOVE YOU...
...AND FALL GENTLY UPON YOUR CHEST.

* "Song of the Wind" by Koutaro Fujishiro

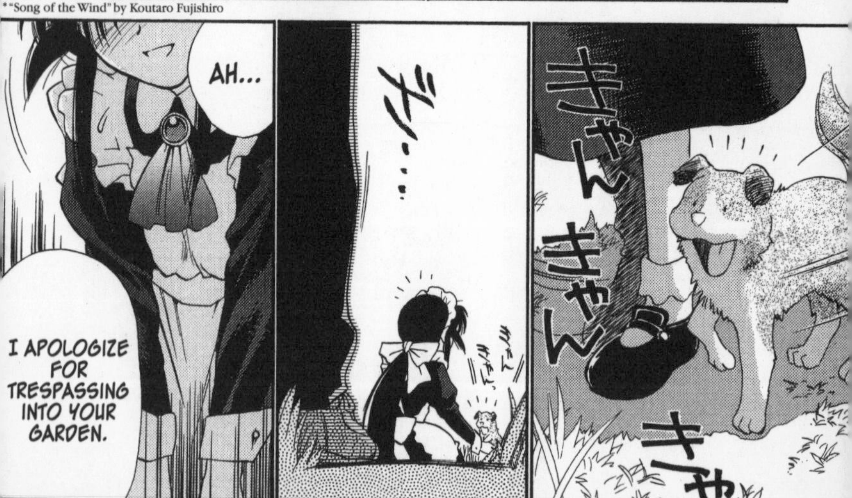
きゃん きゃん
キャ
AH...
I APOLOGIZE FOR TRESPASSING INTO YOUR GARDEN.

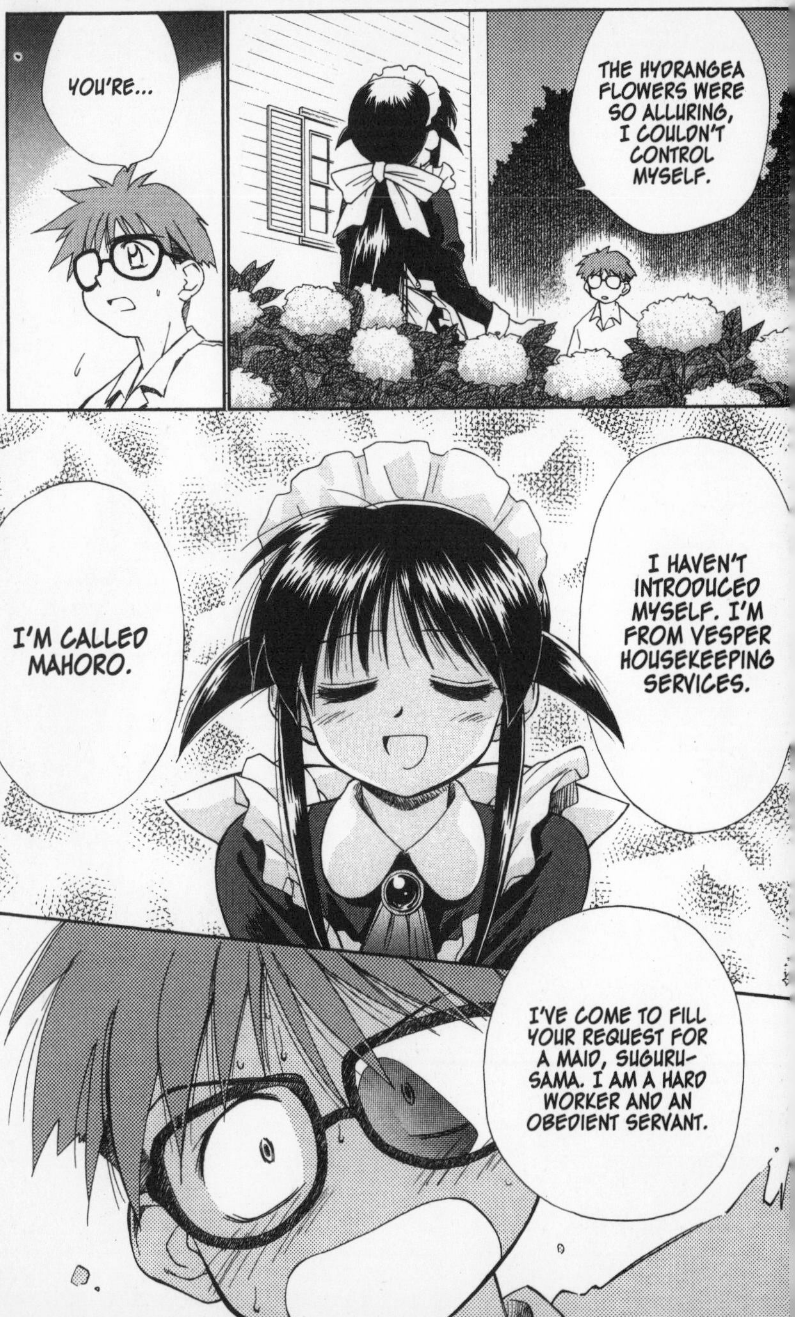
THE HYDRANGEA FLOWERS WERE SO ALLURING, I COULDN'T CONTROL MYSELF.
YOU'RE...
I HAVEN'T INTRODUCED MYSELF. I'M FROM VESPER HOUSEKEEPING SERVICES.
I'M CALLED MAHORO.
I'VE COME TO FILL YOUR REQUEST FOR A MAID, SUGURU-SAMA. I AM A HARD WORKER AND AN OBEDIENT SERVANT.

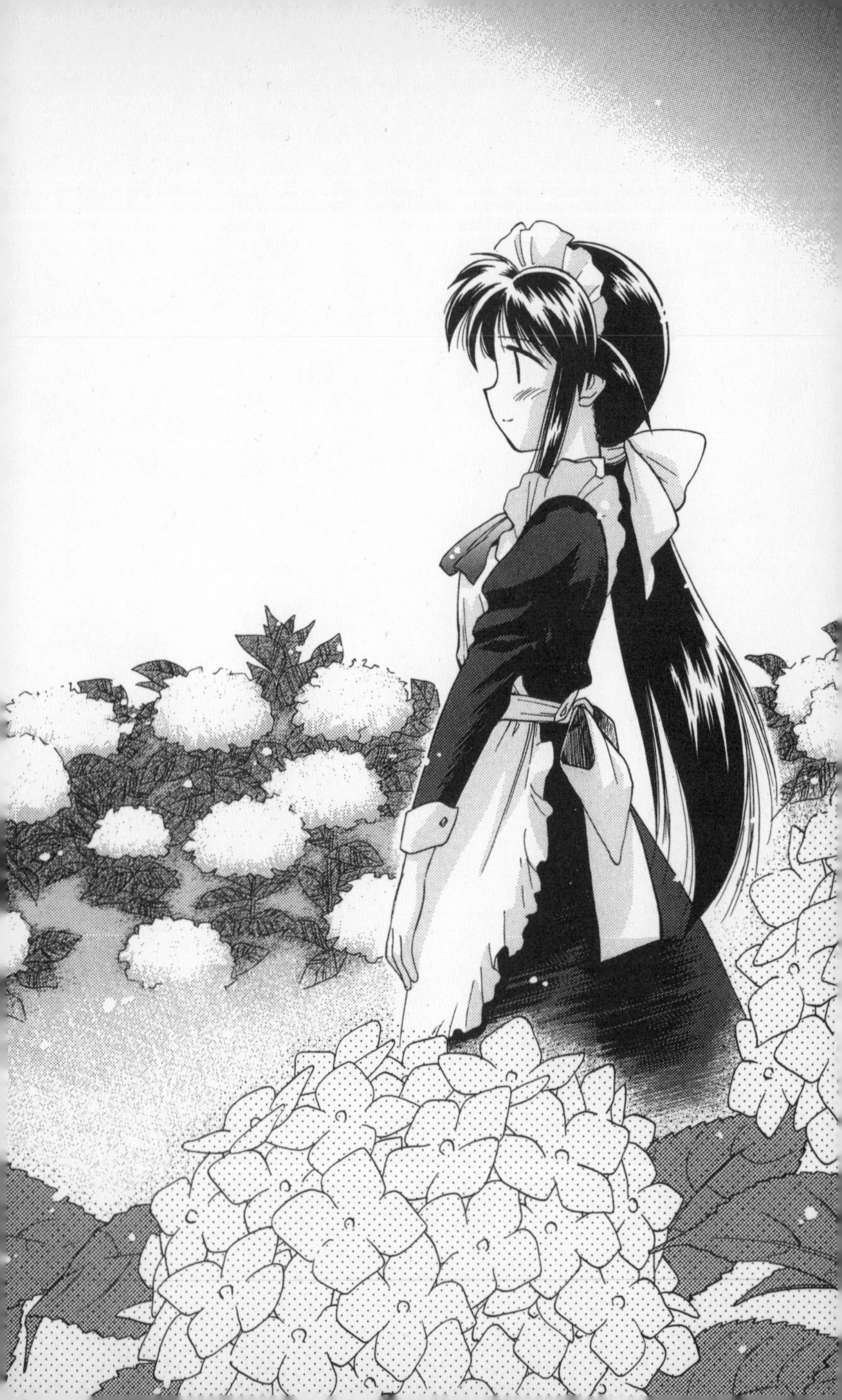

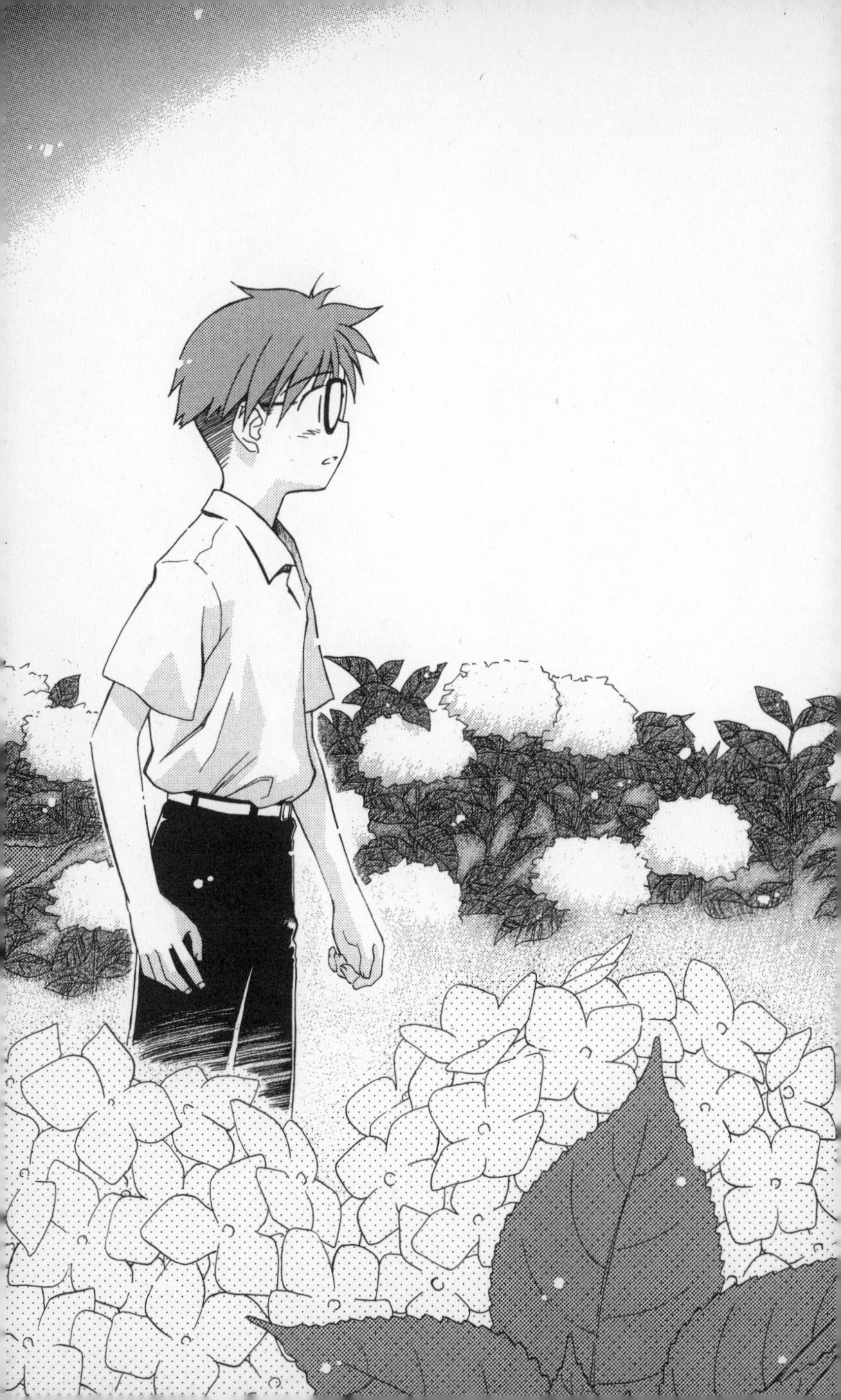

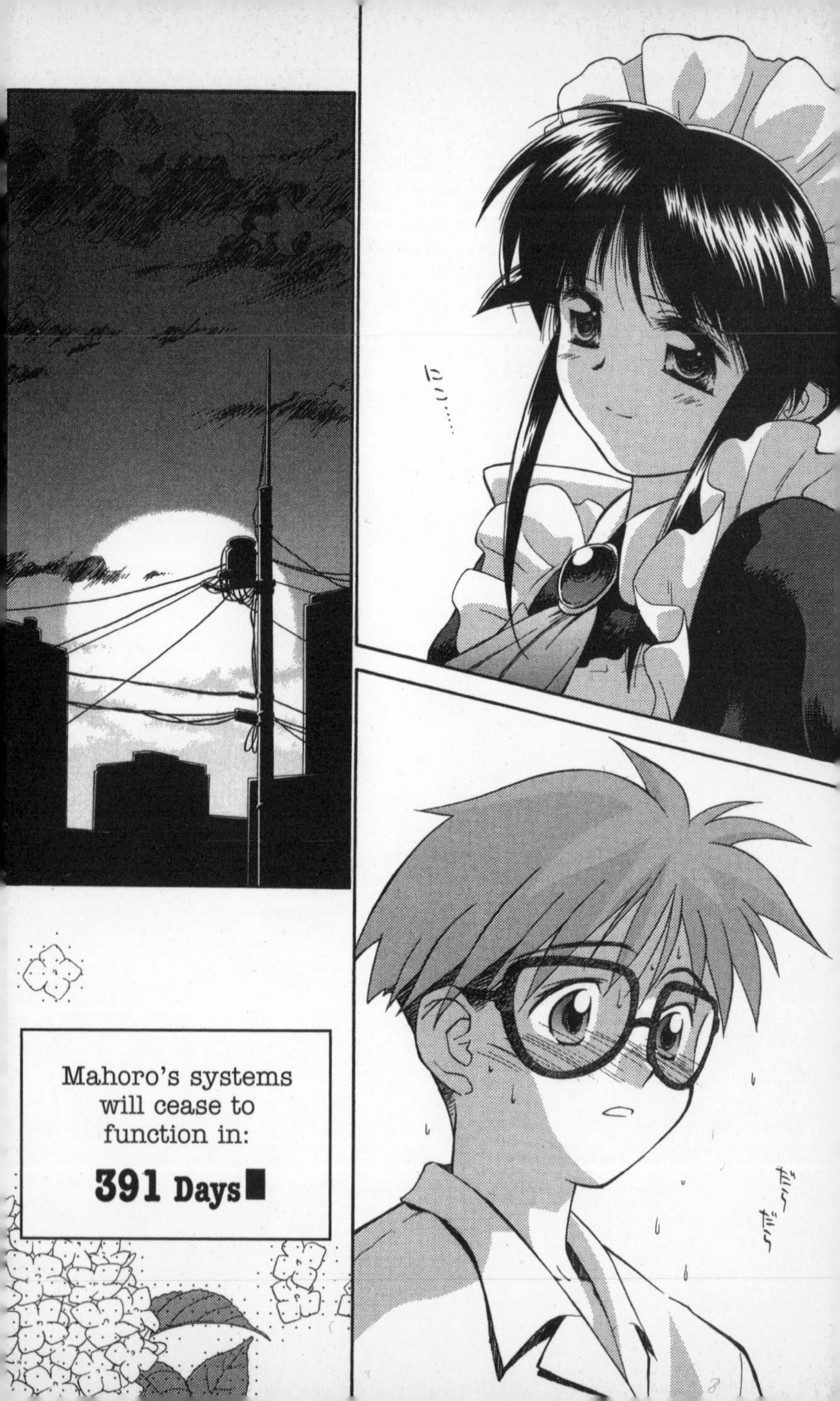
Mahoro's systems will cease to function in:
391 Days

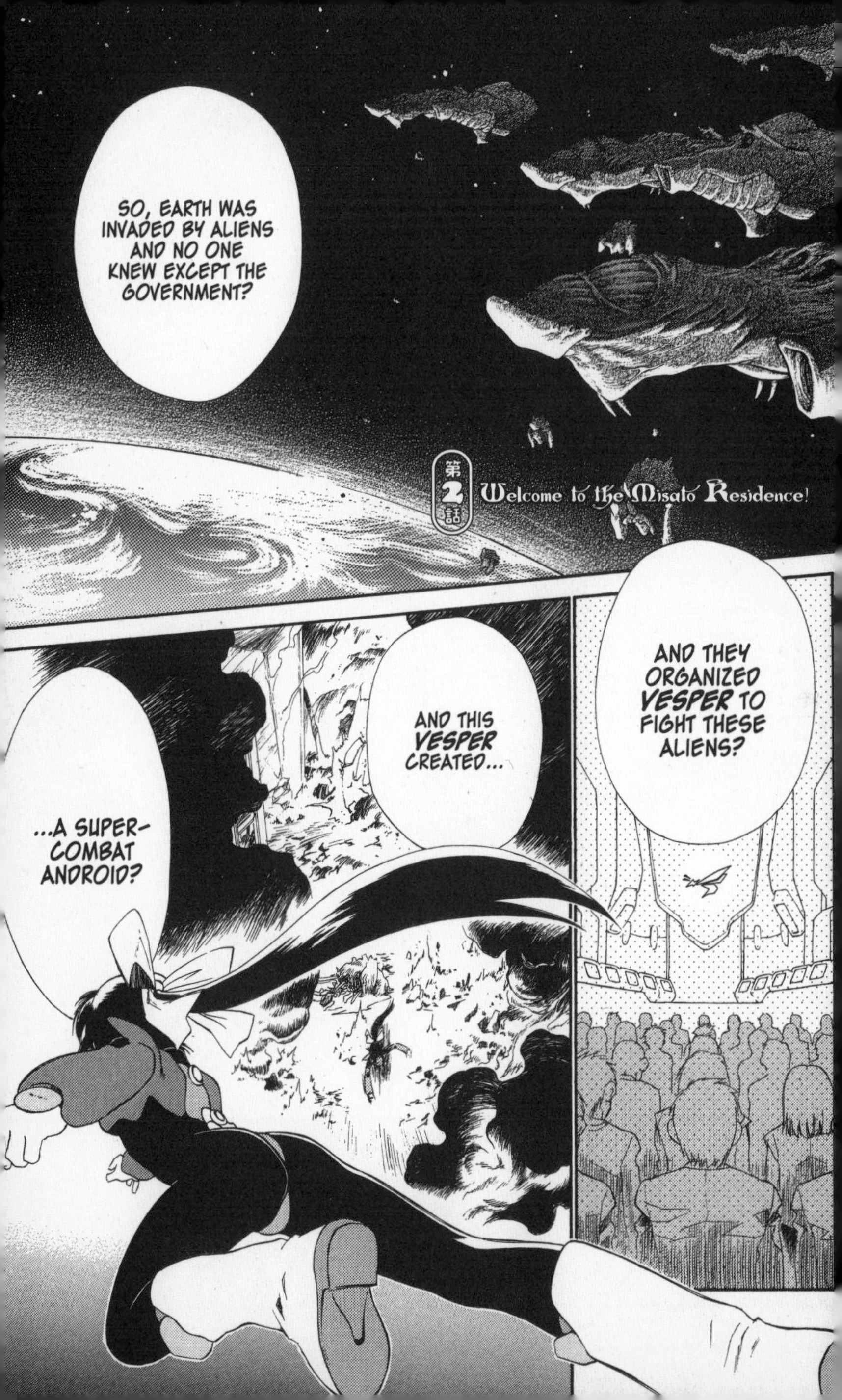
SO, EARTH WAS INVADED BY ALIENS AND NO ONE KNEW EXCEPT THE GOVERNMENT?
第2話 Welcome to the Misato Residence!
AND THEY ORGANIZED VESPER TO FIGHT THESE ALIENS?
AND THIS VESPER CREATED...
...A SUPER-COMBAT ANDROID?

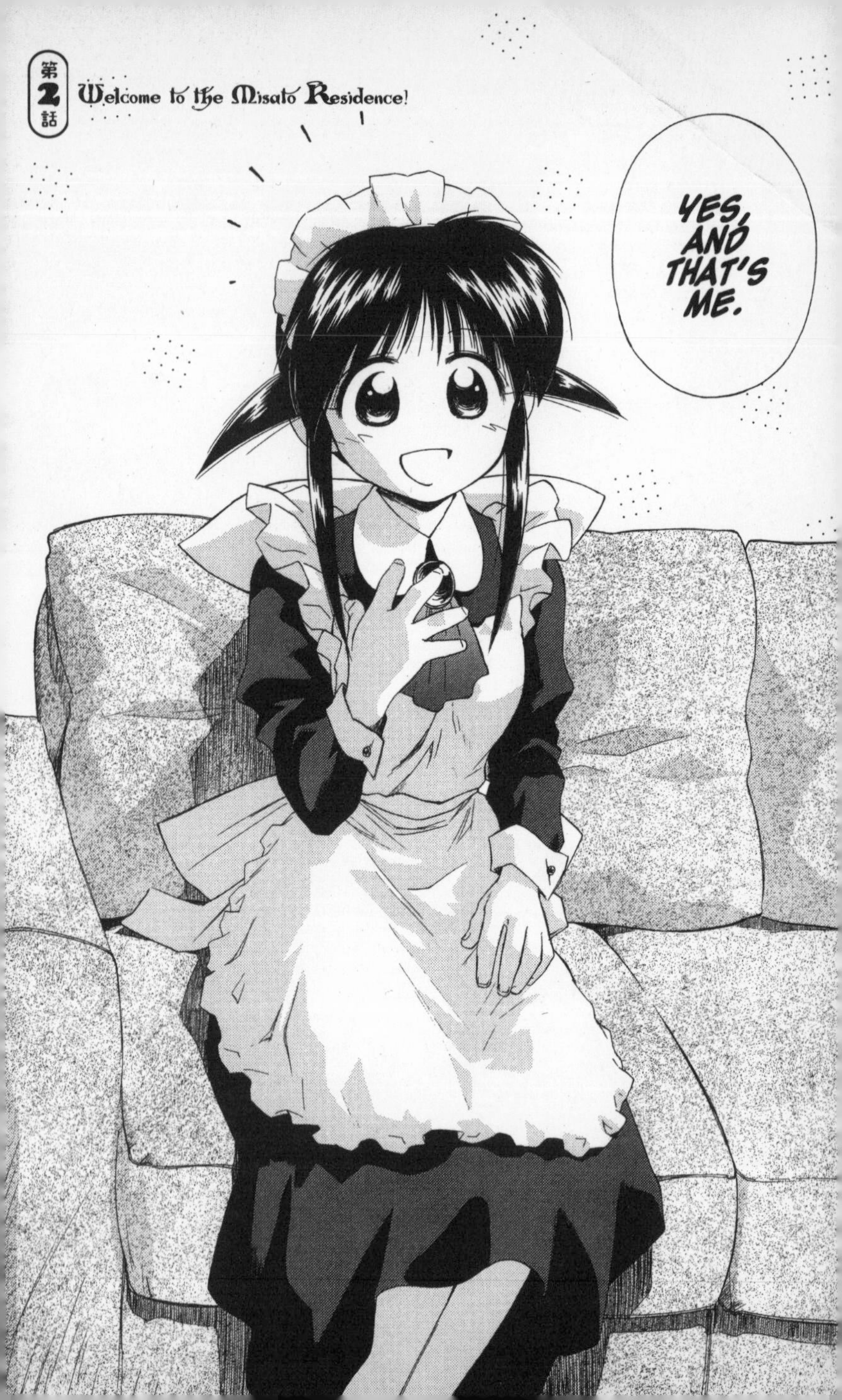
第2話
Welcome to the Misato Residence!
YES, AND THAT'S ME.

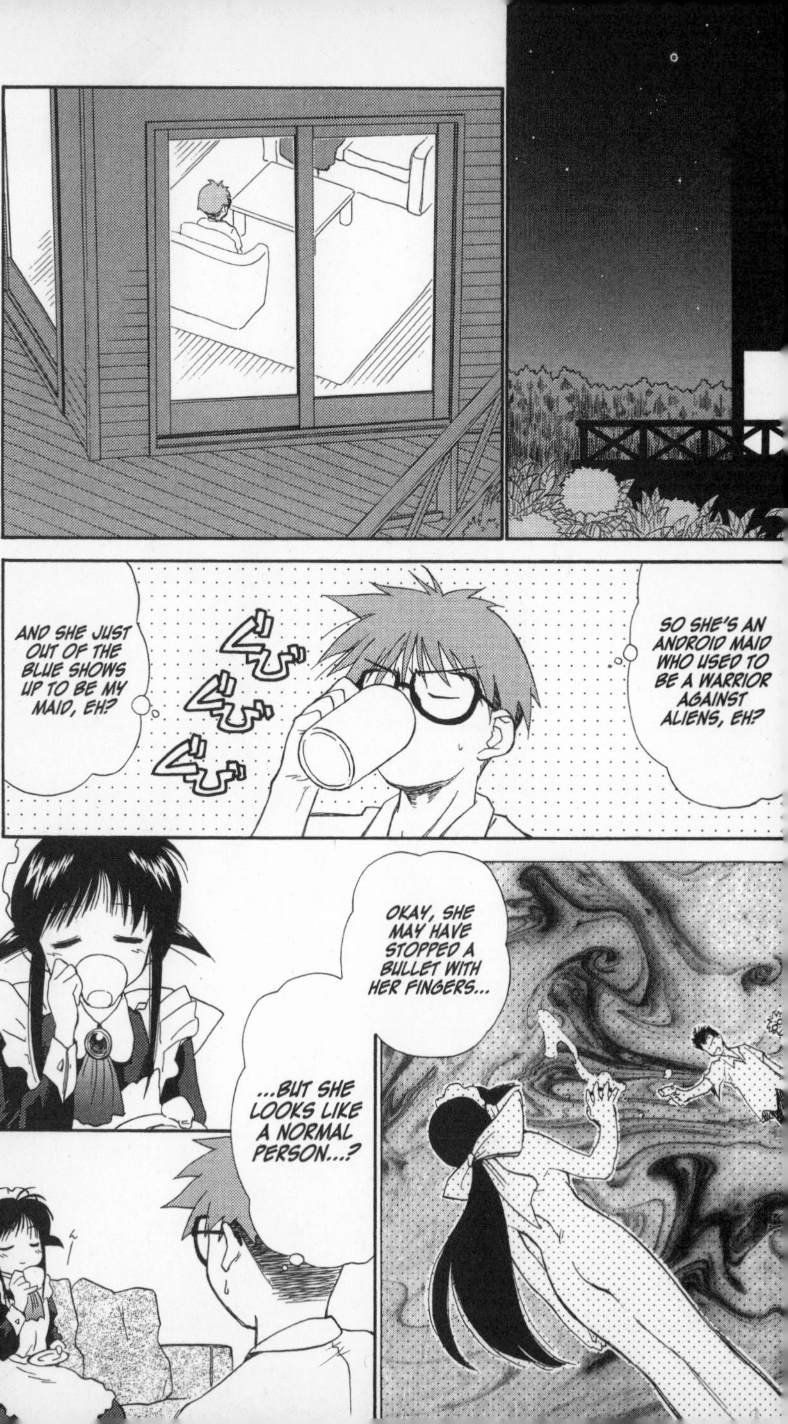
SO SHE'S AN ANDROID MAID WHO USED TO BE A WARRIOR AGAINST ALIENS, EH?
AND SHE JUST OUT OF THE BLUE SHOWS UP TO BE MY MAID, EH?
OKAY, SHE MAY HAVE STOPPED A BULLET WITH HER FINGERS...
...BUT SHE LOOKS LIKE A NORMAL PERSON...?

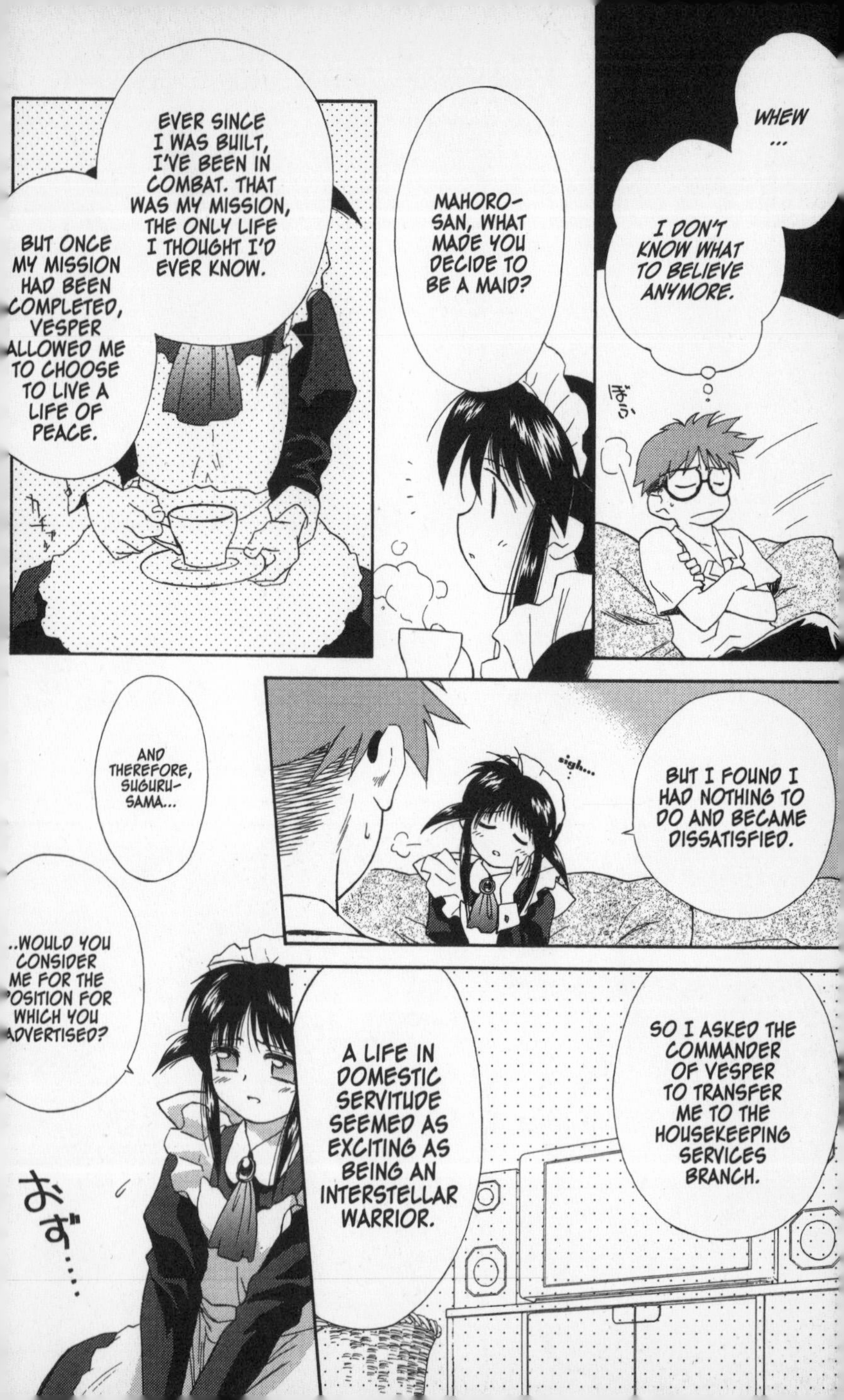
WHEW ...
I DON'T KNOW WHAT TO BELIEVE ANYMORE.
ぼふ
MAHORO-SAN, WHAT MADE YOU DECIDE TO BE A MAID?
EVER SINCE I WAS BUILT, I'VE BEEN IN COMBAT. THAT WAS MY MISSION, THE ONLY LIFE I THOUGHT I'D EVER KNOW.
BUT ONCE MY MISSION HAD BEEN COMPLETED, VESPER ALLOWED ME TO CHOOSE TO LIVE A LIFE OF PEACE.
sigh...
BUT I FOUND I HAD NOTHING TO DO AND BECAME DISSATISFIED.
SO I ASKED THE COMMANDER OF VESPER TO TRANSFER ME TO THE HOUSEKEEPING SERVICES BRANCH.
A LIFE IN DOMESTIC SERVITUDE SEEMED AS EXCITING AS BEING AN INTERSTELLAR WARRIOR.
AND THEREFORE, SUGURU-SAMA...
..WOULD YOU CONSIDER ME FOR THE POSITION FOR WHICH YOU ADVERTISED?
おず…

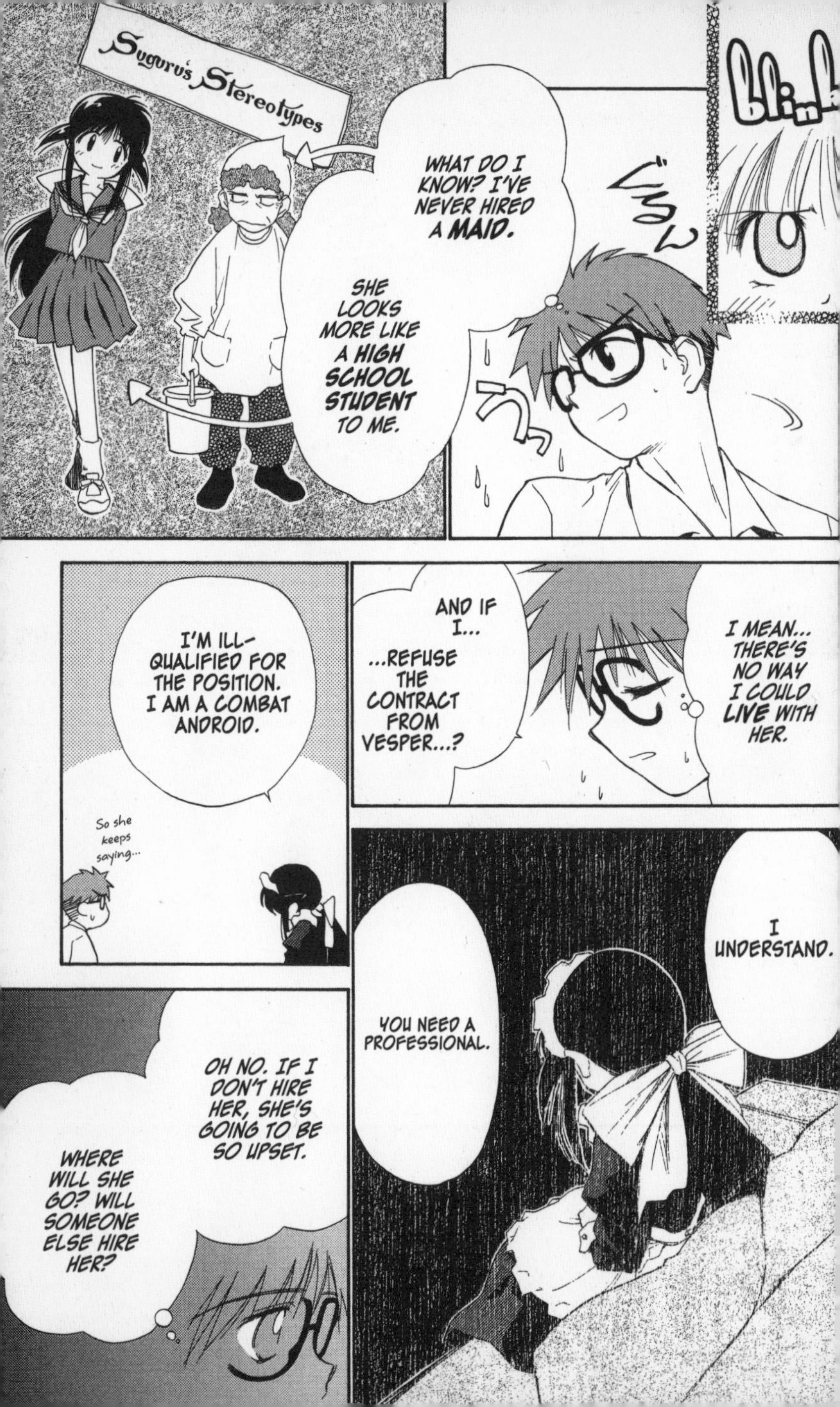
WHAT DO I KNOW? I'VE NEVER HIRED A MAID.
SHE LOOKS MORE LIKE A HIGH SCHOOL STUDENT TO ME.
Suguru's Stereotypes
I MEAN... THERE'S NO WAY I COULD LIVE WITH HER.
AND IF I...
...REFUSE THE CONTRACT FROM VESPER...?
I'M ILL-QUALIFIED FOR THE POSITION. I AM A COMBAT ANDROID.
So she keeps saying...
I UNDERSTAND.
YOU NEED A PROFESSIONAL.
OH NO. IF I DON'T HIRE HER, SHE'S GOING TO BE SO UPSET.
WHERE WILL SHE GO? WILL SOMEONE ELSE HIRE HER?

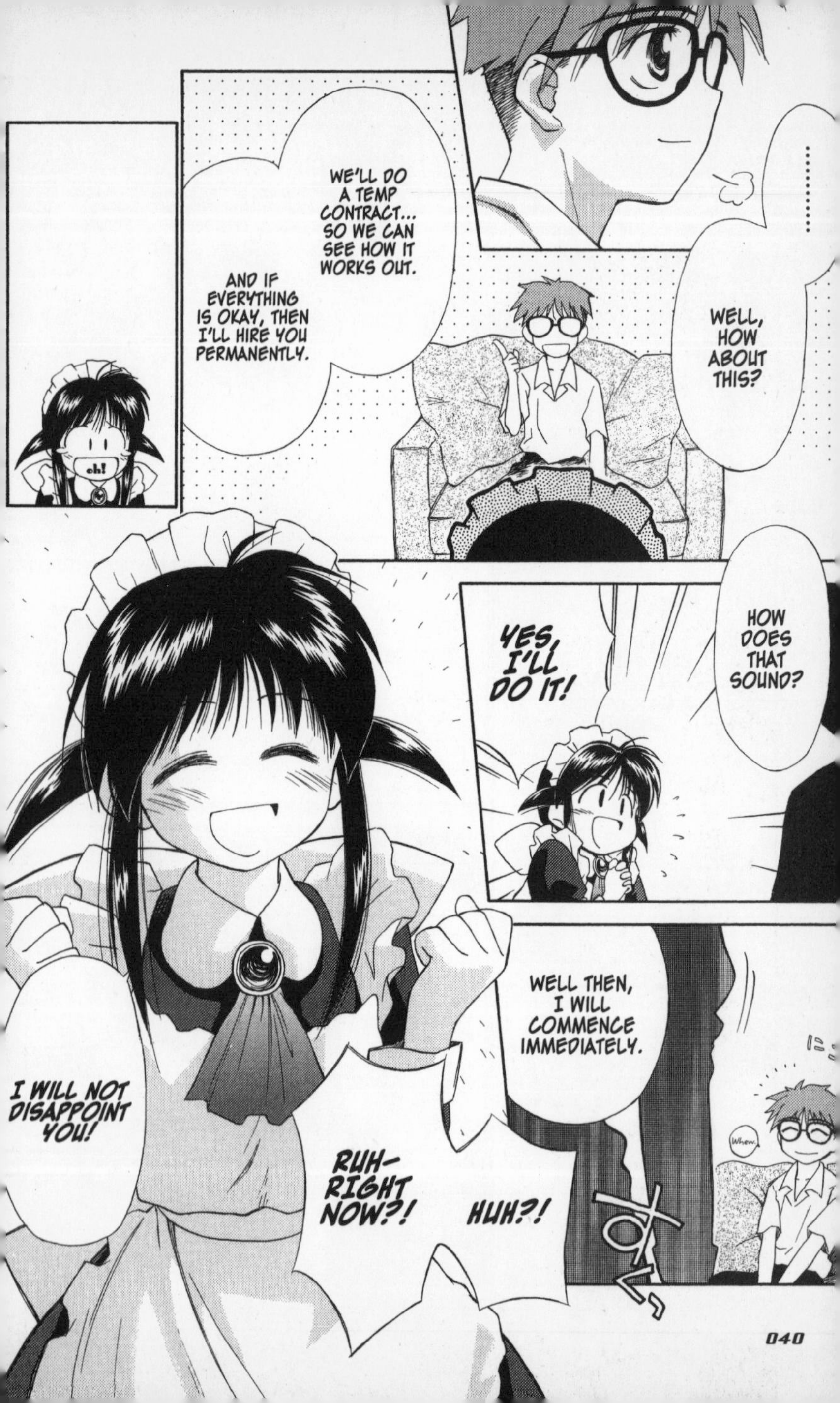
......
WELL, HOW ABOUT THIS?
WE'LL DO A TEMP CONTRACT... SO WE CAN SEE HOW IT WORKS OUT.
AND IF EVERYTHING IS OKAY, THEN I'LL HIRE YOU PERMANENTLY.
oh!
HOW DOES THAT SOUND?
YES, I'LL DO IT!
WELL THEN, I WILL COMMENCE IMMEDIATELY.
Whew.
HUH?!
RUH-RIGHT NOW?!
I WILL NOT DISAPPOINT YOU!

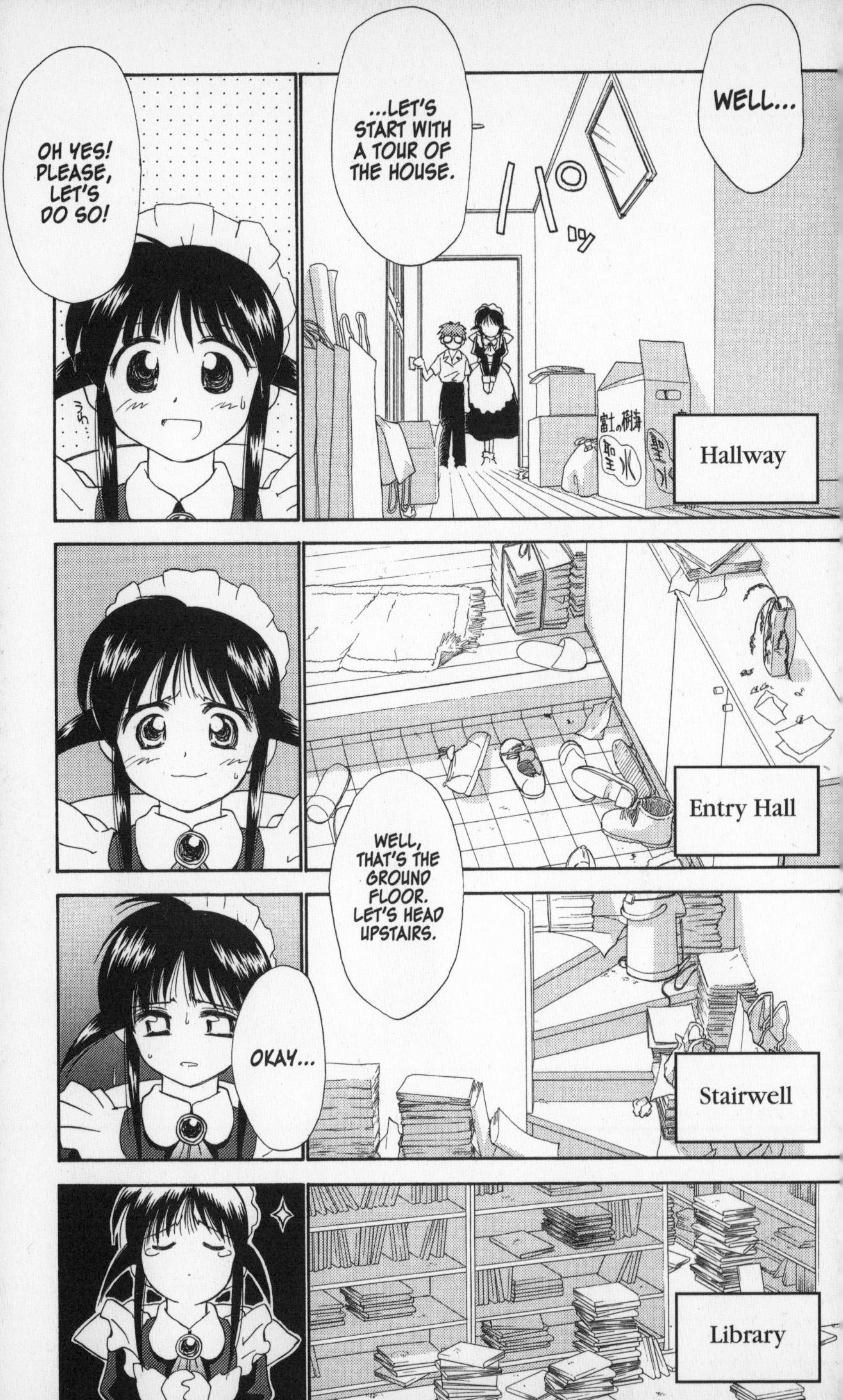
WELL...
...LET'S START WITH A TOUR OF THE HOUSE.
富士の樹海
聖水
聖水
Hallway
OH YES! PLEASE, LET'S DO SO!
Entry Hall
WELL, THAT'S THE GROUND FLOOR. LET'S HEAD UPSTAIRS.
Stairwell
OKAY...
Library

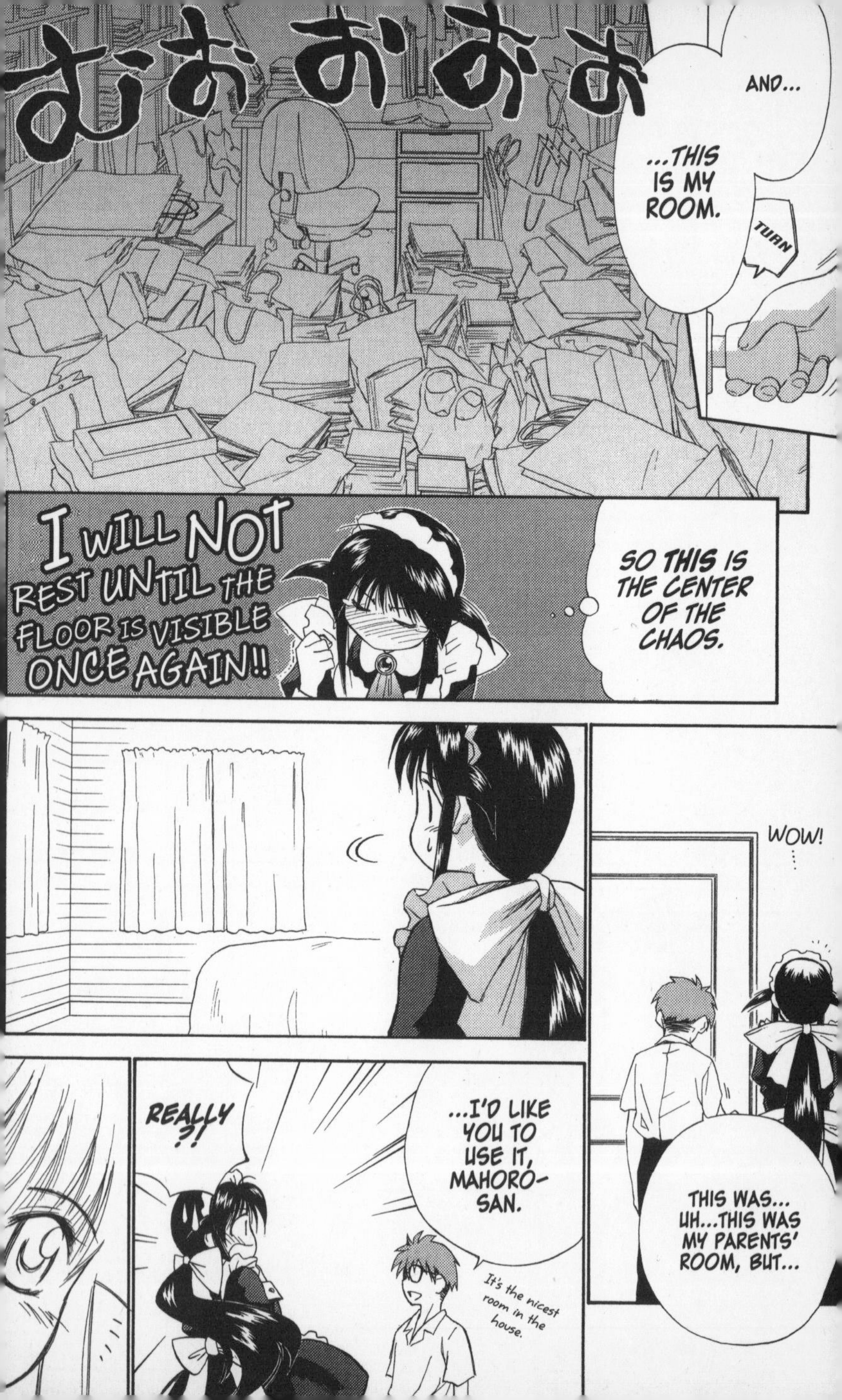
AND...
...THIS IS MY ROOM.
TURN
SO THIS IS THE CENTER OF THE CHAOS.
I WILL NOT REST UNTIL THE FLOOR IS VISIBLE ONCE AGAIN!!
WOW!
THIS WAS... UH...THIS WAS MY PARENTS' ROOM, BUT...
...I'D LIKE YOU TO USE IT, MAHORO-SAN.
It's the nicest room in the house.
REALLY ?!

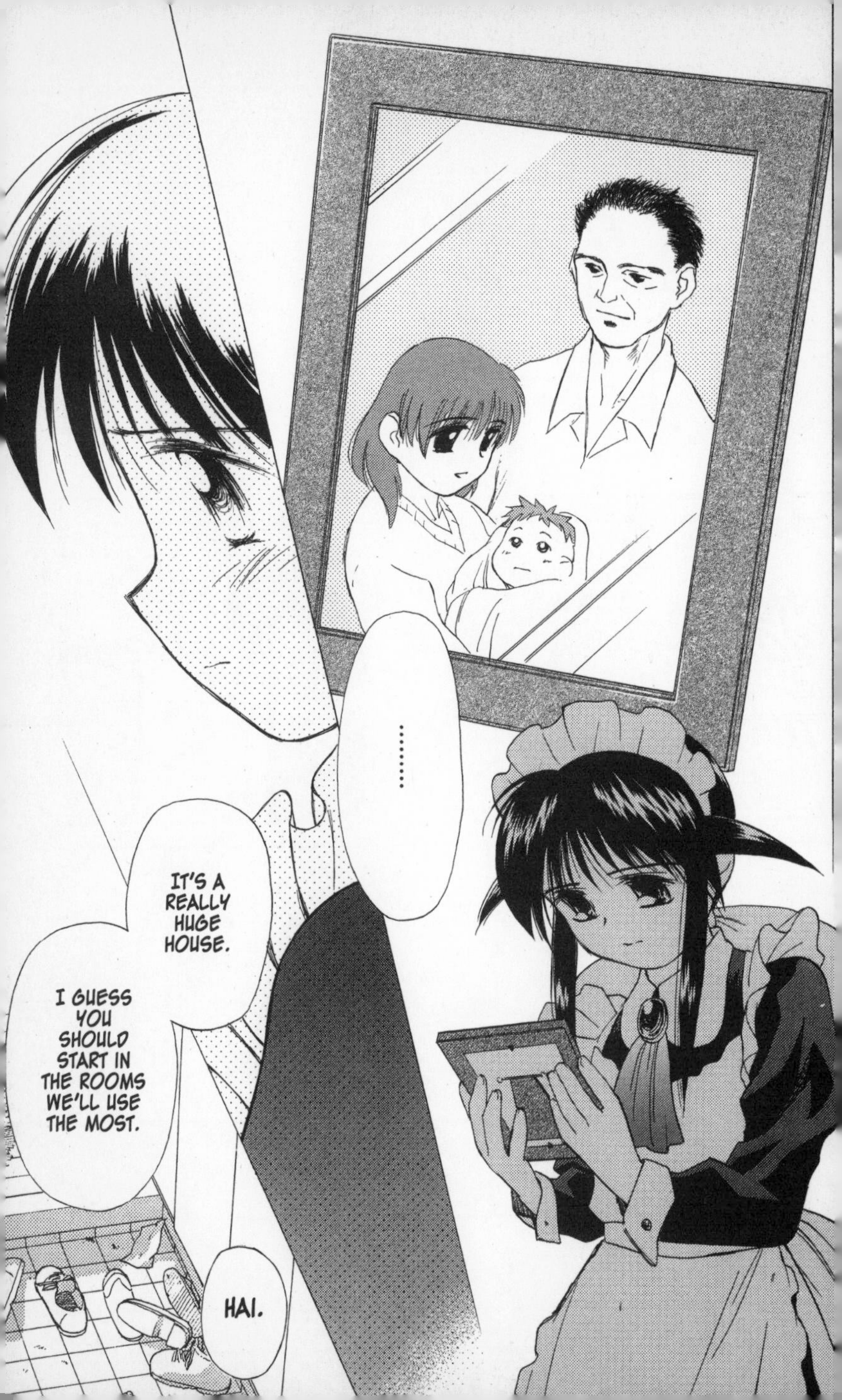

....
IT'S A REALLY HUGE HOUSE.
I GUESS YOU SHOULD START IN THE ROOMS WE'LL USE THE MOST.
HAI.

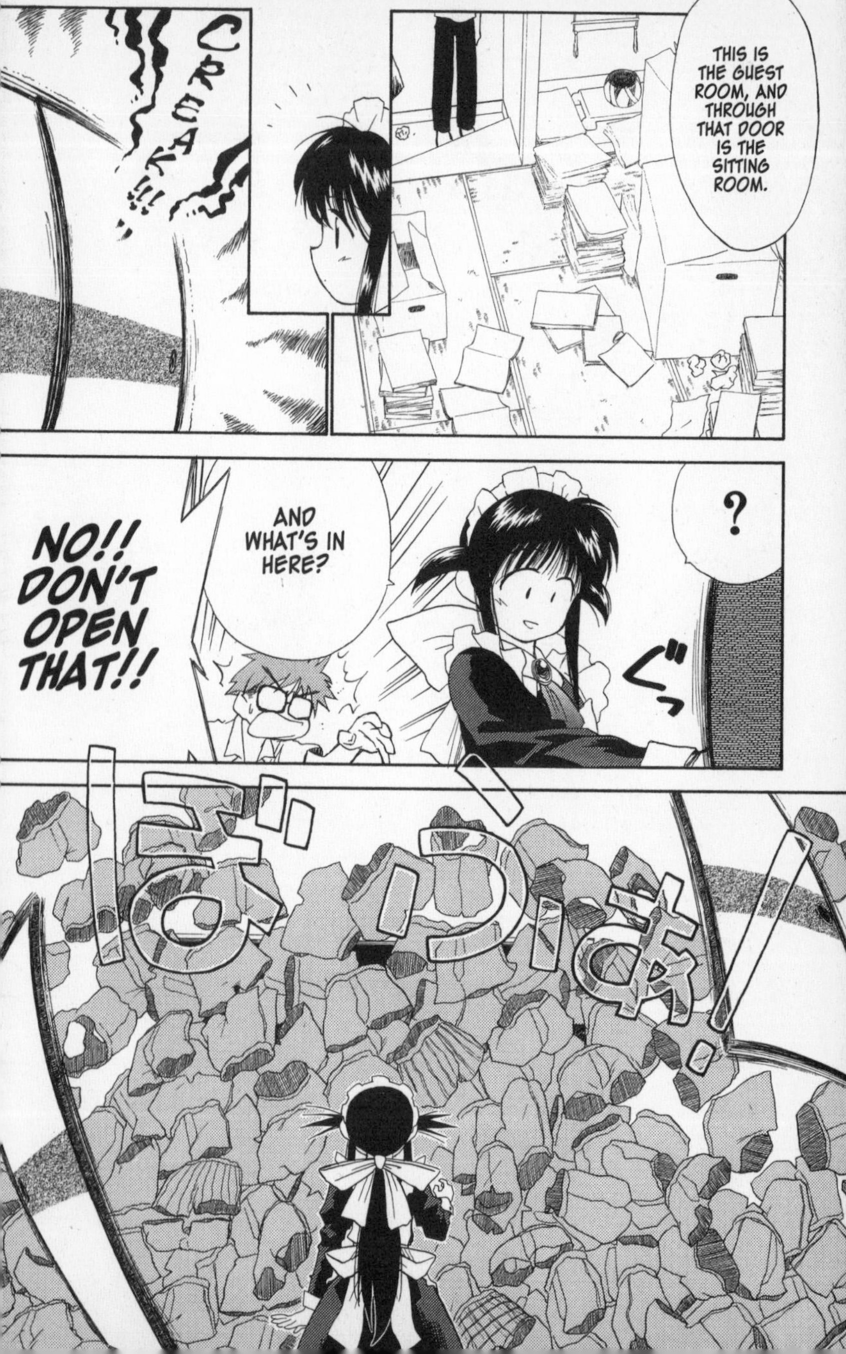
THIS IS THE GUEST ROOM, AND THROUGH THAT DOOR IS THE SITTING ROOM.
CREAK!!!
?
ぐっ
AND WHAT'S IN HERE?
NO!! DON'T OPEN THAT!!

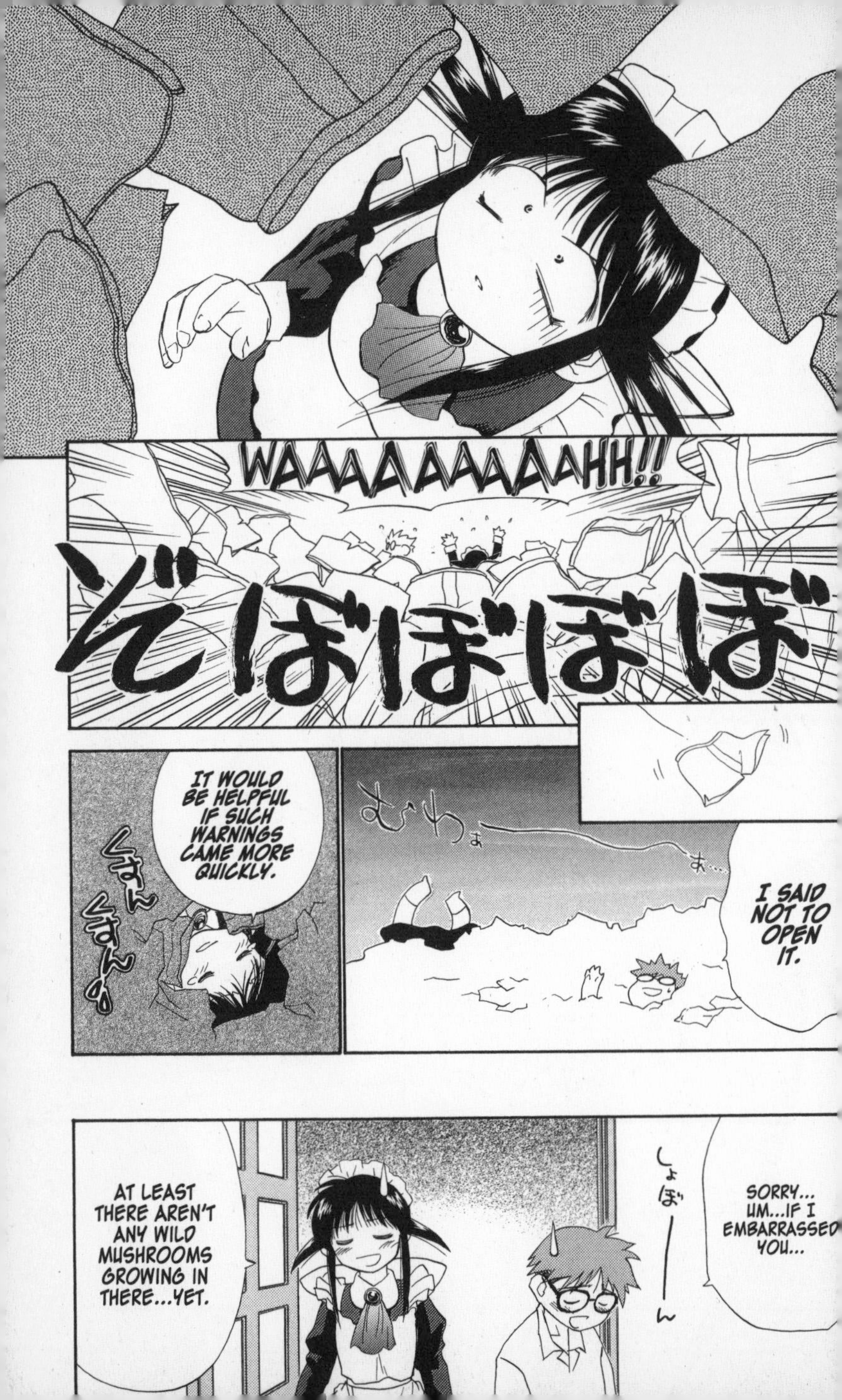
WAAAAAAAAAAAHH!!
ぞぼぼぼぼ
むわぁ―――あ…
I SAID NOT TO OPEN IT.
IT WOULD BE HELPFUL IF SUCH WARNINGS CAME MORE QUICKLY.
くすんくすん
SORRY... UM...IF I EMBARRASSED YOU...
しょぼーん
AT LEAST THERE AREN'T ANY WILD MUSHROOMS GROWING IN THERE...YET.

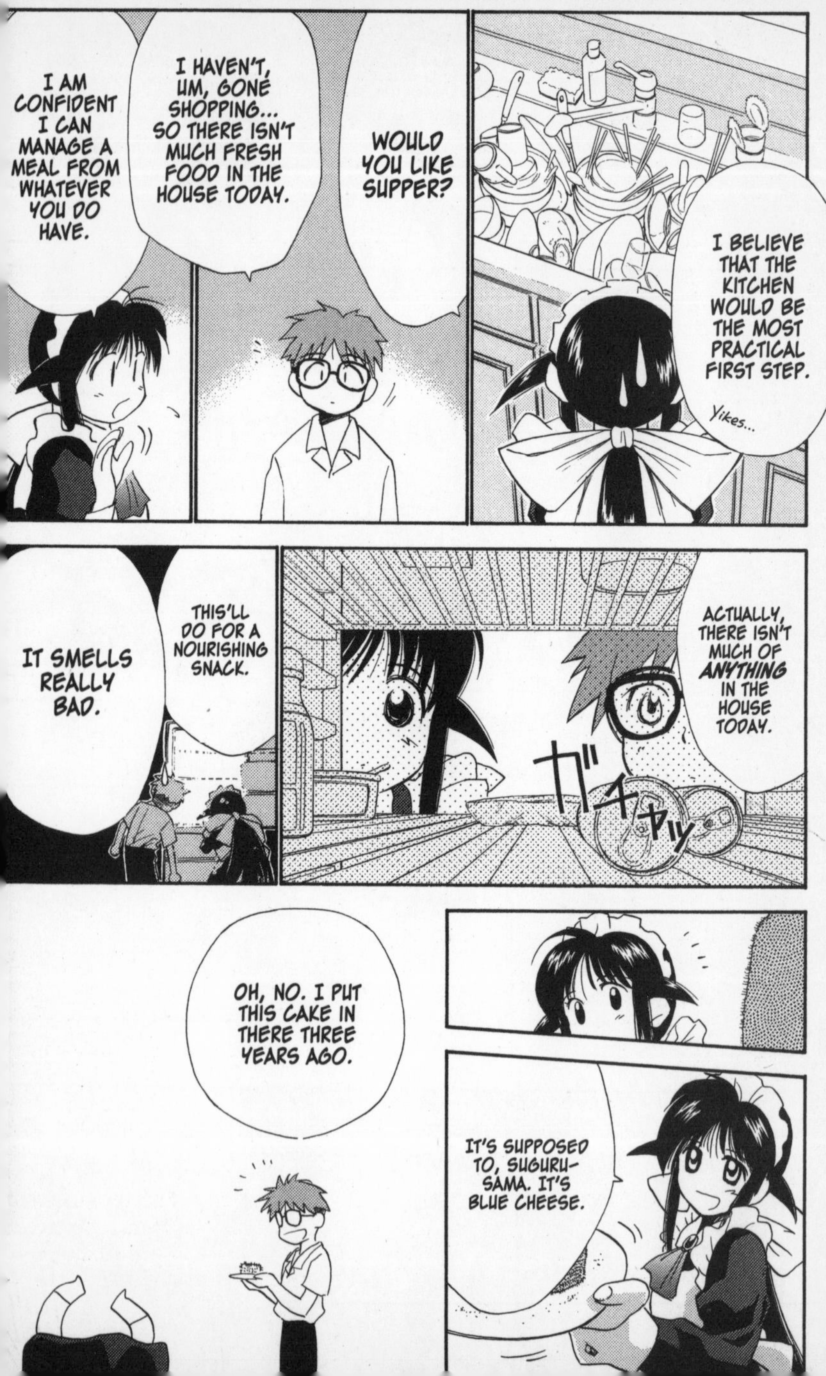
I BELIEVE THAT THE KITCHEN WOULD BE THE MOST PRACTICAL FIRST STEP.
Yikes...
WOULD YOU LIKE SUPPER?
I HAVEN'T, UM, GONE SHOPPING... SO THERE ISN'T MUCH FRESH FOOD IN THE HOUSE TODAY.
I AM CONFIDENT I CAN MANAGE A MEAL FROM WHATEVER YOU DO HAVE.
ACTUALLY, THERE ISN'T MUCH OF *ANYTHING* IN THE HOUSE TODAY.
ガチャッ
THIS'LL DO FOR A NOURISHING SNACK.
IT SMELLS REALLY BAD.
IT'S SUPPOSED TO, SUGURU-SAMA. IT'S BLUE CHEESE.
OH, NO. I PUT THIS CAKE IN THERE THREE YEARS AGO.

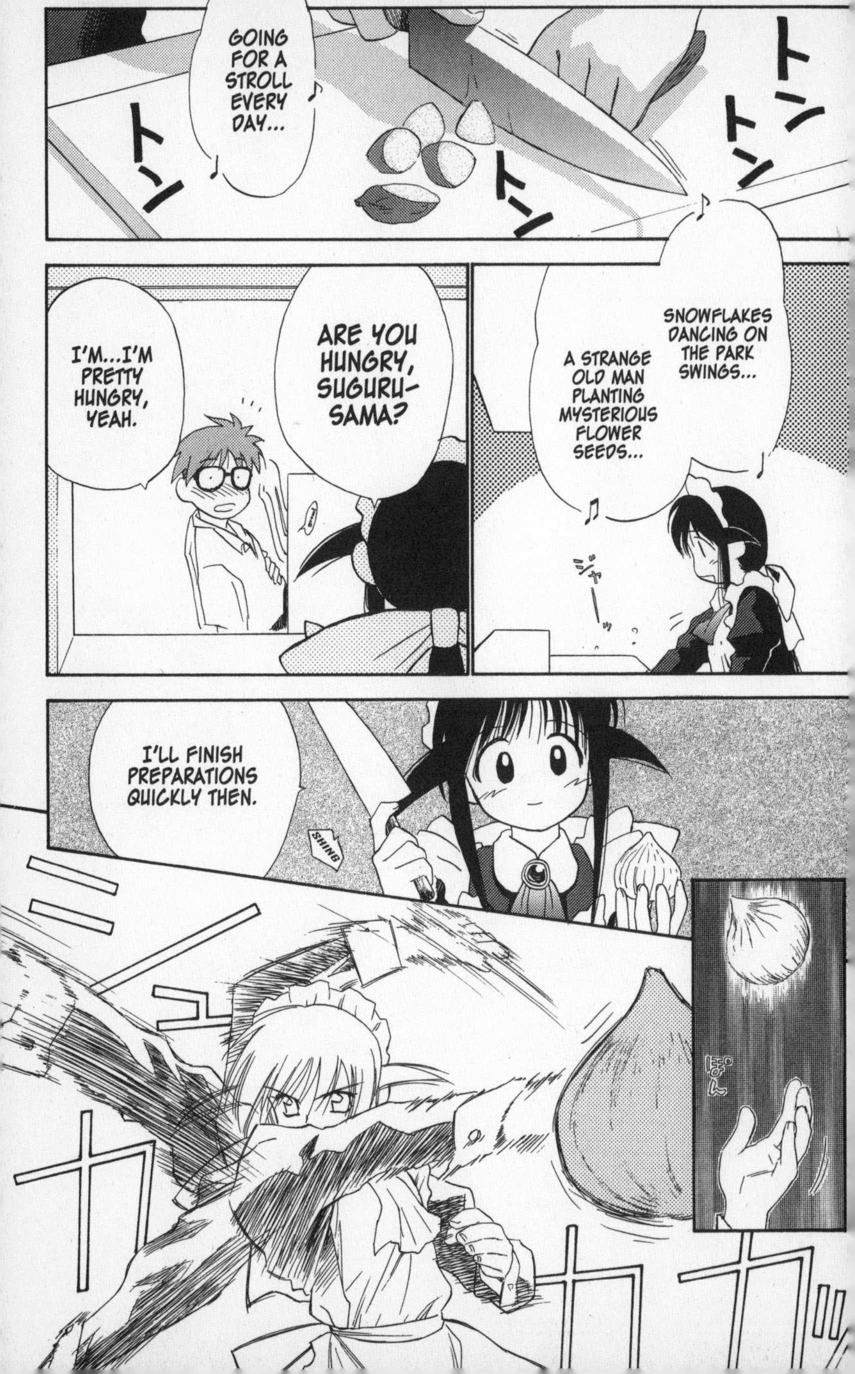
GOING FOR A STROLL EVERY DAY...
トン
トン
トン
SNOWFLAKES DANCING ON THE PARK SWINGS...
A STRANGE OLD MAN PLANTING MYSTERIOUS FLOWER SEEDS...
ARE YOU HUNGRY, SUGURU-SAMA?
I'M...I'M PRETTY HUNGRY, YEAH.
I'LL FINISH PREPARATIONS QUICKLY THEN.
SHING
ぽん

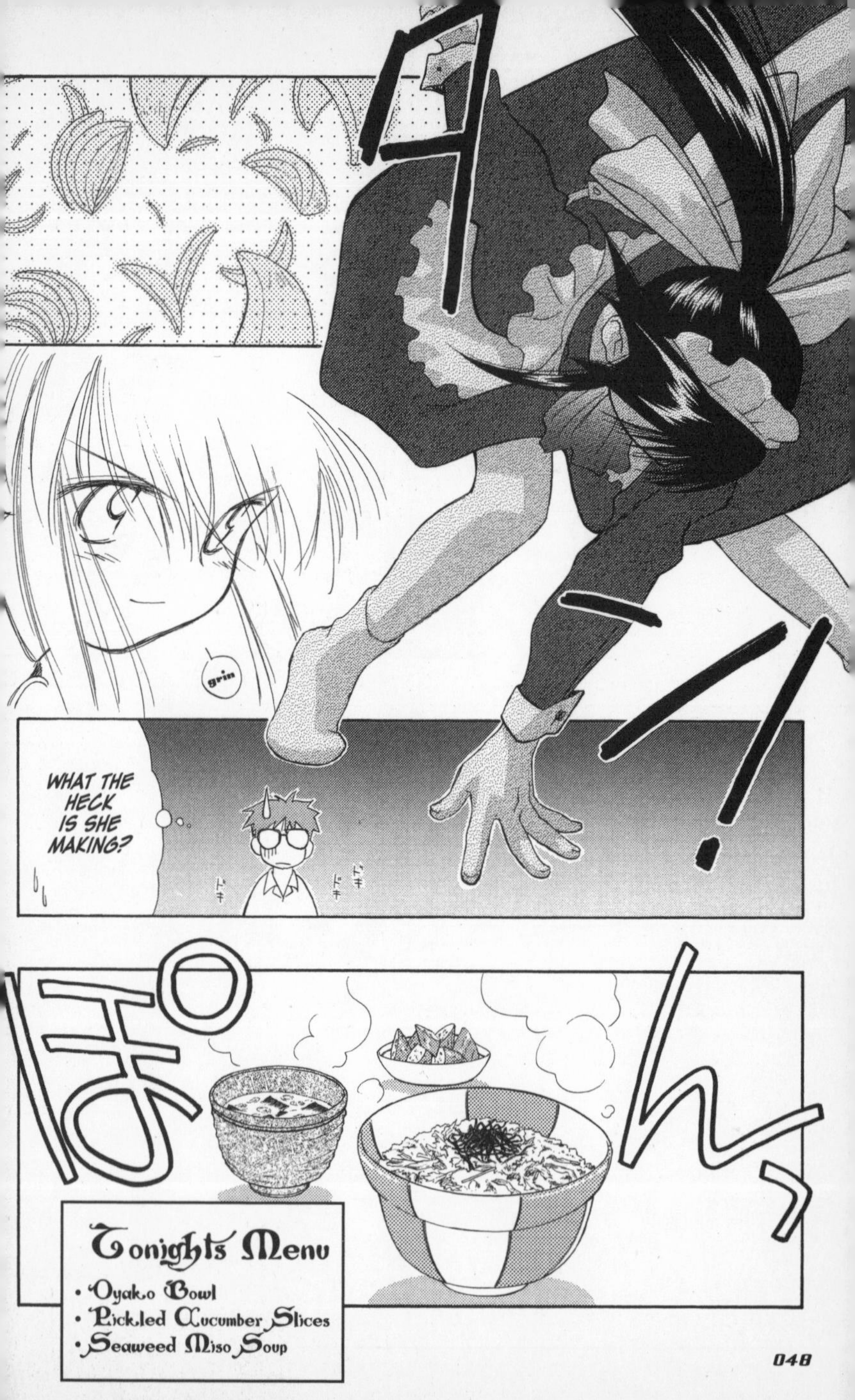
grin
WHAT THE HECK IS SHE MAKING?
ドキ ドキ
ぽん
Tonights Menu
• Oyako Bowl
• Pickled Cucumber Slices
• Seaweed Miso Soup

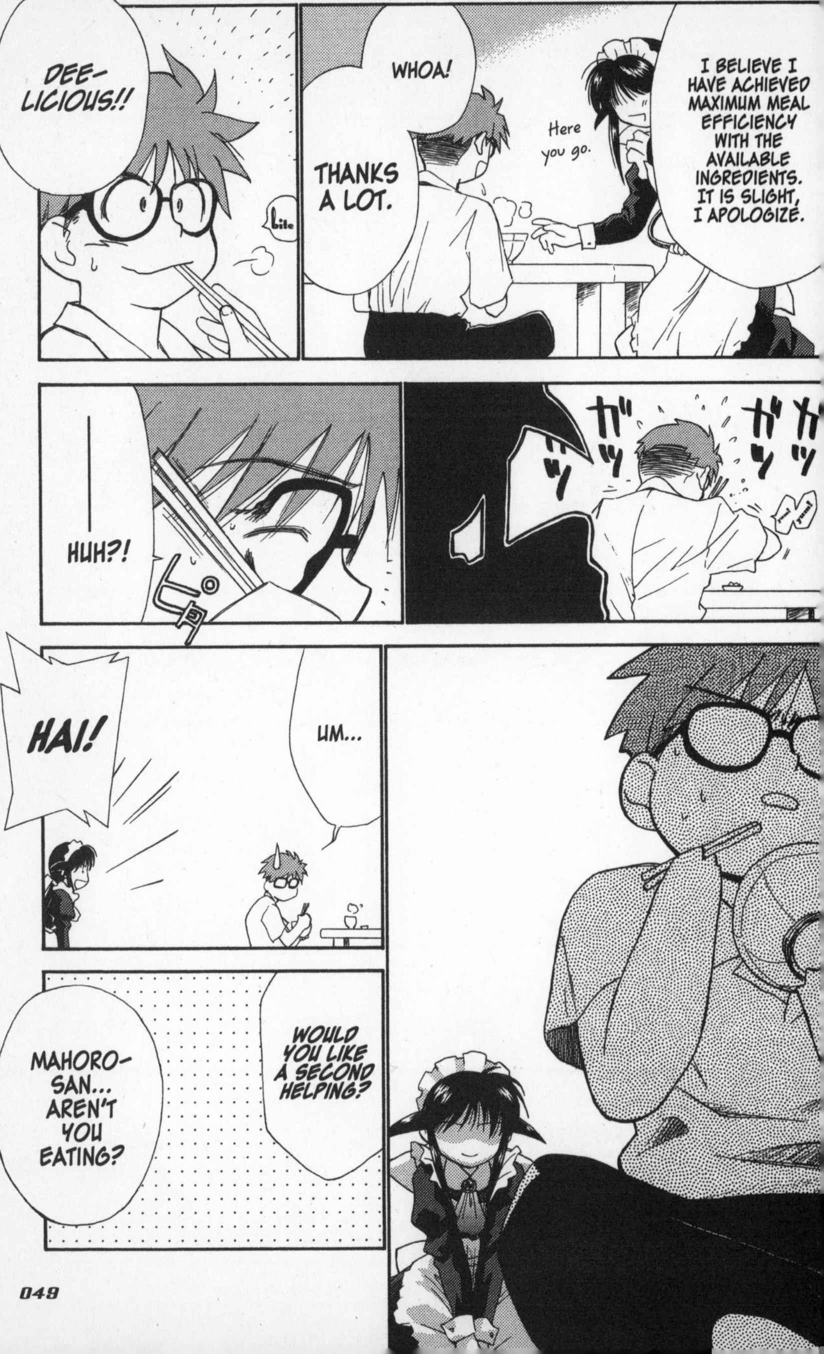
I BELIEVE I HAVE ACHIEVED MAXIMUM MEAL EFFICIENCY WITH THE AVAILABLE INGREDIENTS. IT IS SLIGHT, I APOLOGIZE.
Here you go.
WHOA!
THANKS A LOT.
bite
DEE-LICIOUS!!
ガッ
ガッ
ガッ
ガッ
HUH?!
UM...
HAI!
WOULD YOU LIKE A SECOND HELPING?
MAHORO-SAN... AREN'T YOU EATING?

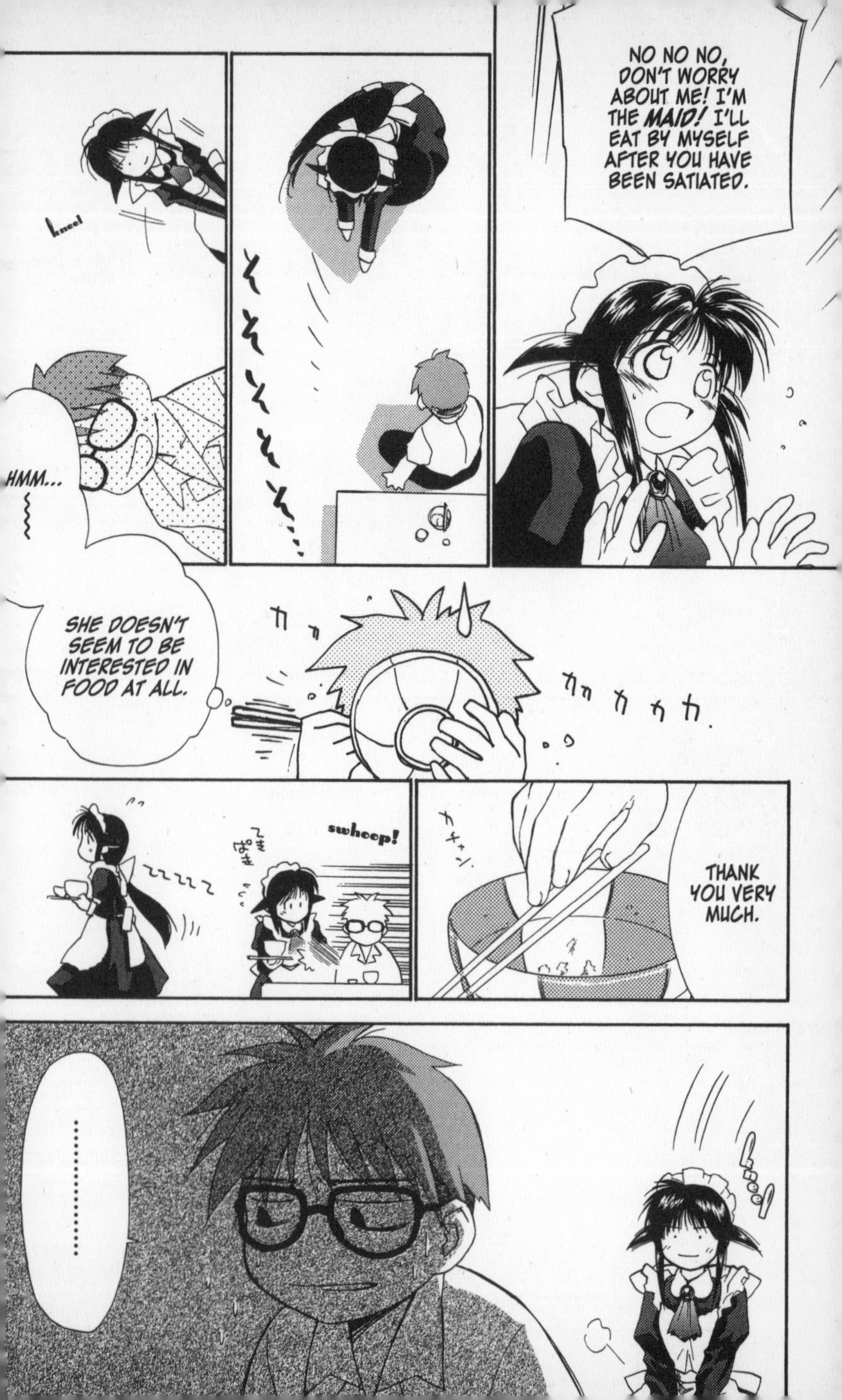
NO NO NO, DON'T WORRY ABOUT ME! I'M THE *MAID!* I'LL EAT BY MYSELF AFTER YOU HAVE BEEN SATIATED.
kneel
HMM...
SHE DOESN'T SEEM TO BE INTERESTED IN FOOD AT ALL.
THANK YOU VERY MUCH.
swhoop!
kneel
....

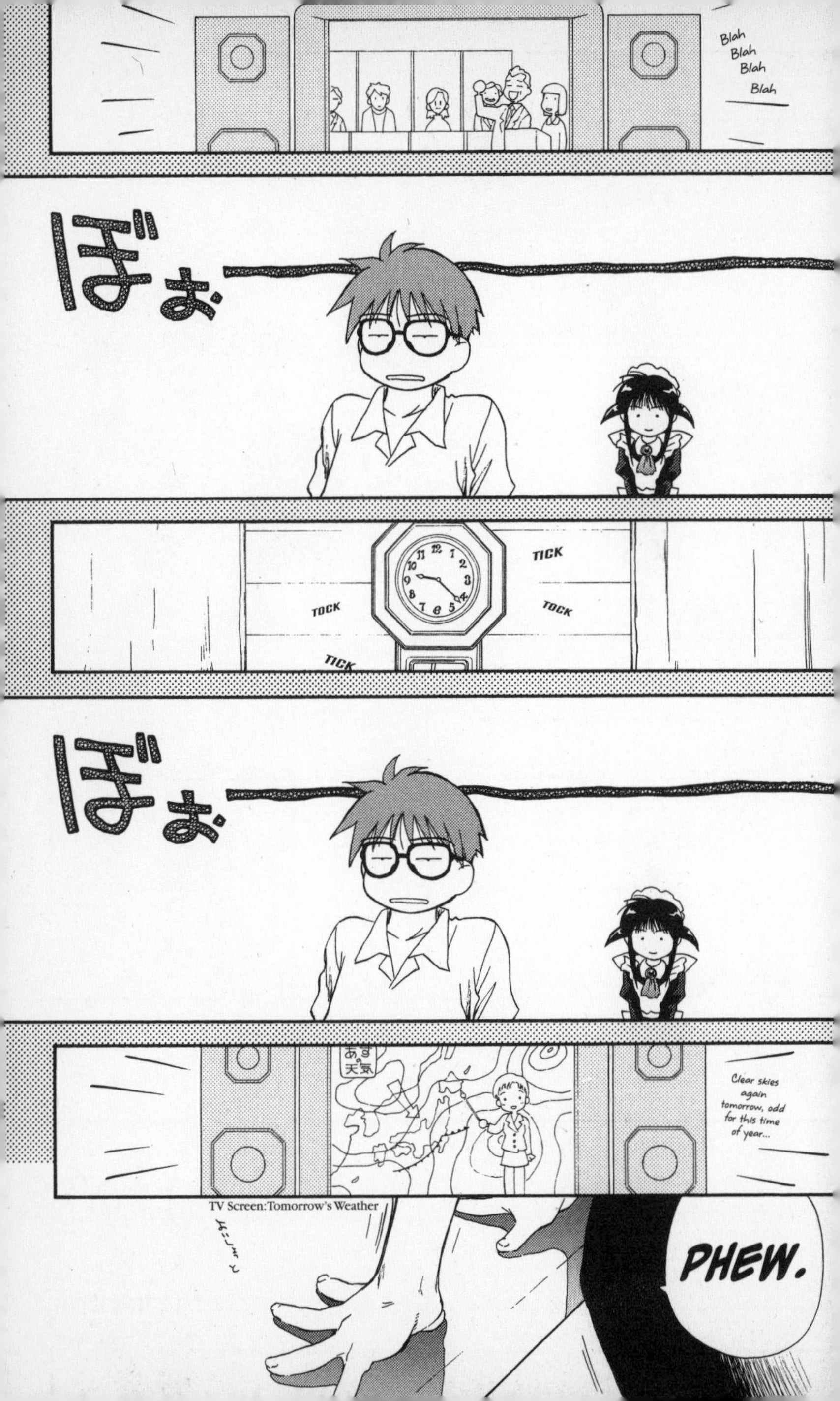
Blah
Blah
Blah
Blah
ぼぉ
TICK
TOCK
TOCK
TICK
ぼぉ
あすの天気
Clear skies again tomorrow, odd for this time of year...
TV Screen: Tomorrow's Weather
PHEW.
よこしょっと

I'M GOING TO TAKE A BATH AND GO TO BED.

I WON'T NEED ANYTHING ELSE TONIGHT, MAHORO-SAN.

....

Towel: Sakura Bath

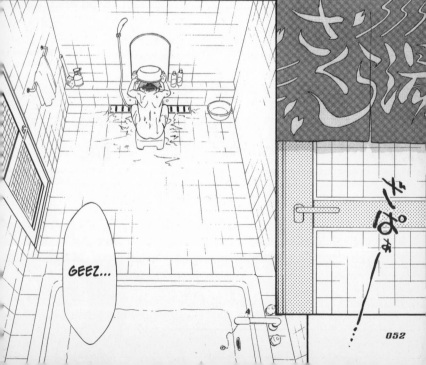

GEEZ...

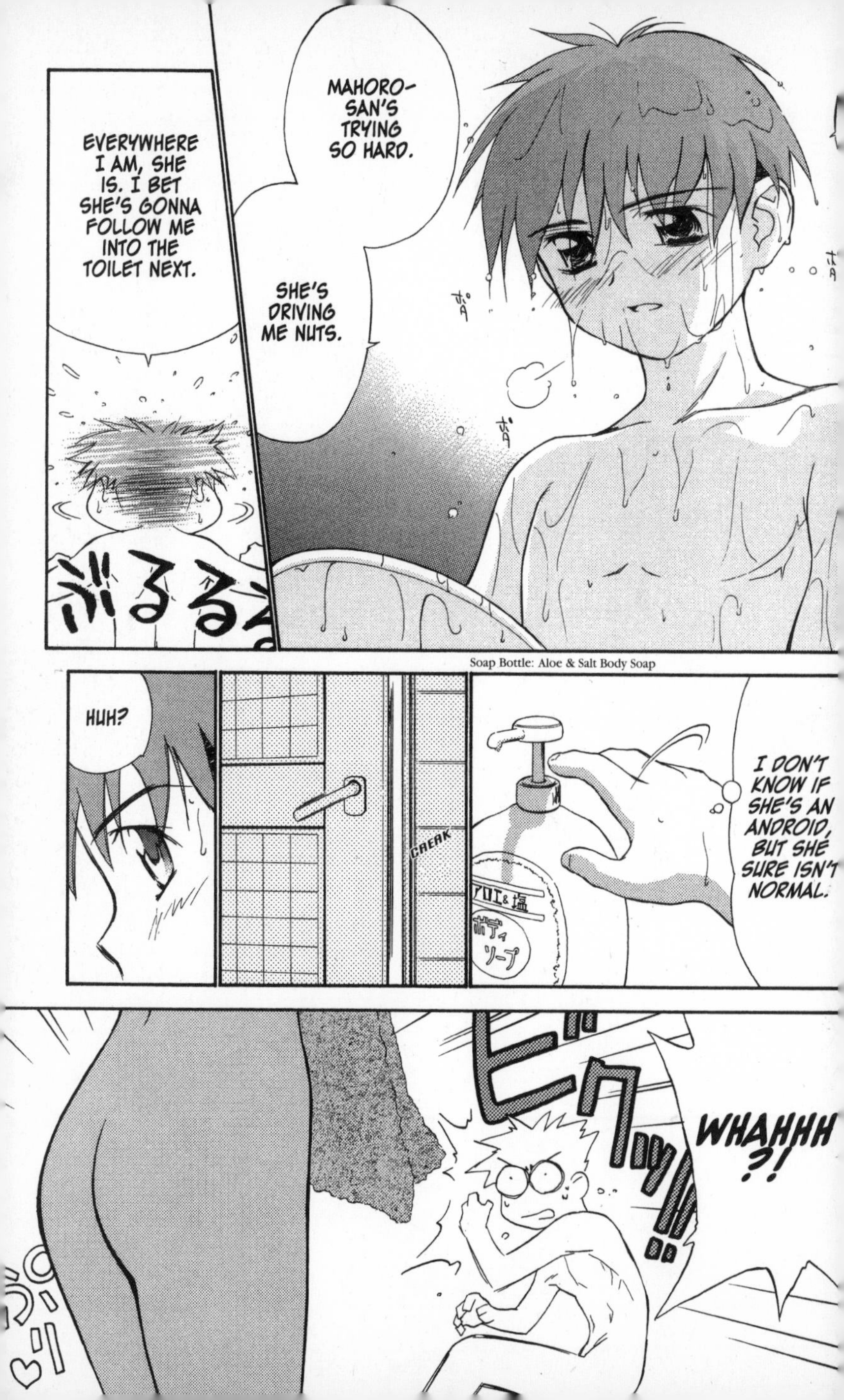
MAHORO-SAN'S TRYING SO HARD.
SHE'S DRIVING ME NUTS.
EVERYWHERE I AM, SHE IS. I BET SHE'S GONNA FOLLOW ME INTO THE TOILET NEXT.
ぶるる
I DON'T KNOW IF SHE'S AN ANDROID, BUT SHE SURE ISN'T NORMAL.
アロエ&塩
ボディソープ
CREAK
HUH?
ビクッ!!
WHAHHH?!
ぷりっ
Soap Bottle: Aloe & Salt Body Soap

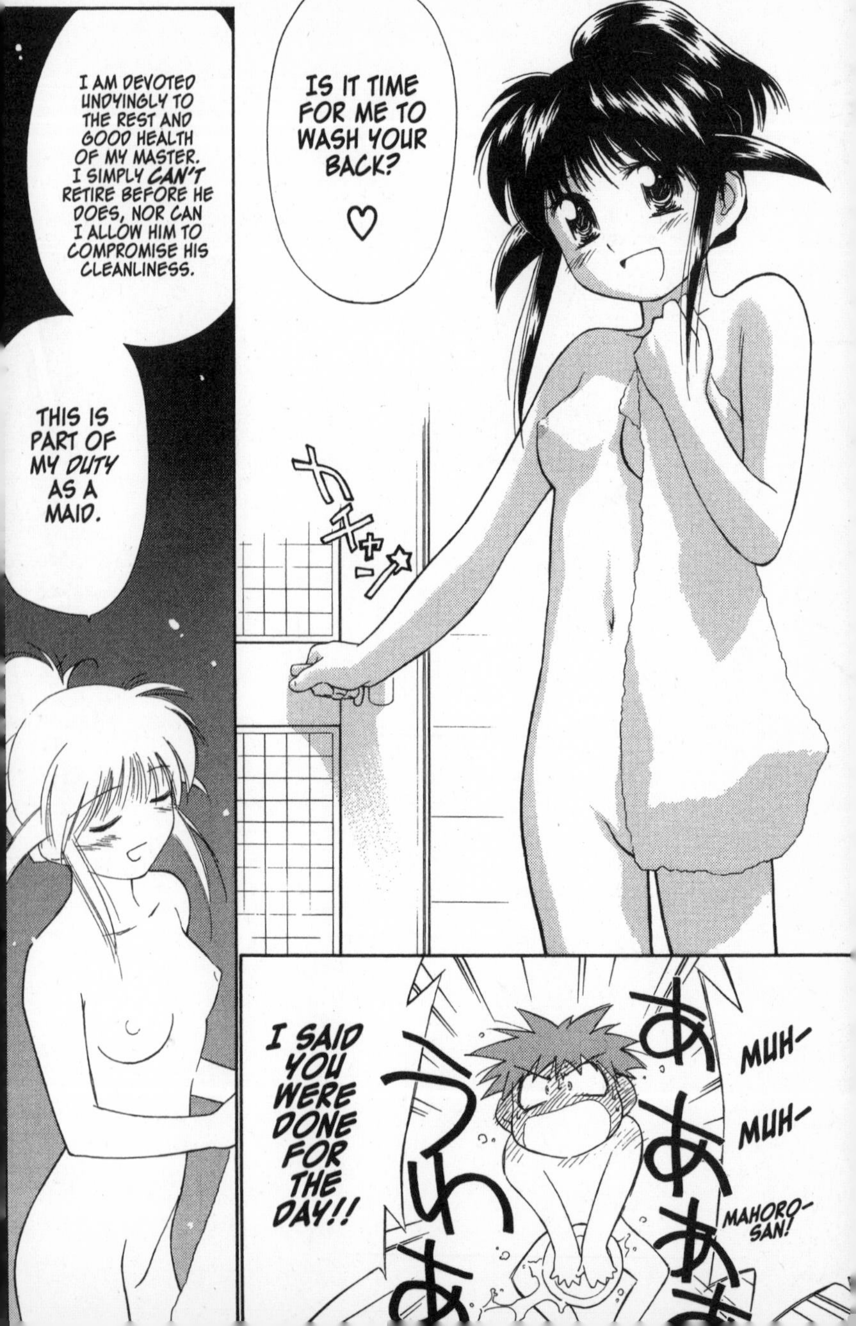

IS IT TIME FOR ME TO WASH YOUR BACK? ♡
ガチャー☆
MUH- MUH- MAHORO-SAN!
I SAID YOU WERE DONE FOR THE DAY!!
I AM DEVOTED UNDYINGLY TO THE REST AND GOOD HEALTH OF MY MASTER. I SIMPLY CAN'T RETIRE BEFORE HE DOES, NOR CAN I ALLOW HIM TO COMPROMISE HIS CLEANLINESS.
THIS IS PART OF MY DUTY AS A MAID.

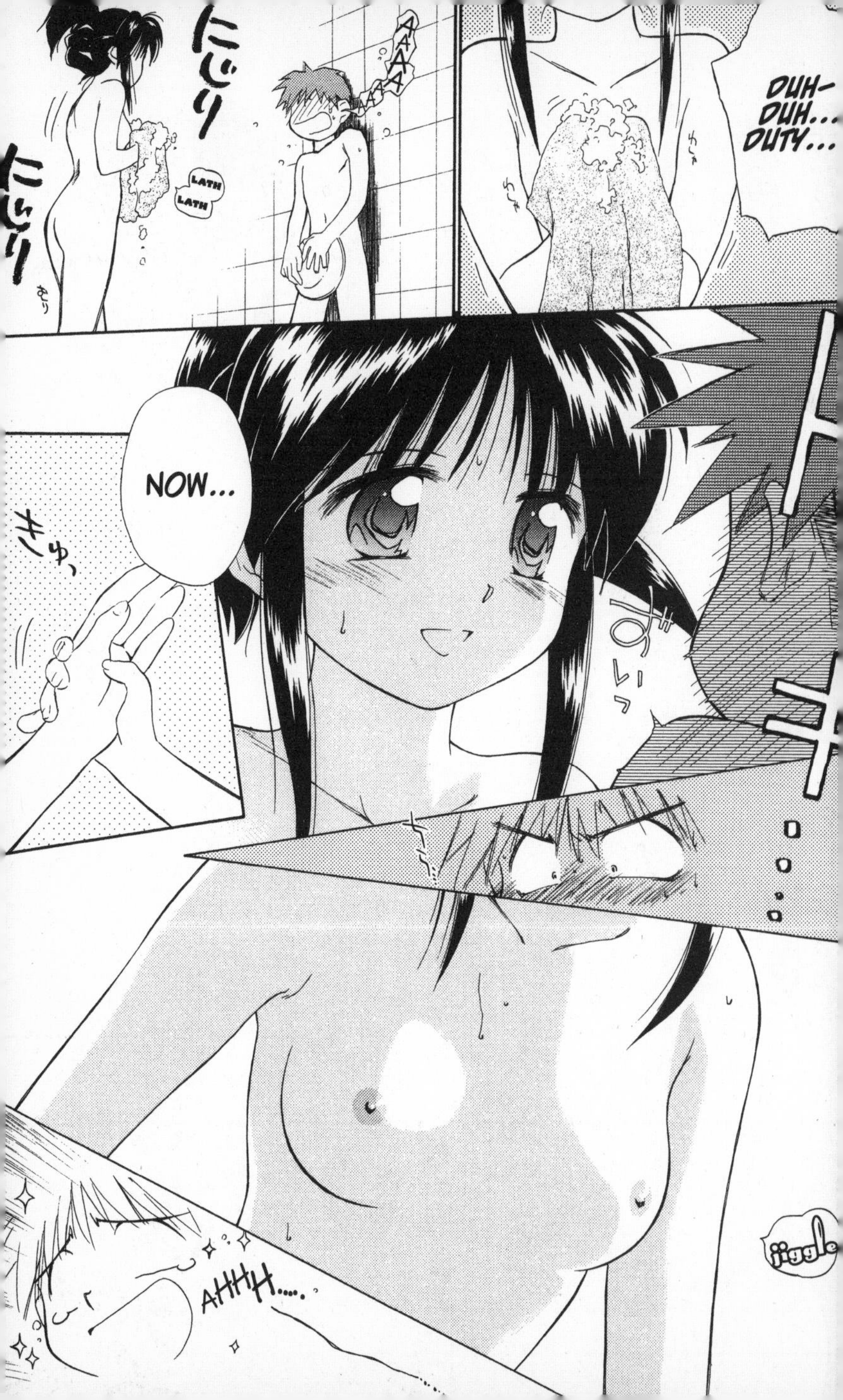

DUH-DUH... DUTY...
にじり
にじり
AAAAA
LATH
LATH
NOW...
AHHH....
jiggle

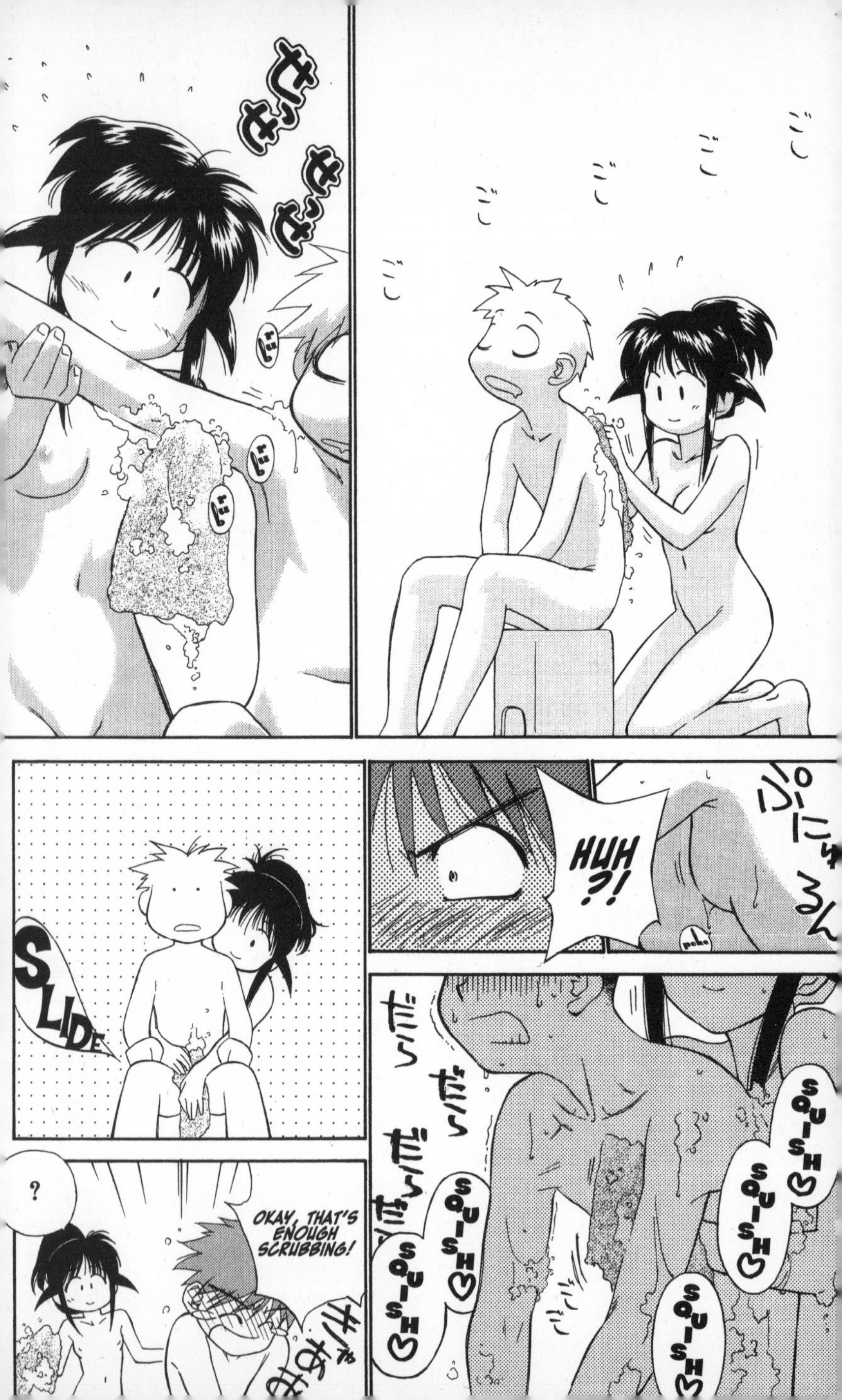
ごし
ごし
ごし
ごし
ごし
ぷにゅるん
poke
HUH?!
だら
だら
だら
だら
SQUISH
SQUISH
SQUISH
SQUISH
SLIDE
?
OKAY, THAT'S ENOUGH SCRUBBING!

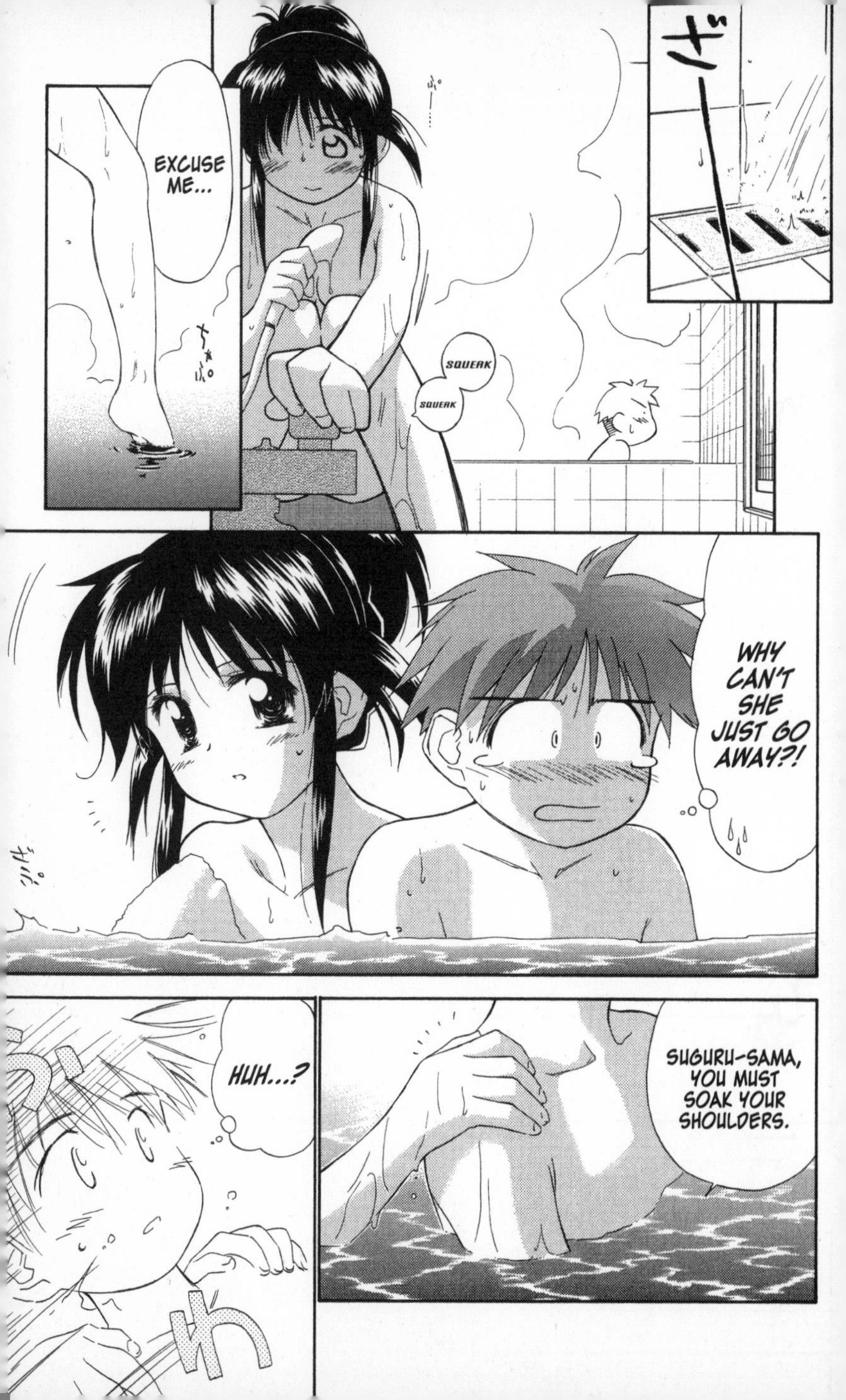
ざー
SQUEAK
SQUEAK
EXCUSE ME...
ちゃぷ
WHY CAN'T SHE JUST GO AWAY?!
SUGURU-SAMA, YOU MUST SOAK YOUR SHOULDERS.
HUH...?

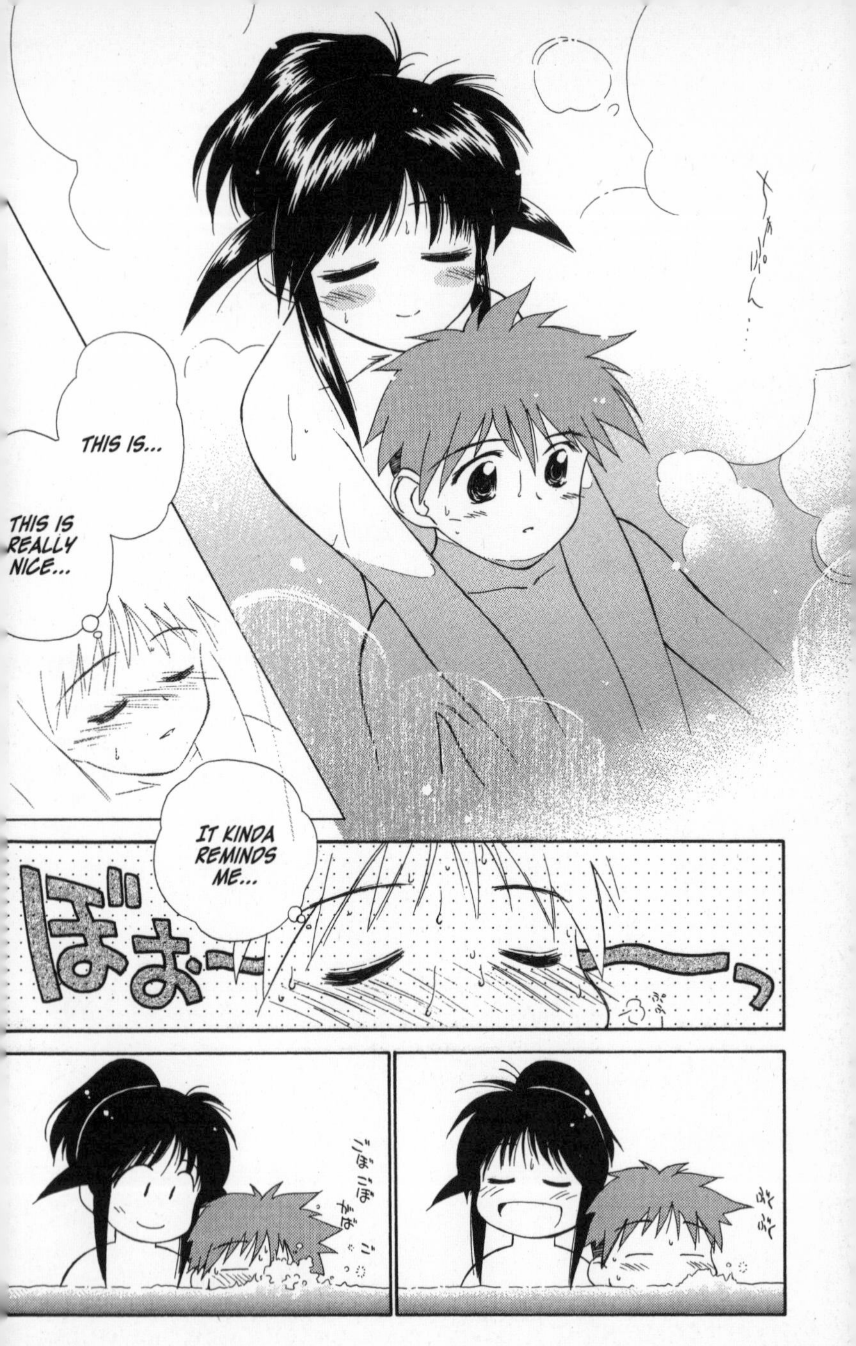

ちゃぷん…
THIS IS...
THIS IS REALLY NICE...
IT KINDA REMINDS ME...
ぼぉ～～～っ
ぷくぷく
ごぼごぼがぼご

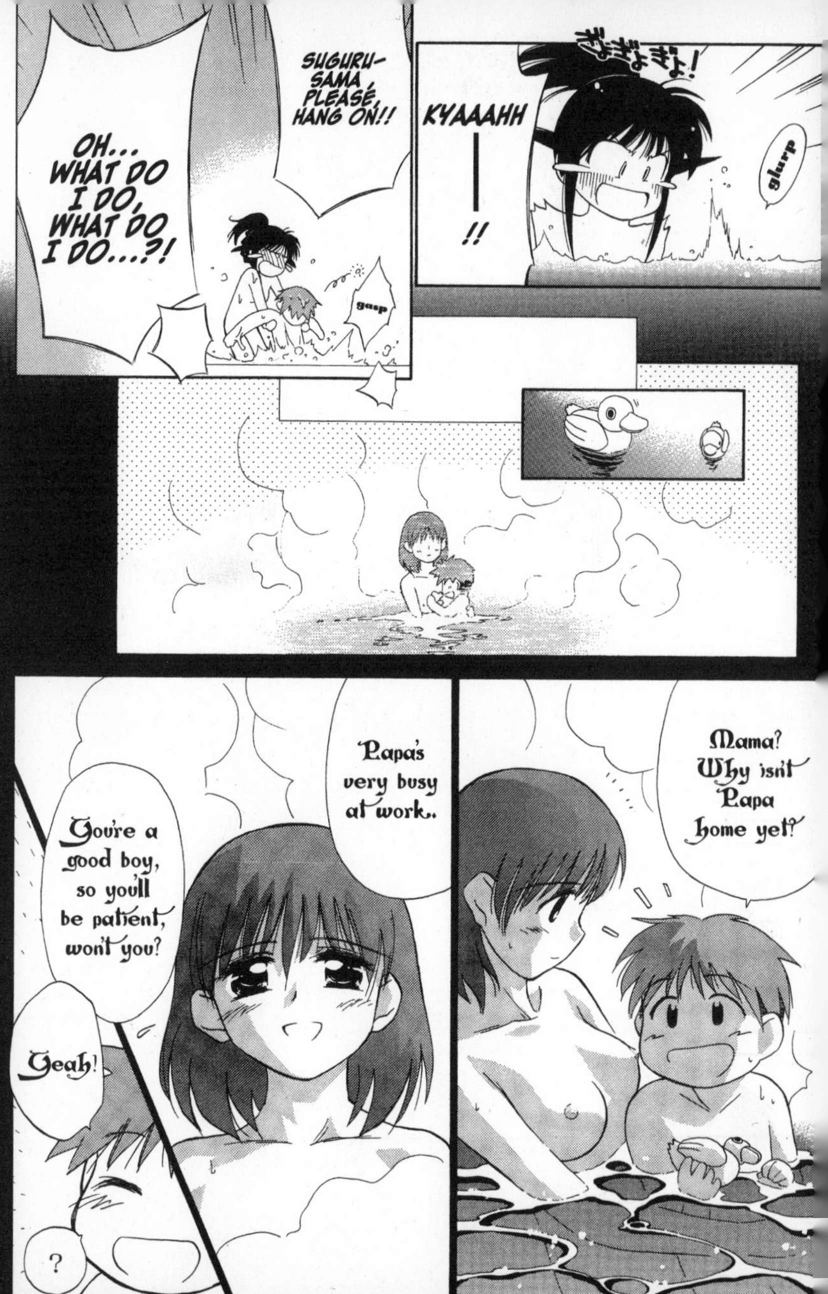
ぎょぎょぎょ!
KYAAAHH—!!
glurp
SUGURU-SAMA, PLEASE, HANG ON!!
OH... WHAT DO I DO, WHAT DO I DO...?!
gasp
Mama? Why isn't Papa home yet?
Papa's very busy at work.
You're a good boy, so you'll be patient, won't you?
Yeah!
?

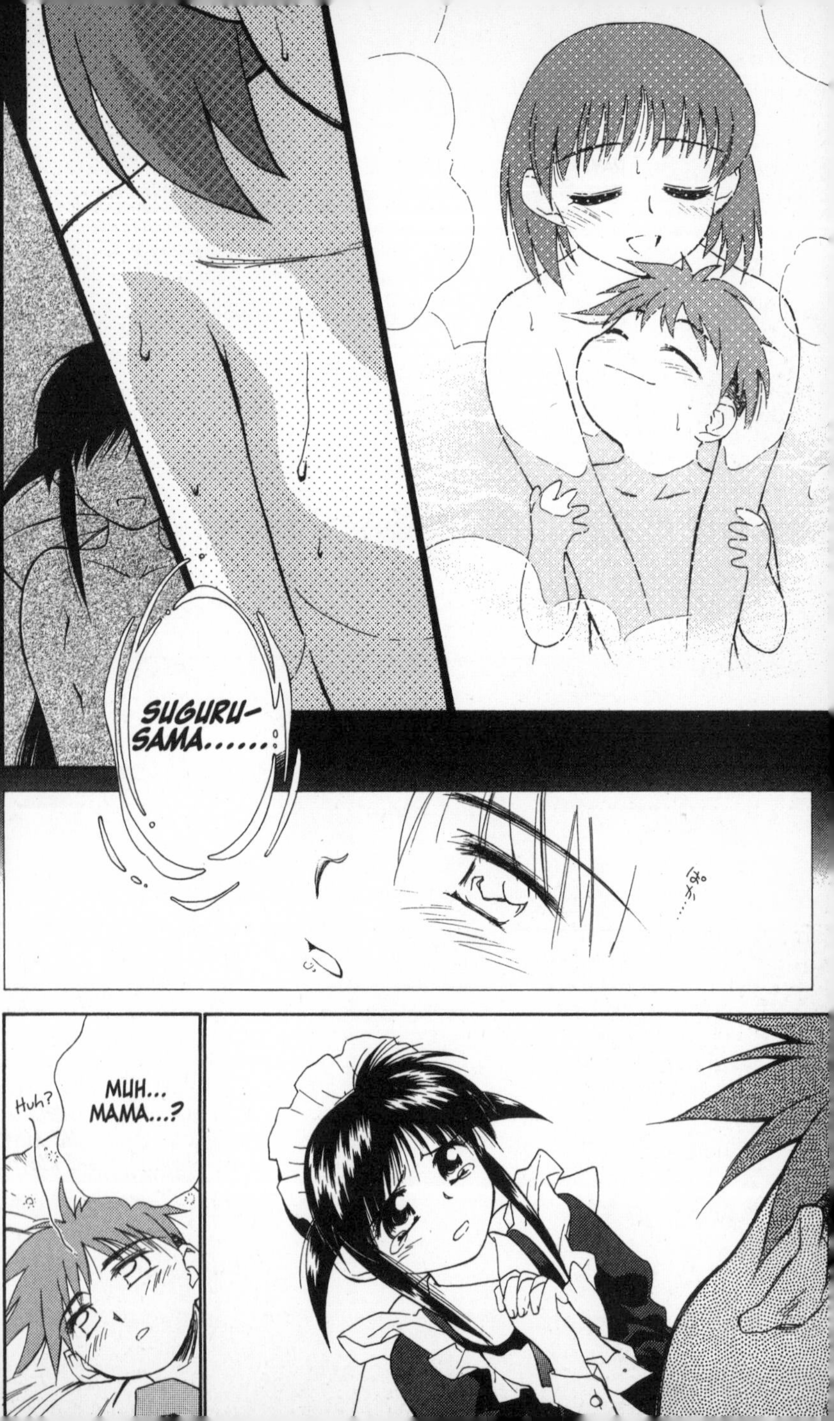
SUGURU-SAMA......
ぱか……
MUH... MAMA...?
Huh?

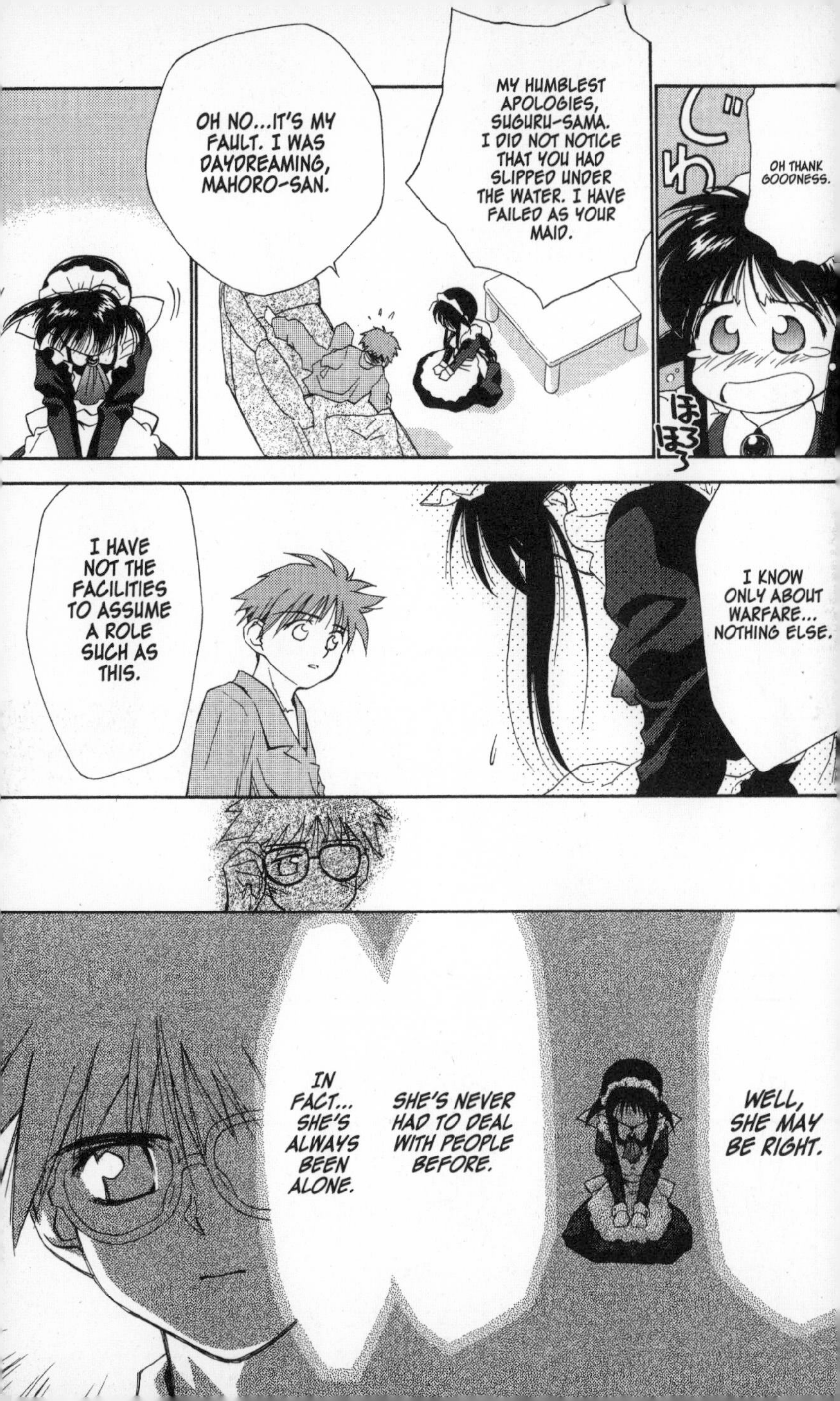
じわ
OH THANK GOODNESS.
ほろほろ
MY HUMBLEST APOLOGIES, SUGURU-SAMA. I DID NOT NOTICE THAT YOU HAD SLIPPED UNDER THE WATER. I HAVE FAILED AS YOUR MAID.
OH NO...IT'S MY FAULT. I WAS DAYDREAMING, MAHORO-SAN.
I KNOW ONLY ABOUT WARFARE... NOTHING ELSE.
I HAVE NOT THE FACILITIES TO ASSUME A ROLE SUCH AS THIS.
WELL, SHE MAY BE RIGHT.
SHE'S NEVER HAD TO DEAL WITH PEOPLE BEFORE.
IN FACT... SHE'S ALWAYS BEEN ALONE.

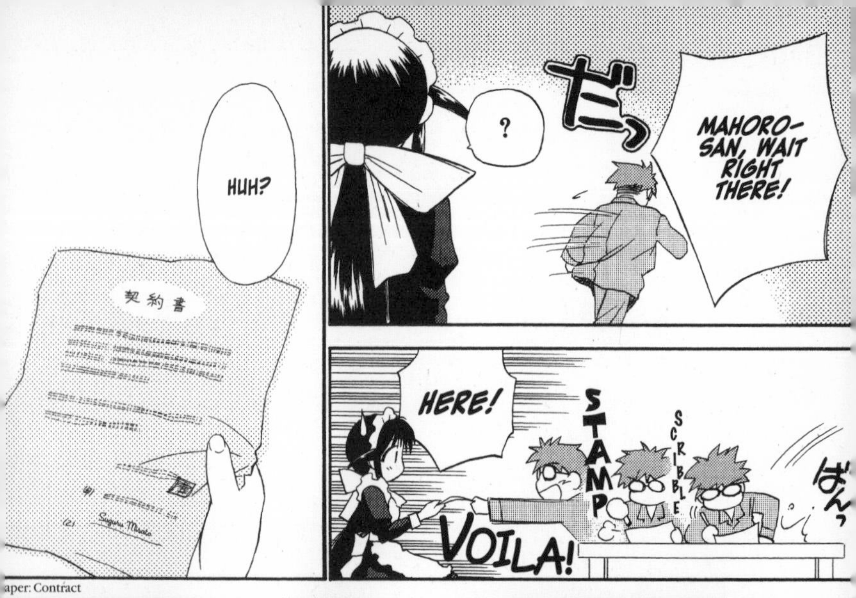

だっ
MAHORO-SAN, WAIT RIGHT THERE!
?
HERE!
STAMP
SCRIBBLE
ばんっ
VOILA!
HUH?
契約書

aper: Contract

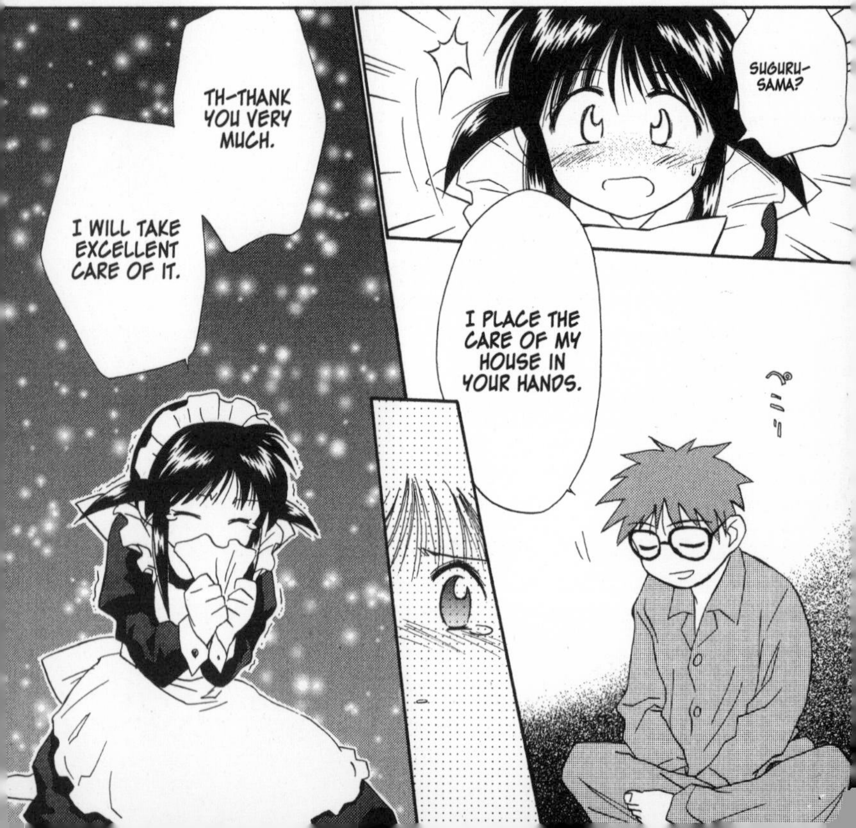

SUGURU-SAMA?
I PLACE THE CARE OF MY HOUSE IN YOUR HANDS.
TH-THANK YOU VERY MUCH.
I WILL TAKE EXCELLENT CARE OF IT.

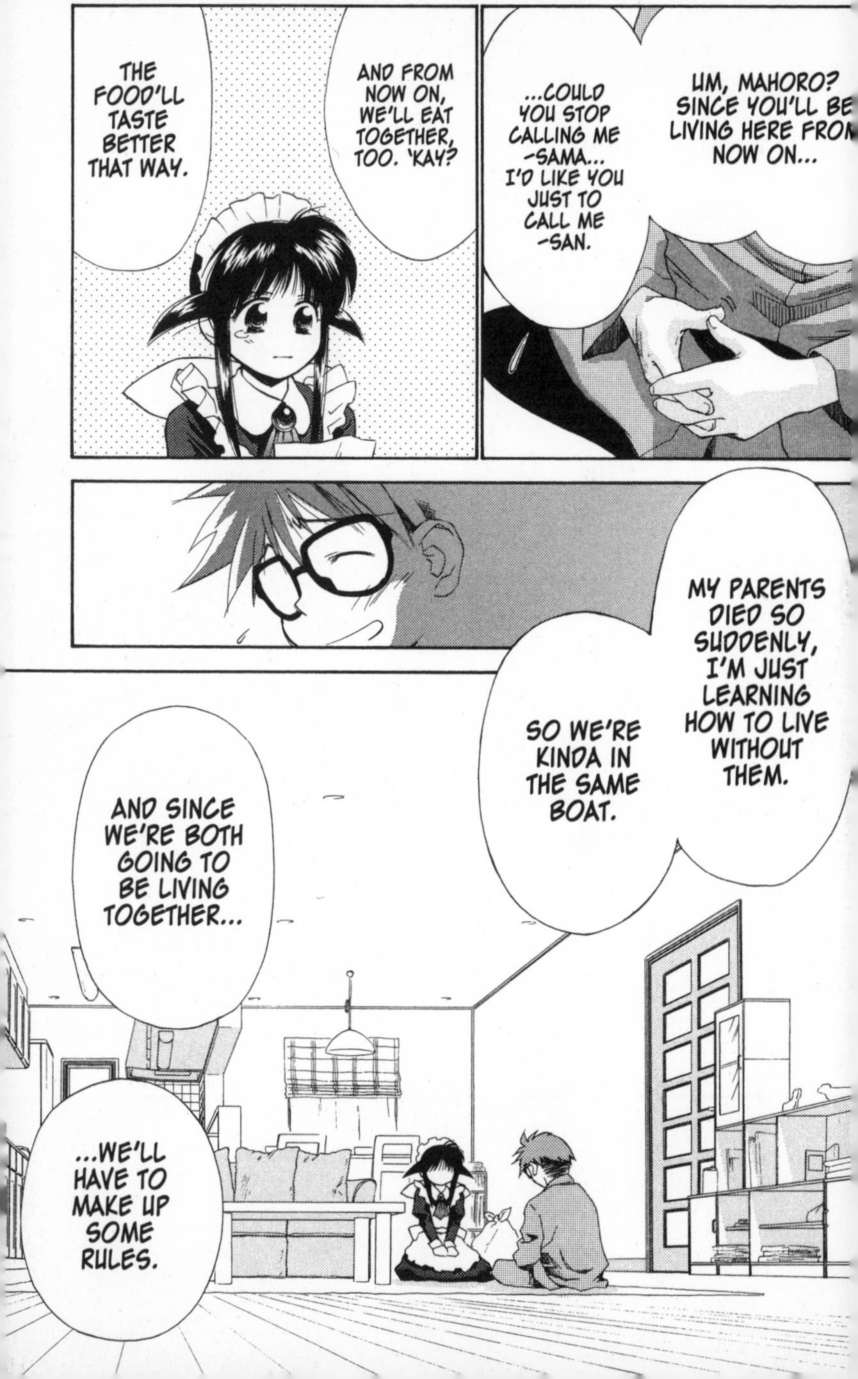
UM, MAHORO? SINCE YOU'LL BE LIVING HERE FROM NOW ON...
...COULD YOU STOP CALLING ME -SAMA... I'D LIKE YOU JUST TO CALL ME -SAN.
AND FROM NOW ON, WE'LL EAT TOGETHER, TOO. 'KAY?
THE FOOD'LL TASTE BETTER THAT WAY.
MY PARENTS DIED SO SUDDENLY, I'M JUST LEARNING HOW TO LIVE WITHOUT THEM.
SO WE'RE KINDA IN THE SAME BOAT.
AND SINCE WE'RE BOTH GOING TO BE LIVING TOGETHER...
...WE'LL HAVE TO MAKE UP SOME RULES.

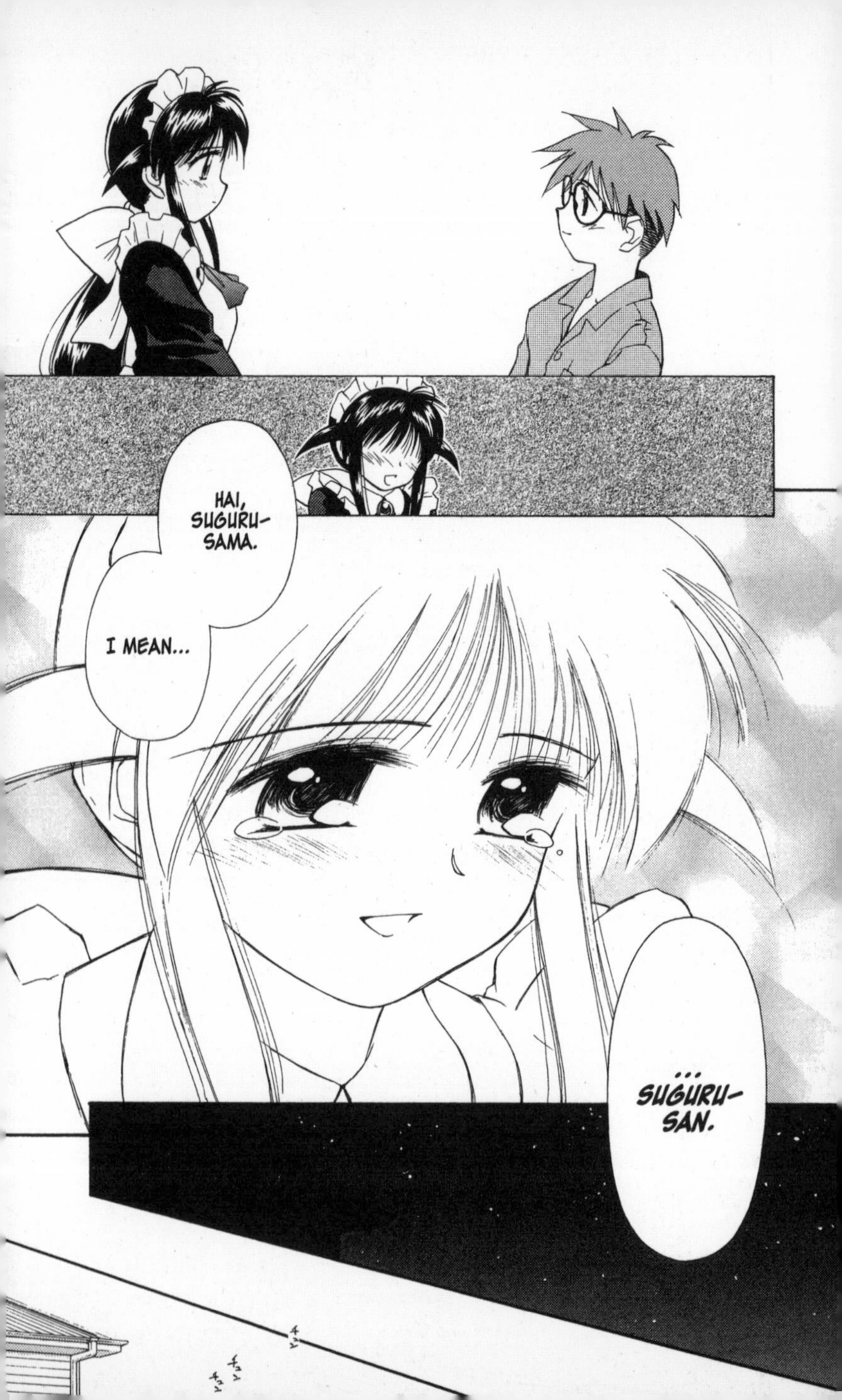
HAI, SUGURU-SAMA.
I MEAN...
...SUGURU-SAN.

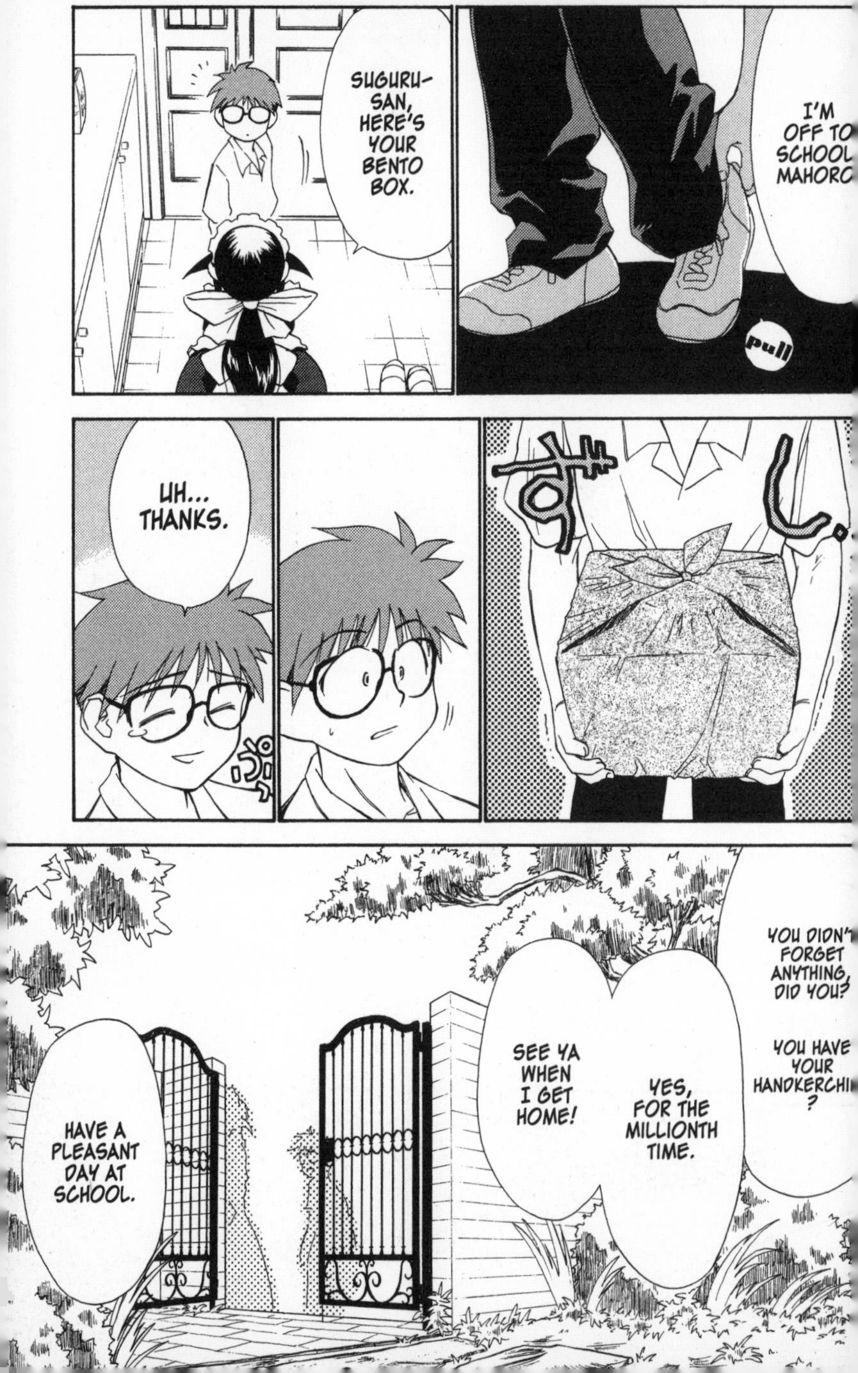

I'M OFF TO SCHOOL MAHORO
pull
SUGURU-SAN, HERE'S YOUR BENTO BOX.
ずし.
UH... THANKS.
YOU DIDN'T FORGET ANYTHING, DID YOU?
YOU HAVE YOUR HANDKERCHI ?
YES, FOR THE MILLIONTH TIME.
SEE YA WHEN I GET HOME!
HAVE A PLEASANT DAY AT SCHOOL.

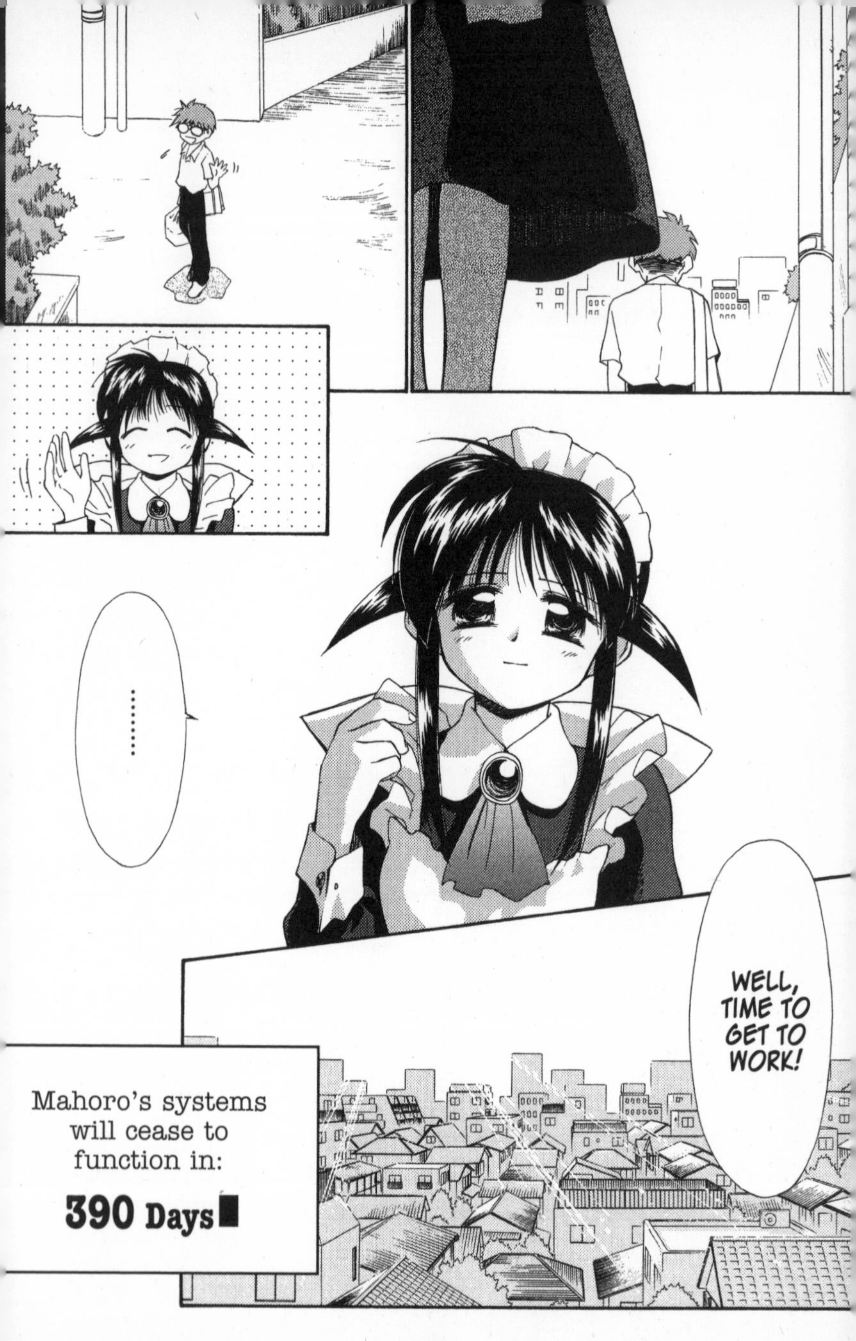
....
WELL, TIME TO GET TO WORK!
Mahoro's systems will cease to function in:
390 Days

CHIZUU

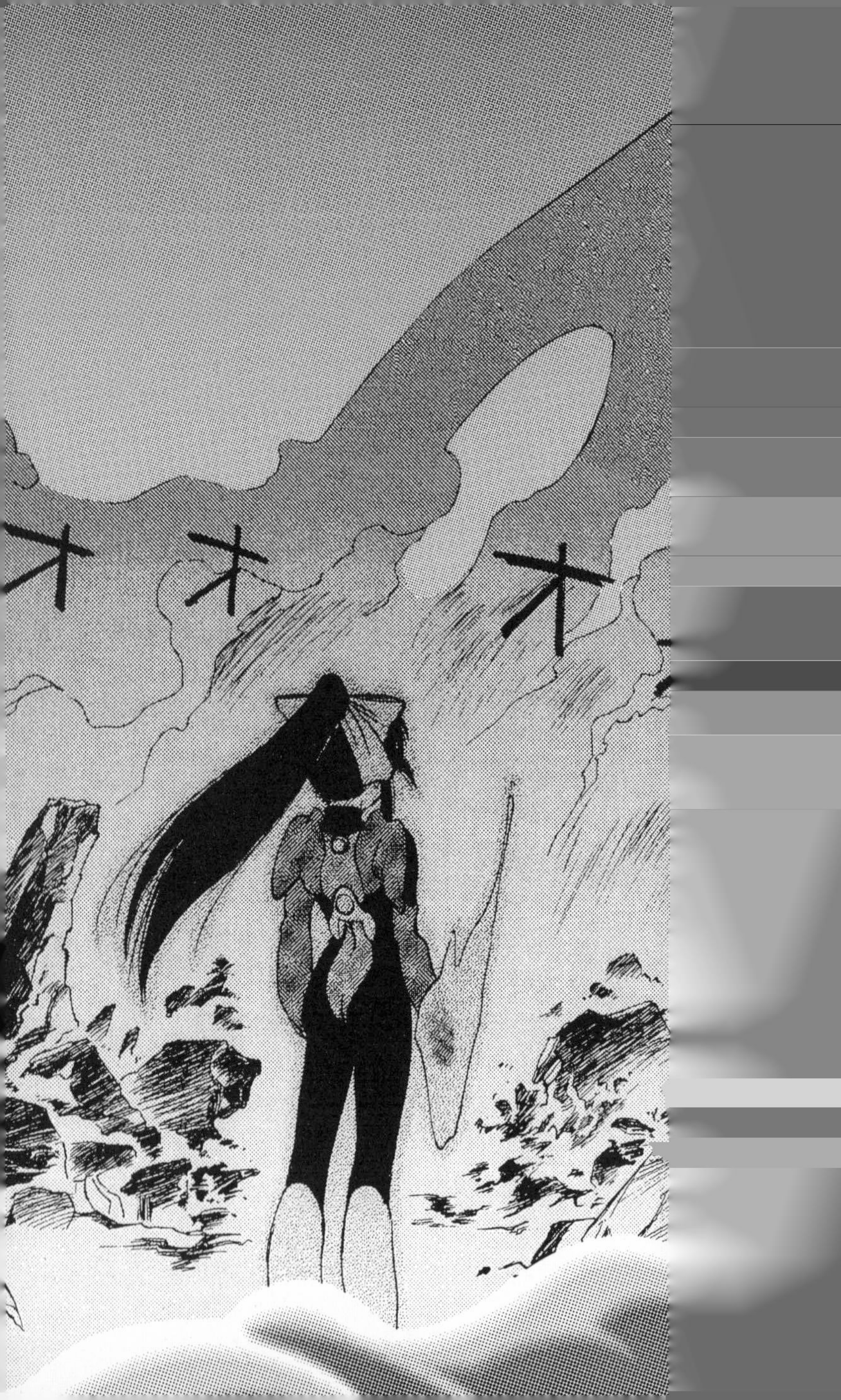
オ
オ
オ
オ

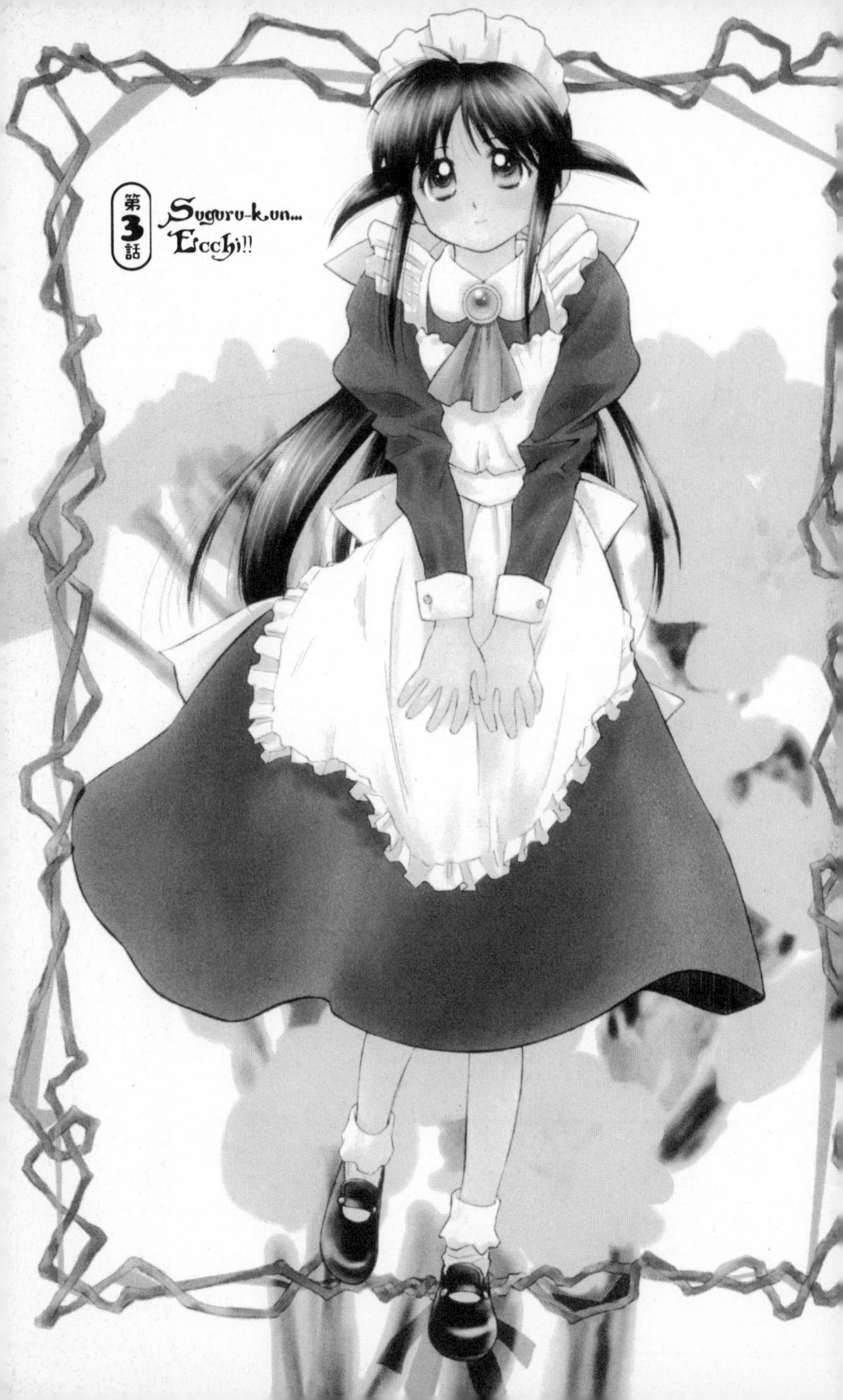
第3話
Suguru-kun...
Ecchi!!

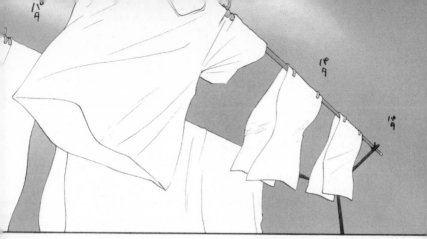

HAI, HERE'S YOUR LUNCH.

HAI HAI

woof!
woof!
woof!
woof!
woof!

SUGURU-SAN SHOULD ALSO BE EATING HIS BENTO RIGHT ABOUT NOW.

SUPPOSE SHOULD HAVE MY LUNCH AS WELL.

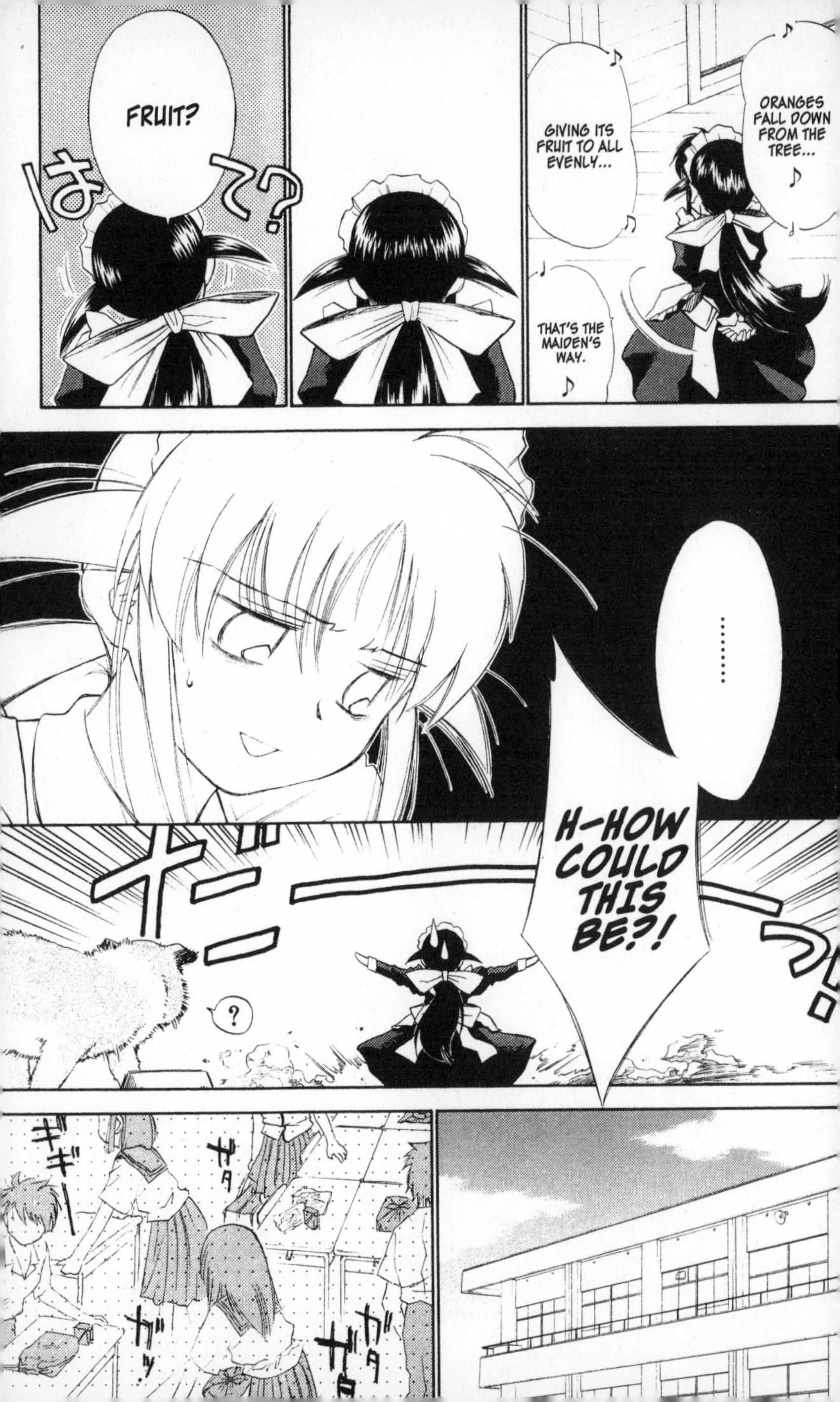
ORANGES FALL DOWN FROM THE TREE... ♪
GIVING ITS FRUIT TO ALL EVENLY... ♪
THAT'S THE MAIDEN'S WAY. ♪
FRUIT?
はて？
....
H-HOW COULD THIS BE?!
?
ギギー
ガタ
ガタ
ガッ

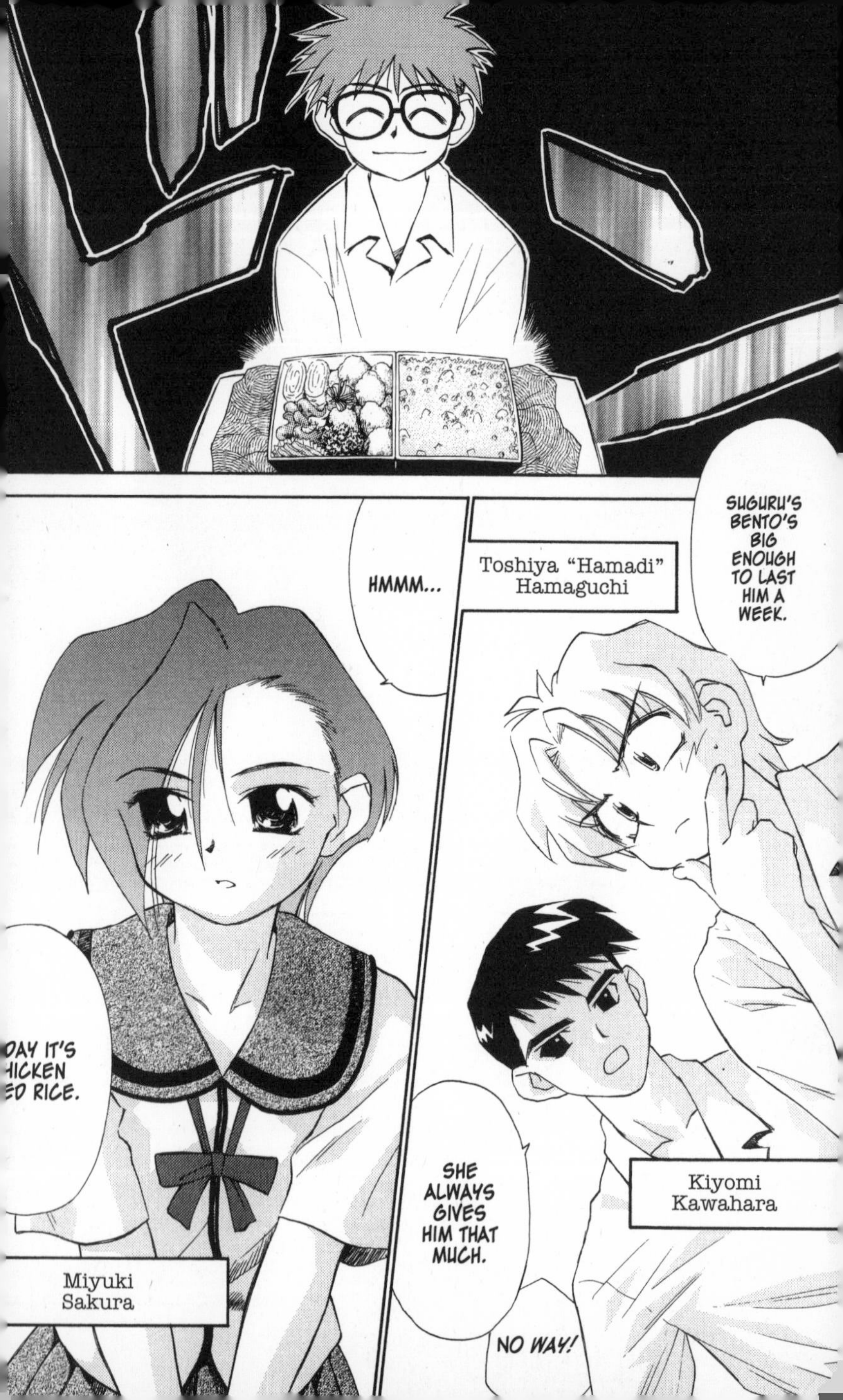

SUGURU'S BENTO'S BIG ENOUGH TO LAST HIM A WEEK.
Toshiya "Hamadi" Hamaguchi
Kiyomi Kawahara
SHE ALWAYS GIVES HIM THAT MUCH.
NO WAY!
HMMM...
DAY IT'S HICKEN ED RICE.
Miyuki Sakura

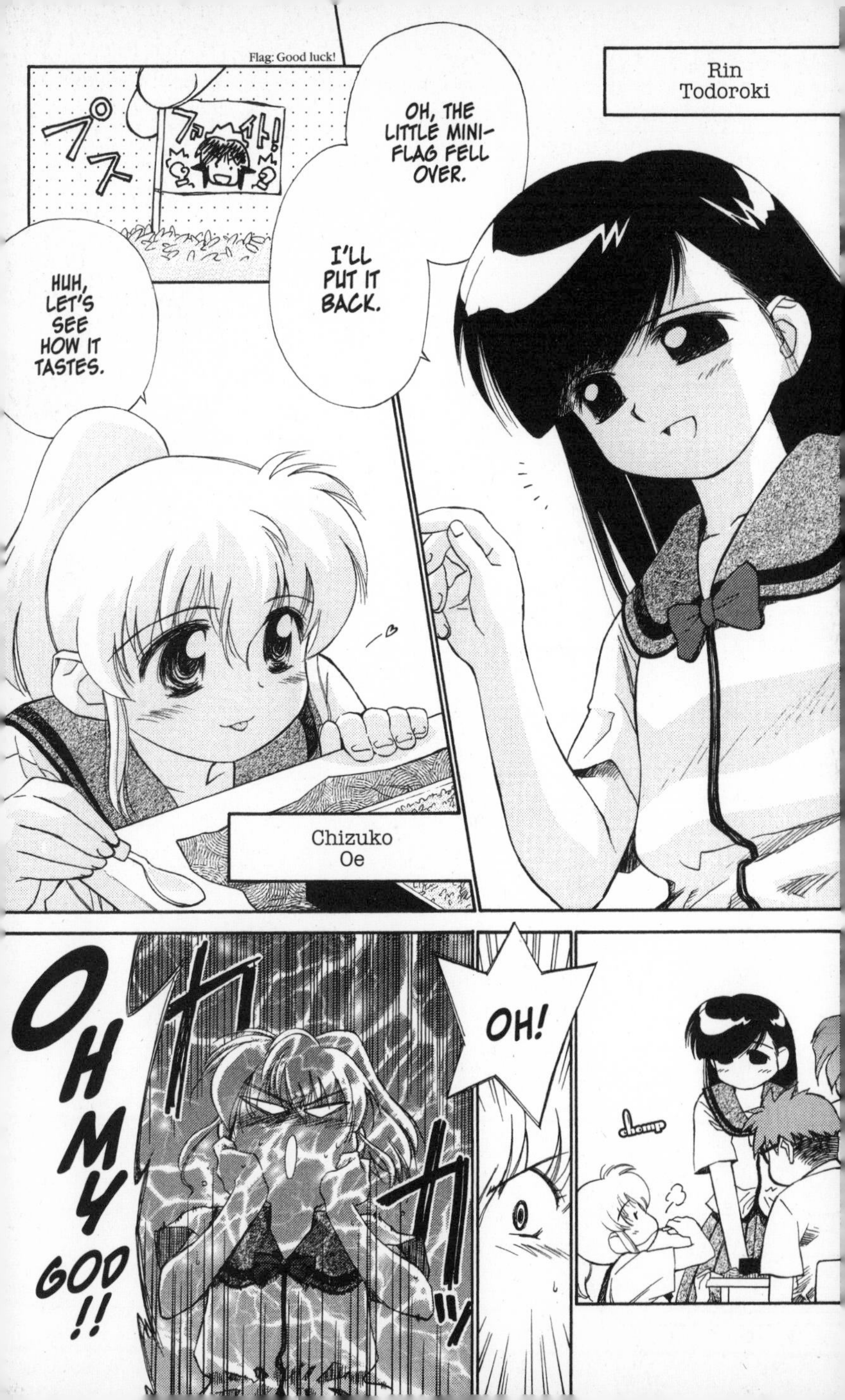

Rin Todoroki
OH, THE LITTLE MINI-FLAG FELL OVER.
I'LL PUT IT BACK.
Flag: Good luck!
プス
ファイト!
HUH, LET'S SEE HOW IT TASTES.
Chizuko Oe
chomp
OH!
OH MY GOD!!

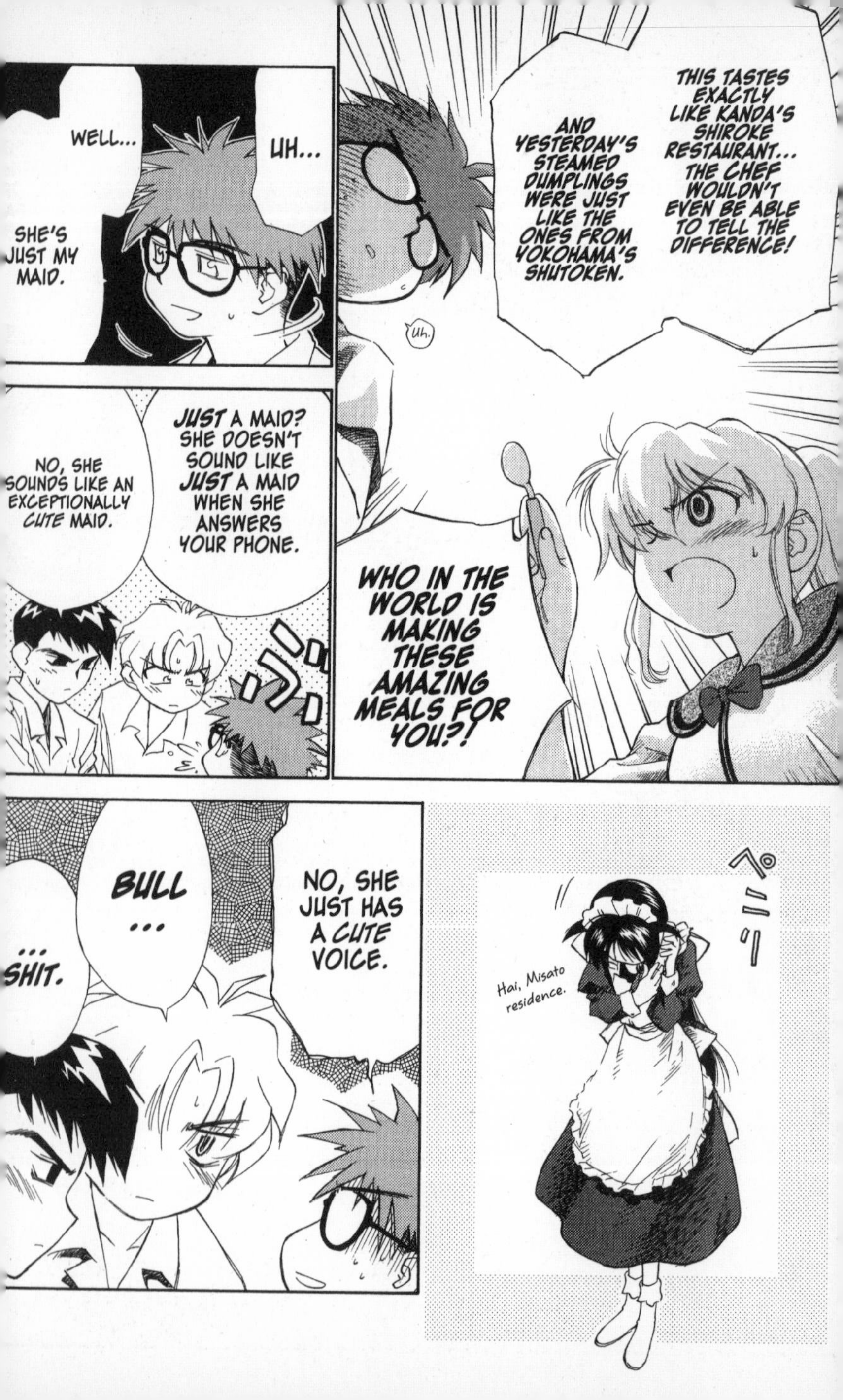
THIS TASTES EXACTLY LIKE KANDA'S SHIROKE RESTAURANT... THE CHEF WOULDN'T EVEN BE ABLE TO TELL THE DIFFERENCE!
AND YESTERDAY'S STEAMED DUMPLINGS WERE JUST LIKE THE ONES FROM YOKOHAMA'S SHUTOKEN.
Uh.
WHO IN THE WORLD IS MAKING THESE AMAZING MEALS FOR YOU?!
UH...
WELL...
SHE'S JUST MY MAID.
JUST A MAID? SHE DOESN'T SOUND LIKE JUST A MAID WHEN SHE ANSWERS YOUR PHONE.
NO, SHE SOUNDS LIKE AN EXCEPTIONALLY CUTE MAID.
Hai, Misato residence.
NO, SHE JUST HAS A CUTE VOICE.
BULL...
...SHIT.

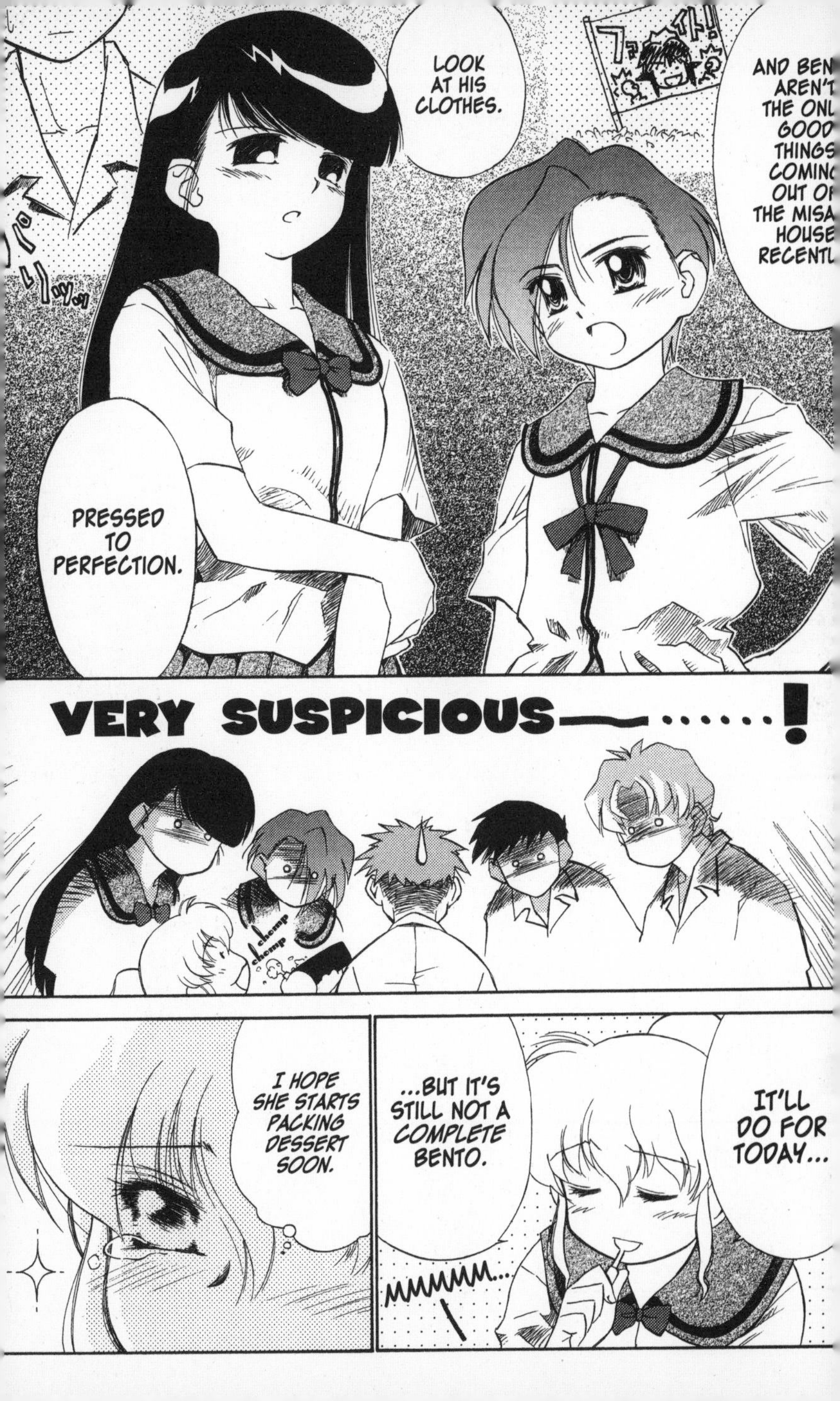
AND BEN AREN'T THE ONL GOOD THINGS COMINC OUT OF THE MISA HOUSE RECENTL
LOOK AT HIS CLOTHES.
PRESSED TO PERFECTION.
VERY SUSPICIOUS——......!
chomp chomp
IT'LL DO FOR TODAY...
...BUT IT'S STILL NOT A COMPLETE BENTO.
MMMMM...
I HOPE SHE STARTS PACKING DESSERT SOON.

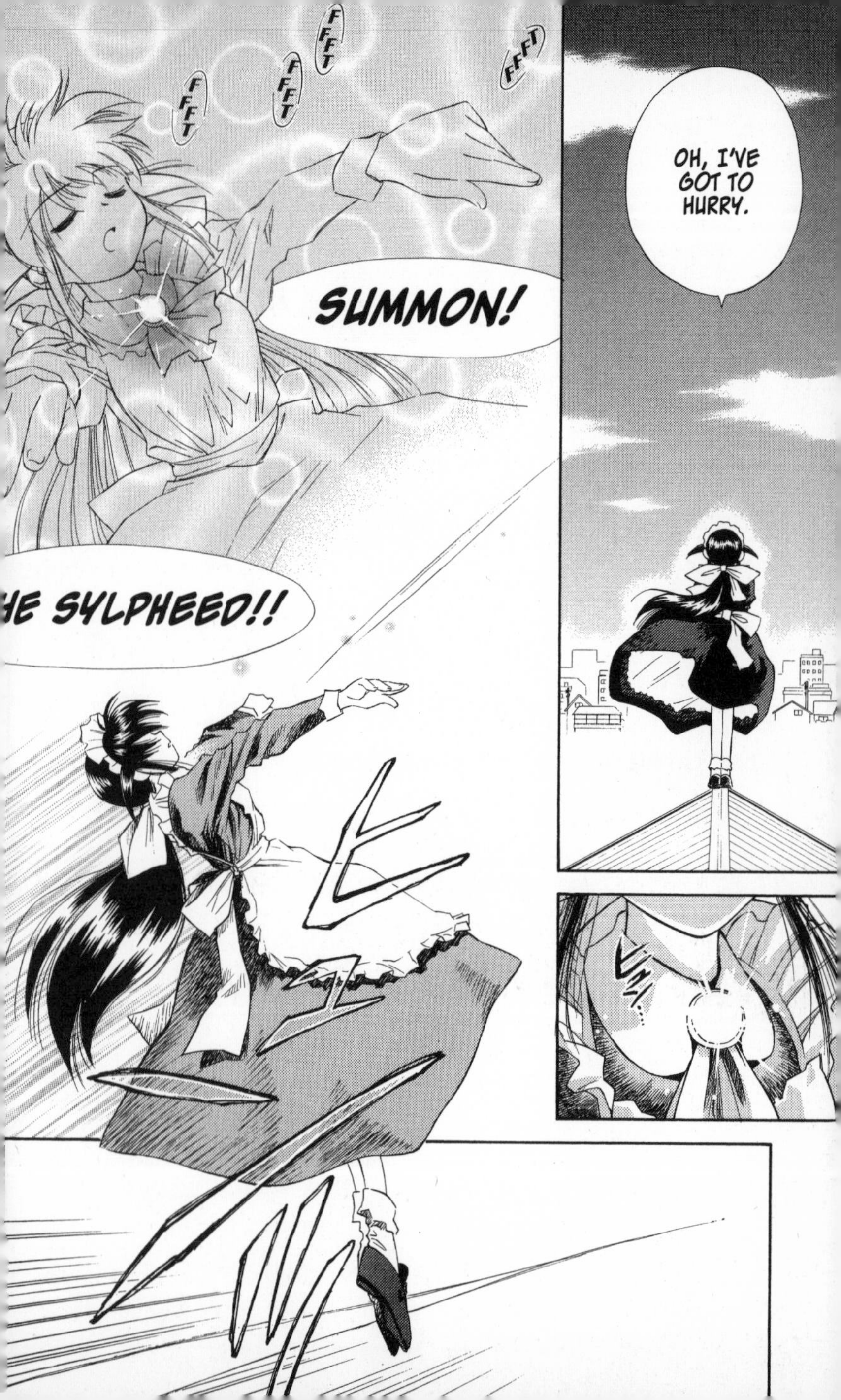
OH, I'VE GOT TO HURRY.
FFFT
FFFT
FFFT
FFFT
SUMMON!
HE SYLPHEED!!

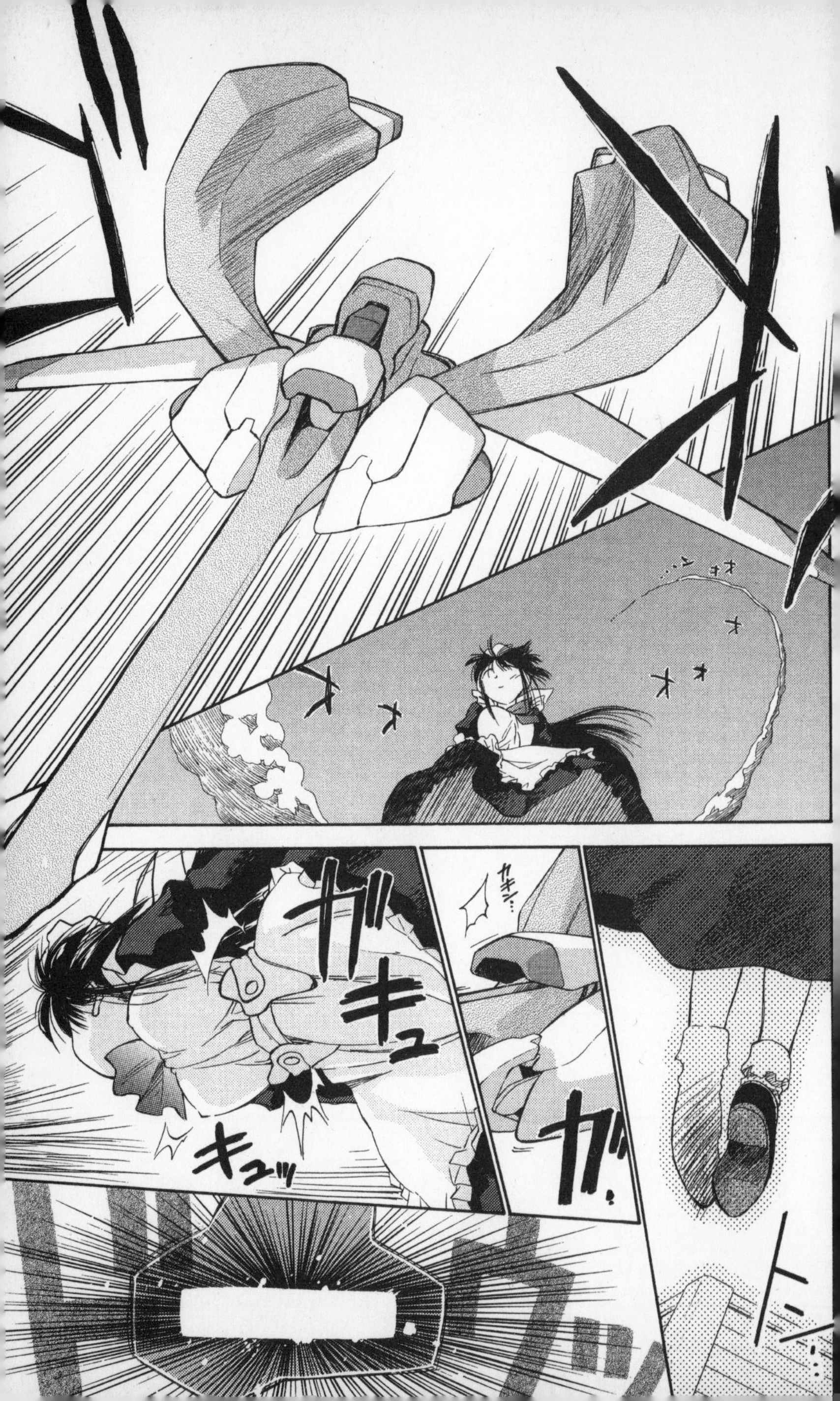
カキン…
ガッ
ガキュ
キュッ

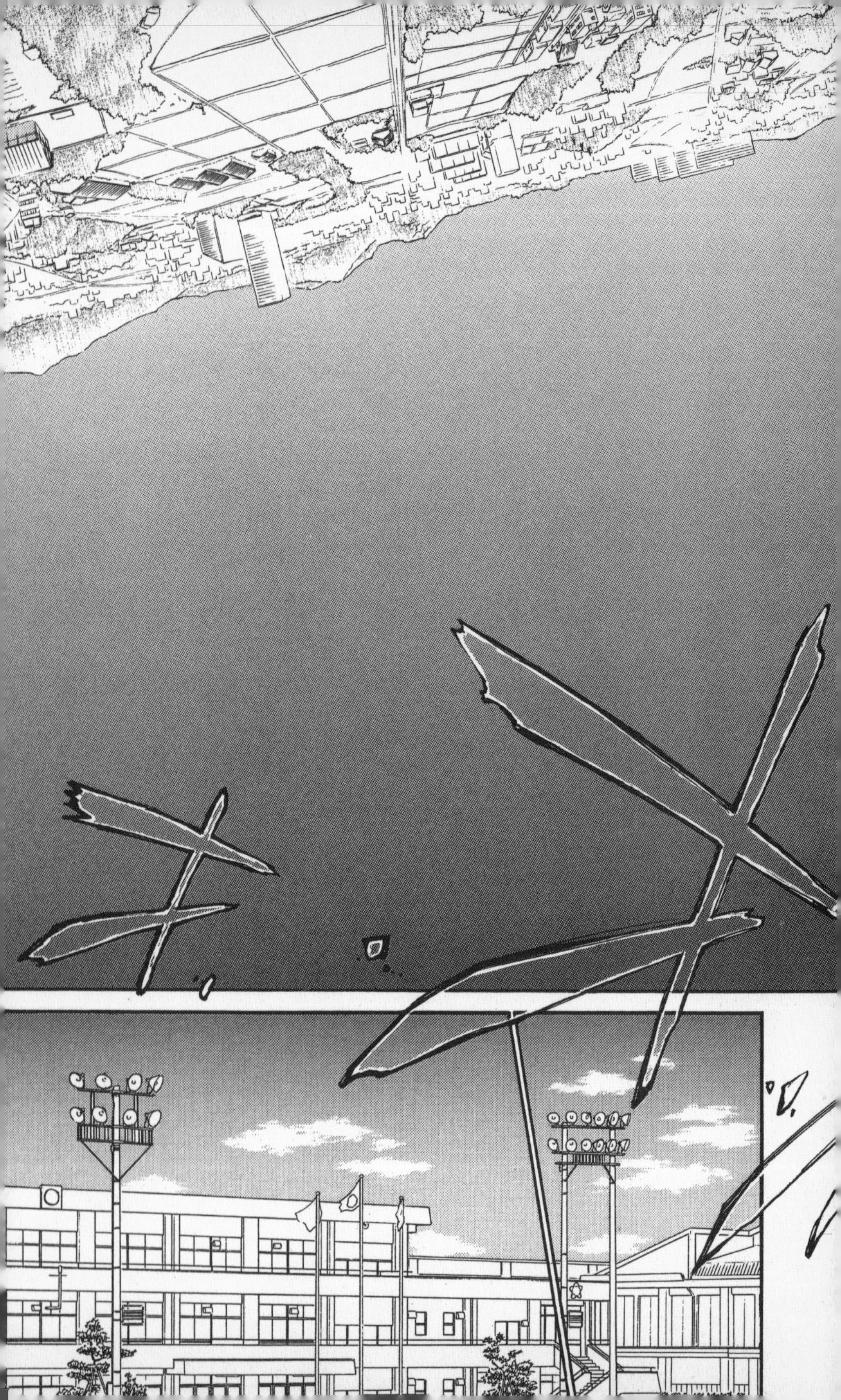

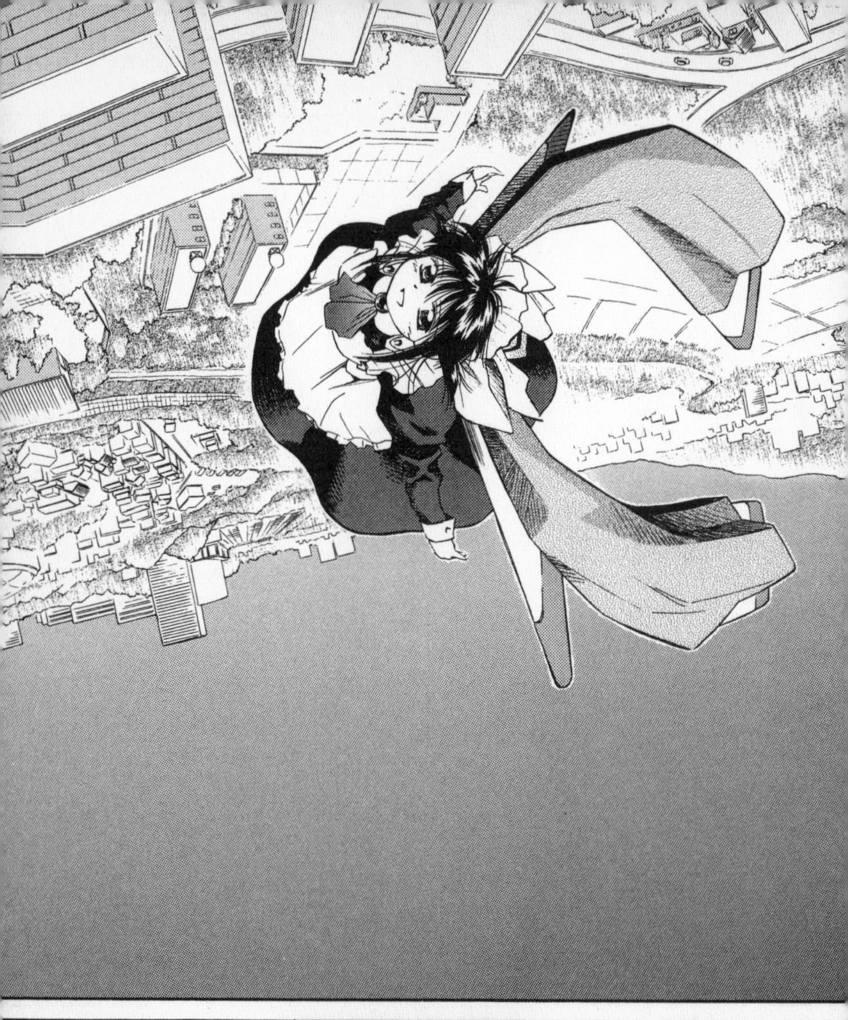

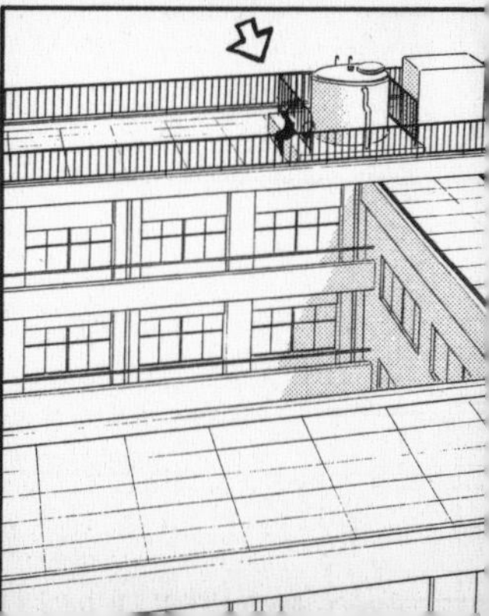

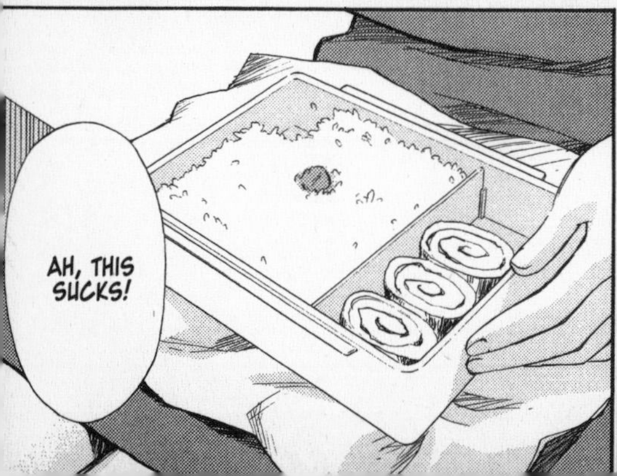
AH, THIS SUCKS!

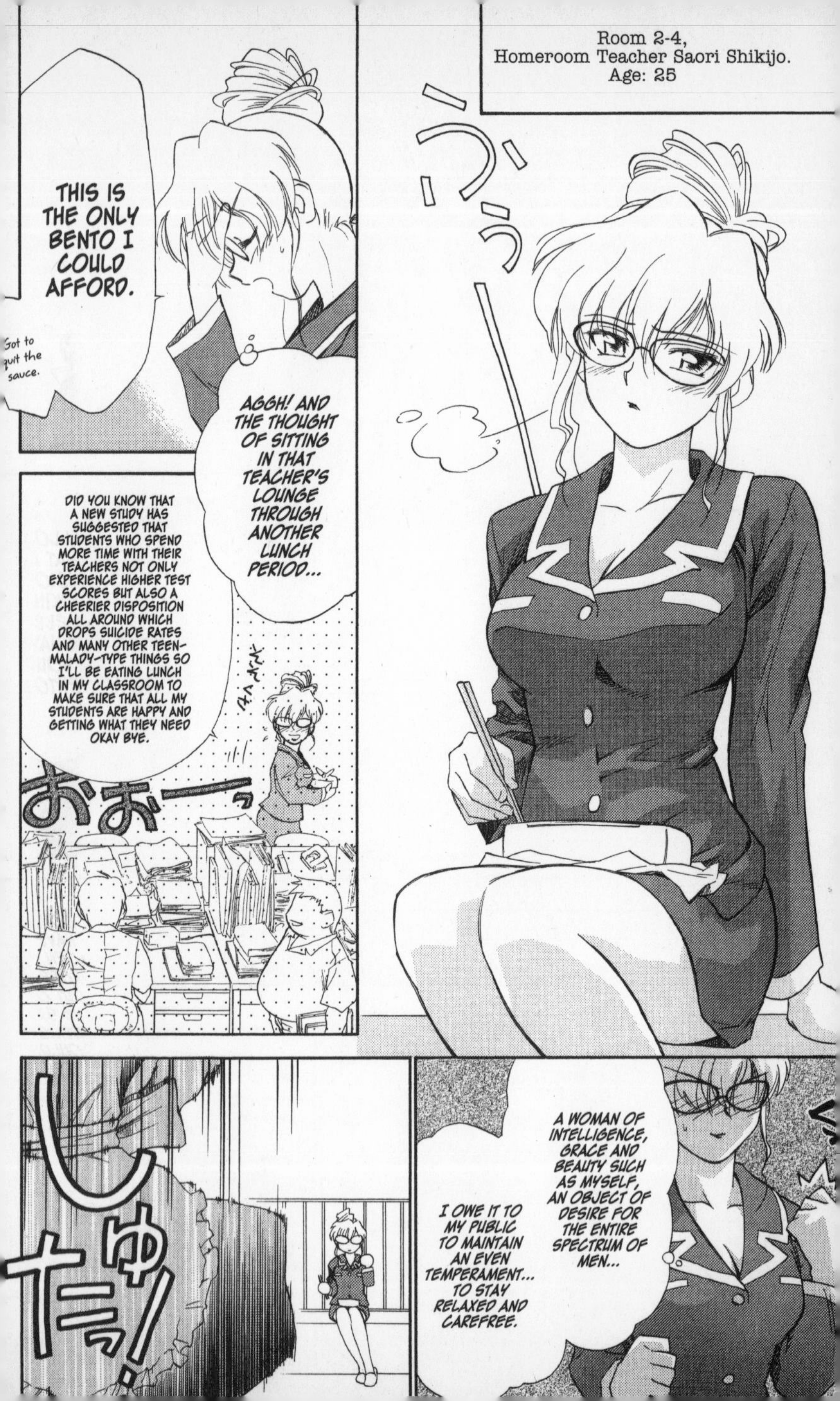

Room 2-4,
Homeroom Teacher Saori Shikijo.
Age: 25
THIS IS THE ONLY BENTO I COULD AFFORD.
Got to quit the sauce.
AGGH! AND THE THOUGHT OF SITTING IN THAT TEACHER'S LOUNGE THROUGH ANOTHER LUNCH PERIOD...
DID YOU KNOW THAT A NEW STUDY HAS SUGGESTED THAT STUDENTS WHO SPEND MORE TIME WITH THEIR TEACHERS NOT ONLY EXPERIENCE HIGHER TEST SCORES BUT ALSO A CHEERIER DISPOSITION ALL AROUND WHICH DROPS SUICIDE RATES AND MANY OTHER TEEN-MALADY-TYPE THINGS SO I'LL BE EATING LUNCH IN MY CLASSROOM TO MAKE SURE THAT ALL MY STUDENTS ARE HAPPY AND GETTING WHAT THEY NEED OKAY BYE.
おおーっ
A WOMAN OF INTELLIGENCE, GRACE AND BEAUTY SUCH AS MYSELF, AN OBJECT OF DESIRE FOR THE ENTIRE SPECTRUM OF MEN...
I OWE IT TO MY PUBLIC TO MAINTAIN AN EVEN TEMPERAMENT... TO STAY RELAXED AND CAREFREE.
しゅたっ!

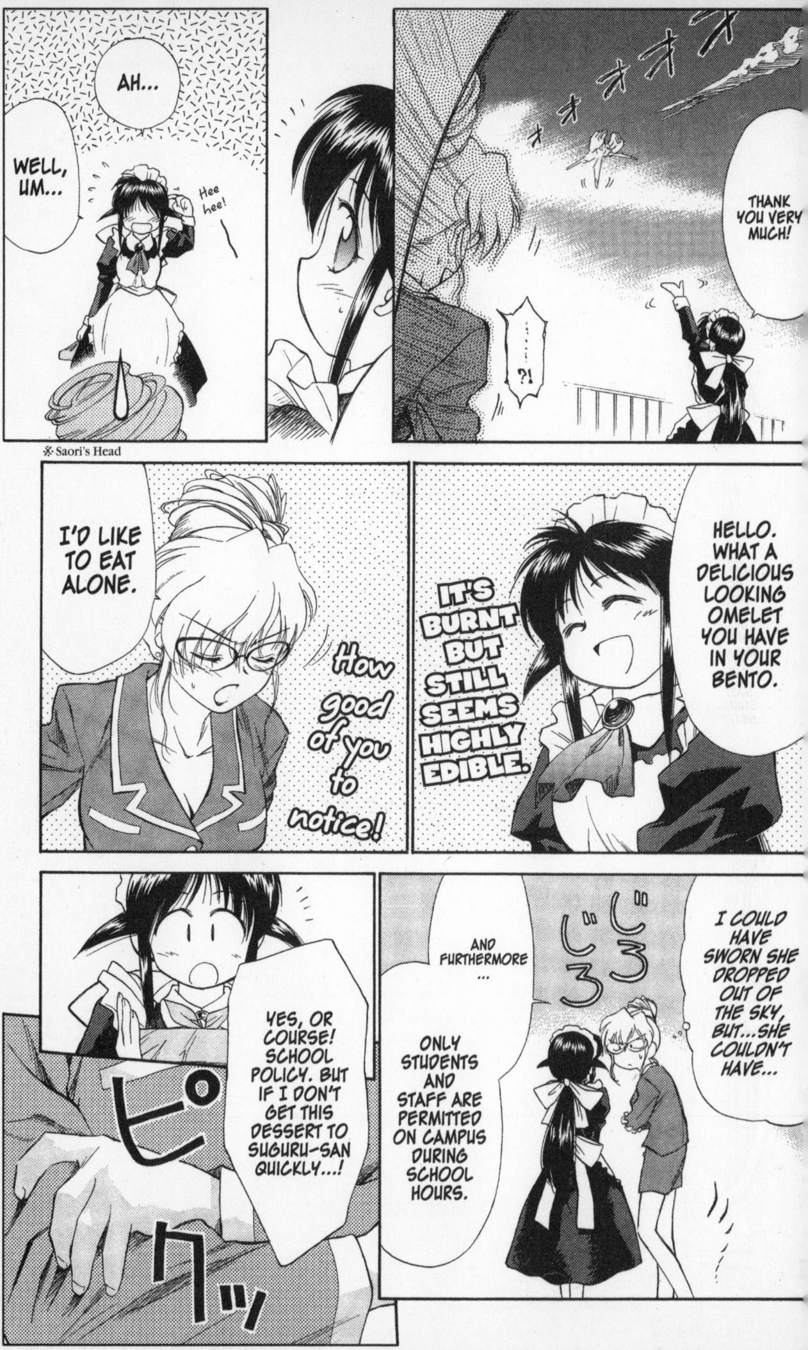

THANK YOU VERY MUCH!
......?!
AH...
WELL, UM...
Hee hee!
HELLO. WHAT A DELICIOUS LOOKING OMELET YOU HAVE IN YOUR BENTO.
IT'S BURNT BUT STILL SEEMS HIGHLY EDIBLE.
How good of you to notice!
I'D LIKE TO EAT ALONE.
I COULD HAVE SWORN SHE DROPPED OUT OF THE SKY, BUT...SHE COULDN'T HAVE...
じろじろ
AND FURTHERMORE ...
ONLY STUDENTS AND STAFF ARE PERMITTED ON CAMPUS DURING SCHOOL HOURS.
YES, OR COURSE! SCHOOL POLICY. BUT IF I DON'T GET THIS DESSERT TO SUGURU-SAN QUICKLY...!
ピクッ

※Saori's Head

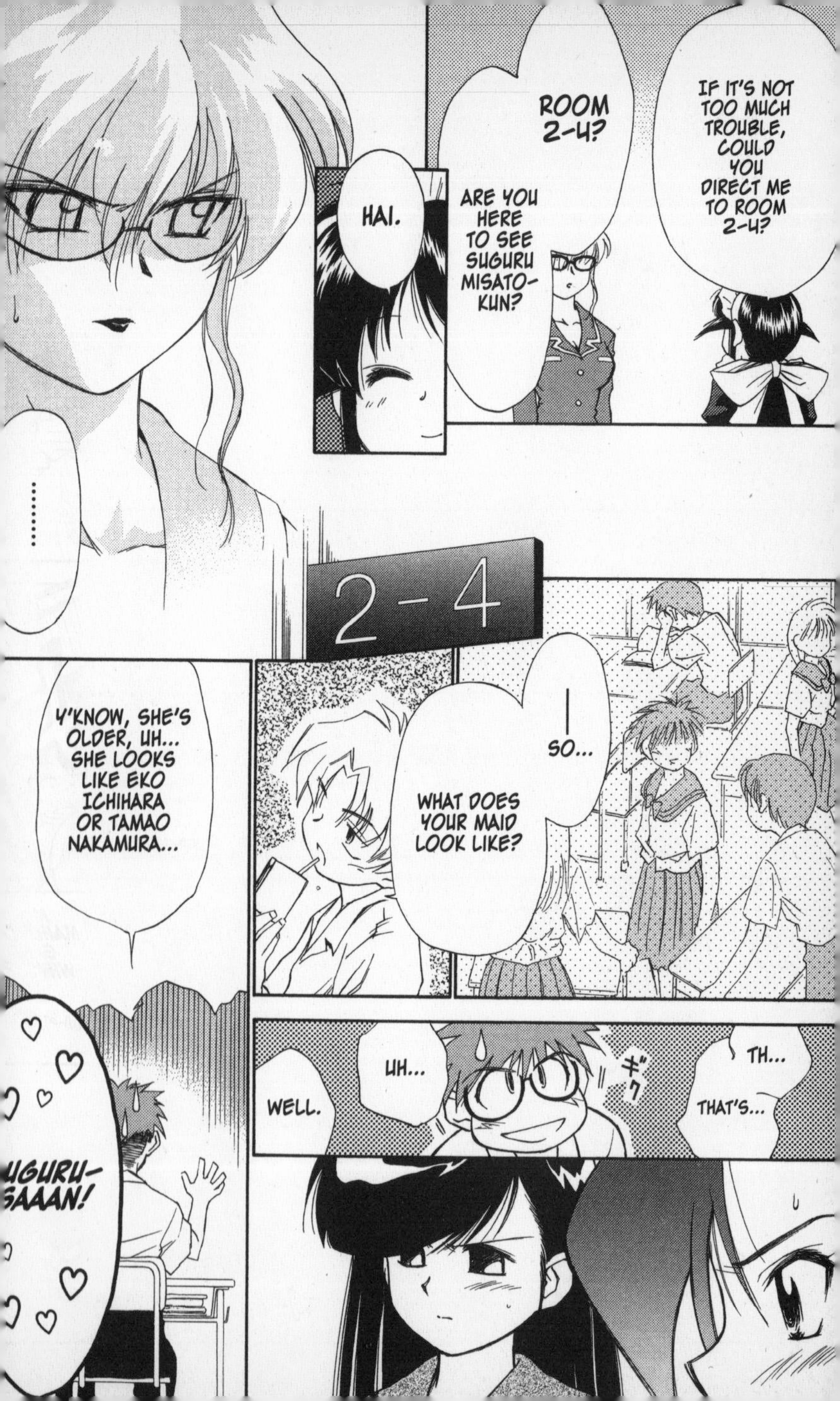
IF IT'S NOT TOO MUCH TROUBLE, COULD YOU DIRECT ME TO ROOM 2-4?
ROOM 2-4?
ARE YOU HERE TO SEE SUGURU MISATO-KUN?
HAI.
......
2-4
—SO...
WHAT DOES YOUR MAID LOOK LIKE?
Y'KNOW, SHE'S OLDER, UH... SHE LOOKS LIKE EKO ICHIHARA OR TAMAO NAKAMURA...
TH... THAT'S...
ギク
UH... WELL.
UGURU-SAAAN!

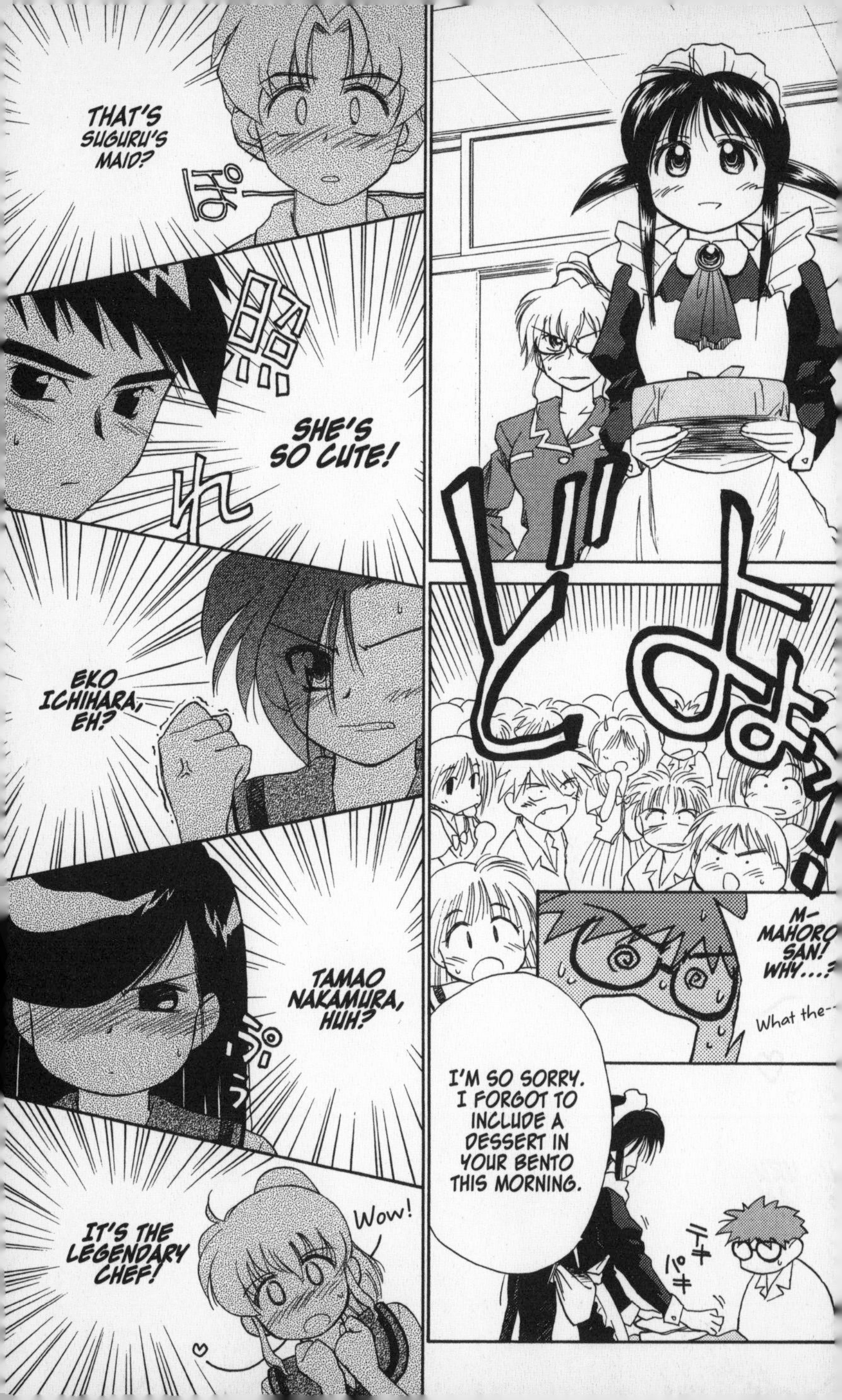

どよっ!!
M-MAHORO SAN! WHY...?
What the--
I'M SO SORRY. I FORGOT TO INCLUDE A DESSERT IN YOUR BENTO THIS MORNING.
テキパキ
THAT'S SUGURU'S MAID?
ぽー
照れ
SHE'S SO CUTE!
EKO ICHIHARA, EH?
TAMAO NAKAMURA, HUH?
ぷぅ
IT'S THE LEGENDARY CHEF!
Wow!

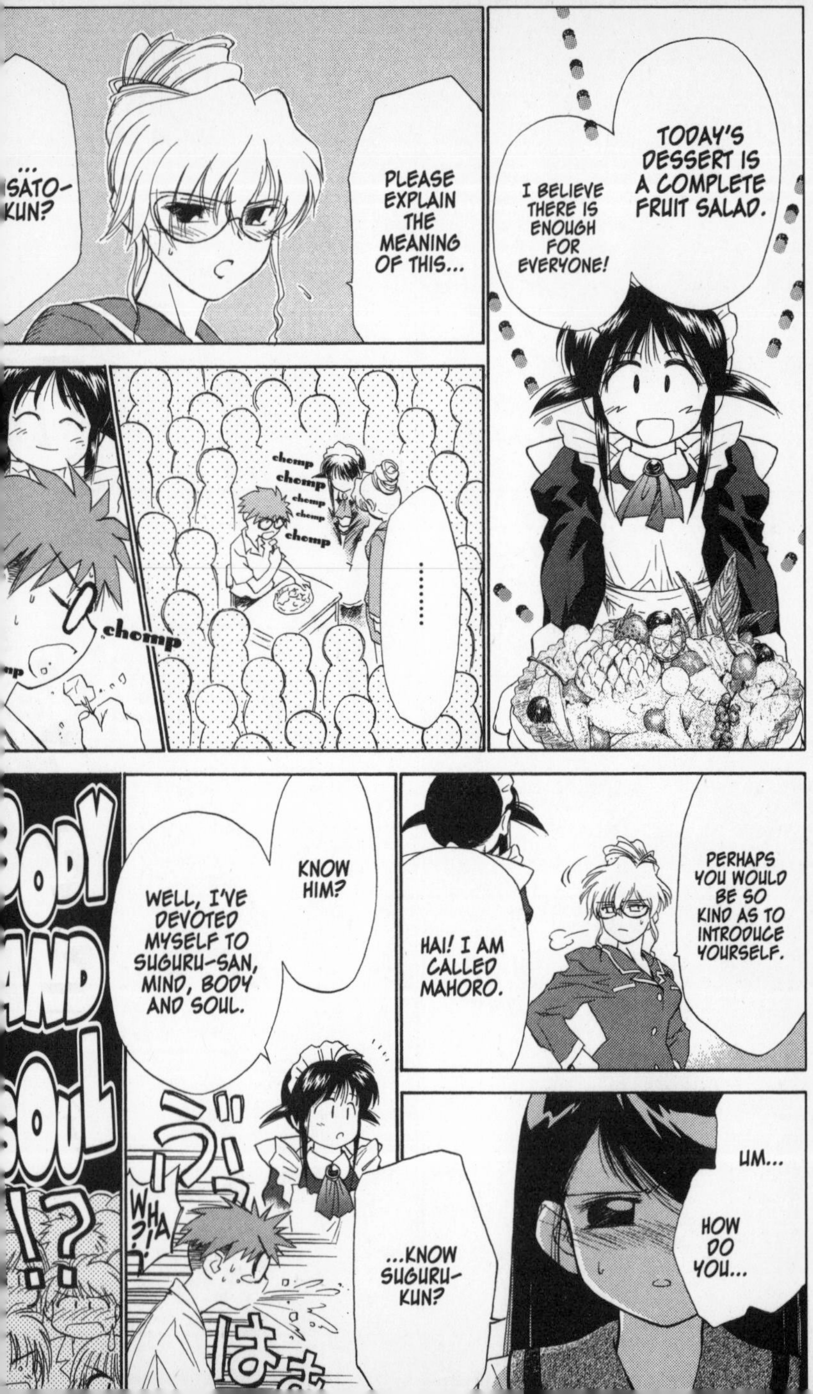
TODAY'S DESSERT IS A COMPLETE FRUIT SALAD.
I BELIEVE THERE IS ENOUGH FOR EVERYONE!
PLEASE EXPLAIN THE MEANING OF THIS...
... SATO-KUN?
chomp
chomp
chomp
chomp
chomp
....
chomp
mp
PERHAPS YOU WOULD BE SO KIND AS TO INTRODUCE YOURSELF.
HAI! I AM CALLED MAHORO.
UM...
HOW DO YOU...
...KNOW SUGURU-KUN?
KNOW HIM?
WELL, I'VE DEVOTED MYSELF TO SUGURU-SAN, MIND, BODY AND SOUL.
WHA ?!
BODY AND SOUL!?

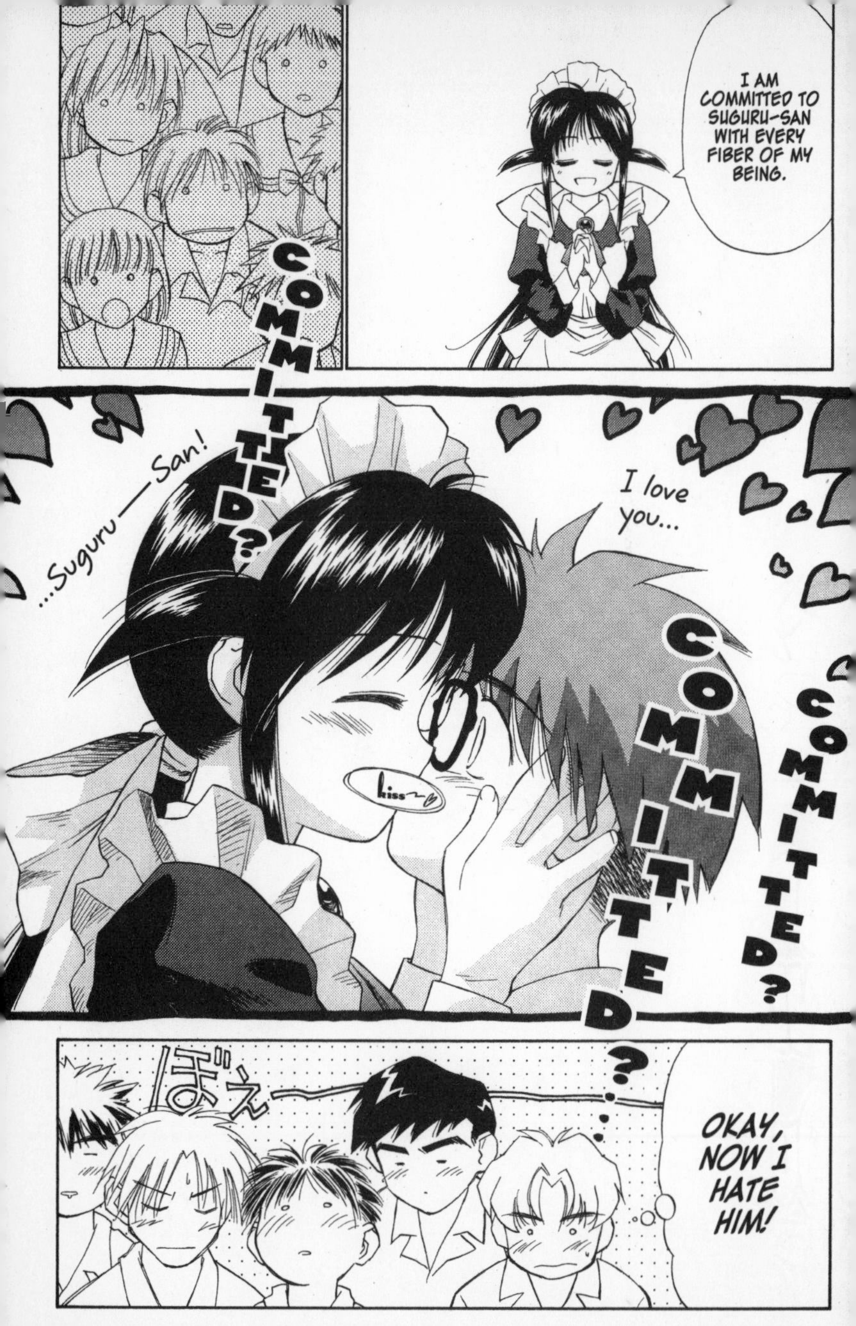

I AM COMMITTED TO SUGURU-SAN WITH EVERY FIBER OF MY BEING.
COMMITTED?
COMMITTED?
COMMITTED?
I love you...
kiss
...Suguru——San!
OKAY, NOW I HATE HIM!
ぼえー

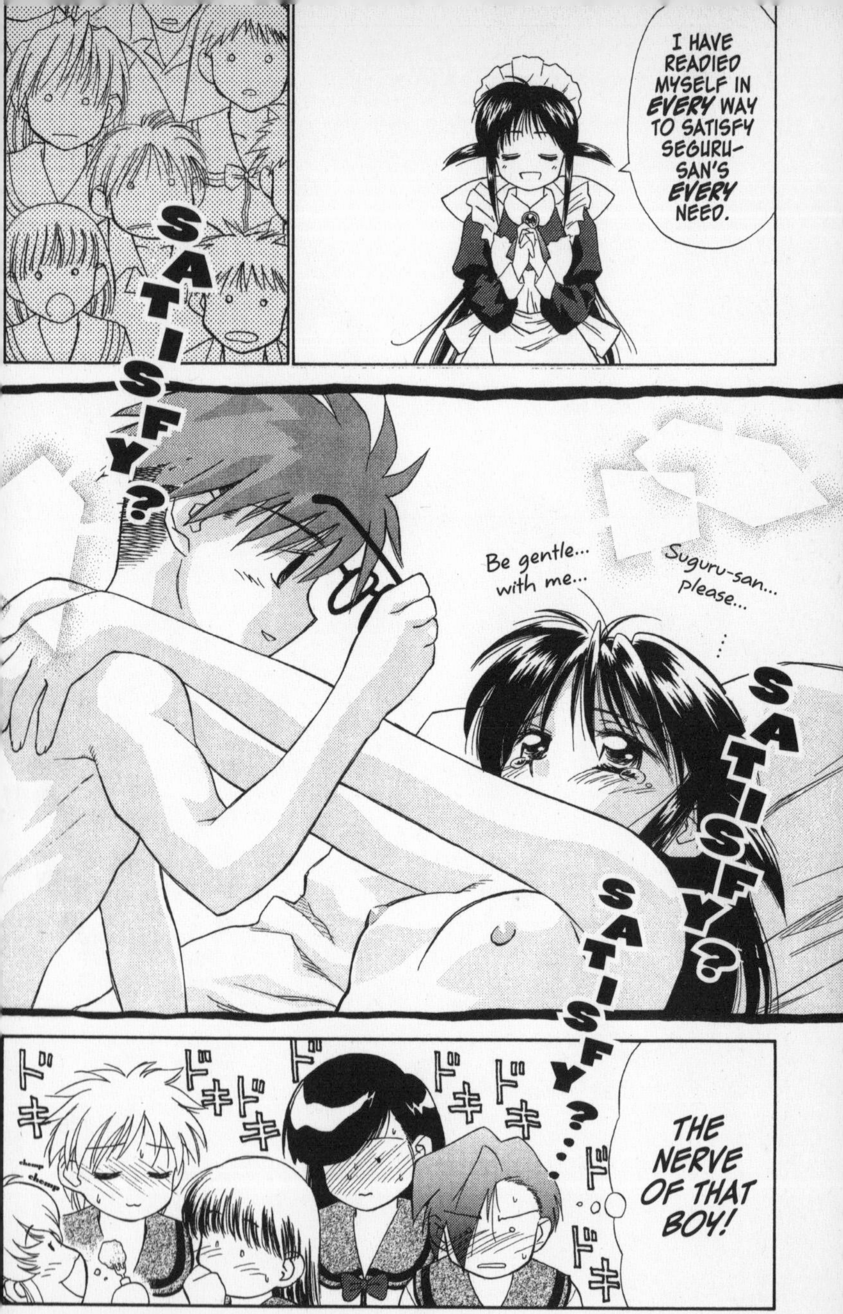
I HAVE READIED MYSELF IN EVERY WAY TO SATISFY SEGURU-SAN'S EVERY NEED.
SATISFY SATISFY?
Suguru-san... please...
Be gentle... with me...
...
SATISFY?
SATISFY SATISFY?...
THE NERVE OF THAT BOY!
ドキドキ
ドキドキ
ドキドキ
ドキドキ
chomp chomp

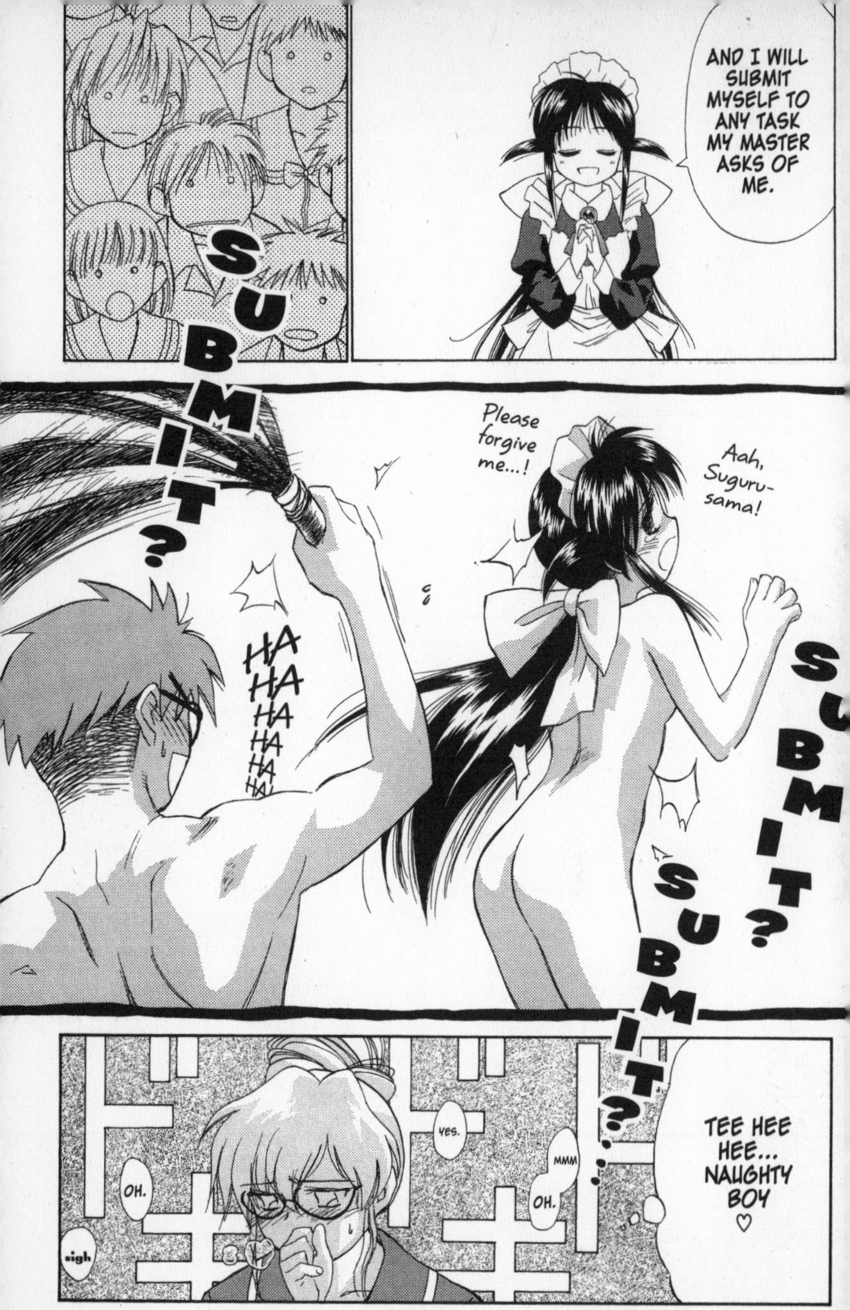
AND I WILL SUBMIT MYSELF TO ANY TASK MY MASTER ASKS OF ME.
SUBMIT?
Please forgive me...!
Aah, Suguru-sama!
HA HA HA HA HA HA
SUBMIT?
SUBMIT?
TEE HEE HEE... NAUGHTY BOY ♡
ドキドキ
yes.
MMM
OH.
OH.
sigh

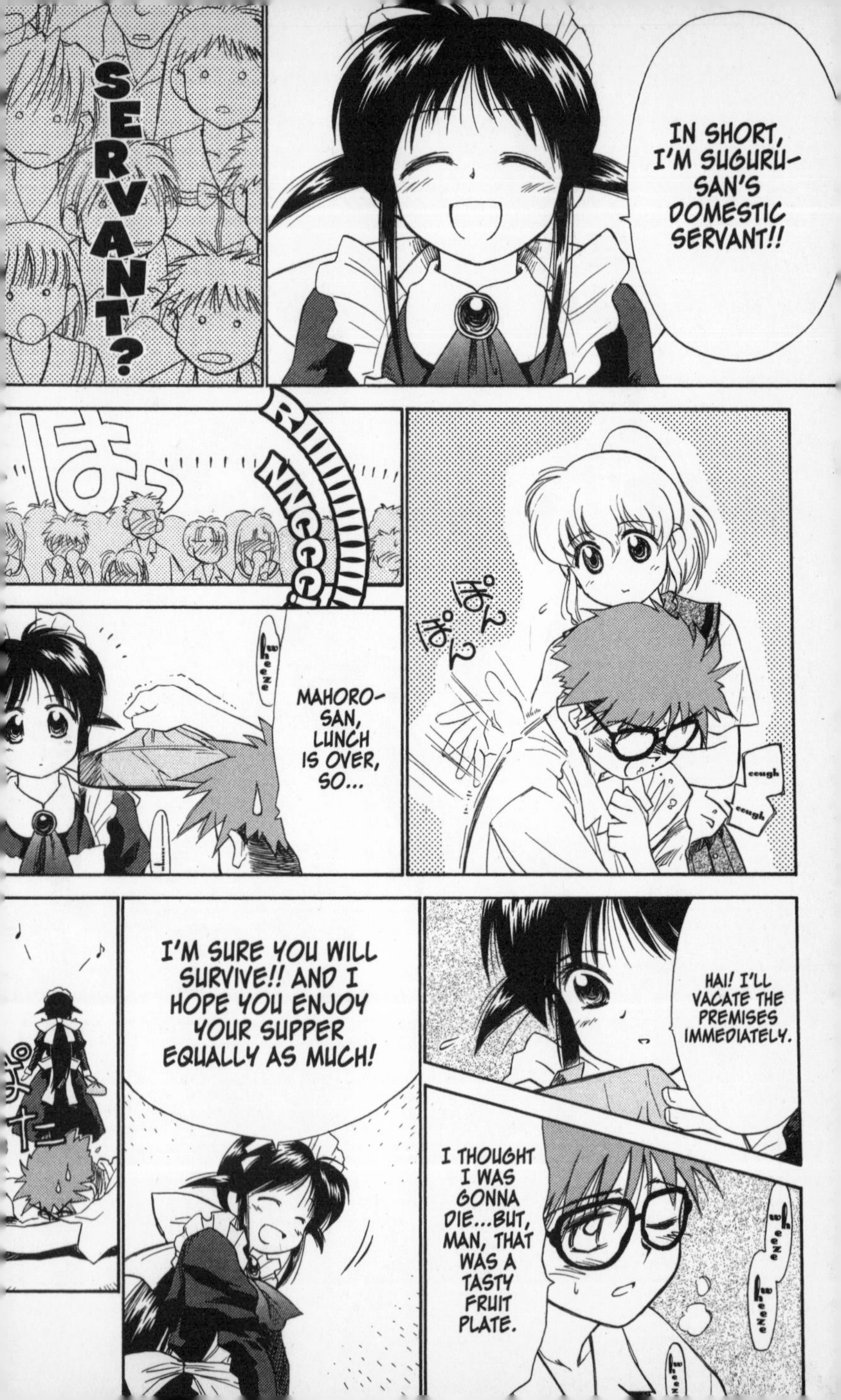
IN SHORT, I'M SUGURU-SAN'S DOMESTIC SERVANT!!
SERVANT?
ぽん ぽん
cough
cough
はっ
RIIIIINNGGG!
wheeze
MAHORO-SAN, LUNCH IS OVER, SO...
HAI! I'LL VACATE THE PREMISES IMMEDIATELY.
I THOUGHT I WAS GONNA DIE...BUT, MAN, THAT WAS A TASTY FRUIT PLATE.
wheeze
wheeze
I'M SURE YOU WILL SURVIVE!! AND I HOPE YOU ENJOY YOUR SUPPER EQUALLY AS MUCH!

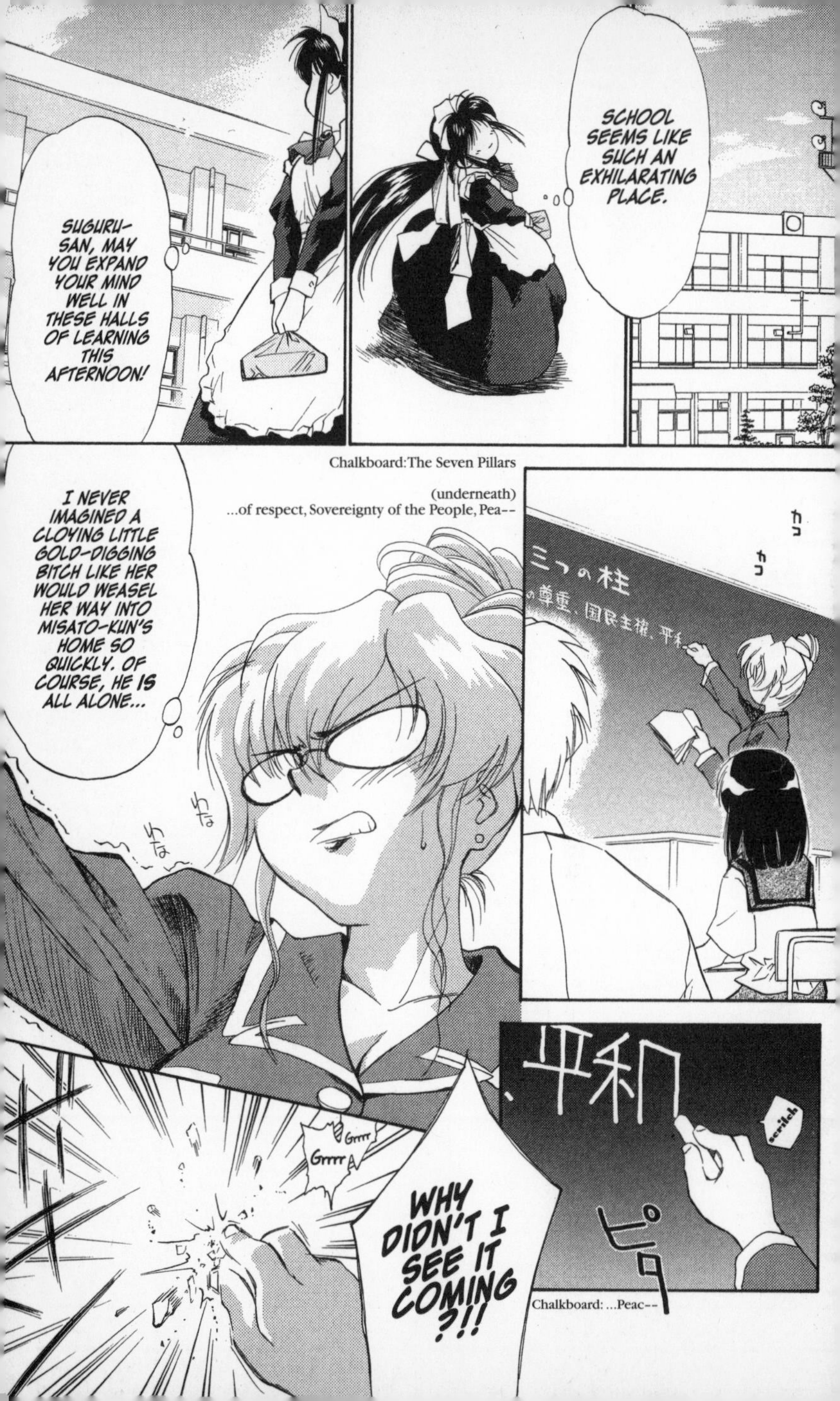
SCHOOL SEEMS LIKE SUCH AN EXHILARATING PLACE.
SUGURU-SAN, MAY YOU EXPAND YOUR MIND WELL IN THESE HALLS OF LEARNING THIS AFTERNOON!
カッ
カッ
三つの柱
の尊重、国民主権、平和
Chalkboard: The Seven Pillars
(underneath)
...of respect, Sovereignty of the People, Pea--
I NEVER IMAGINED A CLOYING LITTLE GOLD-DIGGING BITCH LIKE HER WOULD WEASEL HER WAY INTO MISATO-KUN'S HOME SO QUICKLY. OF COURSE, HE IS ALL ALONE...
わなわな
平和
scritch
ピタ
Chalkboard: ...Peac--
Grrrr
Grrrr
WHY DIDN'T I SEE IT COMING?!!

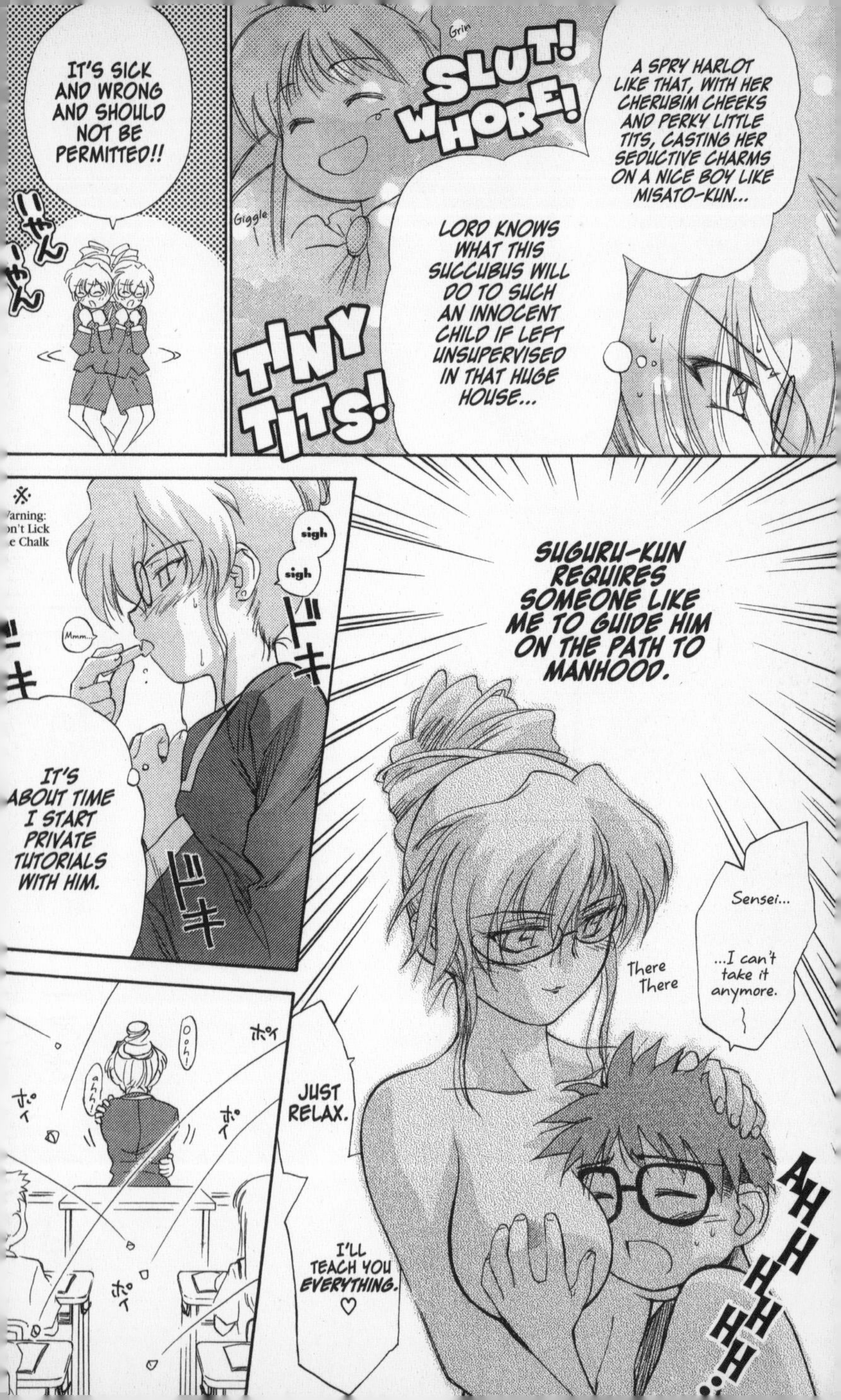

Grin
SLUT! WHORE!
A SPRY HARLOT LIKE THAT, WITH HER CHERUBIM CHEEKS AND PERKY LITTLE TITS, CASTING HER SEDUCTIVE CHARMS ON A NICE BOY LIKE MISATO-KUN...
Giggle
LORD KNOWS WHAT THIS SUCCUBUS WILL DO TO SUCH AN INNOCENT CHILD IF LEFT UNSUPERVISED IN THAT HUGE HOUSE...
TINY TITS!
IT'S SICK AND WRONG AND SHOULD NOT BE PERMITTED!!
にゃんにゃん
SUGURU-KUN REQUIRES SOMEONE LIKE ME TO GUIDE HIM ON THE PATH TO MANHOOD.
Sensei...
...I can't take it anymore.
There There
JUST RELAX.
I'LL TEACH YOU EVERYTHING. ♡
AHHHHHH...
※
sigh
sigh
ドキ
Mmm...
ドキ
IT'S ABOUT TIME I START PRIVATE TUTORIALS WITH HIM.
ドキ
ポイ
ポイ
ポイ
ポイ

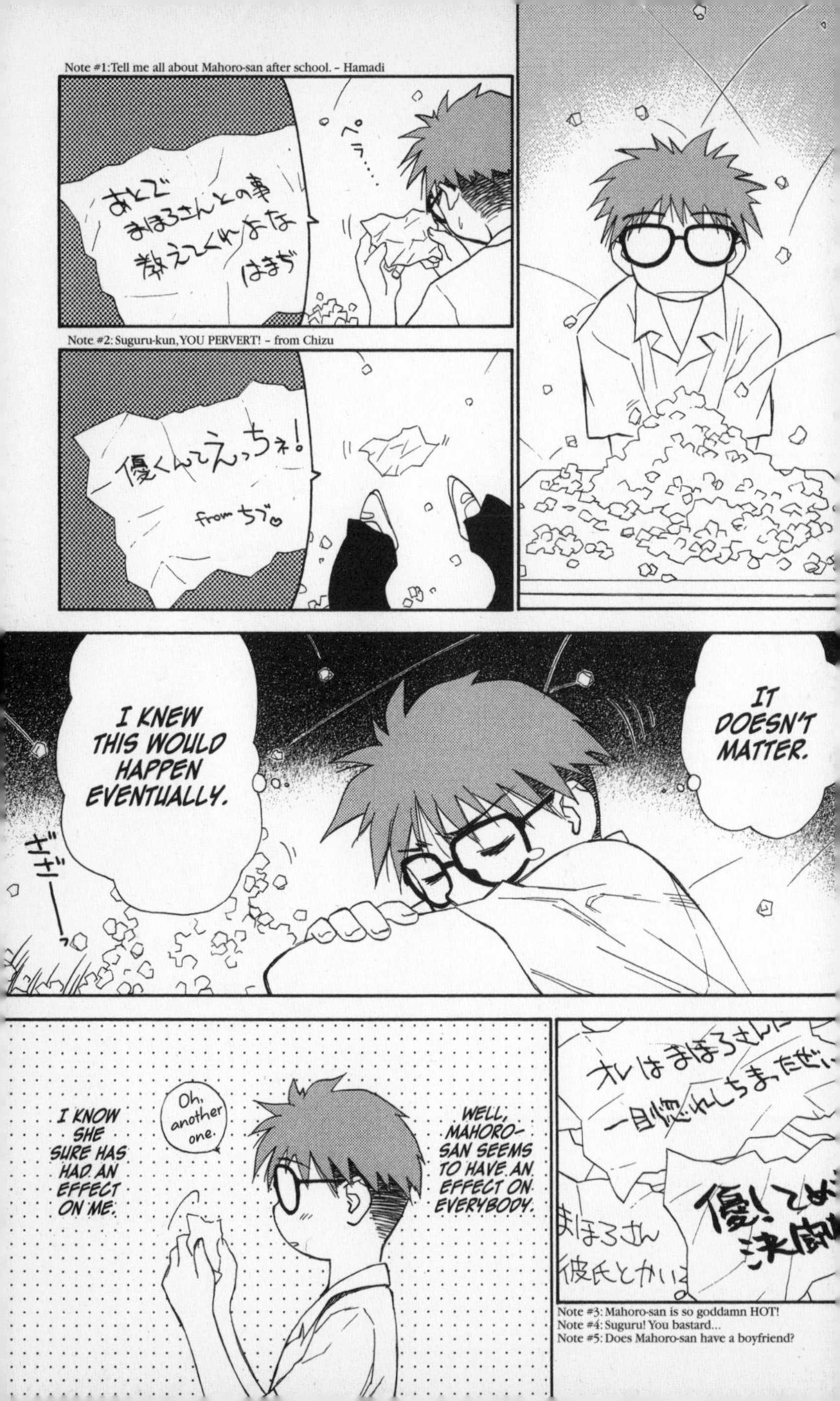
Note #1: Tell me all about Mahoro-san after school. – Hamadi
あとで まほろさんとの事 教えてくれよな
はまぢ
ペラ…
Note #2: Suguru-kun, YOU PERVERT! – from Chizu
優くんてえっちぇ!
from ちづ
IT DOESN'T MATTER.
I KNEW THIS WOULD HAPPEN EVENTUALLY.
ざざー
オレはまほろさんに
一目惚れしちまったぜ
優!てめ
まほろさん
彼氏とかいる
Note #3: Mahoro-san is so goddamn HOT!
Note #4: Suguru! You bastard...
Note #5: Does Mahoro-san have a boyfriend?
WELL, MAHORO-SAN SEEMS TO HAVE AN EFFECT ON EVERYBODY.
Oh, another one.
I KNOW SHE SURE HAS HAD AN EFFECT ON ME.

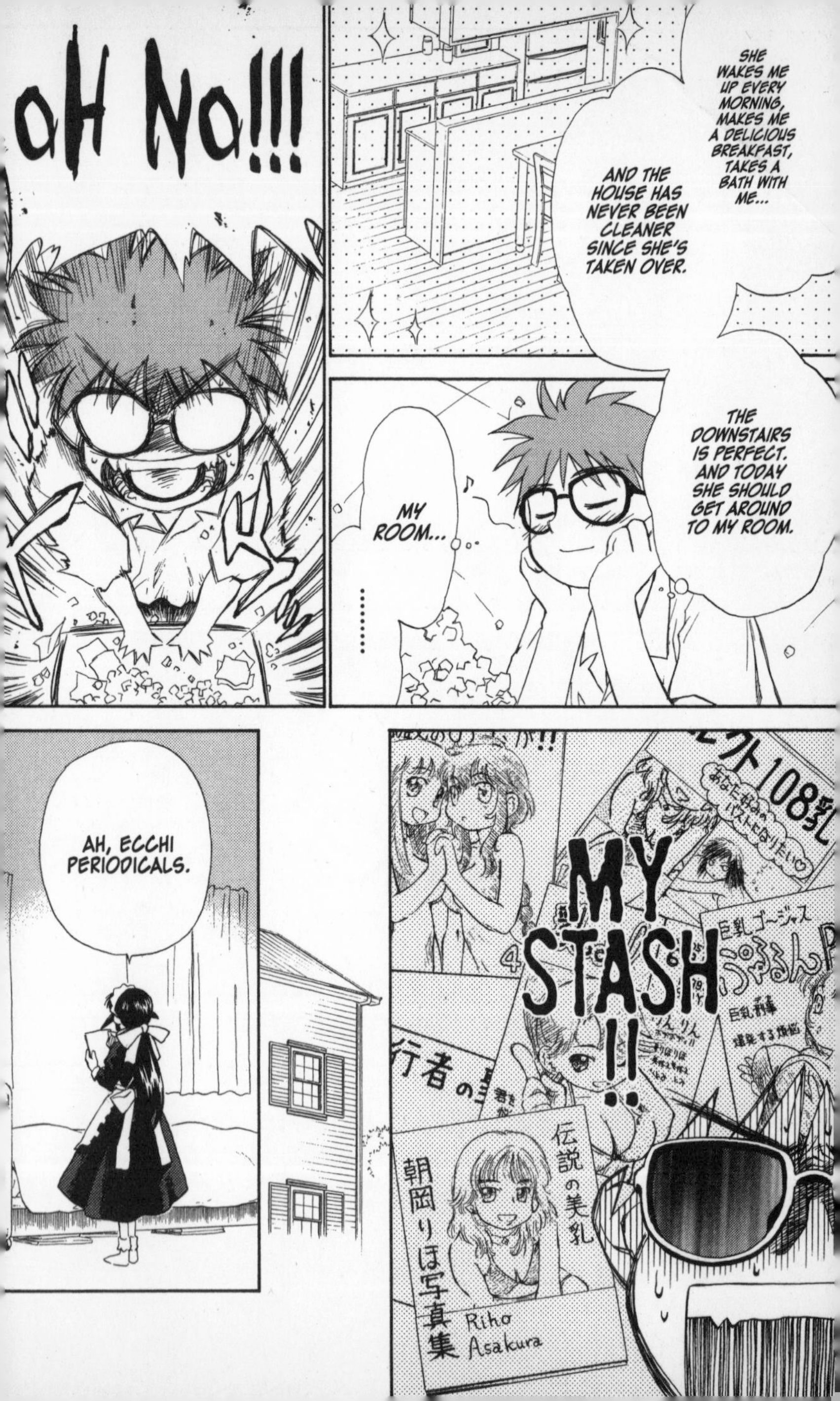
SHE WAKES ME UP EVERY MORNING, MAKES ME A DELICIOUS BREAKFAST, TAKES A BATH WITH ME...
AND THE HOUSE HAS NEVER BEEN CLEANER SINCE SHE'S TAKEN OVER.
THE DOWNSTAIRS IS PERFECT. AND TODAY SHE SHOULD GET AROUND TO MY ROOM.
MY ROOM...
......
oH No!!!
MY STASH!!
108乳
巨乳ゴ～ジャス
伝説の美乳
朝岡りほ写真集
Riho Asakura
AH, ECCHI PERIODICALS.

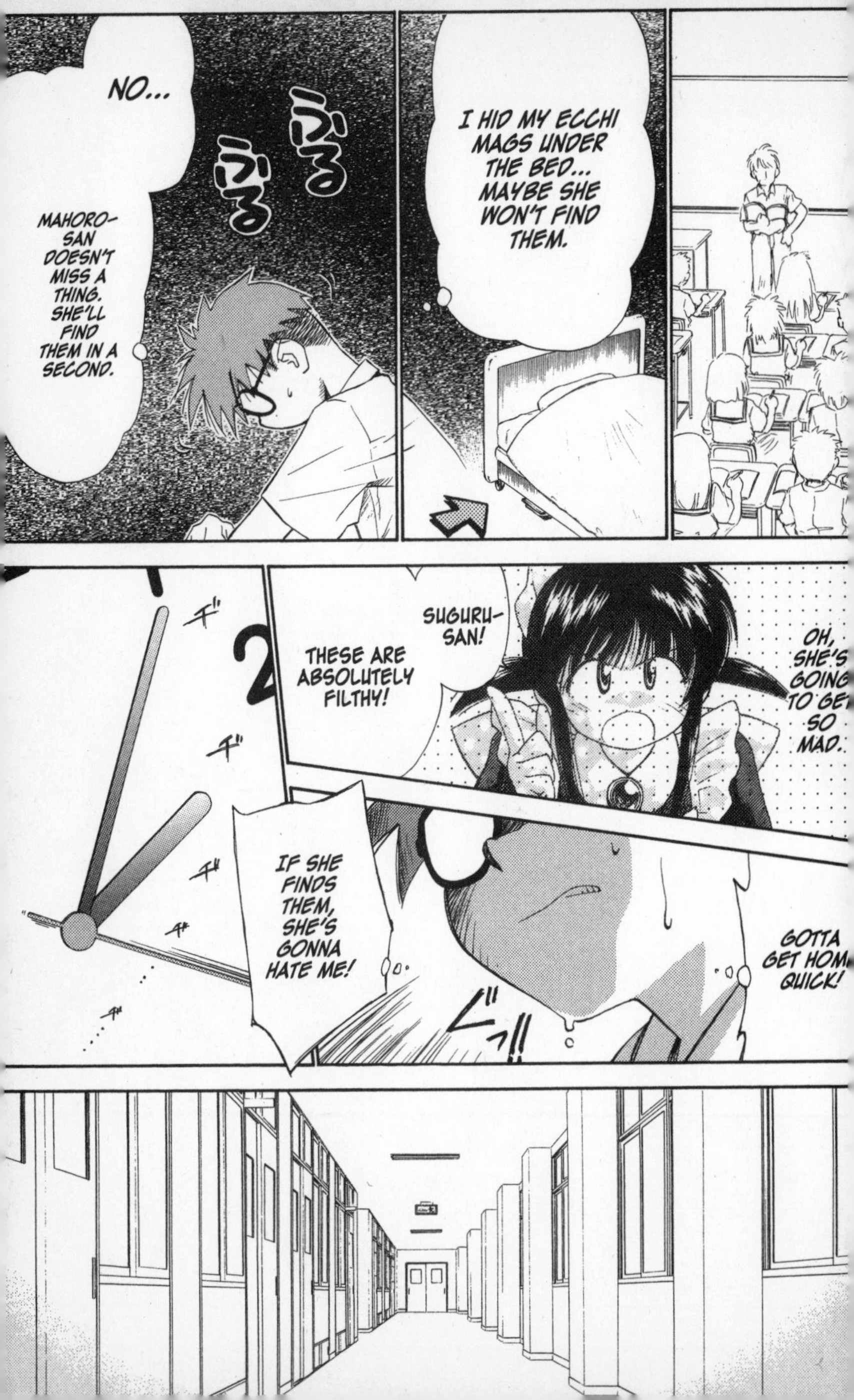
I HID MY ECCHI MAGS UNDER THE BED... MAYBE SHE WON'T FIND THEM.
NO...
ぶる
ぶる
MAHORO-SAN DOESN'T MISS A THING. SHE'LL FIND THEM IN A SECOND.
OH, SHE'S GOING TO GE SO MAD.
SUGURU-SAN!
THESE ARE ABSOLUTELY FILTHY!
GOTTA GET HOM QUICK!
IF SHE FINDS THEM, SHE'S GONNA HATE ME!
ギ
ギ
ギ
ギ

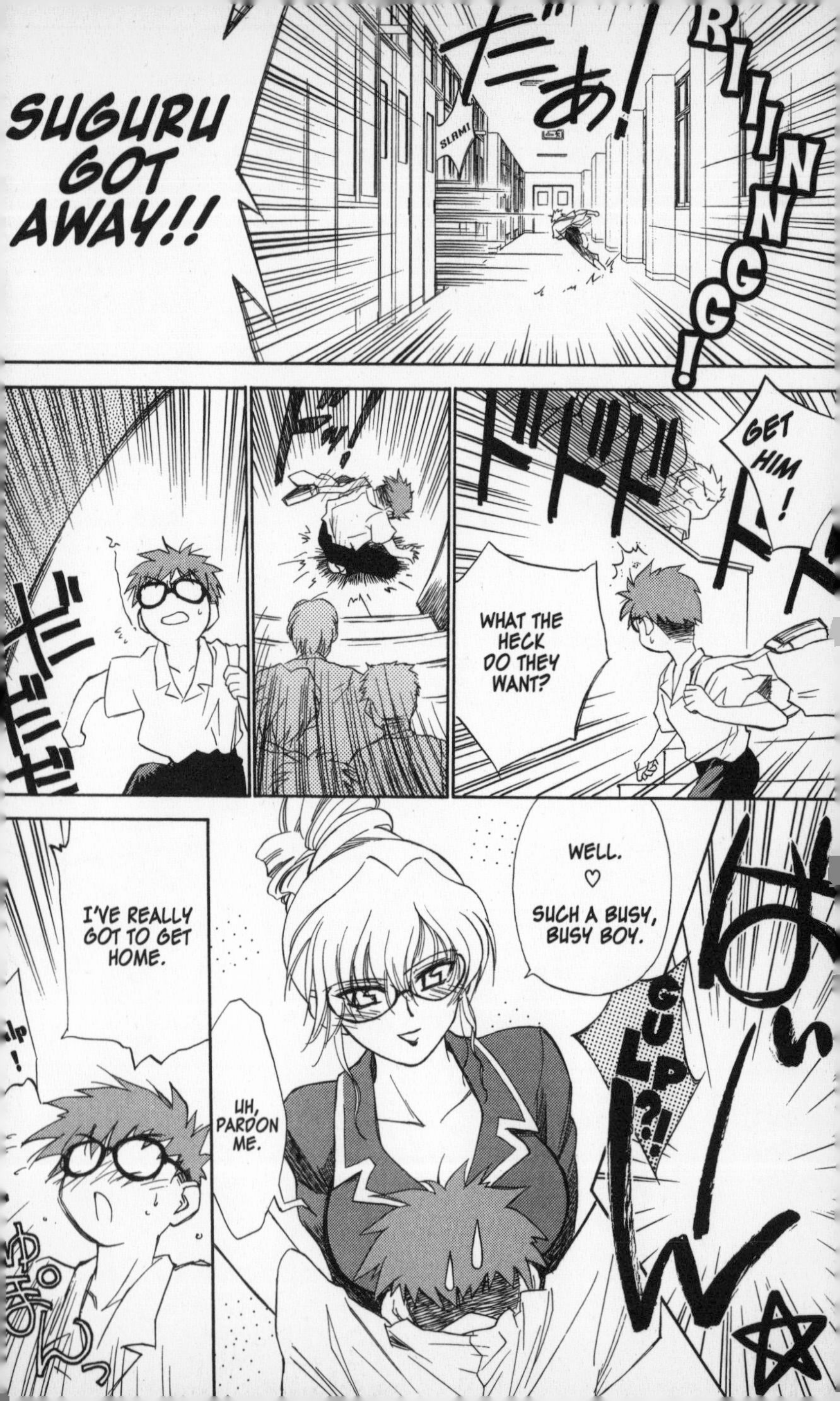
RIIINNNGG!
だぁ!
SLAM!
SUGURU GOT AWAY!!
GET HIM!
WHAT THE HECK DO THEY WANT?
WELL. ♡ SUCH A BUSY, BUSY BOY.
GULP?!
UH, PARDON ME.
I'VE REALLY GOT TO GET HOME.

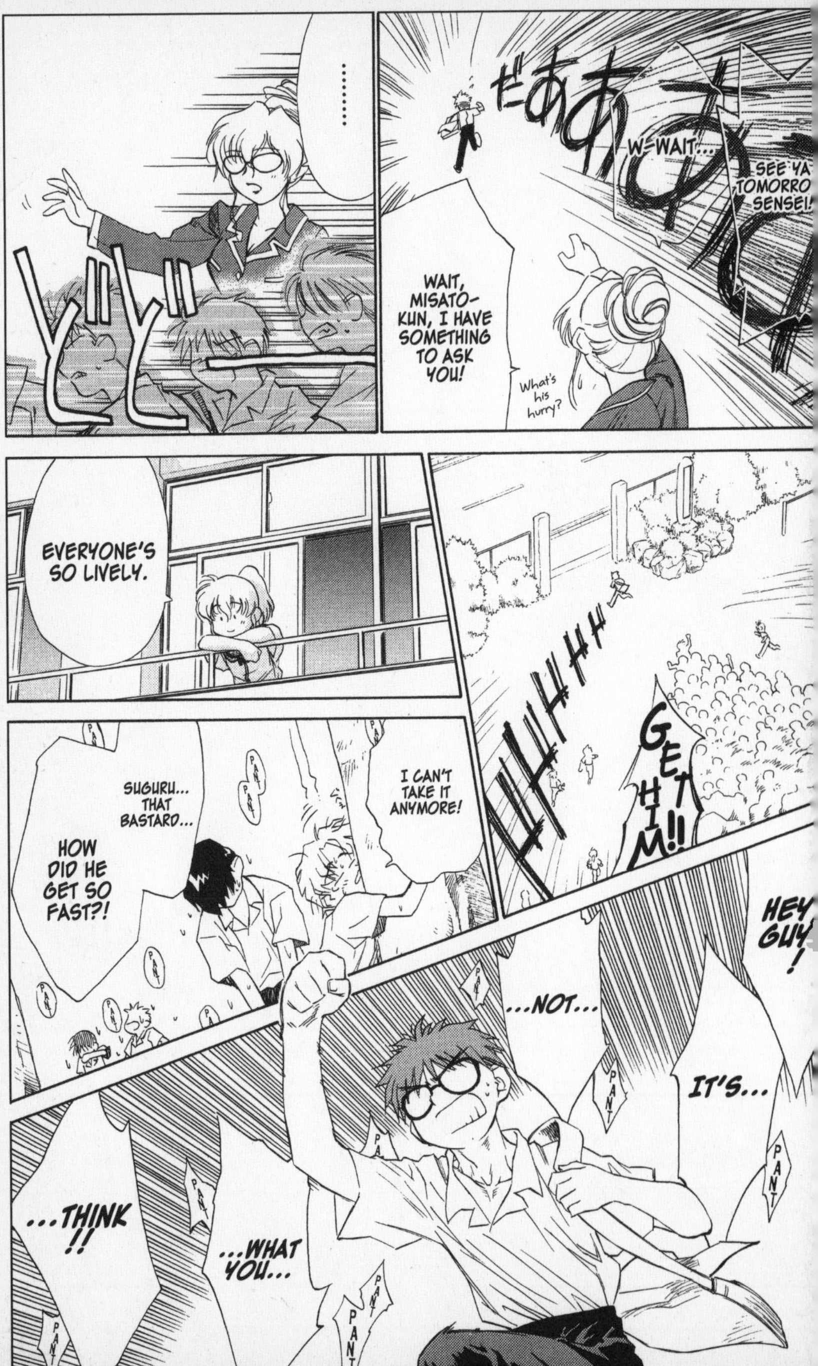
W-WAIT...
SEE YA TOMORRO SENSEI!
WAIT, MISATO-KUN, I HAVE SOMETHING TO ASK YOU!
What's his hurry?
......
GET HIM!!
EVERYONE'S SO LIVELY.
PANT PANT
I CAN'T TAKE IT ANYMORE!
SUGURU... THAT BASTARD...
HOW DID HE GET SO FAST?!
PANT
PANT
HEY GUY!
IT'S...
...NOT...
...WHAT YOU...
...THINK!!
PANT
PANT
PANT

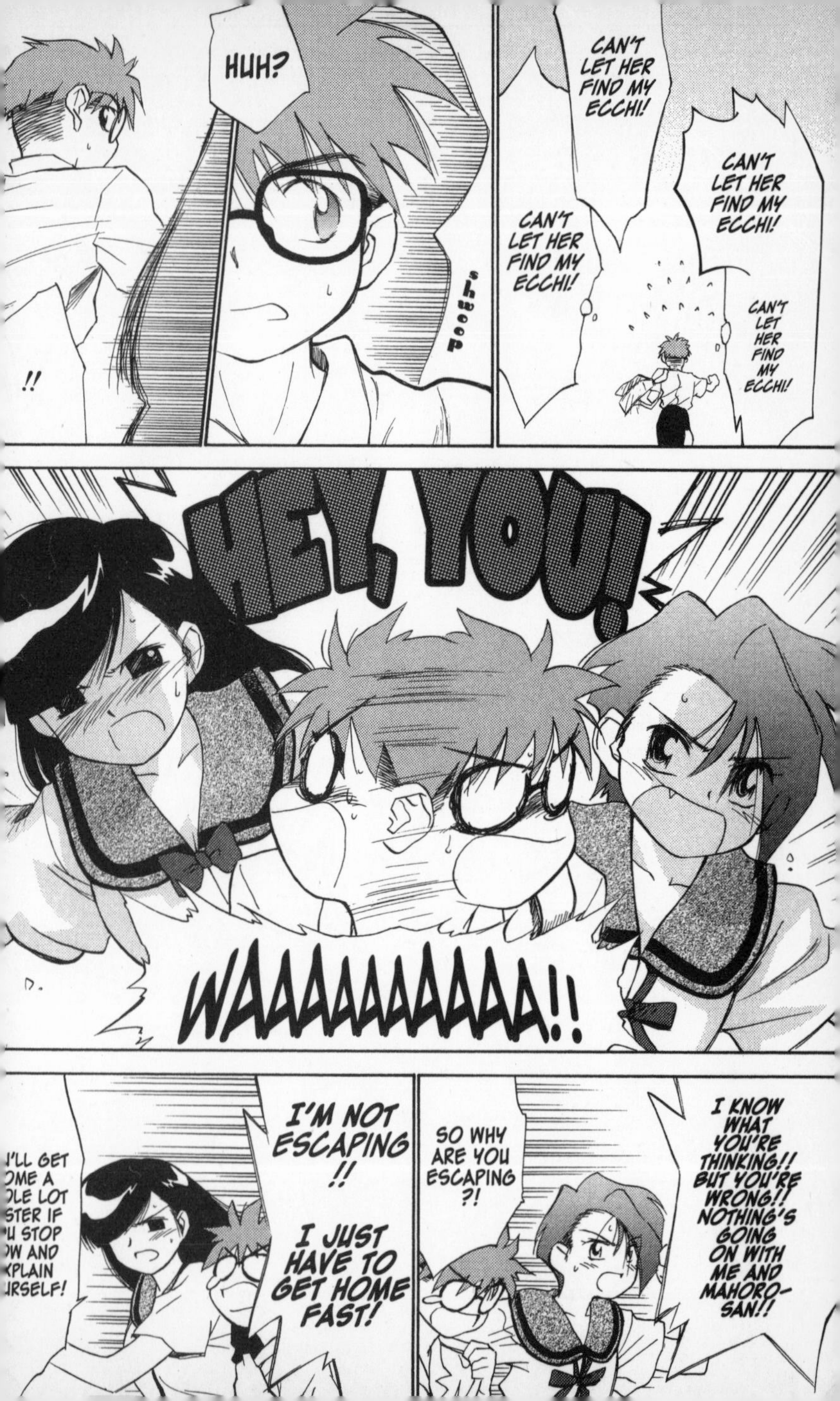
CAN'T LET HER FIND MY ECCHI!
CAN'T LET HER FIND MY ECCHI!
CAN'T LET HER FIND MY ECCHI!
CAN'T LET HER FIND MY ECCHI!
HUH?
shwoop
!!
HEY, YOU!!
WAAAAAAAAAA!!
I KNOW WHAT YOU'RE THINKING!! BUT YOU'RE WRONG!! NOTHING'S GOING ON WITH ME AND MAHORO-SAN!!
SO WHY ARE YOU ESCAPING ?!
I'M NOT ESCAPING !!
I JUST HAVE TO GET HOME FAST!
'LL GET OME A OLE LOT STER IF U STOP OW AND XPLAIN URSELF!

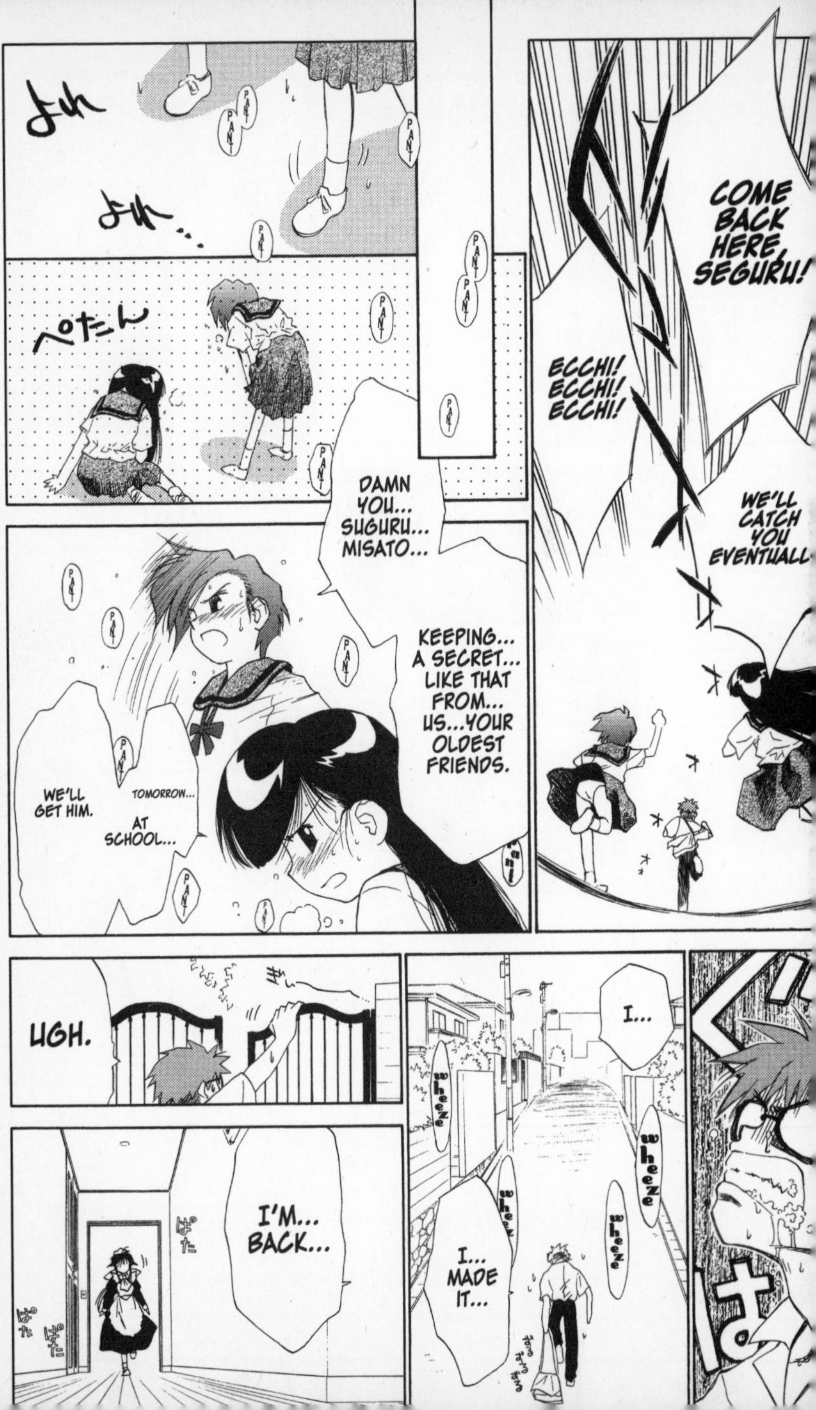

COME BACK HERE, SEGURU!
ECCHI! ECCHI! ECCHI!
WE'LL CATCH YOU EVENTUALL
よれ
よれ...
PANT
PANT
PANT
PANT
PANT
ぺたん
PANT
PANT
PANT
DAMN YOU... SUGURU... MISATO...
KEEPING... A SECRET... LIKE THAT FROM... US...YOUR OLDEST FRIENDS.
PANT
PANT
PANT
TOMORROW...
AT SCHOOL...
WE'LL GET HIM.
PANT
PANT
は
I...
wheeze
wheeze
wheeze
wheeze
I... MADE IT...
UGH.
ぱた
I'M... BACK...
ぱた ぱた

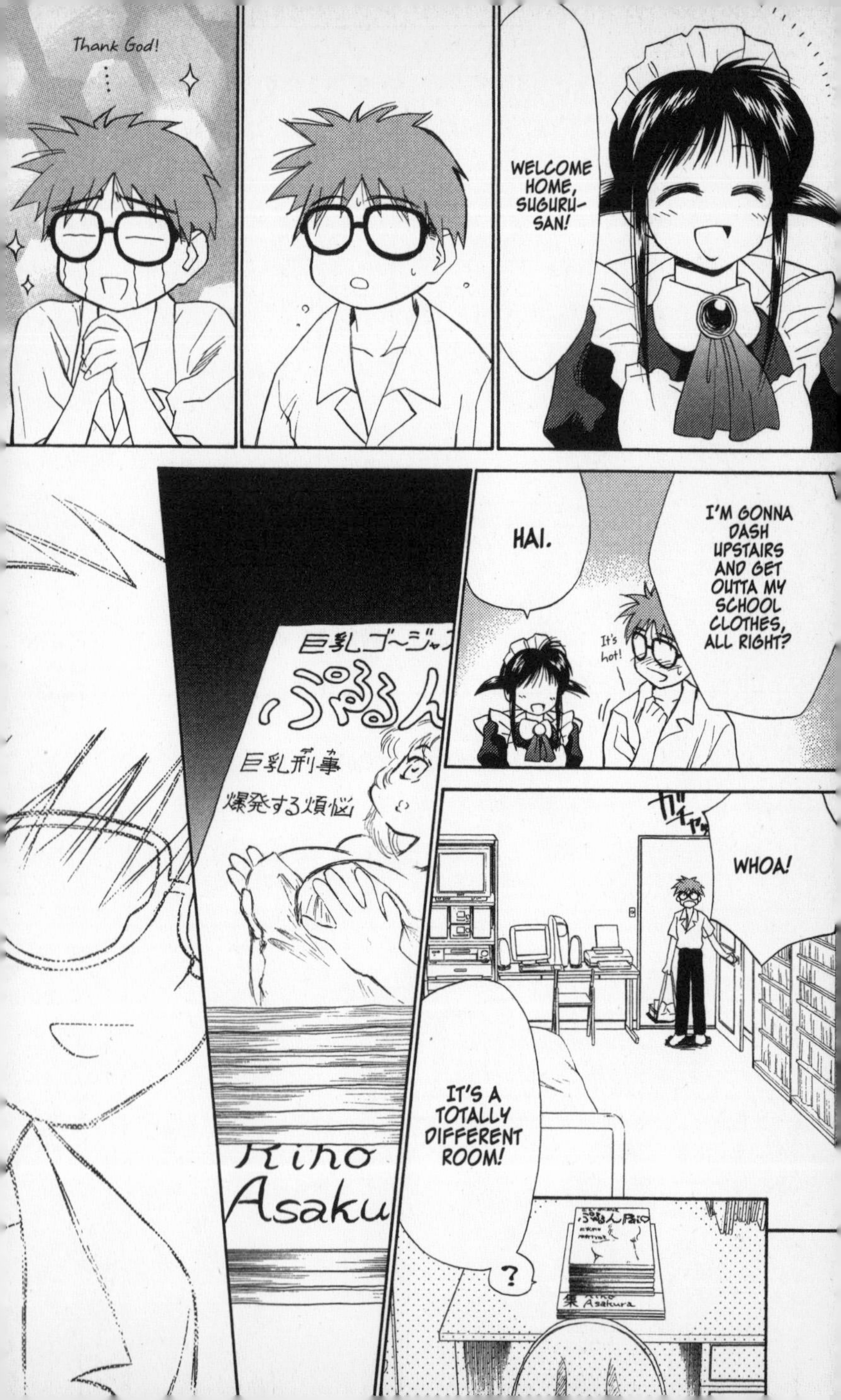
WELCOME HOME, SUGURU-SAN!
Thank God!
...
I'M GONNA DASH UPSTAIRS AND GET OUTTA MY SCHOOL CLOTHES, ALL RIGHT?
It's hot!
HAI.
ガチャッ
WHOA!
IT'S A TOTALLY DIFFERENT ROOM!
?
巨乳ゴ~ジャス
ぷるるん
巨乳刑事
爆発する煩悩
Riho Asaku

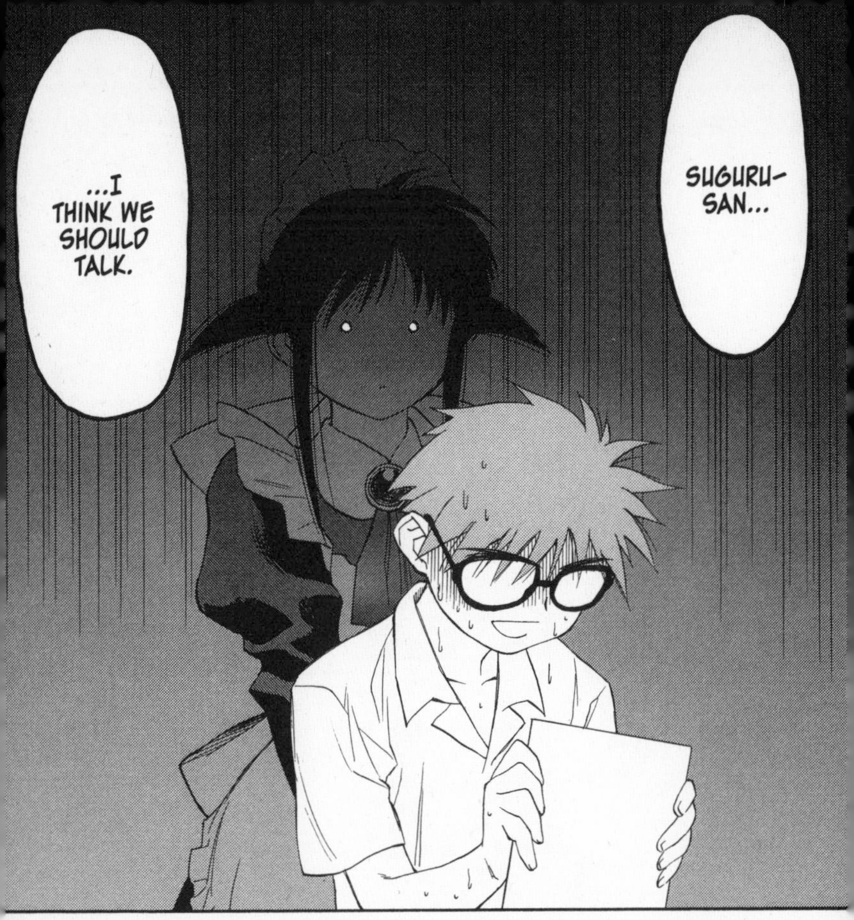
SUGURU-SAN...
...I THINK WE SHOULD TALK.

Banner: Sakura Baths

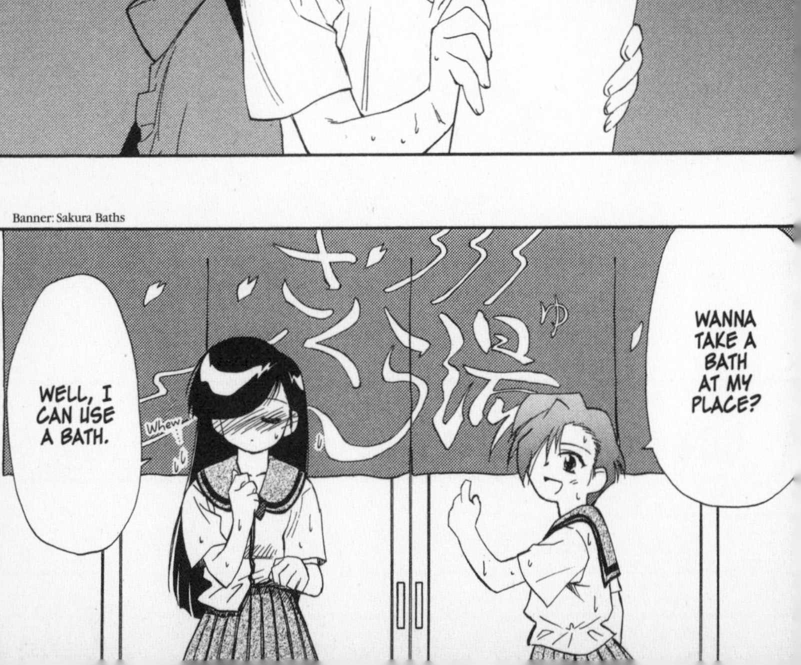
さくら湯
WANNA TAKE A BATH AT MY PLACE?
Whew
WELL, I CAN USE A BATH.

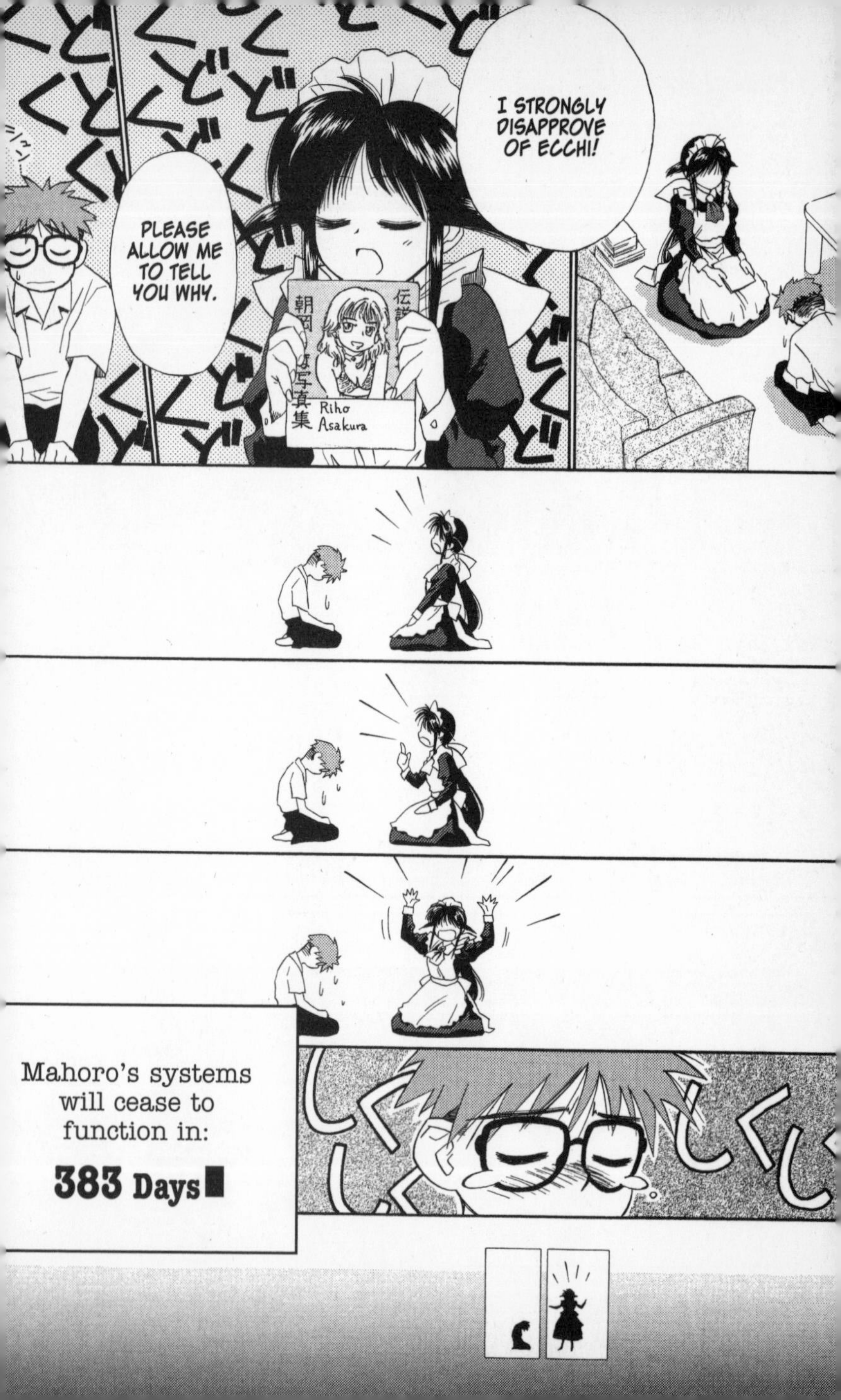
I STRONGLY DISAPPROVE OF ECCHI!
PLEASE ALLOW ME TO TELL YOU WHY.
Riho Asakura
Mahoro's systems will cease to function in:
383 Days

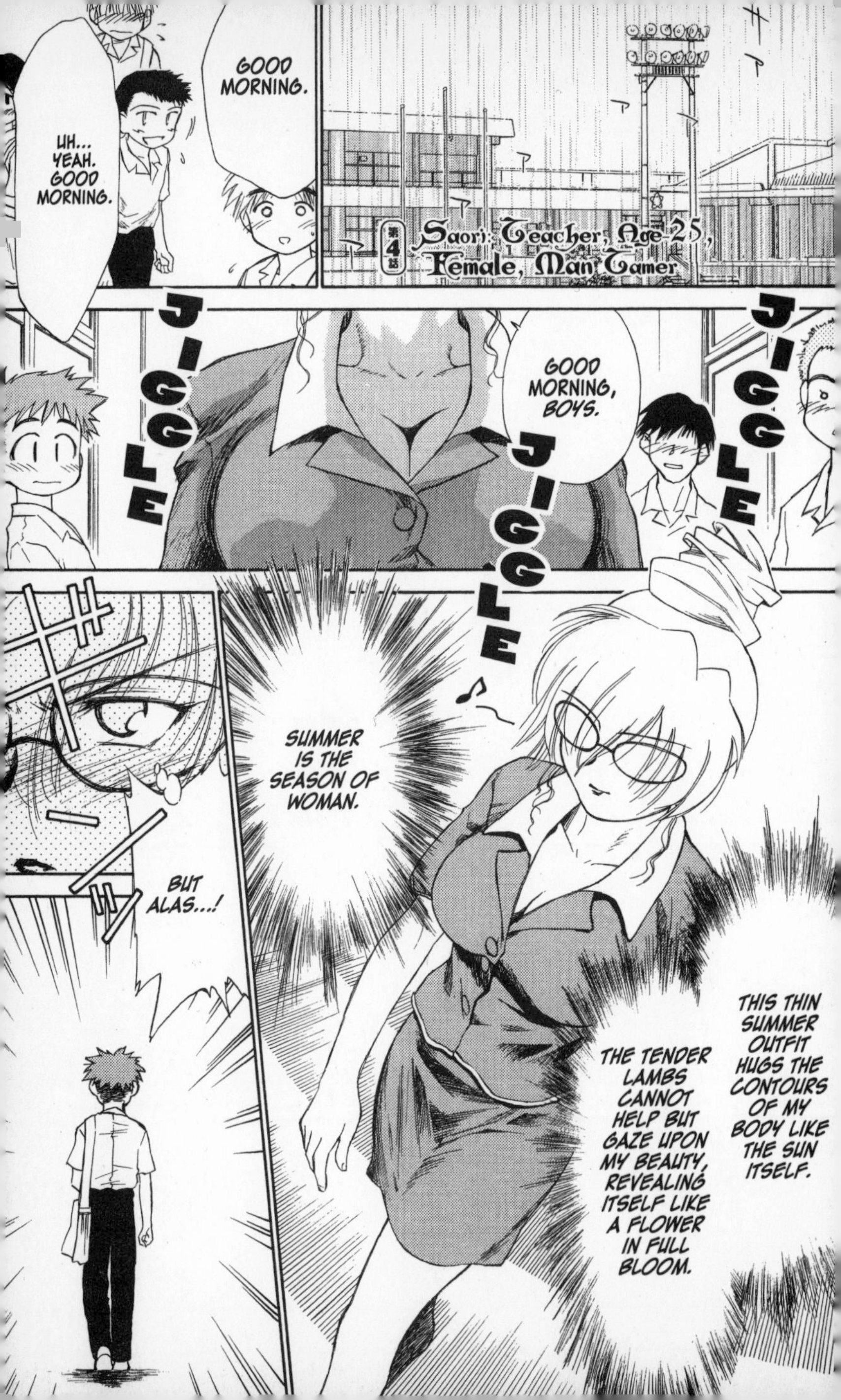

第4話
Saori: Teacher, Age 25, Female, Man Tamer
GOOD MORNING.
UH... YEAH. GOOD MORNING.
JIGGLE
GOOD MORNING, BOYS.
JIGGLE
JIGGLE
SUMMER IS THE SEASON OF WOMAN.
THIS THIN SUMMER OUTFIT HUGS THE CONTOURS OF MY BODY LIKE THE SUN ITSELF.
THE TENDER LAMBS CANNOT HELP BUT GAZE UPON MY BEAUTY, REVEALING ITSELF LIKE A FLOWER IN FULL BLOOM.
BUT ALAS...!

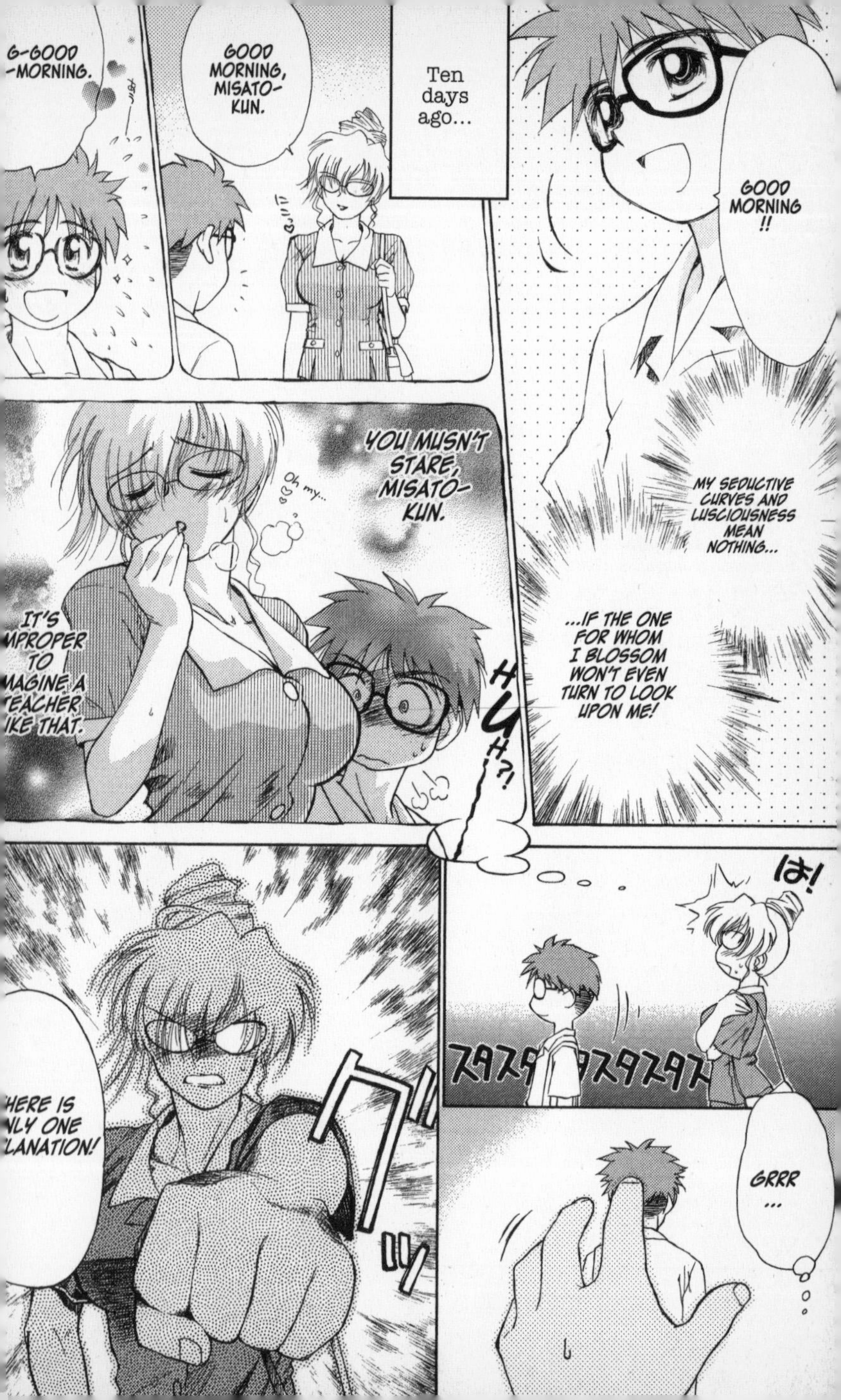
GOOD MORNING !!
MY SEDUCTIVE CURVES AND LUSCIOUSNESS MEAN NOTHING...
...IF THE ONE FOR WHOM I BLOSSOM WON'T EVEN TURN TO LOOK UPON ME!
Ten days ago...
GOOD MORNING, MISATO-KUN.
G-GOOD -MORNING.
YOU MUSN'T STARE, MISATO-KUN.
Oh my...
IT'S MPROPER TO MAGINE A EACHER IKE THAT.
HUH?!
は!
スタスタ タスタスタスタ
GRRR ...
HERE IS NLY ONE LANATION!

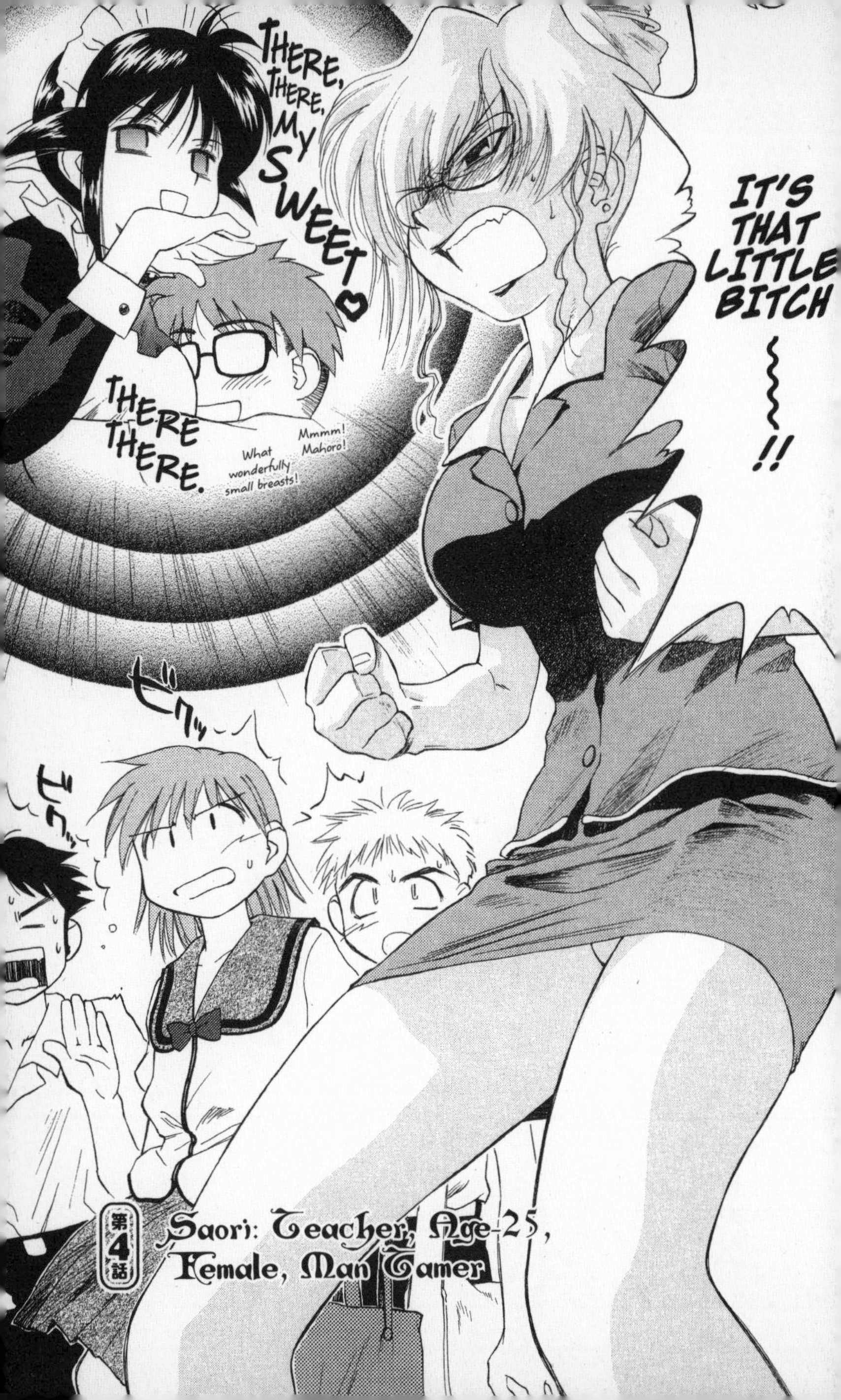
IT'S THAT LITTLE BITCH ~~~!!
THERE, THERE, MY SWEET♡
THERE THERE.
Mmmm! Mahoro!
What wonderfully small breasts!
ビクッ
ビクッ

第4話 Saori: Teacher, Age 25, Female, Man Tamer

Doghouse: Guri-chan

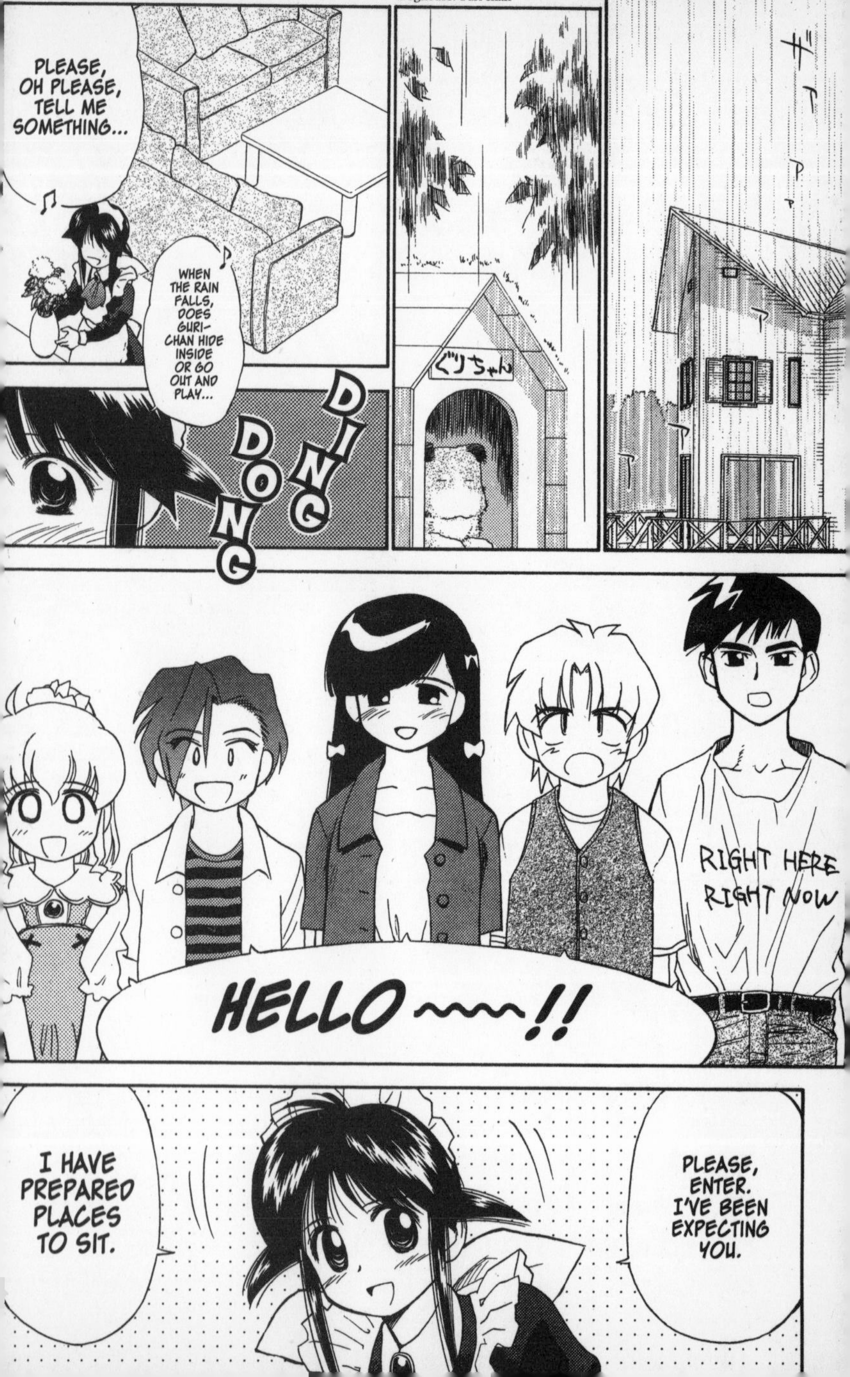
ぐりちゃん
WHEN THE RAIN FALLS, DOES GURI-CHAN HIDE INSIDE OR GO OUT AND PLAY...
PLEASE, OH PLEASE, TELL ME SOMETHING...
DING DONG
RIGHT HERE RIGHT NOW
HELLO~~~!!
PLEASE, ENTER. I'VE BEEN EXPECTING YOU.
I HAVE PREPARED PLACES TO SIT.

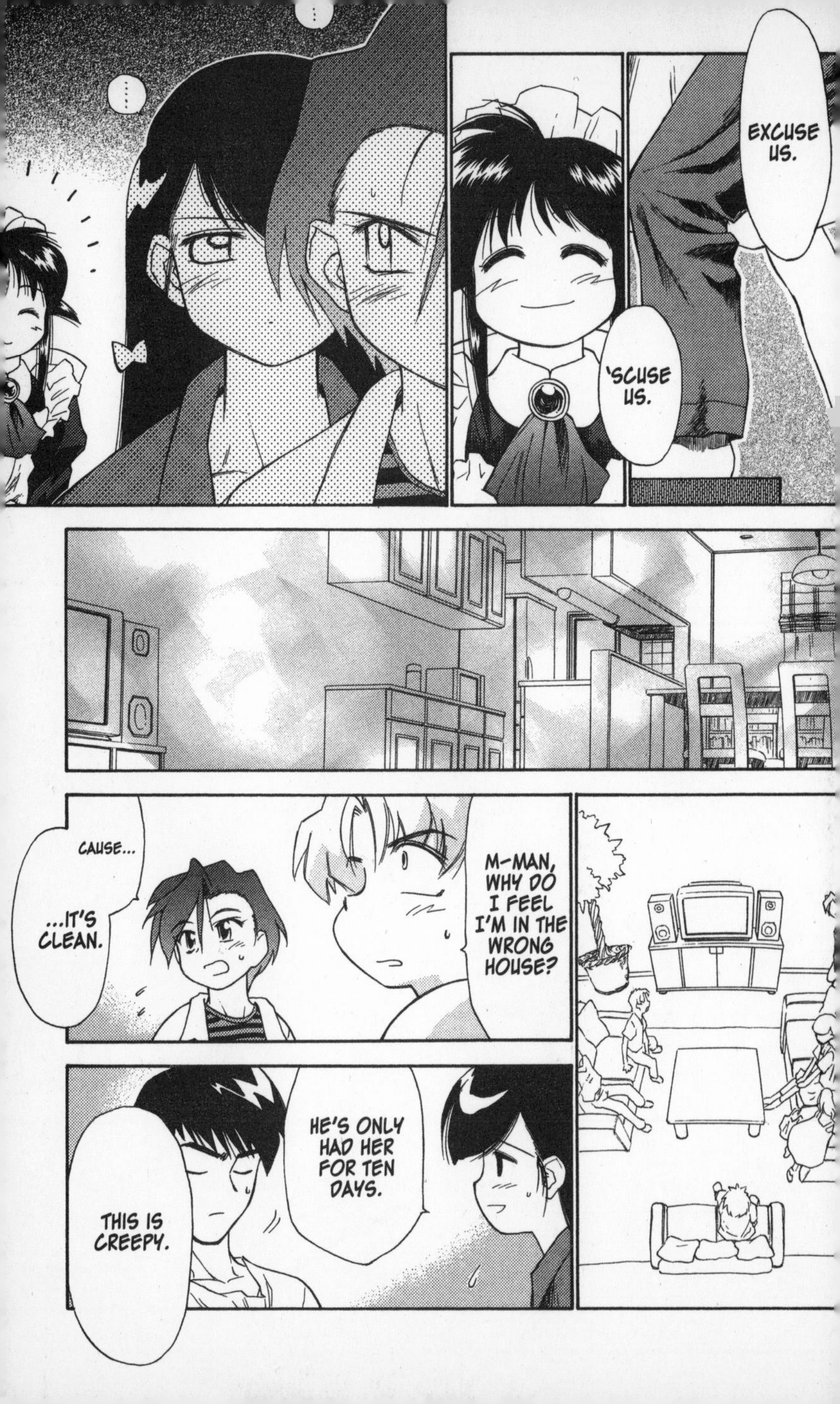
EXCUSE US.
'SCUSE US.
...
...
M-MAN, WHY DO I FEEL I'M IN THE WRONG HOUSE?
CAUSE...
...IT'S CLEAN.
HE'S ONLY HAD HER FOR TEN DAYS.
THIS IS CREEPY.

*Prayer ceremony for a child's artistic development.

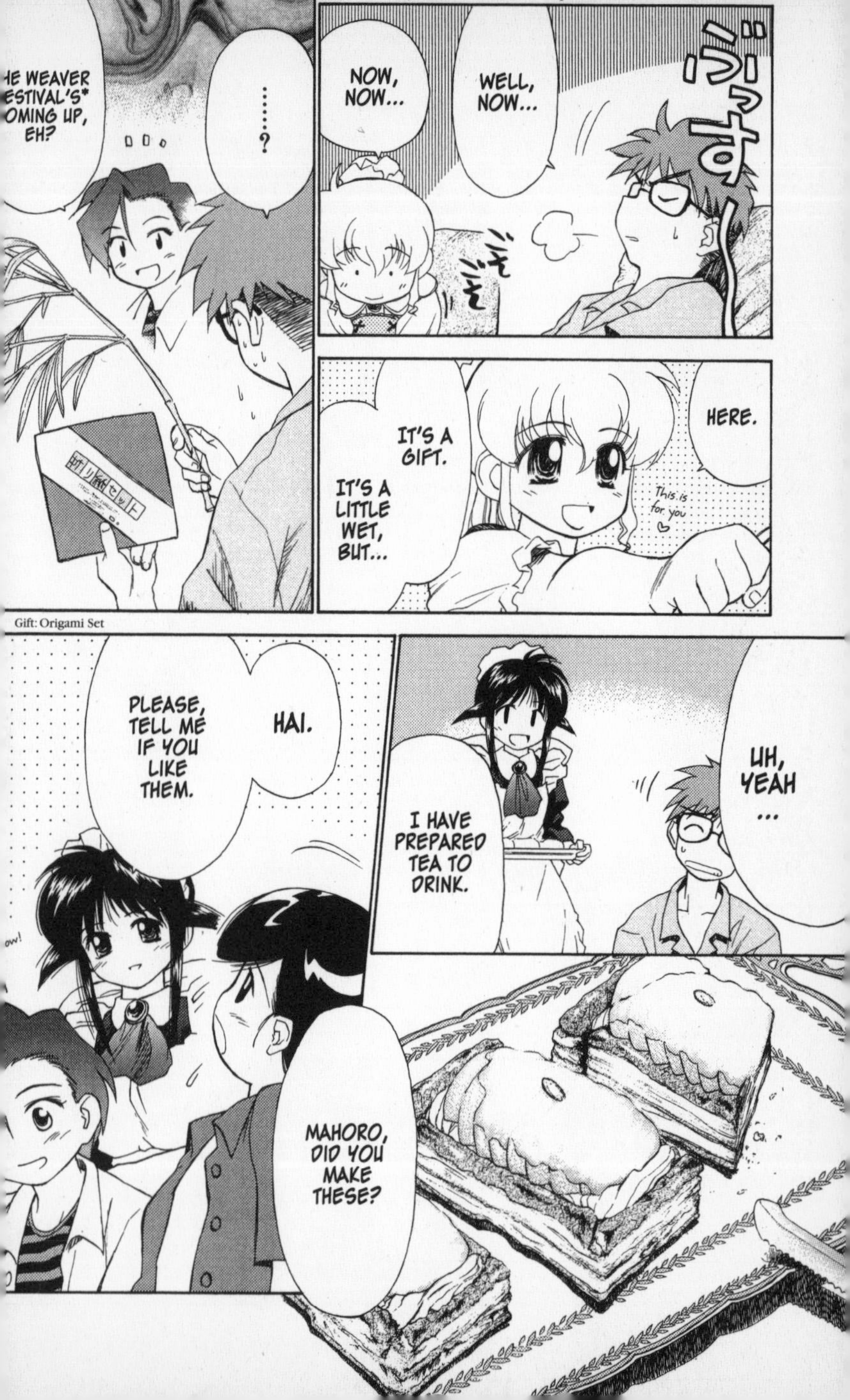

ぶっす
WELL, NOW...
NOW, NOW...
ごそごそ
HERE.
This is for you
IT'S A GIFT.
IT'S A LITTLE WET, BUT...
......?
HE WEAVER ESTIVAL'S* OMING UP, EH?
Gift: Origami Set
UH, YEAH ...
I HAVE PREPARED TEA TO DRINK.
HAI.
PLEASE, TELL ME IF YOU LIKE THEM.
ow!
MAHORO, DID YOU MAKE THESE?

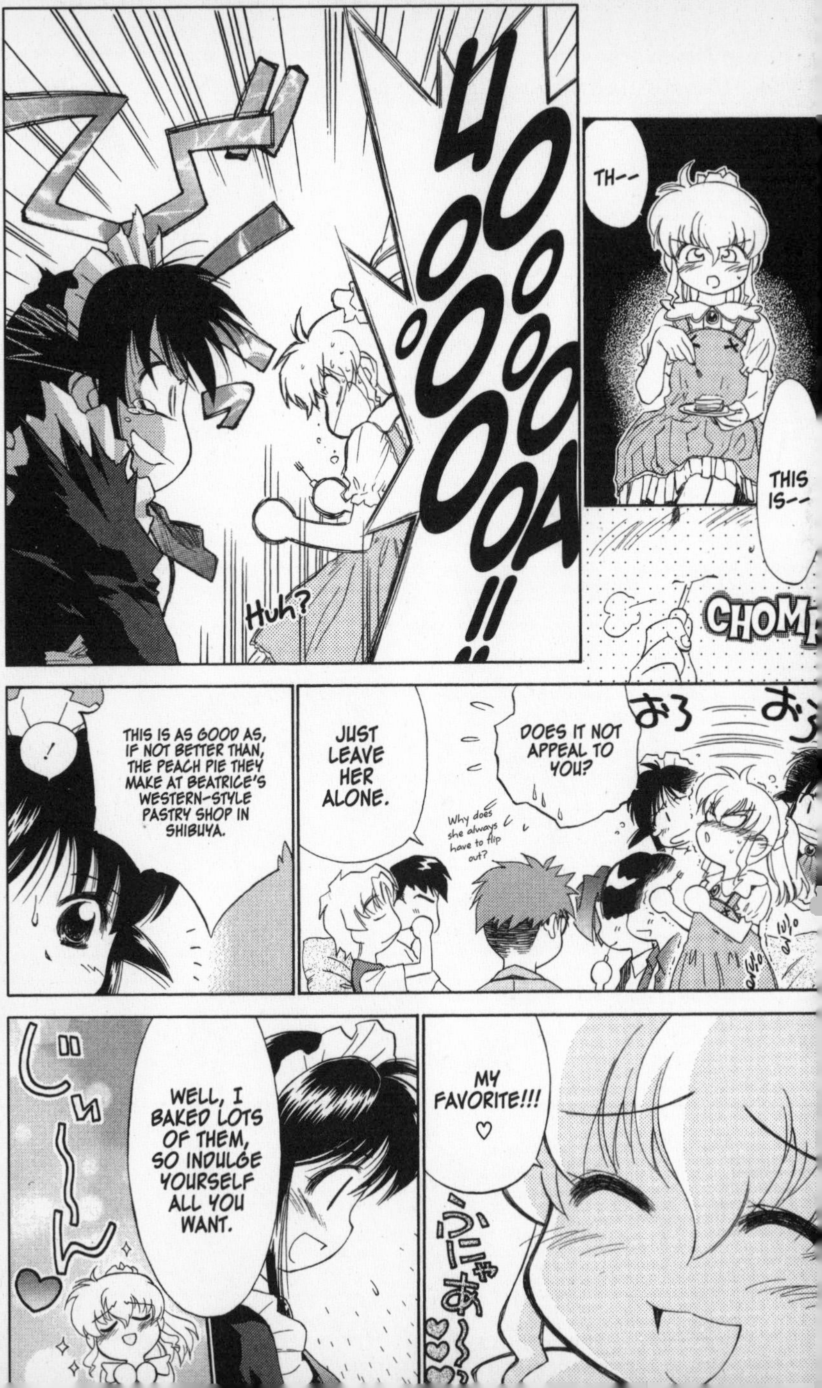
TH--
THIS IS--
CHOM
UOOOOOOOOOA!!
Huh?
おろ
お
DOES IT NOT APPEAL TO YOU?
Why does she always have to flip out?
JUST LEAVE HER ALONE.
!
THIS IS AS GOOD AS, IF NOT BETTER THAN, THE PEACH PIE THEY MAKE AT BEATRICE'S WESTERN-STYLE PASTRY SHOP IN SHIBUYA.
MY FAVORITE!!! ♡
ふにゃあ~~
WELL, I BAKED LOTS OF THEM, SO INDULGE YOURSELF ALL YOU WANT.
じぃ~~ん

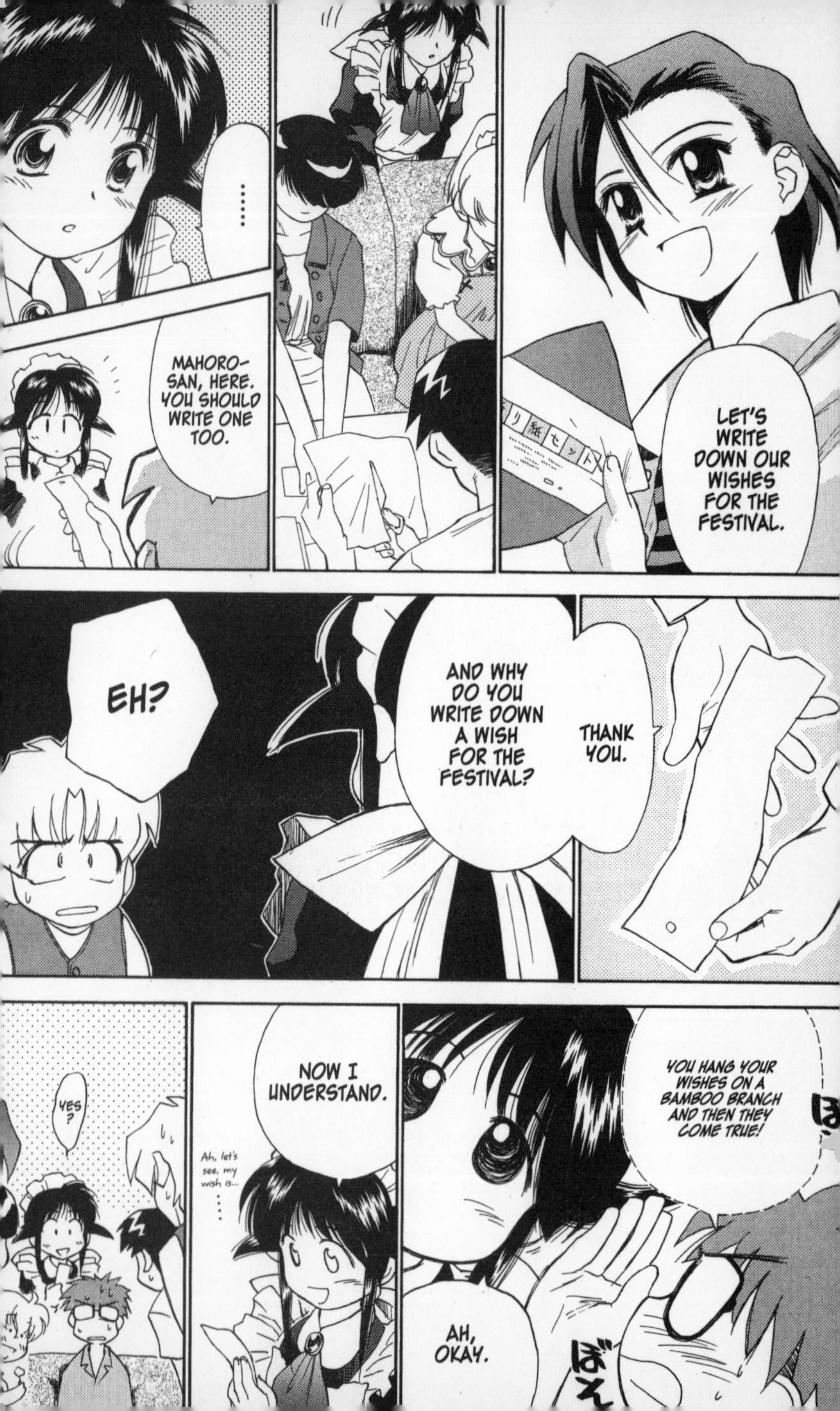
LET'S WRITE DOWN OUR WISHES FOR THE FESTIVAL.
......
MAHORO-SAN, HERE. YOU SHOULD WRITE ONE TOO.
THANK YOU.
AND WHY DO YOU WRITE DOWN A WISH FOR THE FESTIVAL?
EH?
YOU HANG YOUR WISHES ON A BAMBOO BRANCH AND THEN THEY COME TRUE!
NOW I UNDERSTAND.
AH, OKAY.
YES?
Ah, let's see, my wish is...
....

I wish for lots and lots of tasty snacks! ♡ - Chizu

I wish to be a bride. - Rin

I wish to fall madly in love! - Hamadi

I wish to have fun on summer break!! - Miyuk

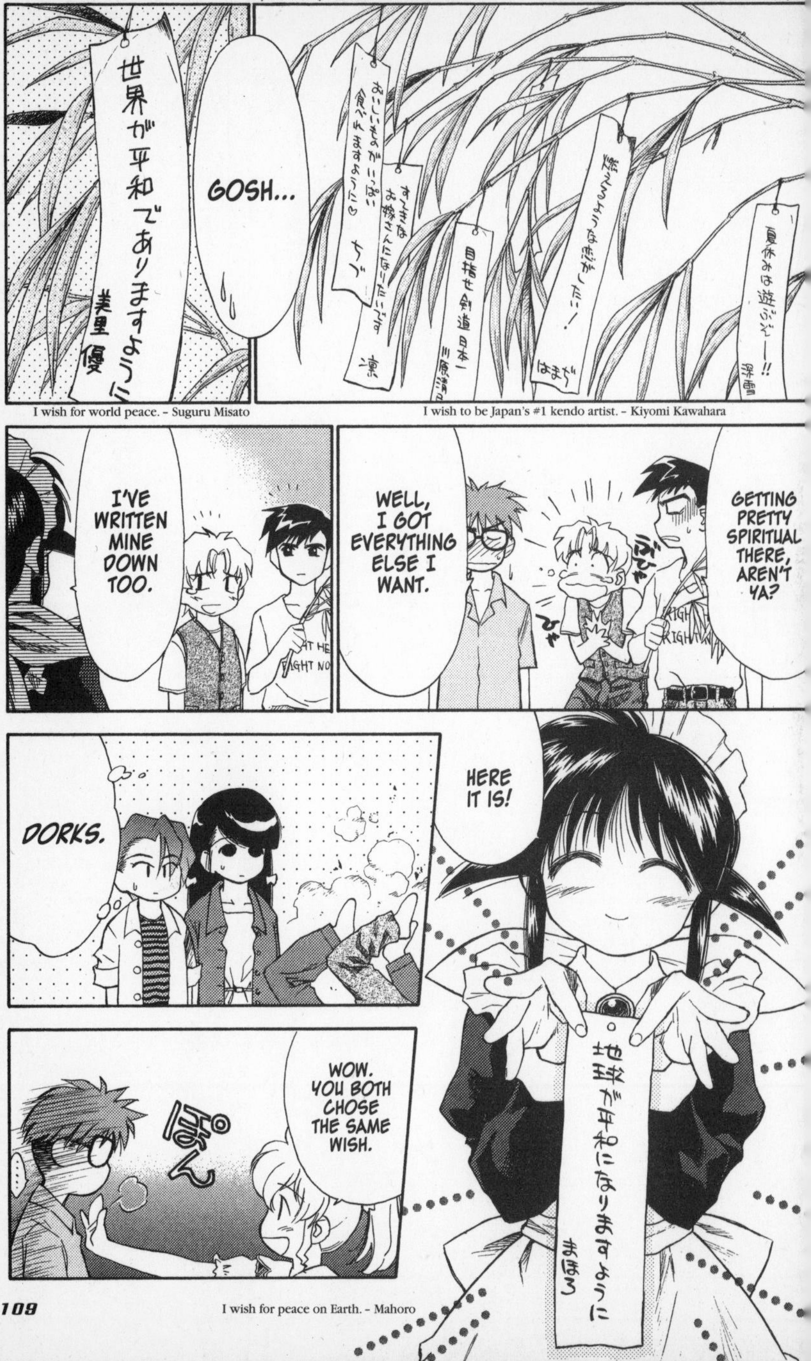

夏休みは遊ぶぞー!! 深雪
燃えるような恋がしたい! はまだ
目指せ剣道日本一 川原清
すてきなお嫁さんになりたいです 凛
おいしいものがいっぱい食べれますように♡ ちづ
GOSH...
世界が平和でありますように 美里優
GETTING PRETTY SPIRITUAL THERE, AREN'T YA?
WELL, I GOT EVERYTHING ELSE I WANT.
I'VE WRITTEN MINE DOWN TOO.
HERE IT IS!
地球が平和になりますように まほろ
DORKS.
WOW. YOU BOTH CHOSE THE SAME WISH.
ぽん

I wish for world peace. - Suguru Misato

I wish to be Japan's #1 kendo artist. - Kiyomi Kawahara

I wish for peace on Earth. - Mahoro

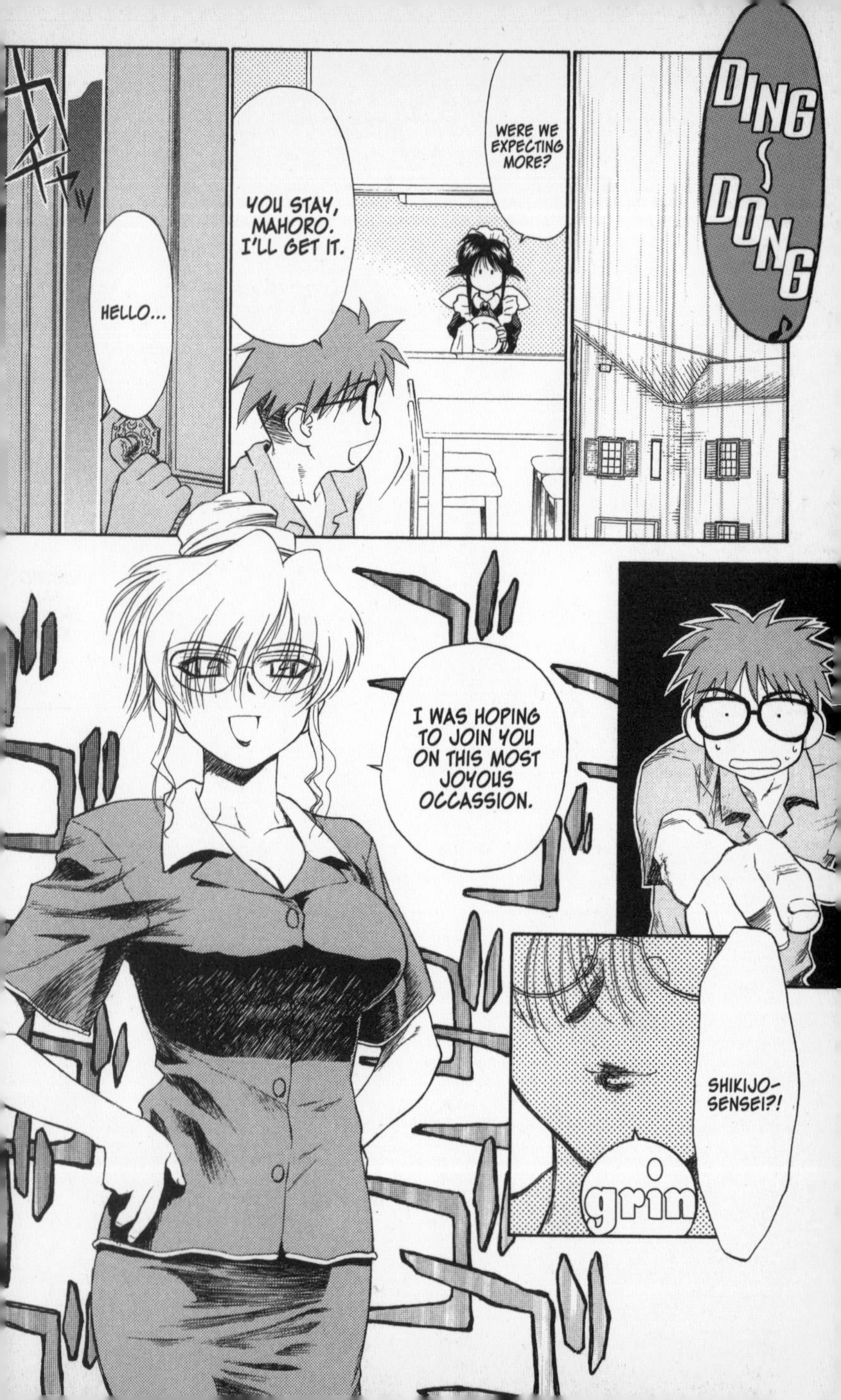
DING ~ DONG
WERE WE EXPECTING MORE?
YOU STAY, MAHORO. I'LL GET IT.
HELLO...
SHIKIJO-SENSEI?!
grin
I WAS HOPING TO JOIN YOU ON THIS MOST JOYOUS OCCASSION.

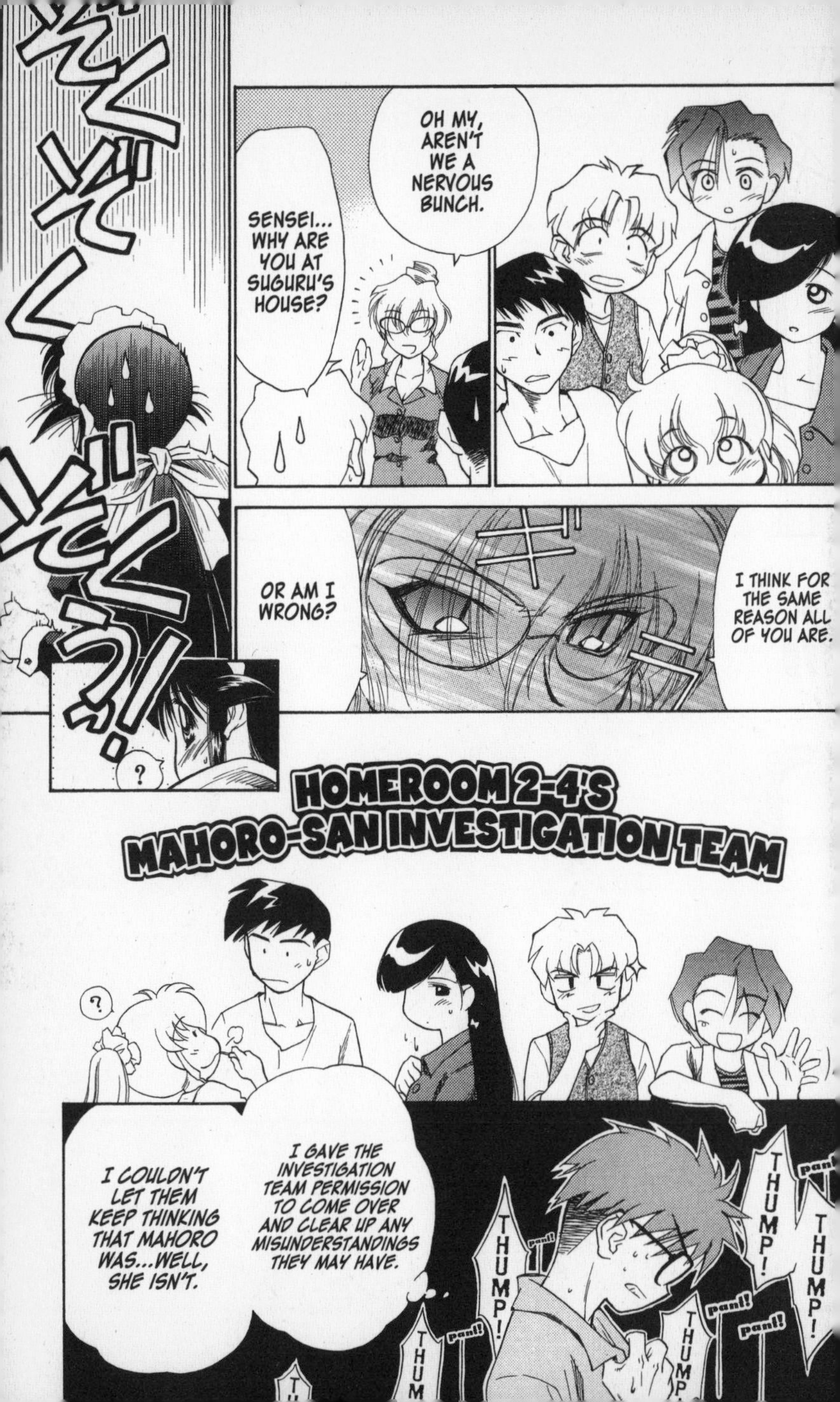
OH MY, AREN'T WE A NERVOUS BUNCH.
SENSEI... WHY ARE YOU AT SUGURU'S HOUSE?
I THINK FOR THE SAME REASON ALL OF YOU ARE.
OR AM I WRONG?
ぞくぞくぞくっ!
?
HOMEROOM 2-4'S MAHORO-SAN INVESTIGATION TEAM
?
THUMP! pan!
THUMP! pan!
THUMP! pan!
THUMP! pan!
THUMP! pan!
THUM
I GAVE THE INVESTIGATION TEAM PERMISSION TO COME OVER AND CLEAR UP ANY MISUNDERSTANDINGS THEY MAY HAVE.
I COULDN'T LET THEM KEEP THINKING THAT MAHORO WAS...WELL, SHE ISN'T.

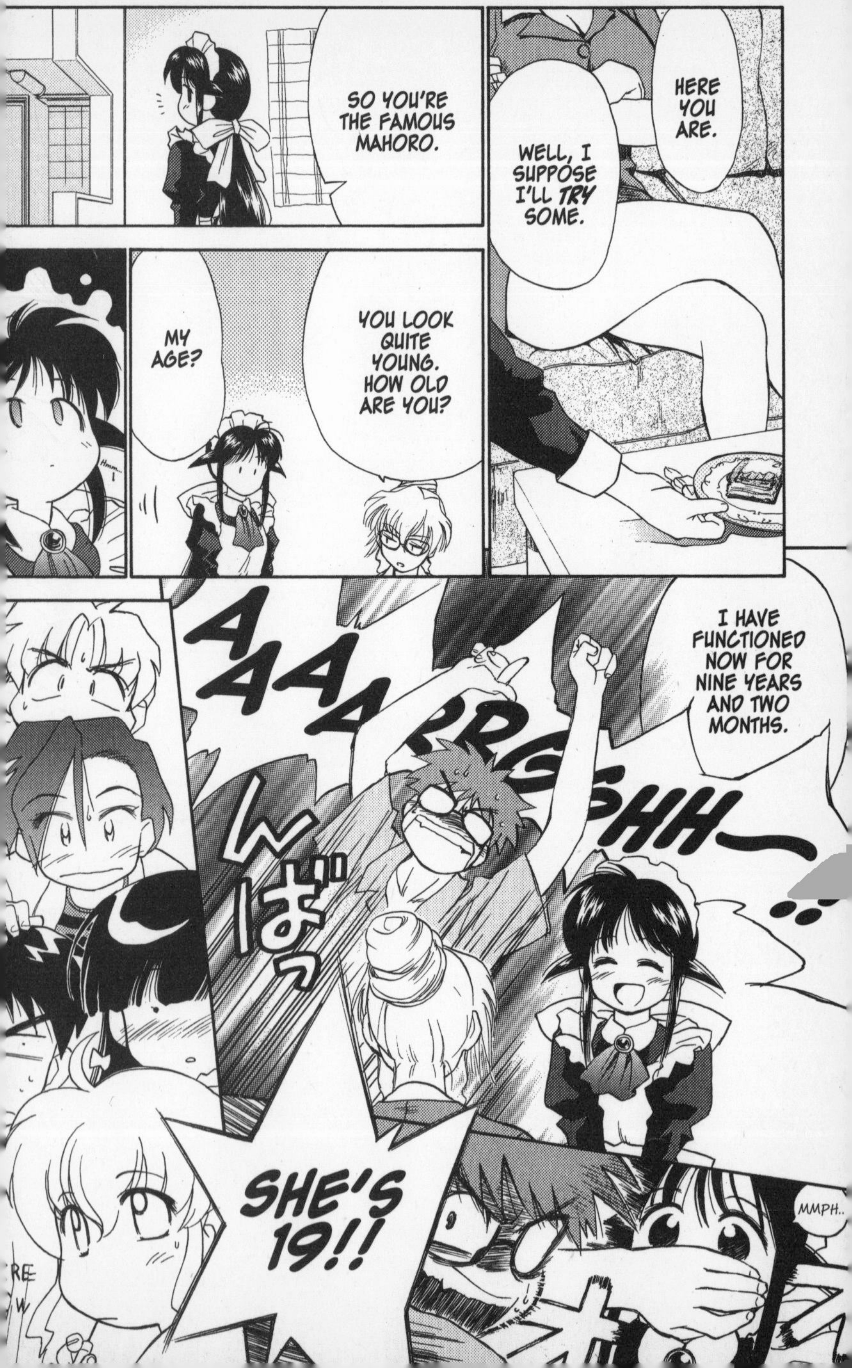
HERE YOU ARE.
WELL, I SUPPOSE I'LL *TRY* SOME.
SO YOU'RE THE FAMOUS MAHORO.
YOU LOOK QUITE YOUNG. HOW OLD ARE YOU?
Hmm...
MY AGE?
I HAVE FUNCTIONED NOW FOR NINE YEARS AND TWO MONTHS.
AAAARRGSHH—
んぱっ
SHE'S 19!!
MMPH..

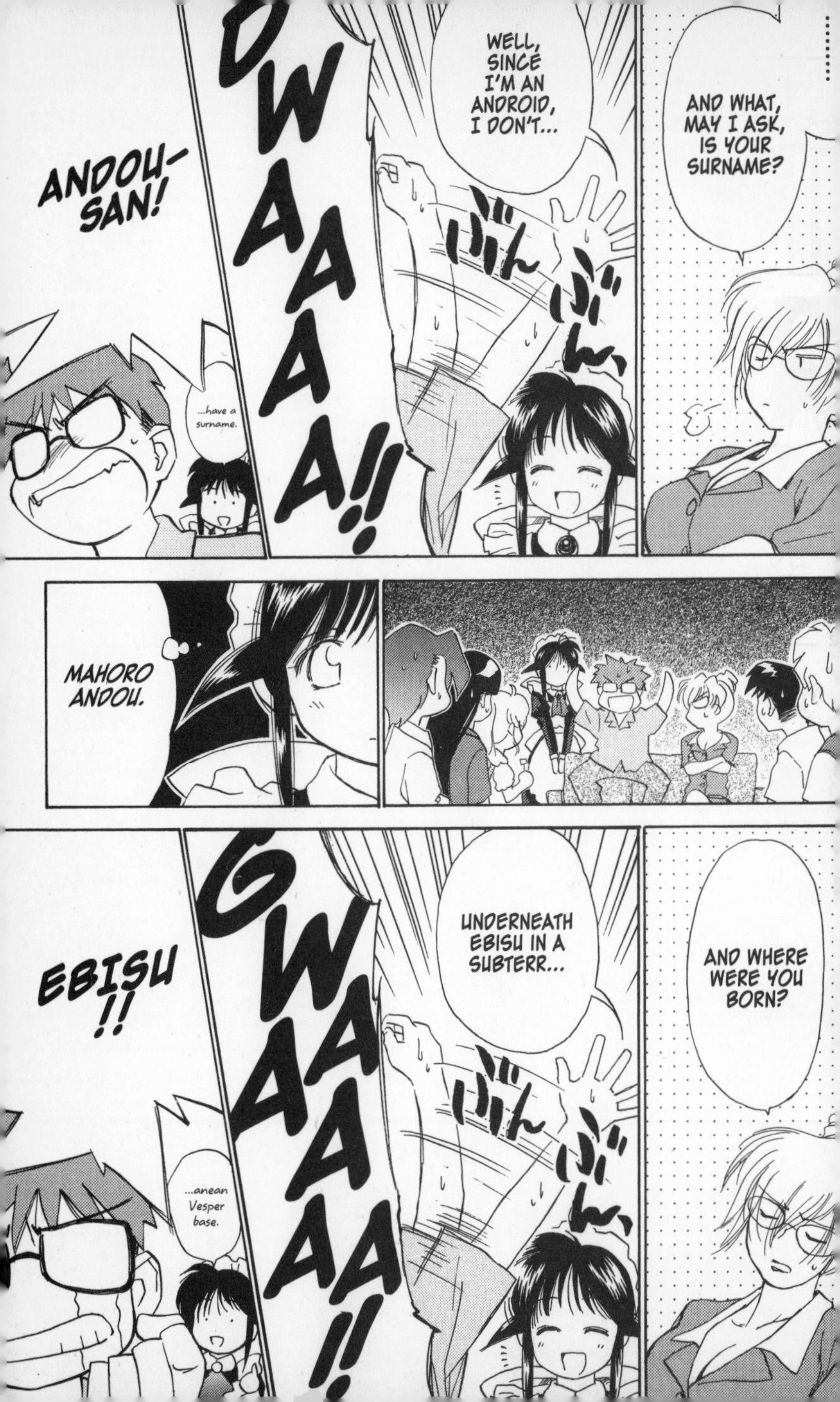
AND WHAT, MAY I ASK, IS YOUR SURNAME?
WELL, SINCE I'M AN ANDROID, I DON'T...
ぶんぶん
DWAAAA!!
ANDOU-SAN!
...have a surname.
MAHORO ANDOU.
AND WHERE WERE YOU BORN?
UNDERNEATH EBISU IN A SUBTERR...
ぶんぶん
GWAAAAA!!
EBISU!!
...anean Vesper base.

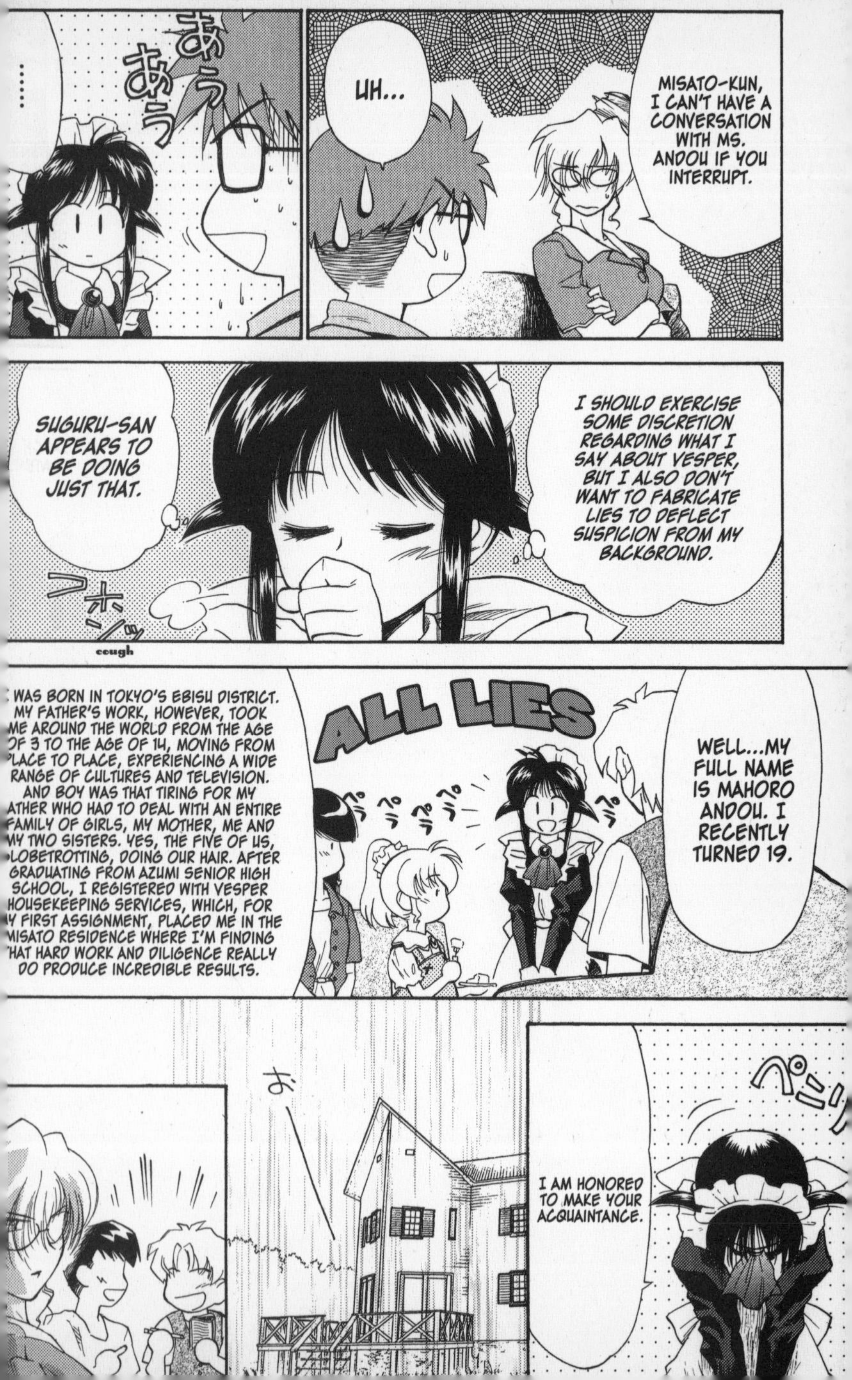
MISATO-KUN, I CAN'T HAVE A CONVERSATION WITH MS. ANDOU IF YOU INTERRUPT.
UH...
あう あう
......
I SHOULD EXERCISE SOME DISCRETION REGARDING WHAT I SAY ABOUT VESPER, BUT I ALSO DON'T WANT TO FABRICATE LIES TO DEFLECT SUSPICION FROM MY BACKGROUND.
SUGURU-SAN APPEARS TO BE DOING JUST THAT.
コホンッ
cough
WELL...MY FULL NAME IS MAHORO ANDOU. I RECENTLY TURNED 19.
ALL LIES
ぺら ぺら ぺら ぺら ぺら
WAS BORN IN TOKYO'S EBISU DISTRICT. MY FATHER'S WORK, HOWEVER, TOOK ME AROUND THE WORLD FROM THE AGE OF 3 TO THE AGE OF 14, MOVING FROM PLACE TO PLACE, EXPERIENCING A WIDE RANGE OF CULTURES AND TELEVISION. AND BOY WAS THAT TIRING FOR MY ATHER WHO HAD TO DEAL WITH AN ENTIRE FAMILY OF GIRLS, MY MOTHER, ME AND MY TWO SISTERS. YES, THE FIVE OF US, LOBETROTTING, DOING OUR HAIR. AFTER GRADUATING FROM AZUMI SENIOR HIGH SCHOOL, I REGISTERED WITH VESPER HOUSEKEEPING SERVICES, WHICH, FOR Y FIRST ASSIGNMENT, PLACED ME IN THE MISATO RESIDENCE WHERE I'M FINDING HAT HARD WORK AND DILIGENCE REALLY DO PRODUCE INCREDIBLE RESULTS.
ペこり
I AM HONORED TO MAKE YOUR ACQUAINTANCE.
お

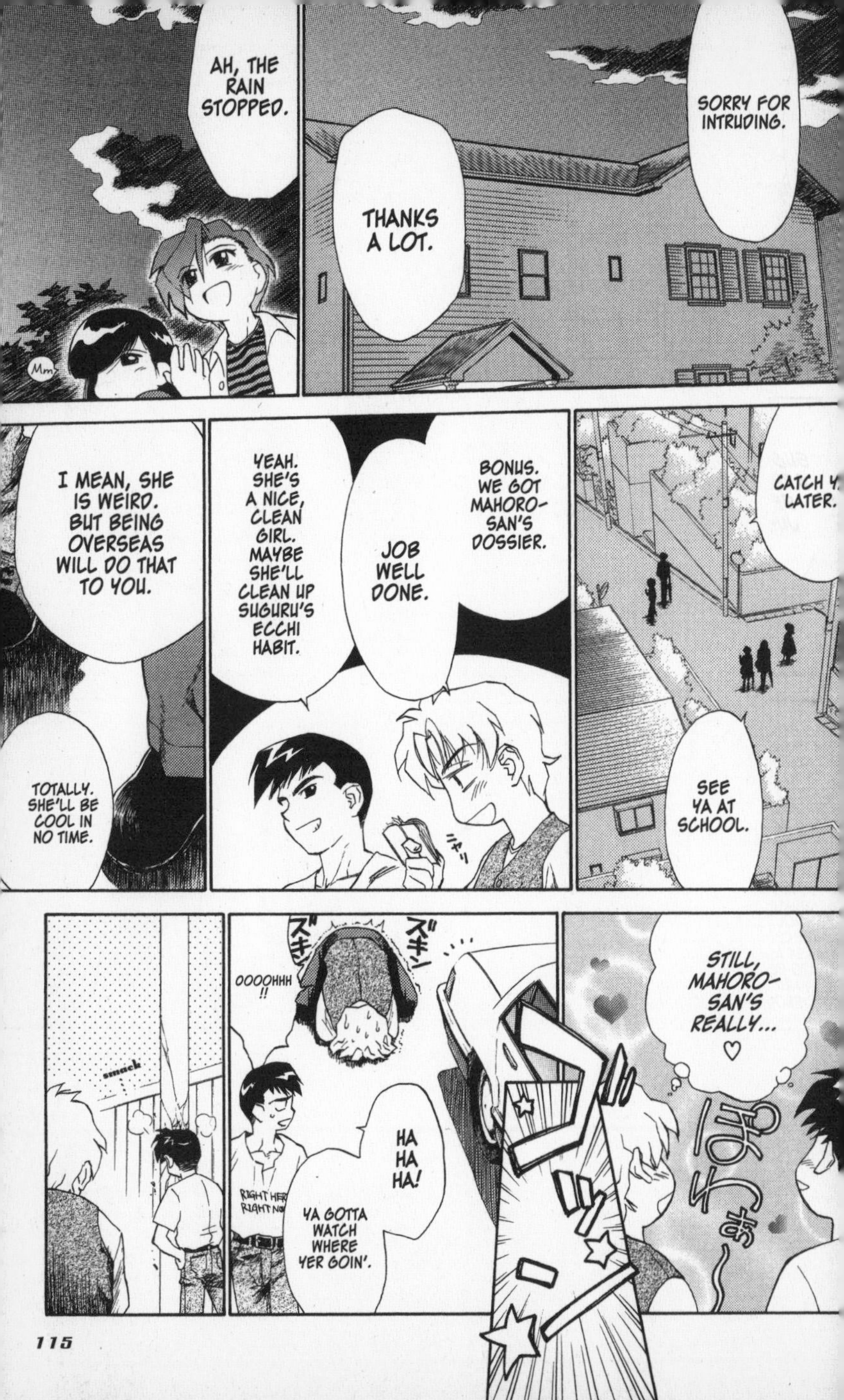
SORRY FOR INTRUDING.
THANKS A LOT.
AH, THE RAIN STOPPED.
Mm
CATCH Y LATER.
SEE YA AT SCHOOL.
BONUS. WE GOT MAHORO-SAN'S DOSSIER.
JOB WELL DONE.
YEAH. SHE'S A NICE, CLEAN GIRL. MAYBE SHE'LL CLEAN UP SUGURU'S ECCHI HABIT.
ニヤリ
I MEAN, SHE IS WEIRD. BUT BEING OVERSEAS WILL DO THAT TO YOU.
TOTALLY. SHE'LL BE COOL IN NO TIME.
STILL, MAHORO-SAN'S REALLY... ♡
ぽわぁ～
ズキン
ズキ
OOOOHHH !!
HA HA HA!
YA GOTTA WATCH WHERE YER GOIN'.
smack

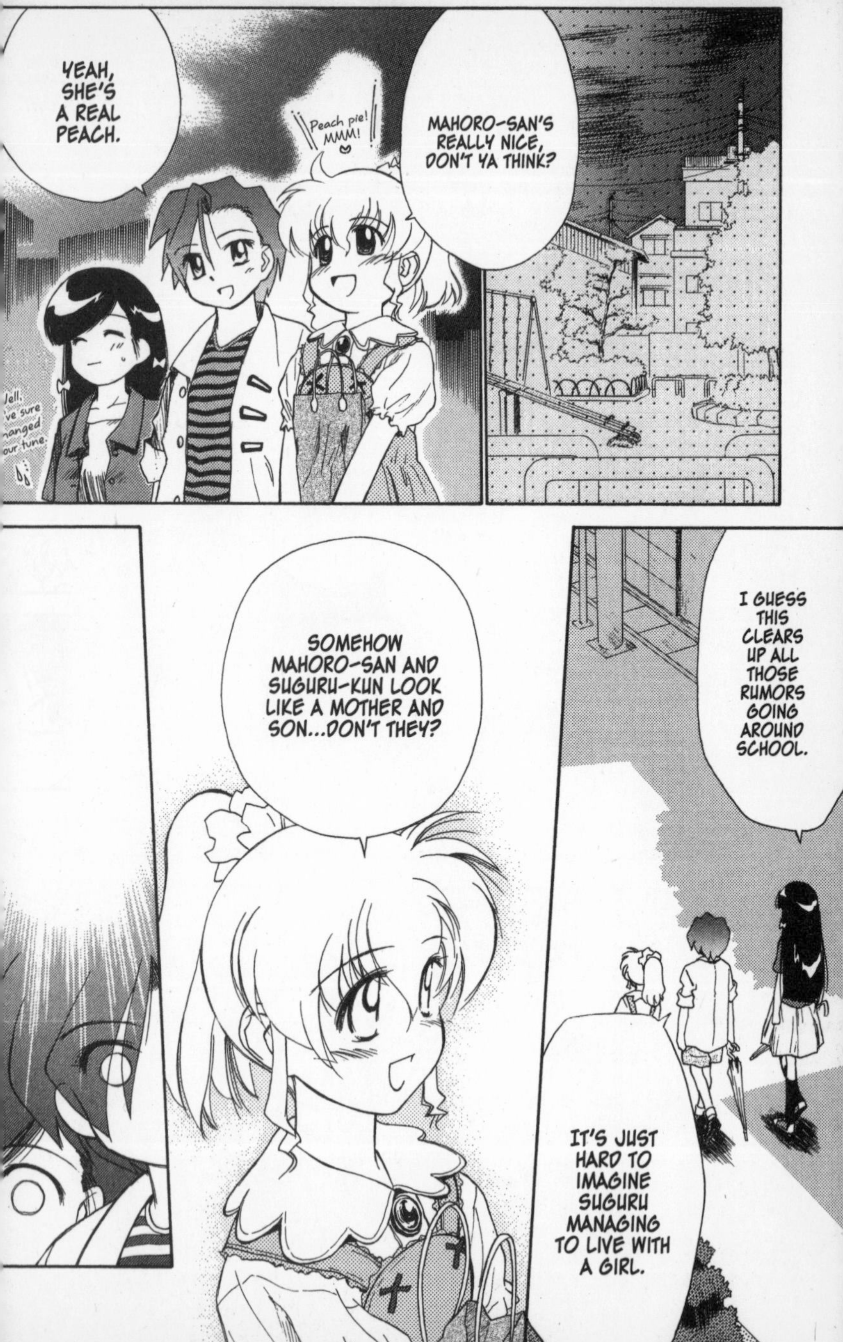
MAHORO-SAN'S REALLY NICE, DON'T YA THINK?
Peach pie! MMM!
YEAH, SHE'S A REAL PEACH.
I GUESS THIS CLEARS UP ALL THOSE RUMORS GOING AROUND SCHOOL.
IT'S JUST HARD TO IMAGINE SUGURU MANAGING TO LIVE WITH A GIRL.
SOMEHOW MAHORO-SAN AND SUGURU-KUN LOOK LIKE A MOTHER AND SON...DON'T THEY?

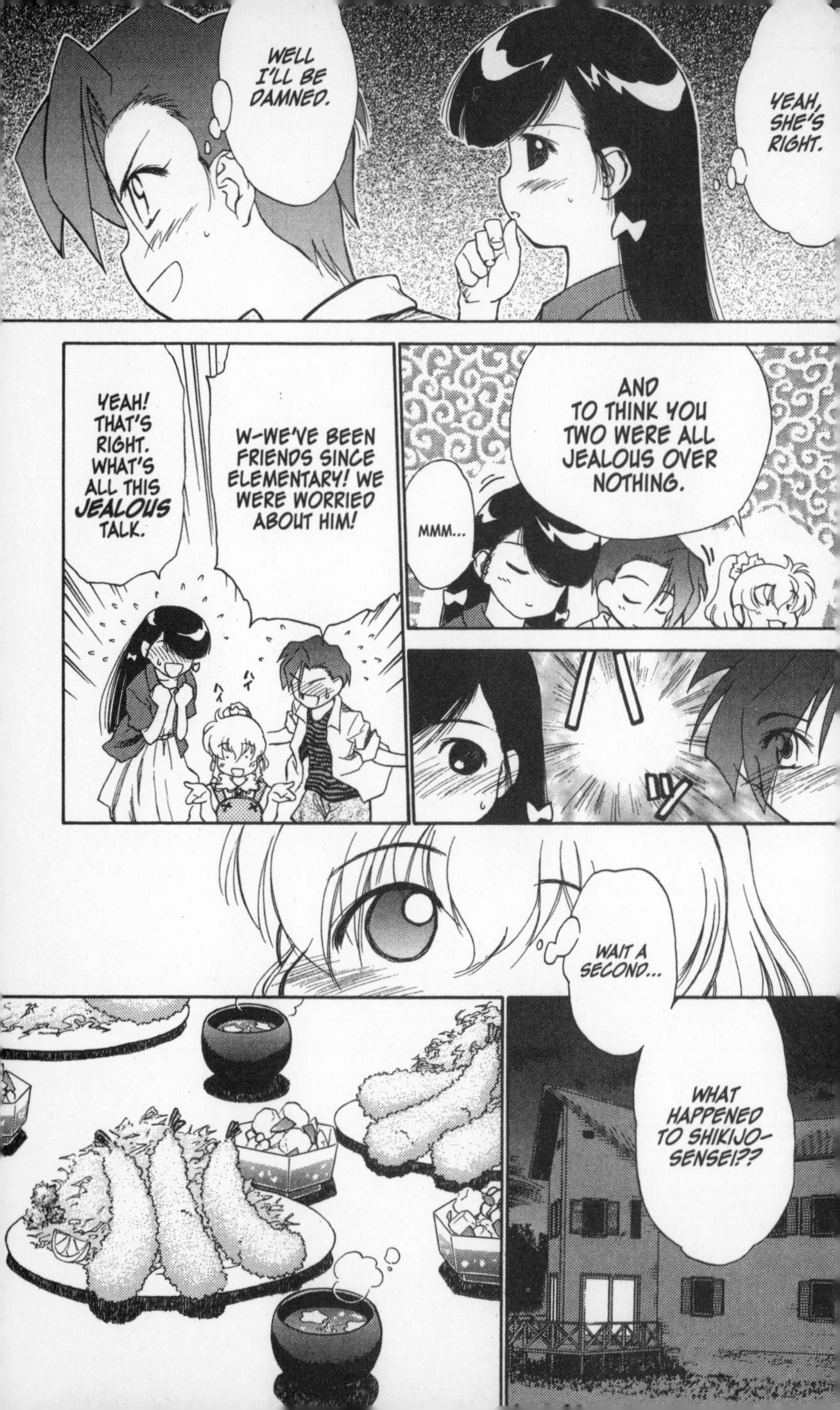
YEAH, SHE'S RIGHT.
WELL I'LL BE DAMNED.
AND TO THINK YOU TWO WERE ALL JEALOUS OVER NOTHING.
MMM...
W-WE'VE BEEN FRIENDS SINCE ELEMENTARY! WE WERE WORRIED ABOUT HIM!
YEAH! THAT'S RIGHT. WHAT'S ALL THIS JEALOUS TALK.
WAIT A SECOND...
WHAT HAPPENED TO SHIKIJO-SENSEI??

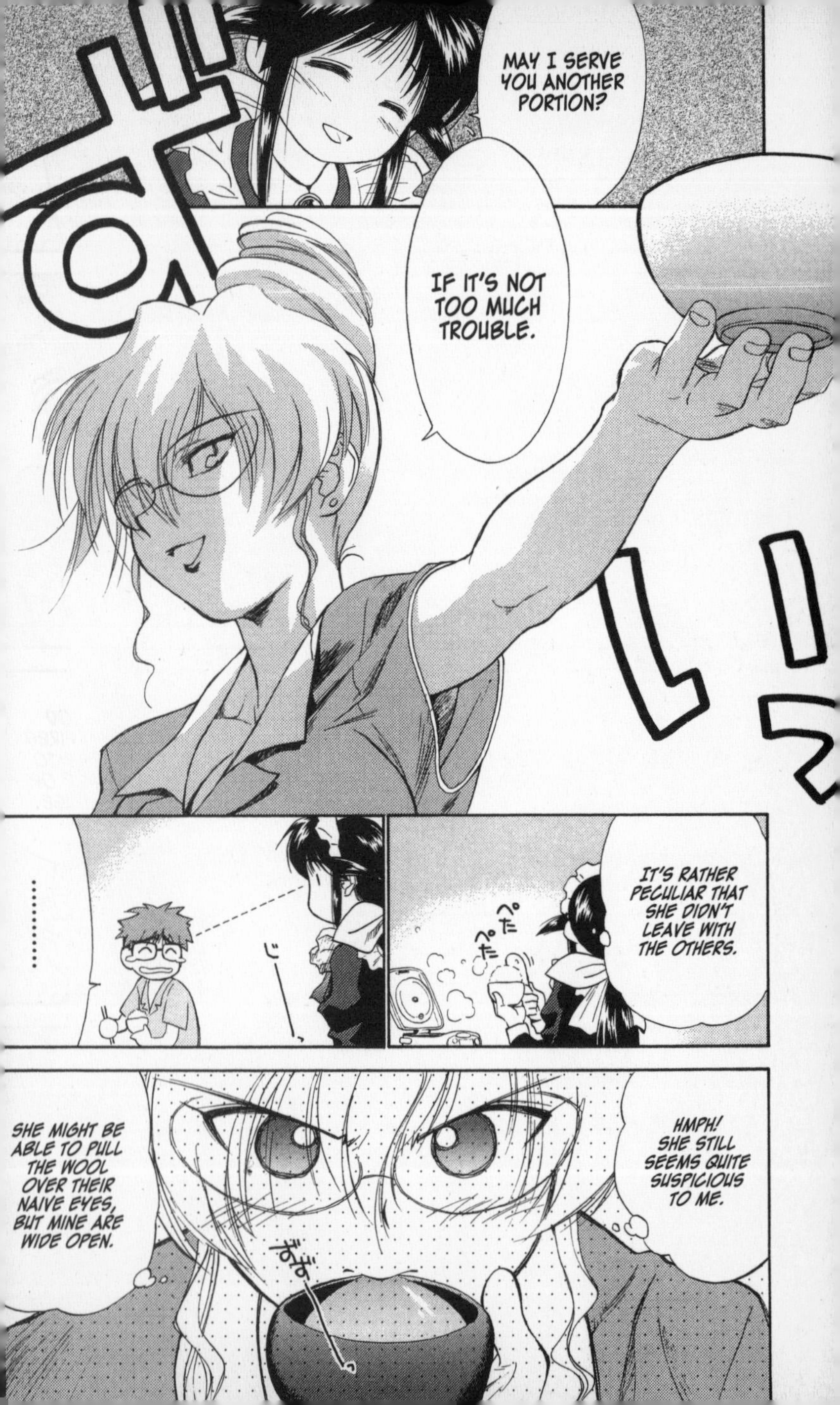
MAY I SERVE YOU ANOTHER PORTION?
IF IT'S NOT TOO MUCH TROUBLE.
IT'S RATHER PECULIAR THAT SHE DIDN'T LEAVE WITH THE OTHERS.
へた
へた
......
じー
HMPH! SHE STILL SEEMS QUITE SUSPICIOUS TO ME.
SHE MIGHT BE ABLE TO PULL THE WOOL OVER THEIR NAIVE EYES, BUT MINE ARE WIDE OPEN.
ずず

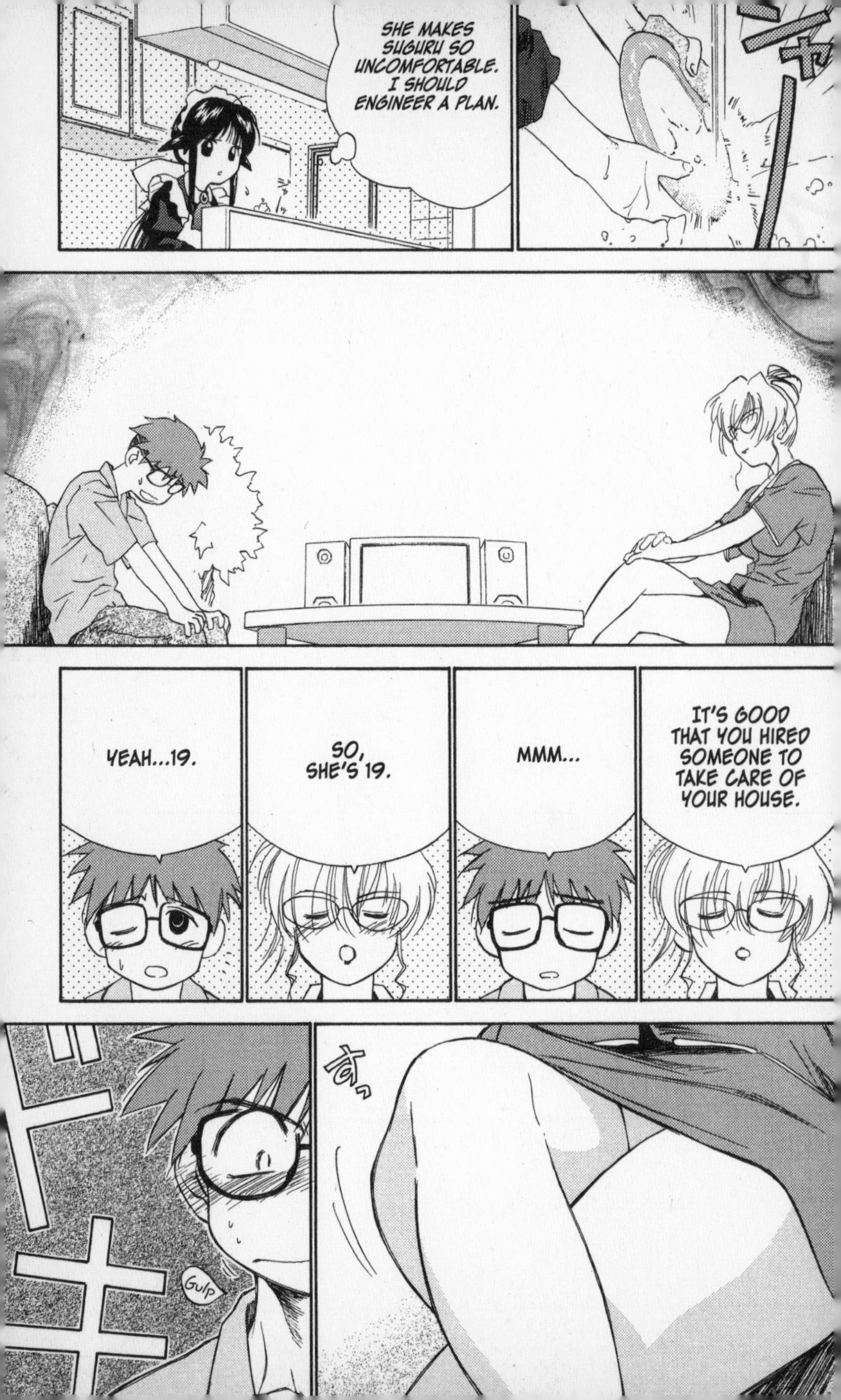
SHE MAKES SUGURU SO UNCOMFORTABLE. I SHOULD ENGINEER A PLAN.
IT'S GOOD THAT YOU HIRED SOMEONE TO TAKE CARE OF YOUR HOUSE.
MMM...
SO, SHE'S 19.
YEAH...19.
すっ
Gulp

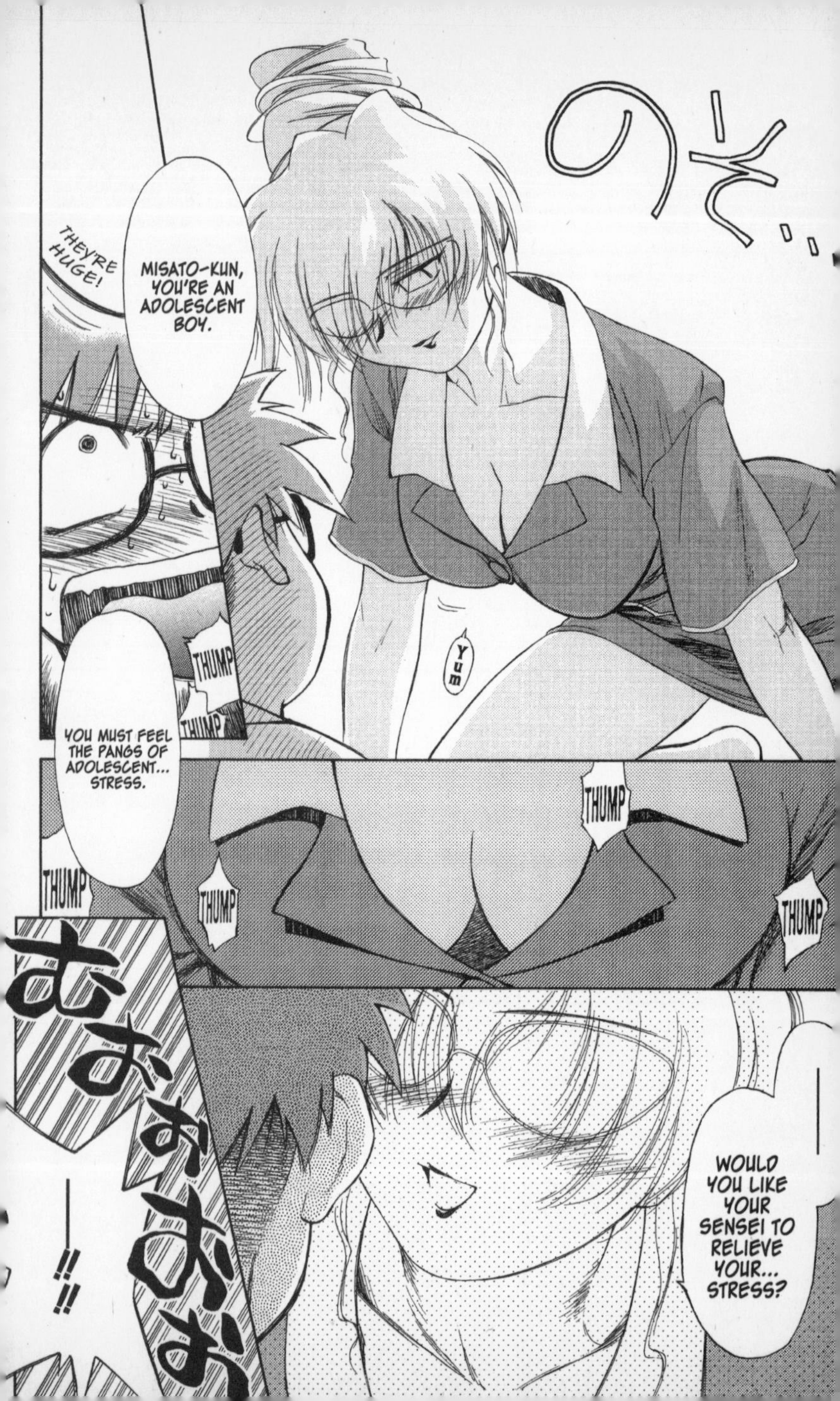
のそ…
MISATO-KUN, YOU'RE AN ADOLESCENT BOY.
Yum
THEY'RE HUGE!
THUMP
THUMP
YOU MUST FEEL THE PANGS OF ADOLESCENT... STRESS.
THUMP
THUMP
THUMP
THUMP
WOULD YOU LIKE YOUR SENSEI TO RELIEVE YOUR... STRESS?
むおおおお――!!

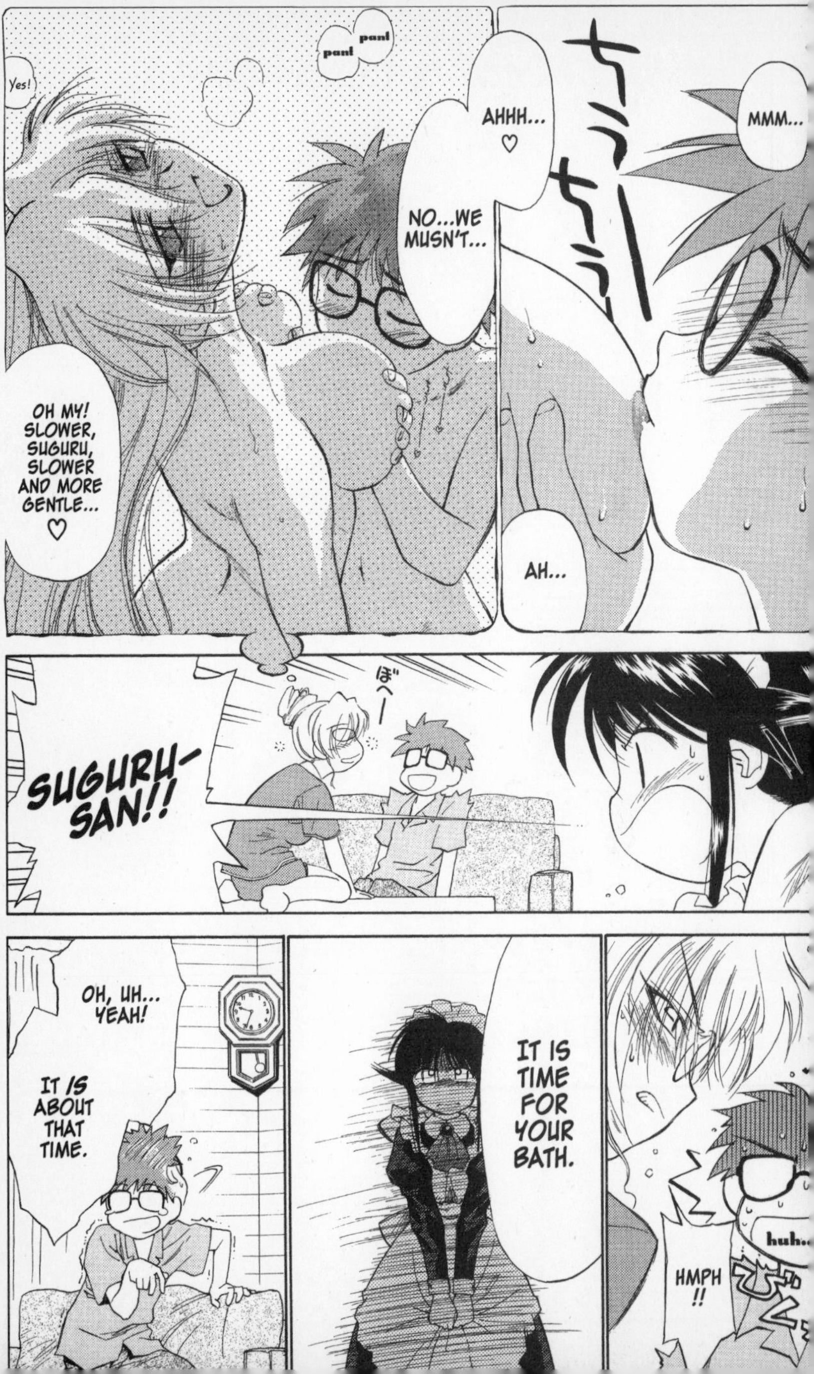

MMM...
AH...
AHHH... ♡
NO...WE MUSN'T...
pant pant
Yes!
OH MY! SLOWER, SUGURU, SLOWER AND MORE GENTLE... ♡
ぼへー
SUGURH-SAN!!
huh...
HMPH!!
IT IS TIME FOR YOUR BATH.
OH, UH... YEAH!
IT IS ABOUT THAT TIME.

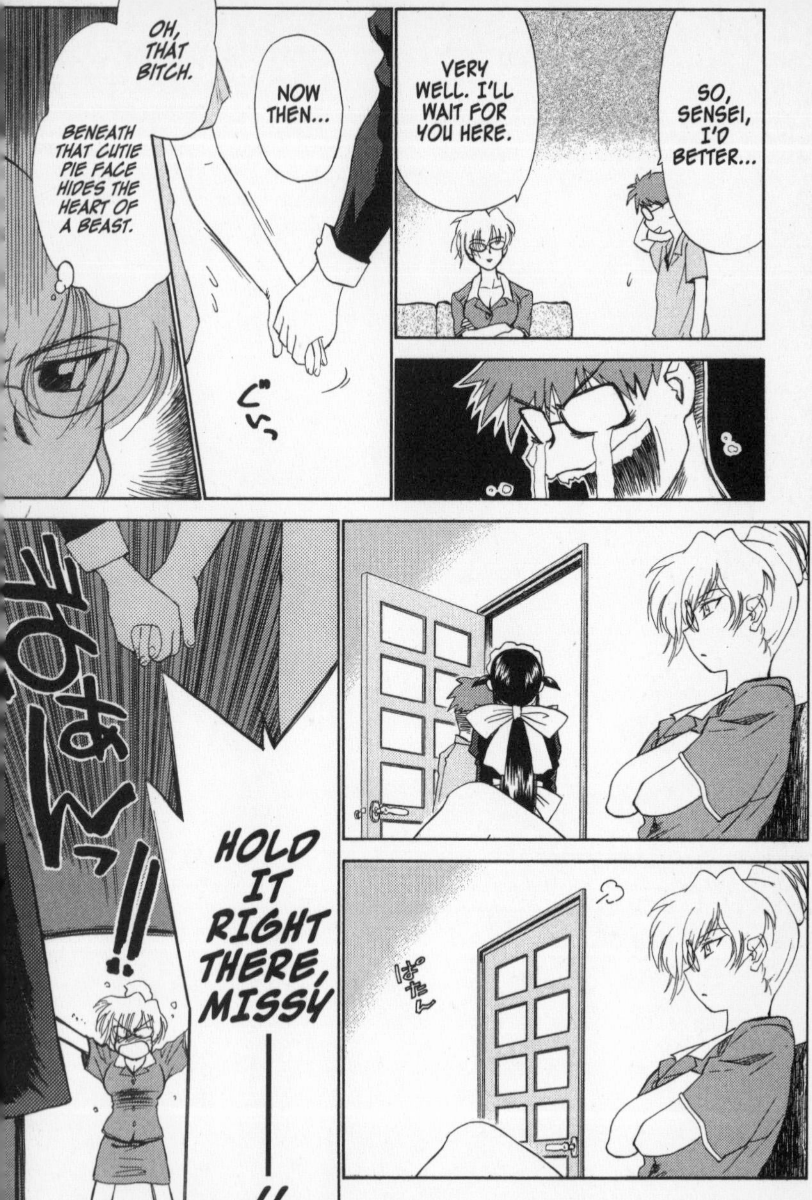

SO, SENSEI, I'D BETTER...
VERY WELL. I'LL WAIT FOR YOU HERE.
NOW THEN...
OH, THAT BITCH.
BENEATH THAT CUTIE PIE FACE HIDES THE HEART OF A BEAST.
じぃっ
ぱたん
ずおんっ!!
HOLD IT RIGHT THERE, MISSY——!!

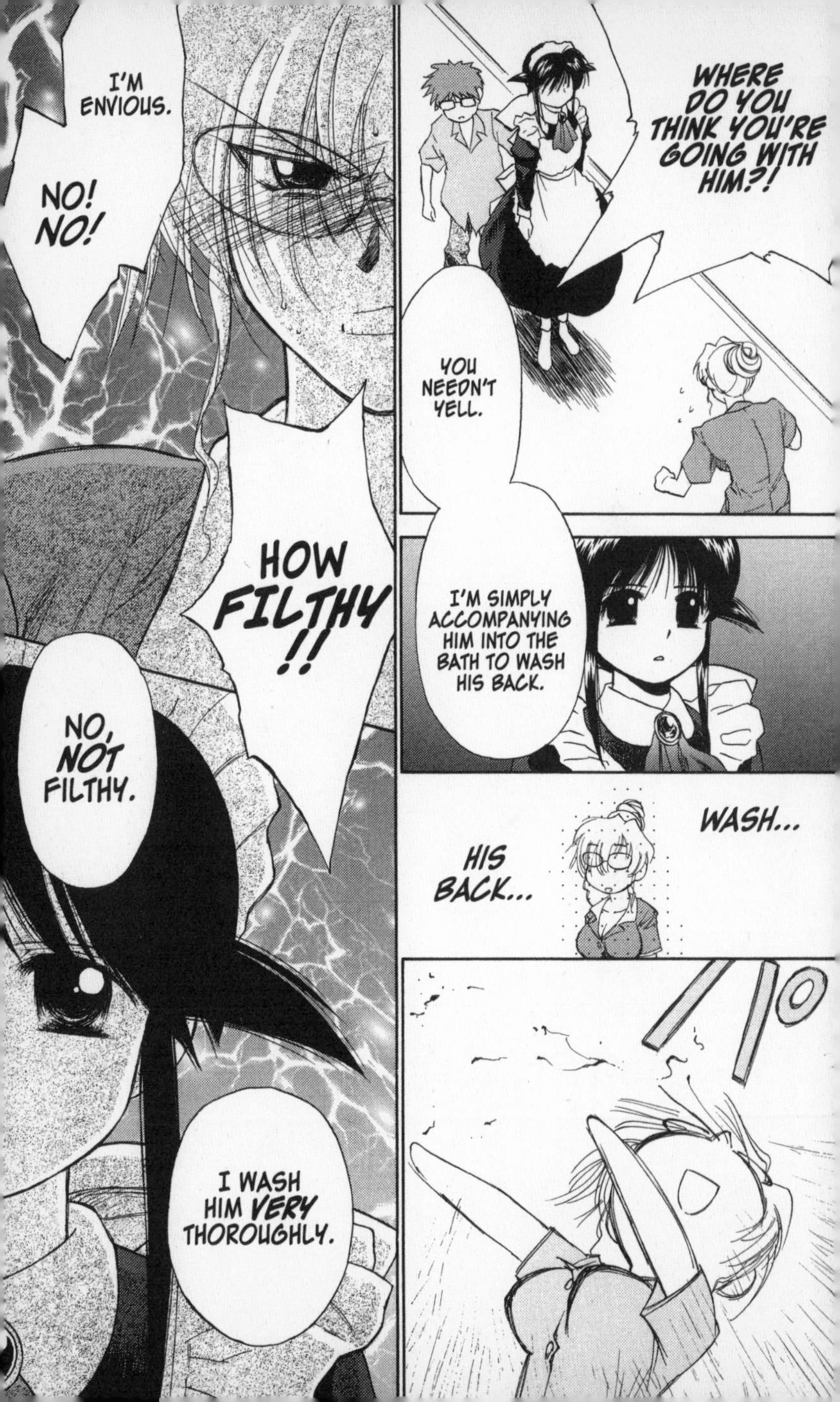
WHERE DO YOU THINK YOU'RE GOING WITH HIM?!
YOU NEEDN'T YELL.
I'M SIMPLY ACCOMPANYING HIM INTO THE BATH TO WASH HIS BACK.
WASH...
HIS BACK...
I'M ENVIOUS.
NO! NO!
HOW FILTHY!!
NO, NOT FILTHY.
I WASH HIM VERY THOROUGHLY.

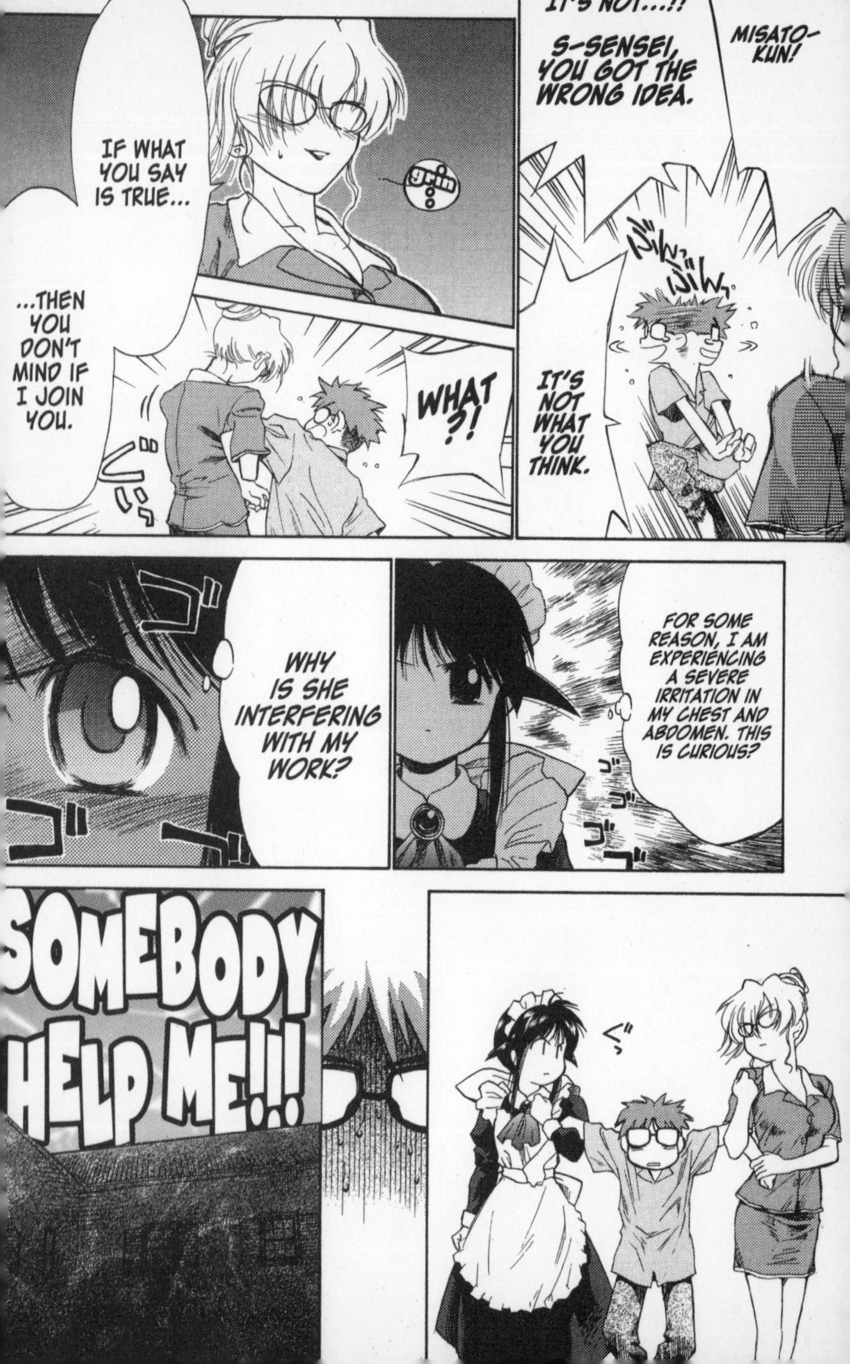
MISATO-KUN!
IT'S NOT...!!
S-SENSEI, YOU GOT THE WRONG IDEA.
IT'S NOT WHAT YOU THINK.
IF WHAT YOU SAY IS TRUE...
grin
...THEN YOU DON'T MIND IF I JOIN YOU.
WHAT?!
FOR SOME REASON, I AM EXPERIENCING A SEVERE IRRITATION IN MY CHEST AND ABDOMEN. THIS IS CURIOUS?
WHY IS SHE INTERFERING WITH MY WORK?
SOMEBODY HELP ME!!!

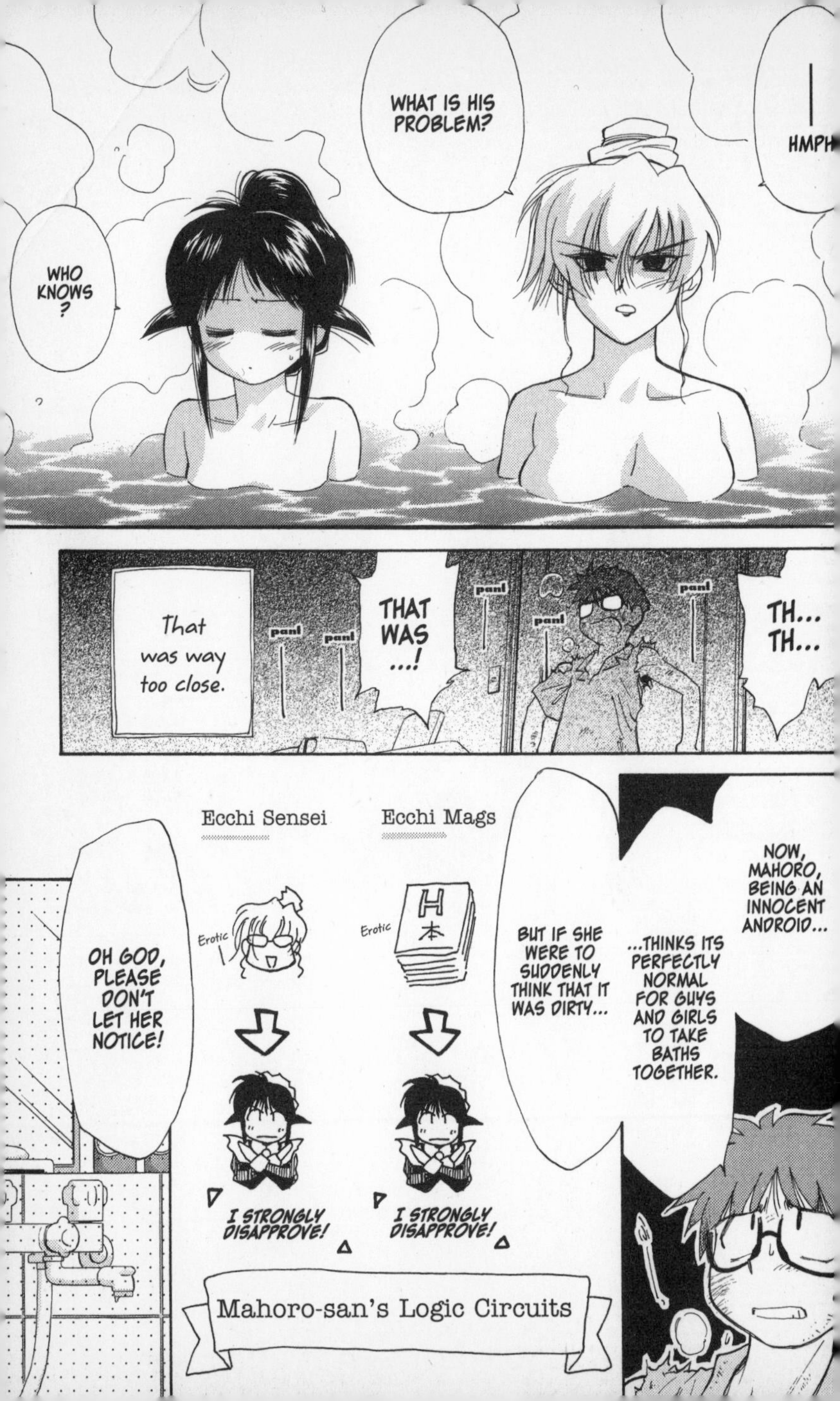
HMPH
WHAT IS HIS PROBLEM?
WHO KNOWS?
TH... TH...
pant
pant
THAT WAS ...!
pant
pant
That was way too close.
NOW, MAHORO, BEING AN INNOCENT ANDROID...
...THINKS ITS PERFECTLY NORMAL FOR GUYS AND GIRLS TO TAKE BATHS TOGETHER.
BUT IF SHE WERE TO SUDDENLY THINK THAT IT WAS DIRTY...
Mahoro-san's Logic Circuits
Ecchi Mags
Erotic
H 本
I STRONGLY DISAPPROVE!
Ecchi Sensei
Erotic
I STRONGLY DISAPPROVE!
OH GOD, PLEASE DON'T LET HER NOTICE!

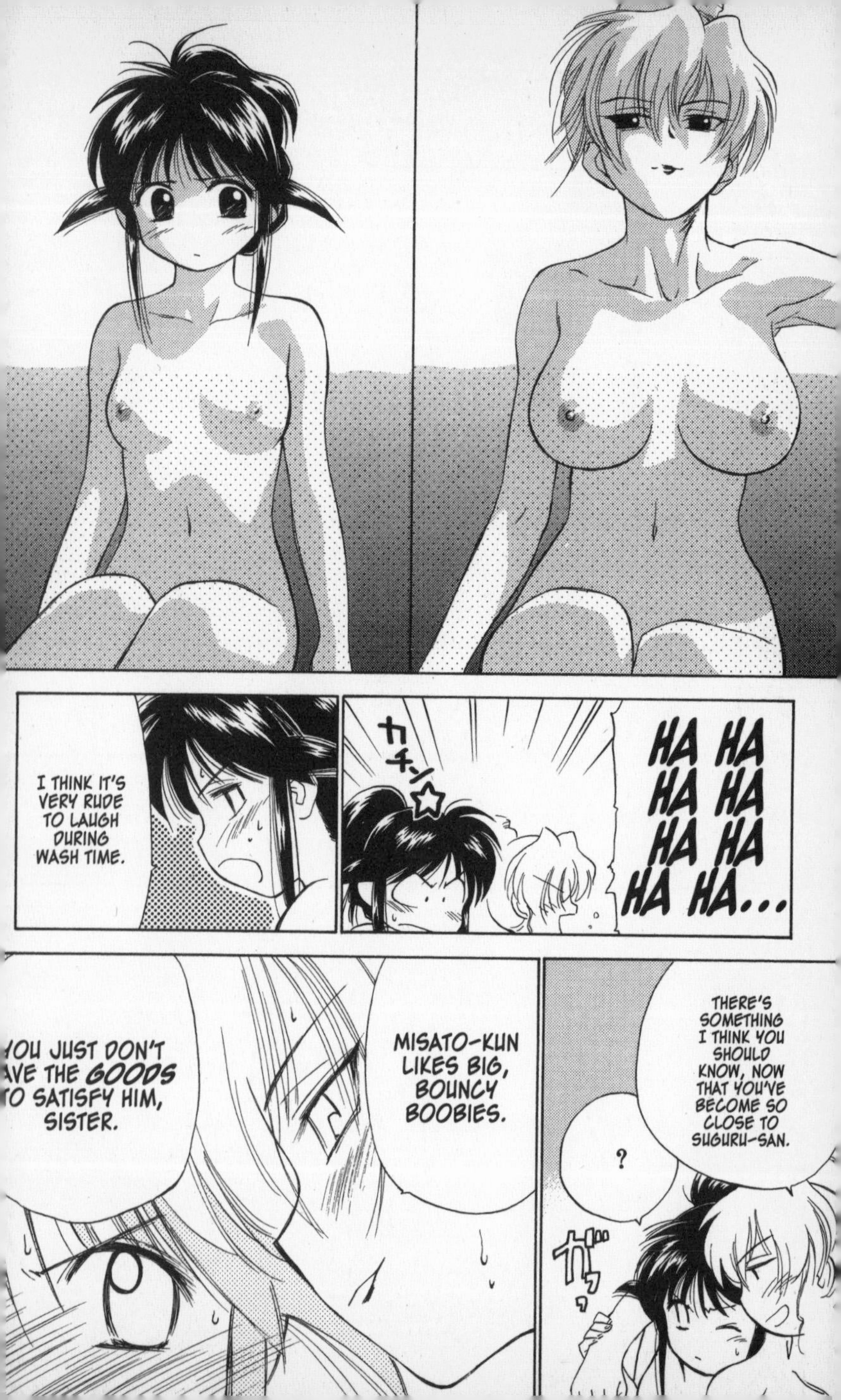
HA HA HA HA HA HA HA HA...
カチン
I THINK IT'S VERY RUDE TO LAUGH DURING WASH TIME.
THERE'S SOMETHING I THINK YOU SHOULD KNOW, NOW THAT YOU'VE BECOME SO CLOSE TO SUGURU-SAN.
?
ガッ
MISATO-KUN LIKES BIG, BOUNCY BOOBIES.
OU JUST DON'T AVE THE *GOODS* O SATISFY HIM, SISTER.

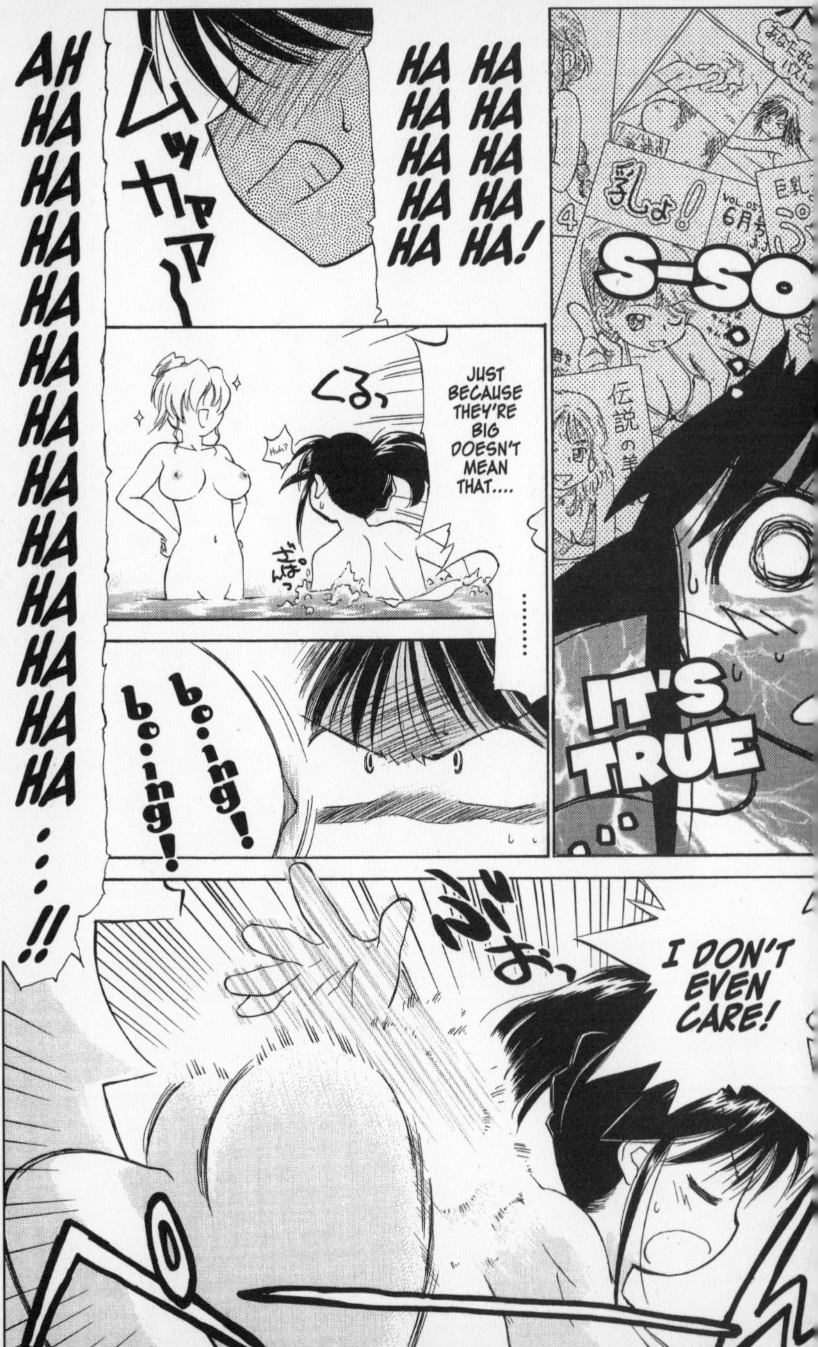
S-SO
IT'S TRUE
HA HA HA HA HA HA HA HA HA HA!
ムッカァ~
JUST BECAUSE THEY'RE BIG DOESN'T MEAN THAT....
くるっ
Huh?
ざぽんっ
......
bo-ing! bo-ing!
AH HA HA HA HA HA HA HA HA HA HA HA HA HA HA HA HA HA HA HA ...!!
ぶおっ
I DON'T EVEN CARE!

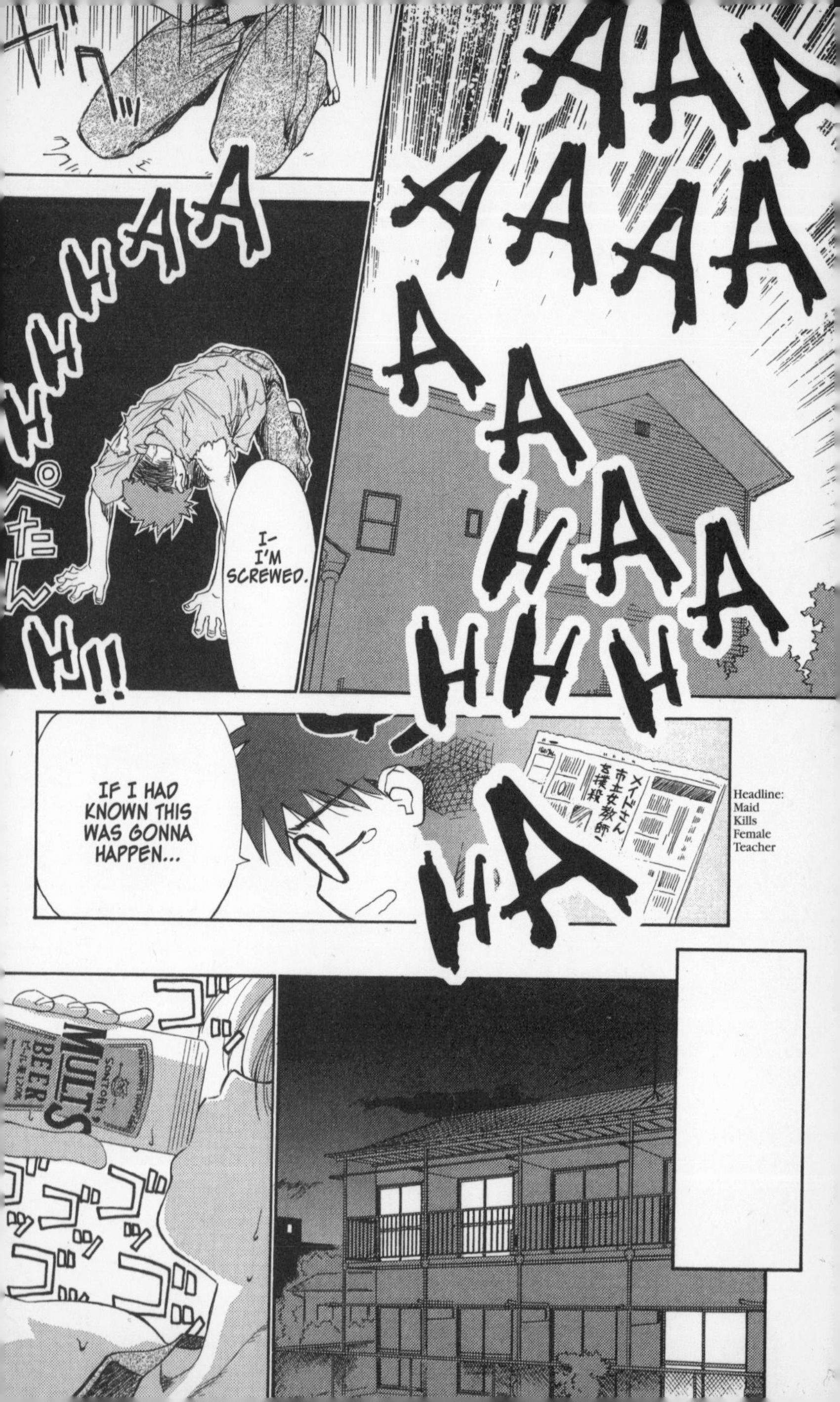

AAAAAAAAAAAHAHAHAHA
HHHHAAA
I- I'M SCREWED.
ぺたん
H!!
Headline: Maid Kills Female Teacher
IF I HAD KNOWN THIS WAS GONNA HAPPEN...

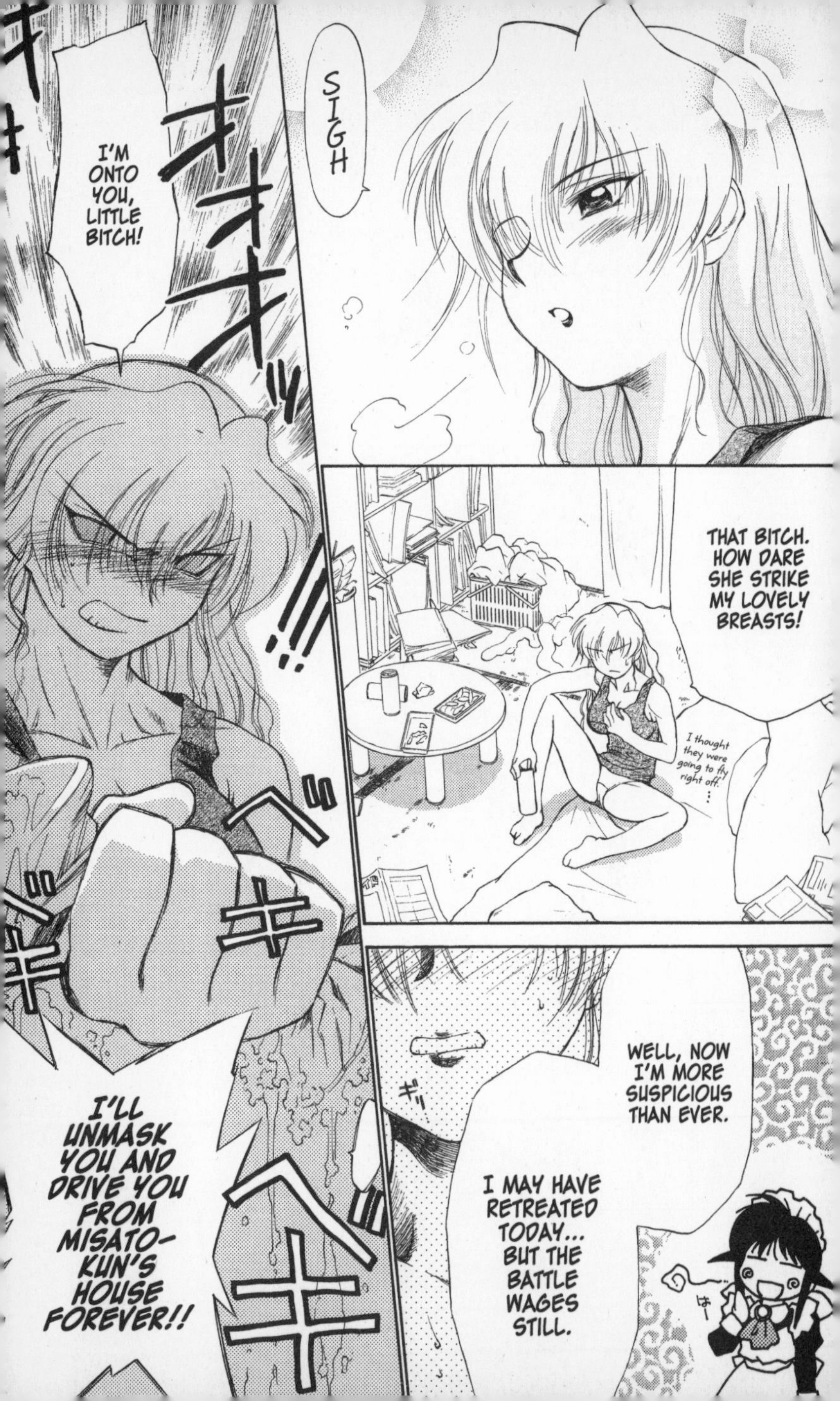
SIGH
THAT BITCH. HOW DARE SHE STRIKE MY LOVELY BREASTS!
I thought they were going to fly right off...
WELL, NOW I'M MORE SUSPICIOUS THAN EVER.
I MAY HAVE RETREATED TODAY... BUT THE BATTLE WAGES STILL.
I'M ONTO YOU, LITTLE BITCH!
I'LL UNMASK YOU AND DRIVE YOU FROM MISATO-KUN'S HOUSE FOREVER!!

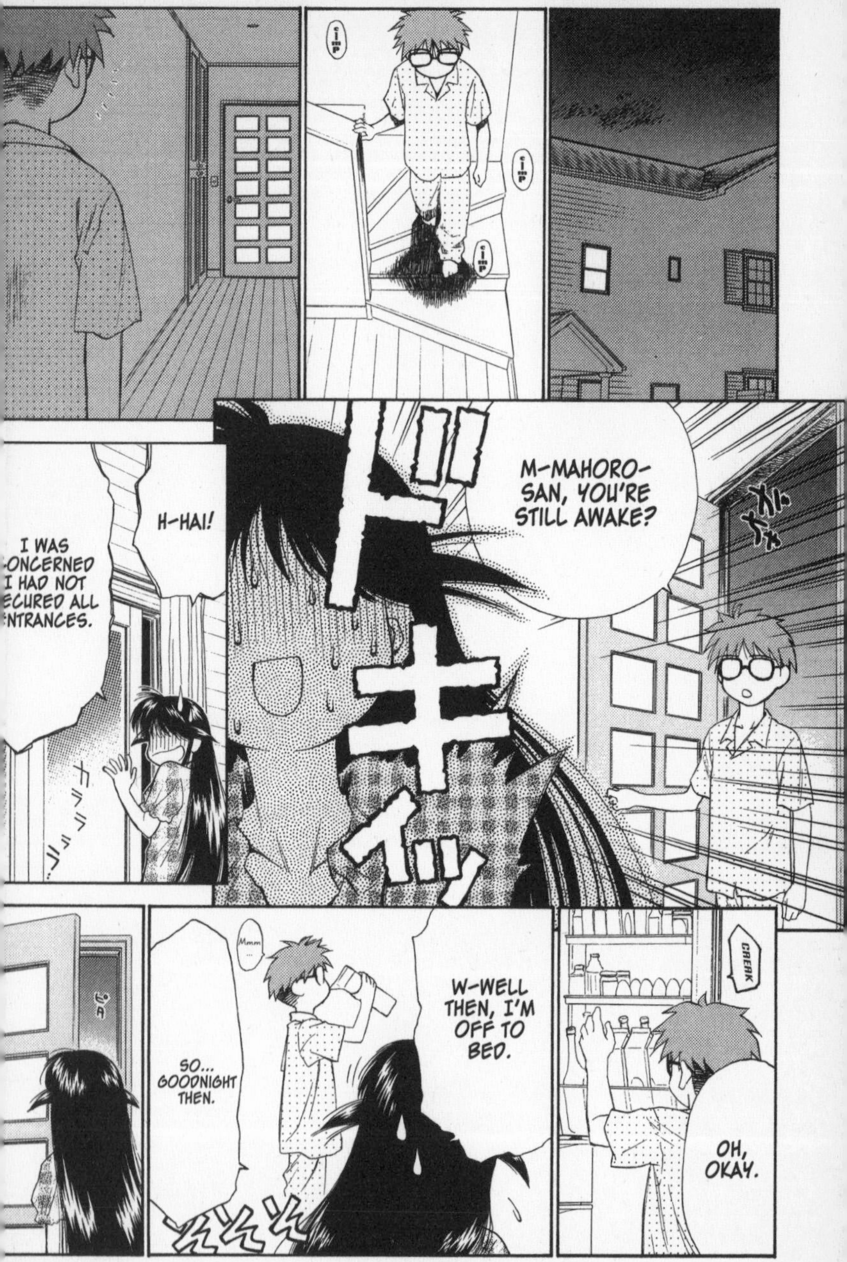
clmp
clmp
clmp
M-MAHORO-SAN, YOU'RE STILL AWAKE?
ドキッ
H-HAI!
I WAS
ONCERNED
I HAD NOT
ECURED ALL
NTRANCES.
CREAK
OH, OKAY.
Mmm...
W-WELL THEN, I'M OFF TO BED.
SO... GOODNIGHT THEN.

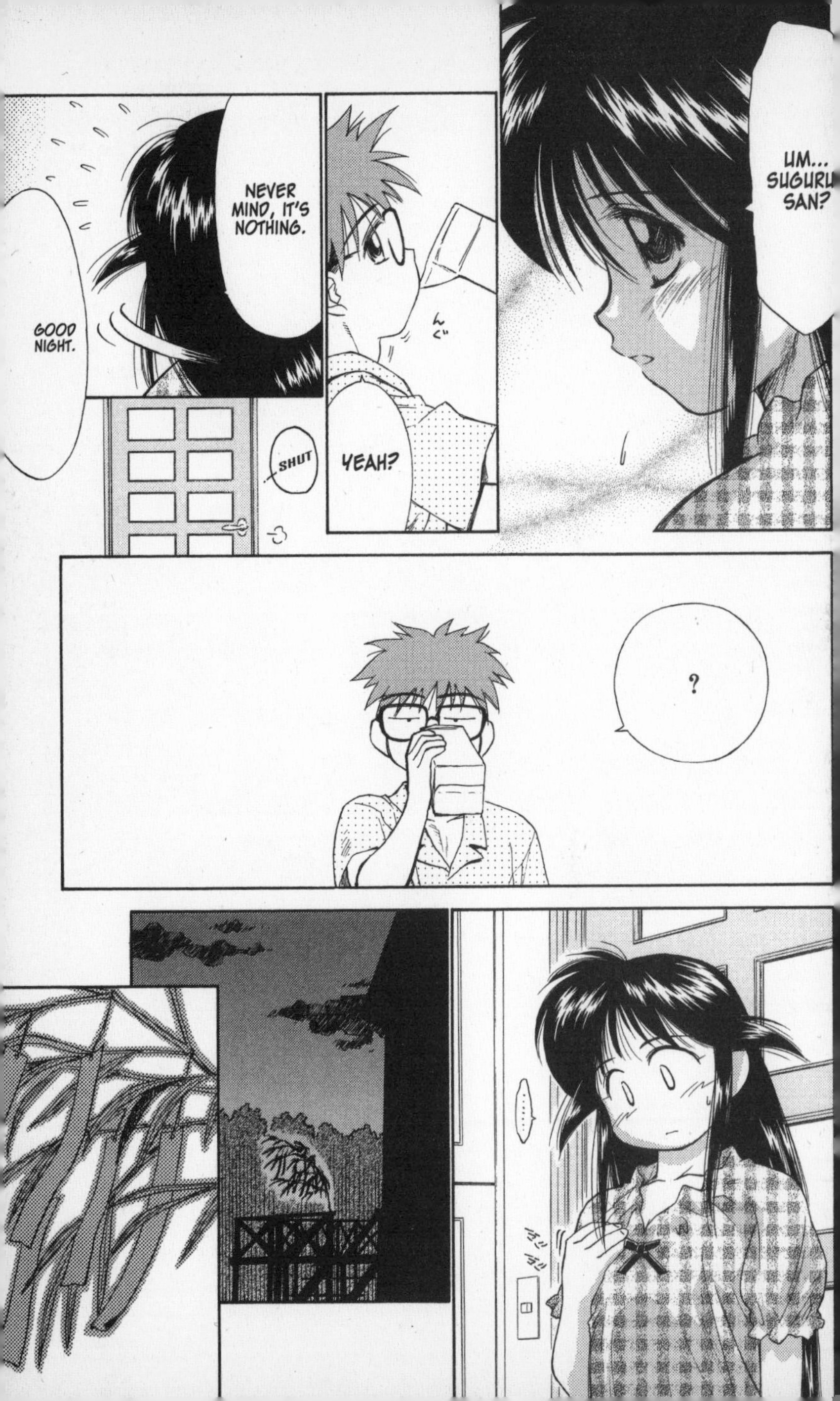
UM... SUGURU SAN?
YEAH?
NEVER MIND, IT'S NOTHING.
GOOD NIGHT.
SHUT

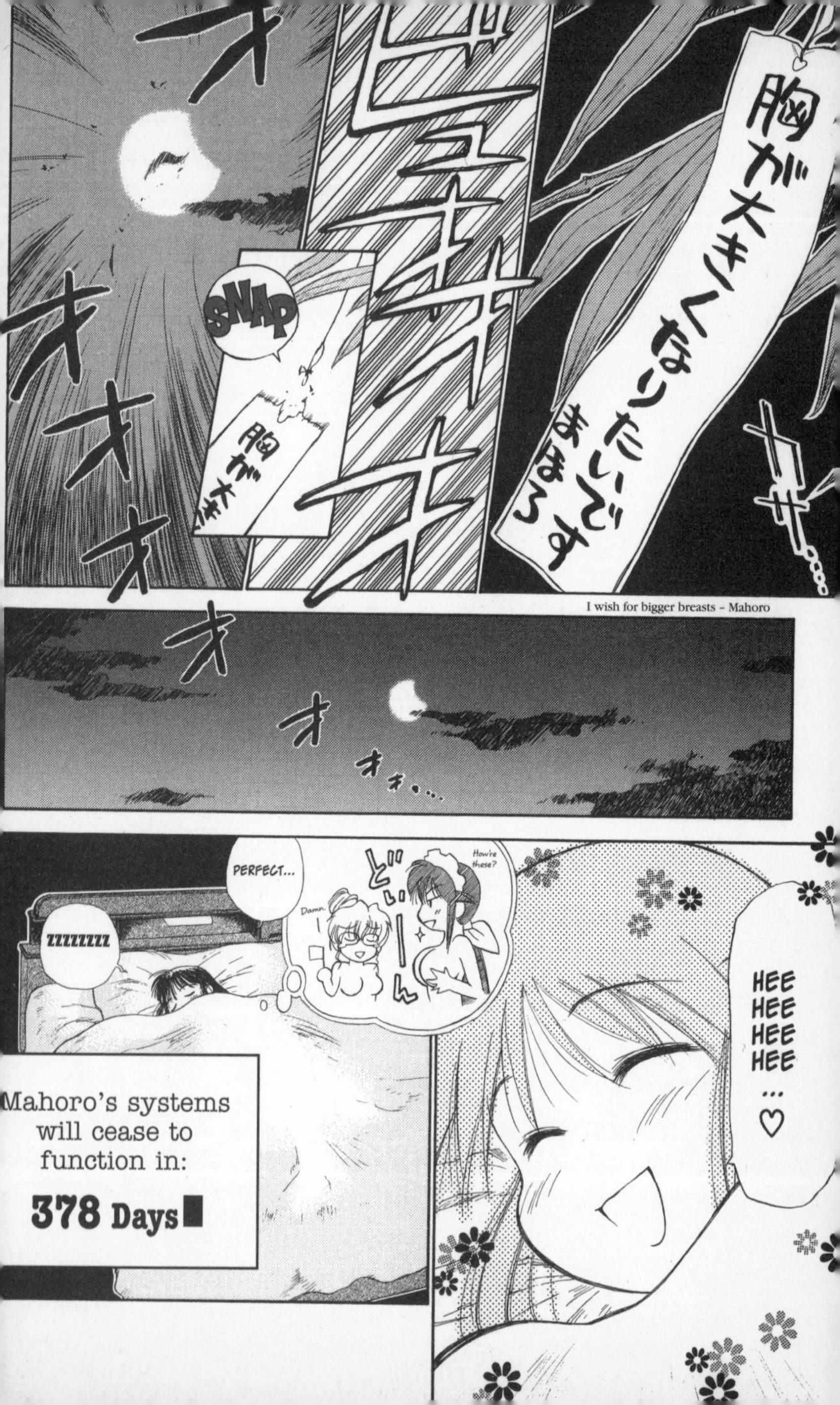
胸が大きくなりたいです まほろ
I wish for bigger breasts - Mahoro
SNAP
胸が大き
オ
オオオオ
オ
オ
オォ...
HEE HEE HEE HEE ...♡
PERFECT...
How're these?
Damn.
ZZZZZZZ
Mahoro's systems will cease to function in:
378 Days

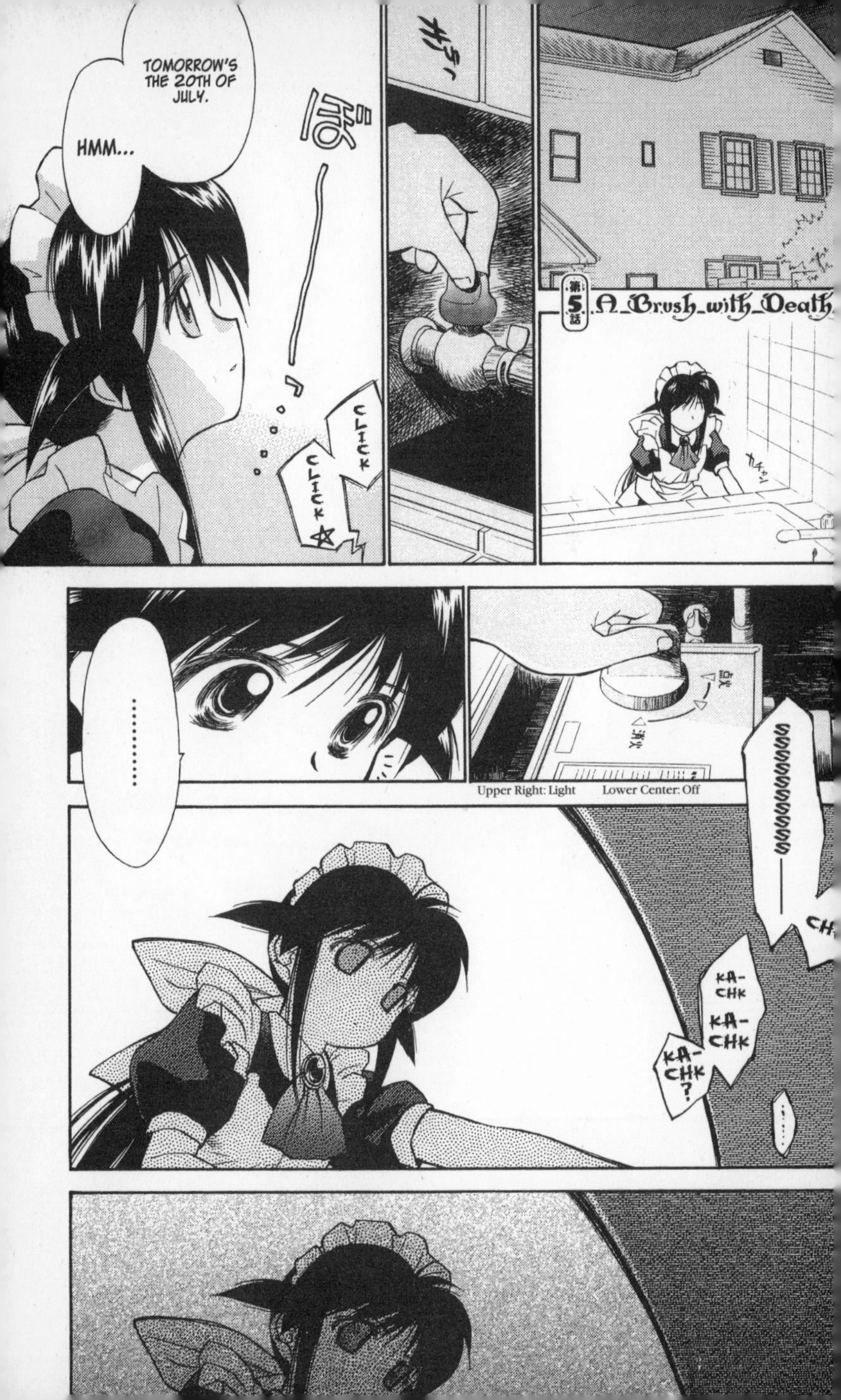

第5話
A Brush with Death
ぼー
TOMORROW'S THE 20TH OF JULY.
HMM...
CLICK
CLICK
点火
消火
Upper Right: Light   Lower Center: Off
......
SSSSSSSSSSSS——
CH
KA-CHK
KA-CHK
KA-CHK?
......

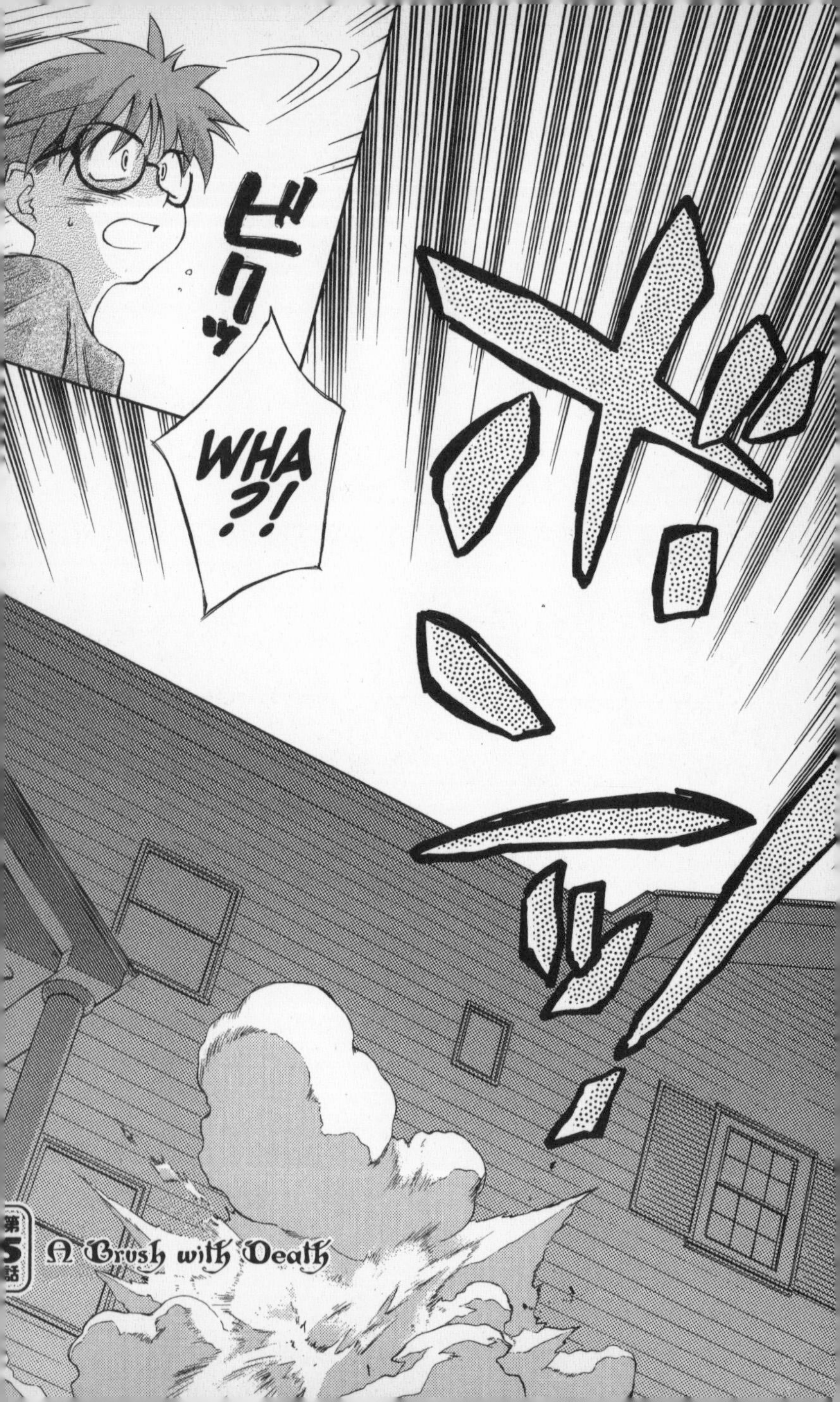
ビクッ
WHA?!
第5話
A Brush with Death

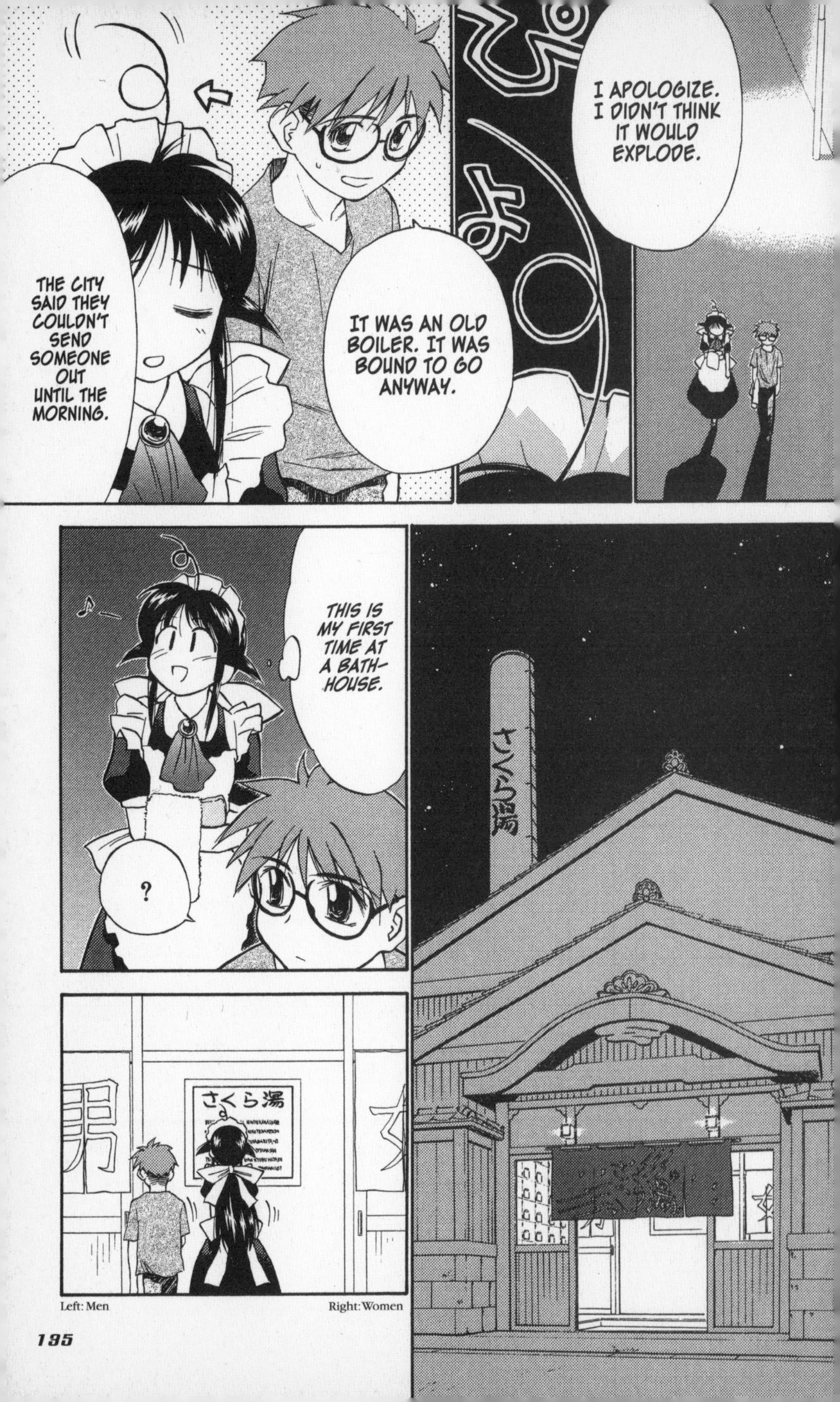

I APOLOGIZE. I DIDN'T THINK IT WOULD EXPLODE.
IT WAS AN OLD BOILER. IT WAS BOUND TO GO ANYWAY.
THE CITY SAID THEY COULDN'T SEND SOMEONE OUT UNTIL THE MORNING.
さくら湯
THIS IS MY FIRST TIME AT A BATH-HOUSE.
?
さくら湯

Left: Men

Right: Women

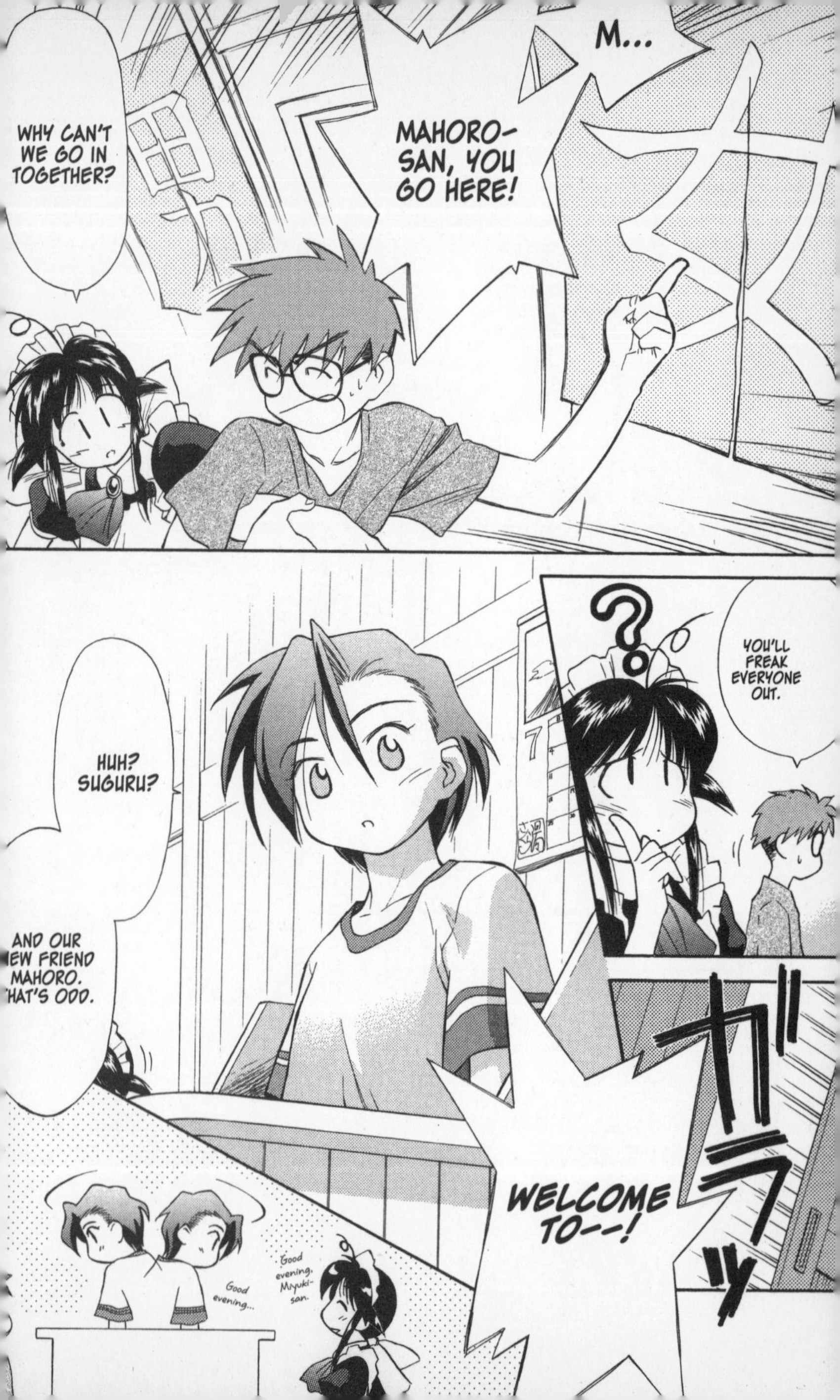
M...
MAHORO-SAN, YOU GO HERE!
WHY CAN'T WE GO IN TOGETHER?
YOU'LL FREAK EVERYONE OUT.
ガラッ
WELCOME TO--!
HUH? SUGURU?
AND OUR
EW FRIEND
MAHORO.
HAT'S ODD.
Good evening, Miyuki-san.
Good evening...

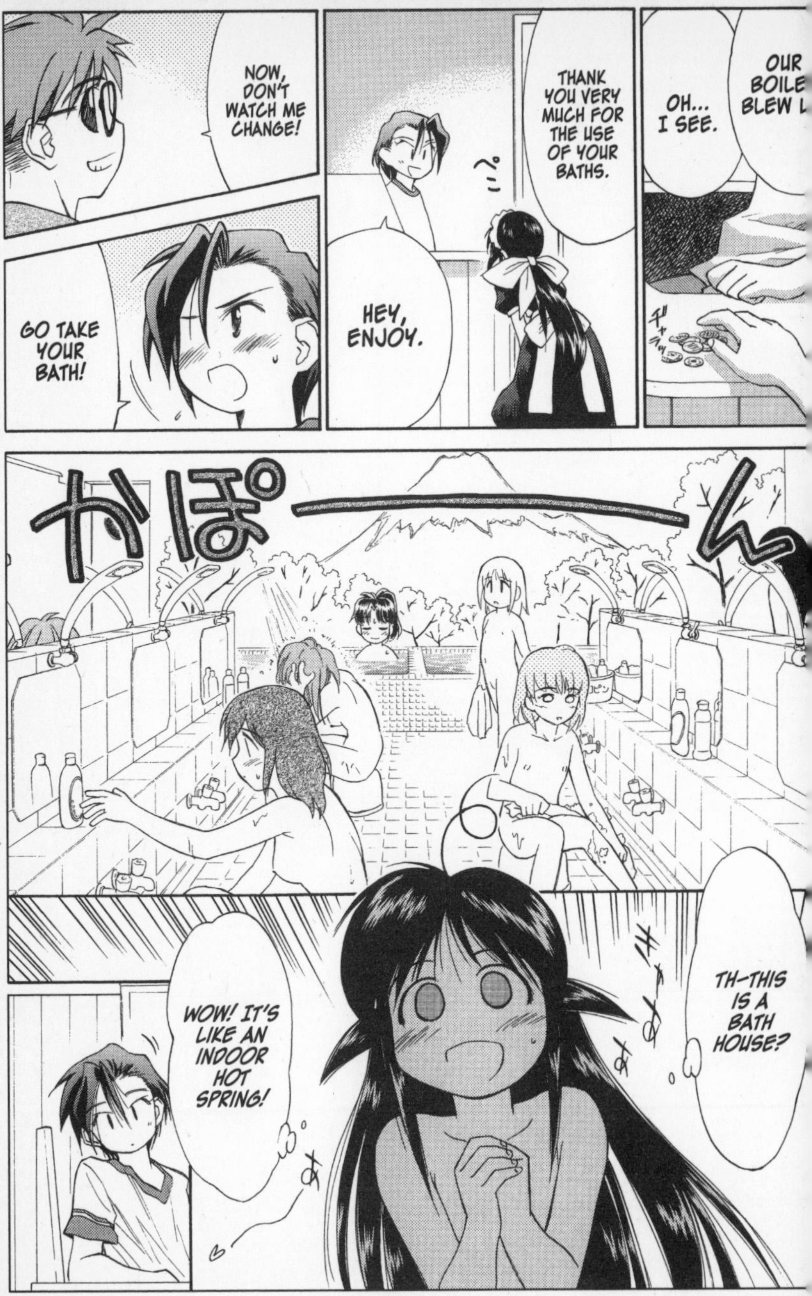
OUR BOILE
BLEW L
OH... I SEE.
THANK YOU VERY MUCH FOR THE USE OF YOUR BATHS.
ぺこ
HEY, ENJOY.
NOW, DON'T WATCH ME CHANGE!
GO TAKE YOUR BATH!
かぽーーーん
TH-THIS IS A BATH HOUSE?
WOW! IT'S LIKE AN INDOOR HOT SPRING!

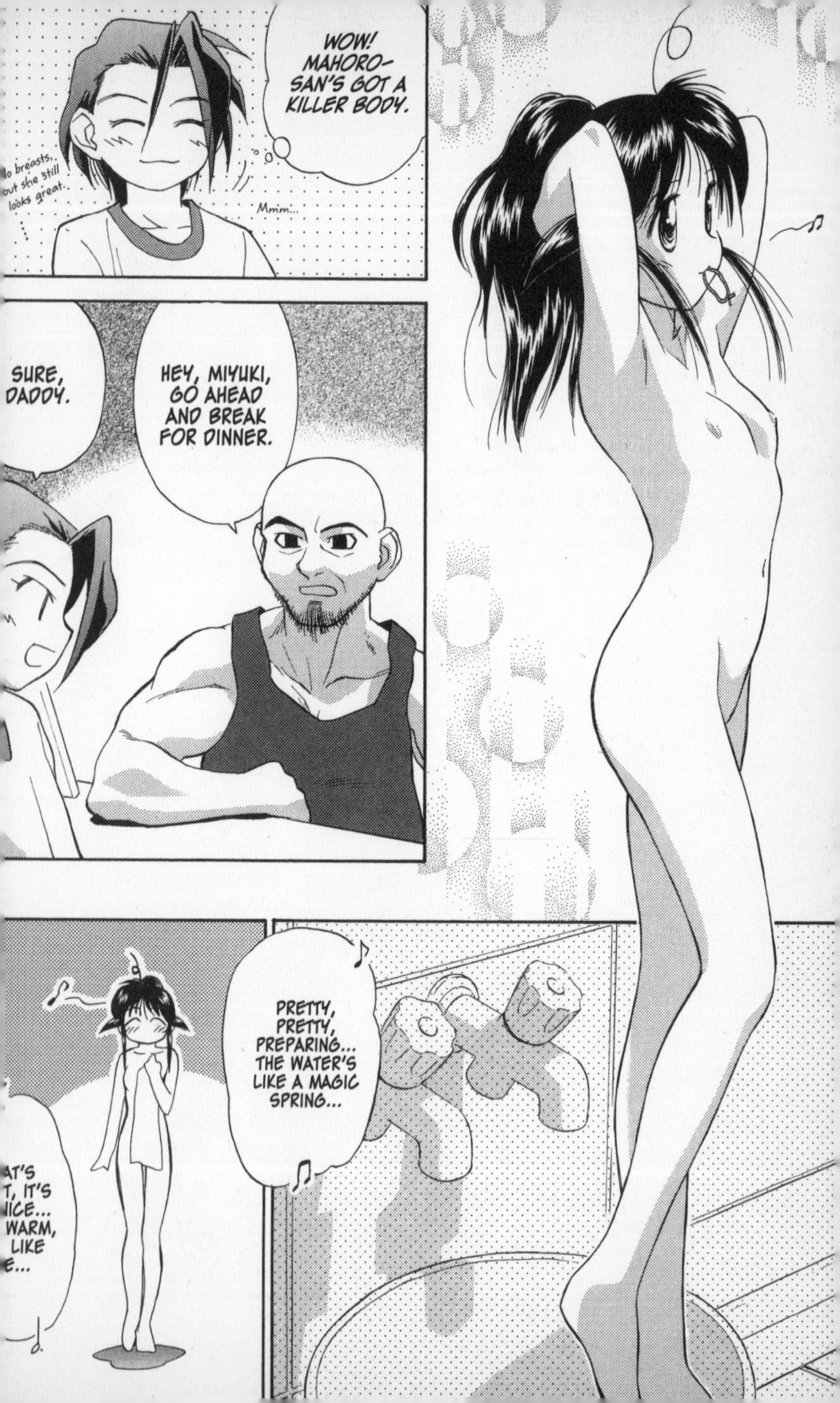
WOW! MAHORO-SAN'S GOT A KILLER BODY.
Mmm...
HEY, MIYUKI, GO AHEAD AND BREAK FOR DINNER.
SURE, DADDY.
PRETTY, PRETTY, PREPARING... THE WATER'S LIKE A MAGIC SPRING...

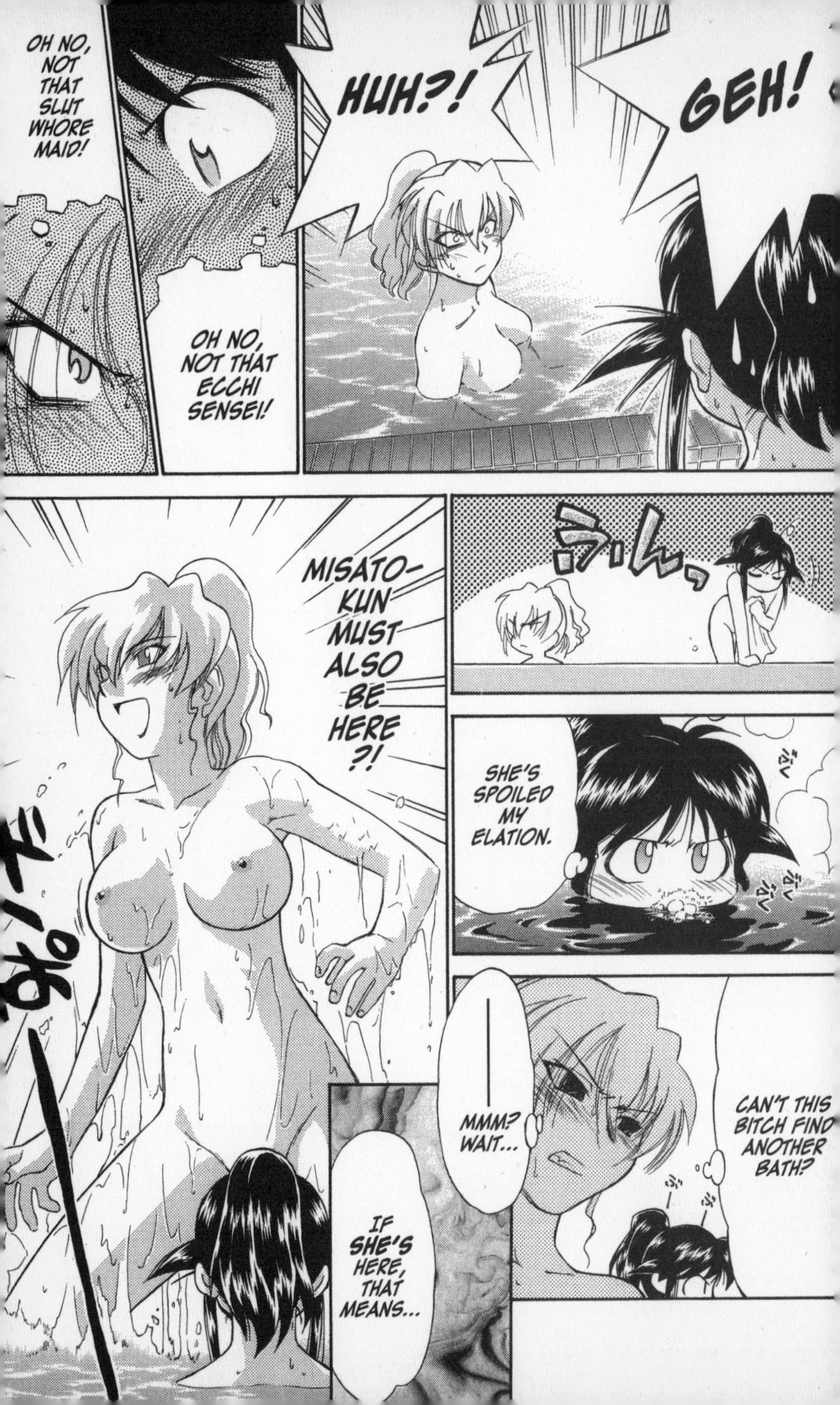
GEH!
HUH?!
OH NO, NOT THAT ECCHI SENSEI!
OH NO, NOT THAT SLUT WHORE MAID!
ふんっ
SHE'S SPOILED MY ELATION.
CAN'T THIS BITCH FIND ANOTHER BATH?
MMM? WAIT...
IF SHE'S HERE, THAT MEANS...
MISATO-KUN MUST ALSO BE HERE?!

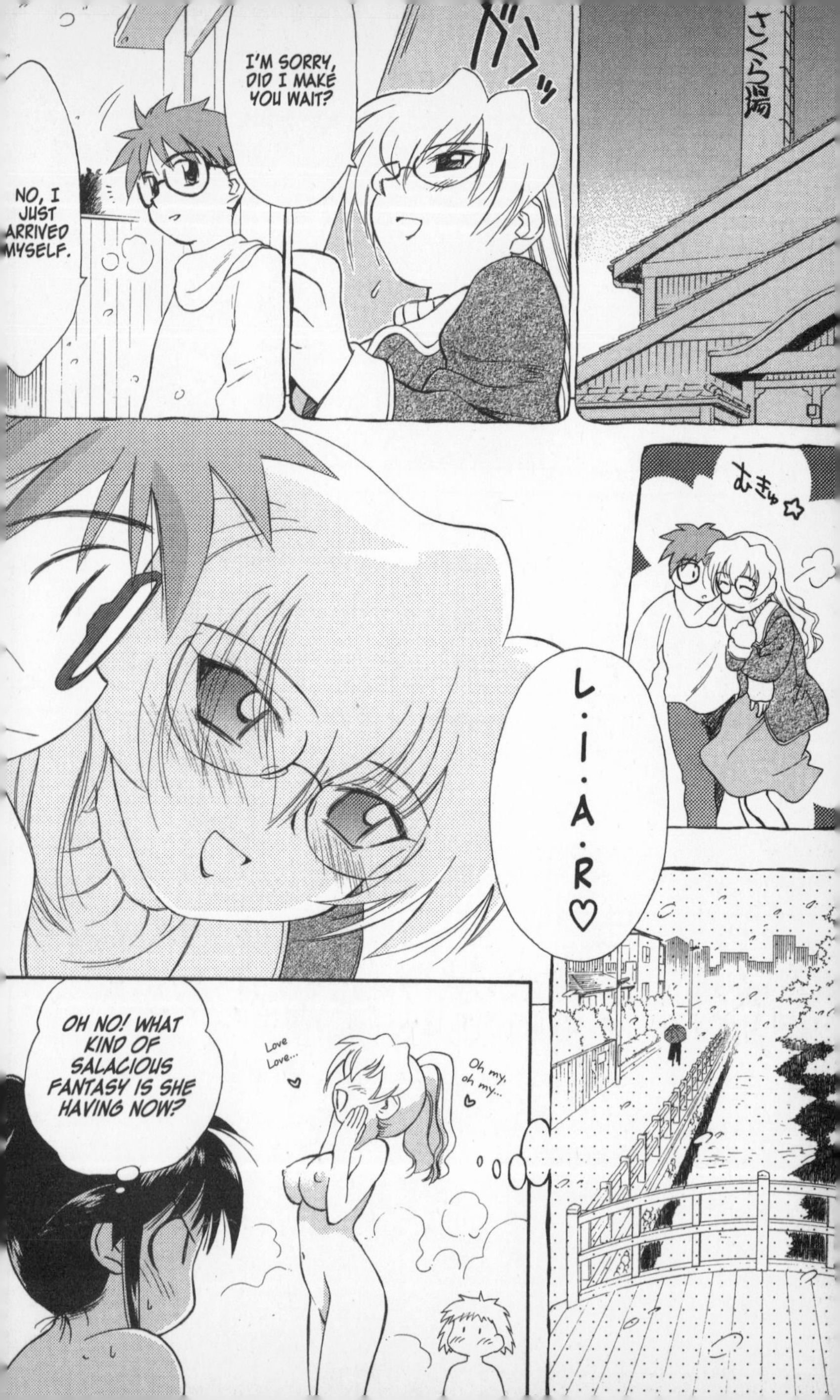

さくら湯
ガラッ
I'M SORRY, DID I MAKE YOU WAIT?
NO, I JUST ARRIVED MYSELF.
むぎゅ☆
L.I.A.R♡
OH NO! WHAT KIND OF SALACIOUS FANTASY IS SHE HAVING NOW?
Love Love...♡
Oh my, oh my...♡

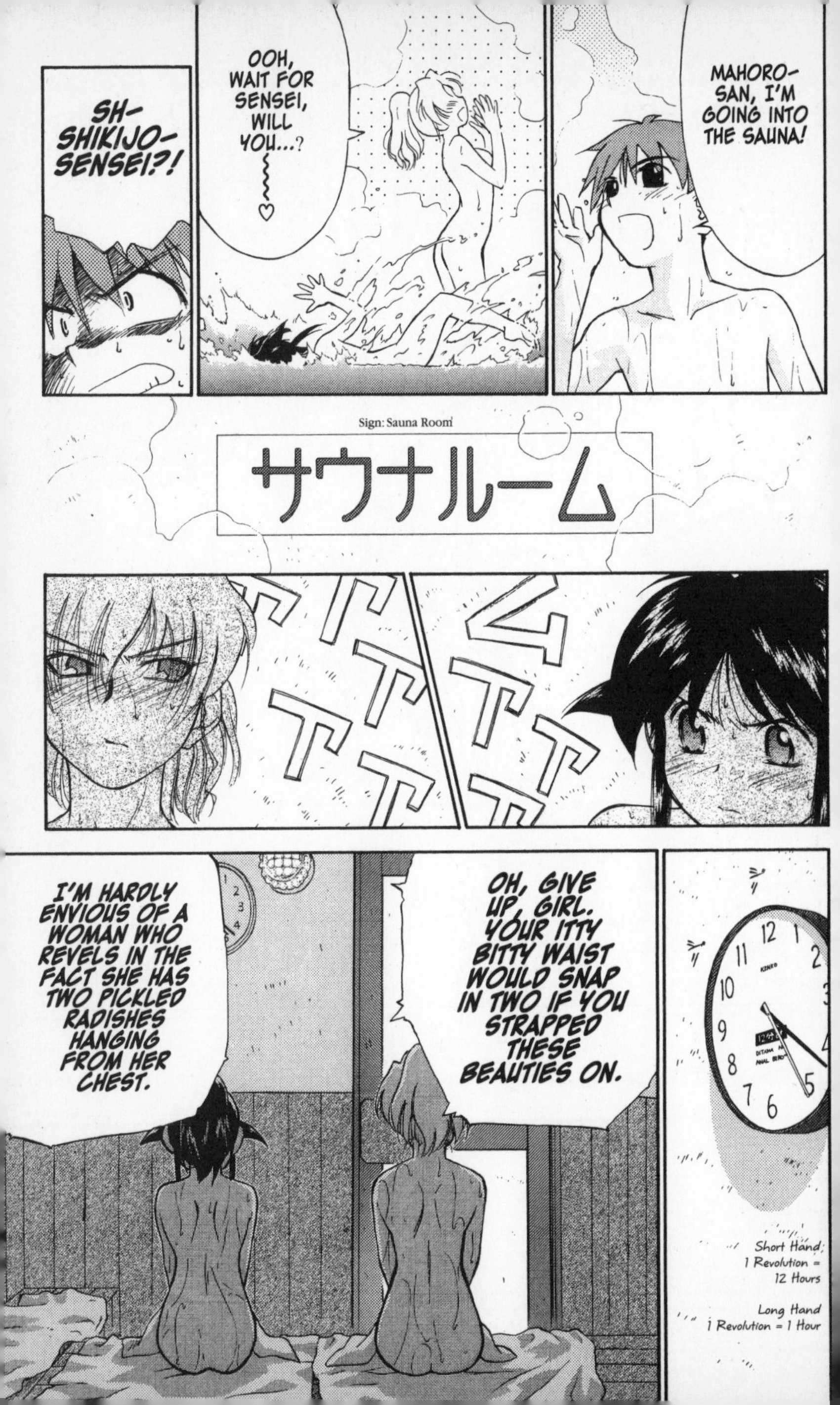

MAHORO-SAN, I'M GOING INTO THE SAUNA!
OOH, WAIT FOR SENSEI, WILL YOU...? ~♥
SH-SHIKIJO-SENSEI?!
Sign: Sauna Room
サウナルーム
Short Hand: 1 Revolution = 12 Hours
Long Hand 1 Revolution = 1 Hour
OH, GIVE UP, GIRL. YOUR ITTY BITTY WAIST WOULD SNAP IN TWO IF YOU STRAPPED THESE BEAUTIES ON.
I'M HARDLY ENVIOUS OF A WOMAN WHO REVELS IN THE FACT SHE HAS TWO PICKLED RADISHES HANGING FROM HER CHEST.

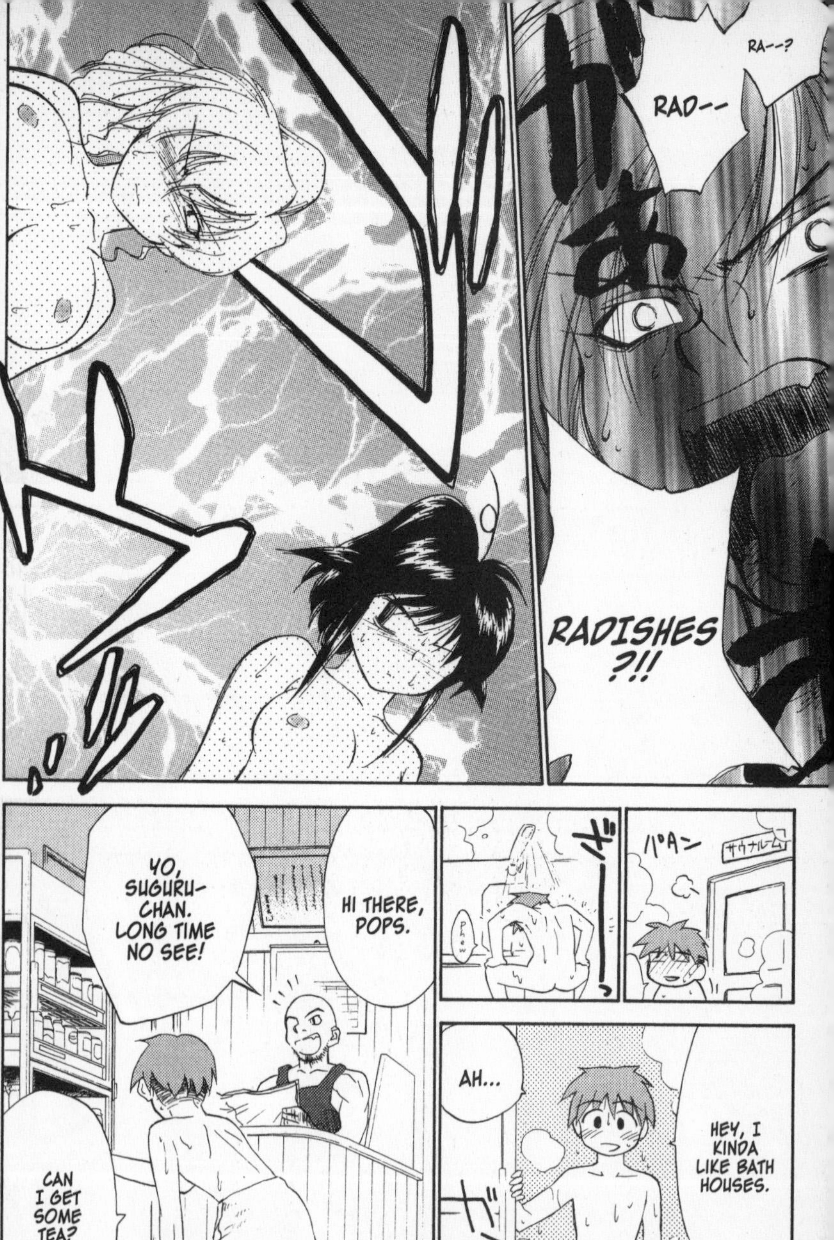
RA--?
RAD--
RADISHES ?!!
サウナルーム
Phew
AH...
HEY, I KINDA LIKE BATH HOUSES.
YO, SUGURU-CHAN. LONG TIME NO SEE!
HI THERE, POPS.
CAN I GET SOME TEA?

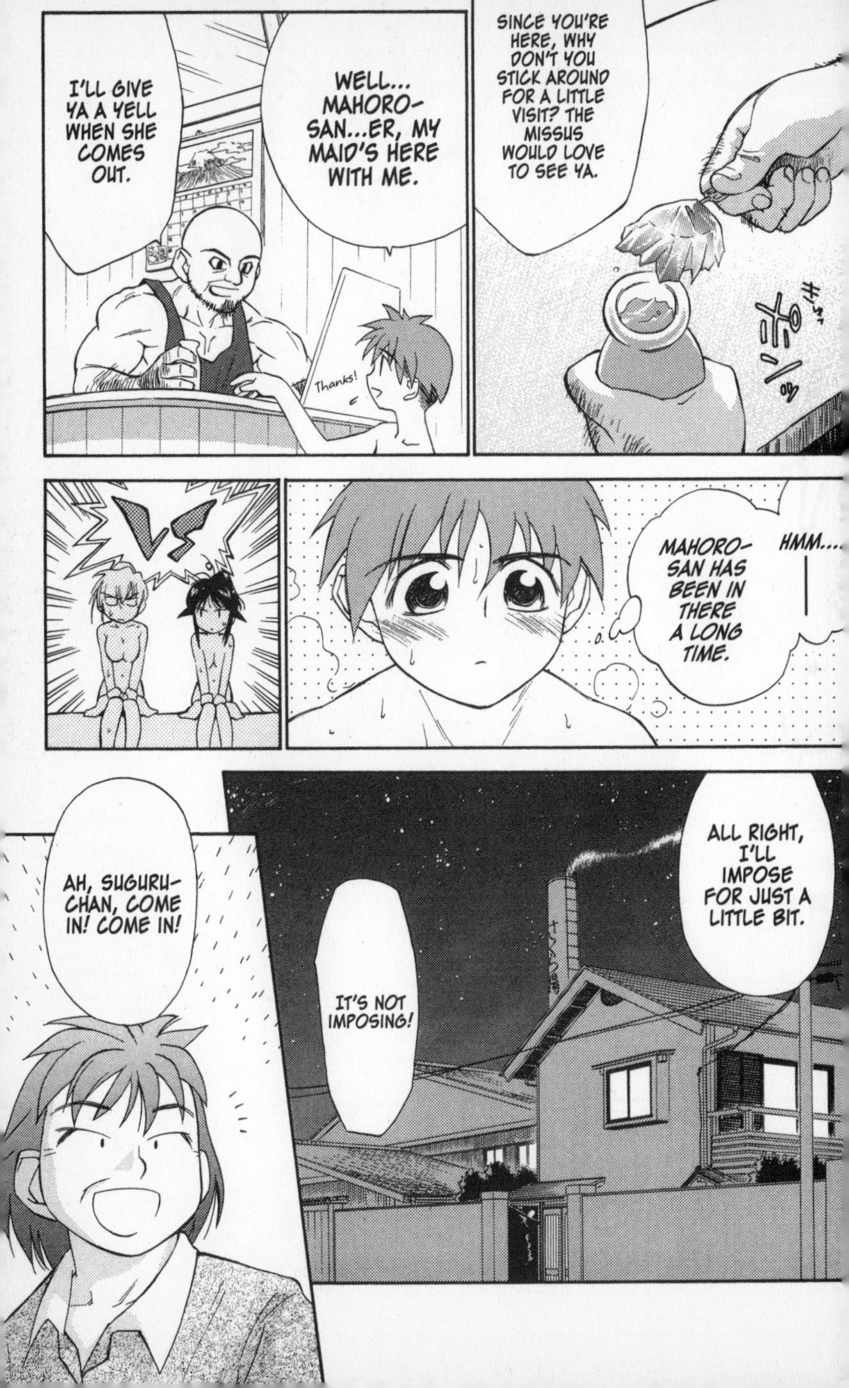
SINCE YOU'RE HERE, WHY DON'T YOU STICK AROUND FOR A LITTLE VISIT? THE MISSUS WOULD LOVE TO SEE YA.
WELL... MAHORO-SAN...ER, MY MAID'S HERE WITH ME.
I'LL GIVE YA A YELL WHEN SHE COMES OUT.
Thanks!
HMM....
MAHORO-SAN HAS BEEN IN THERE A LONG TIME.
VS
ALL RIGHT, I'LL IMPOSE FOR JUST A LITTLE BIT.
IT'S NOT IMPOSING!
AH, SUGURU-CHAN, COME IN! COME IN!

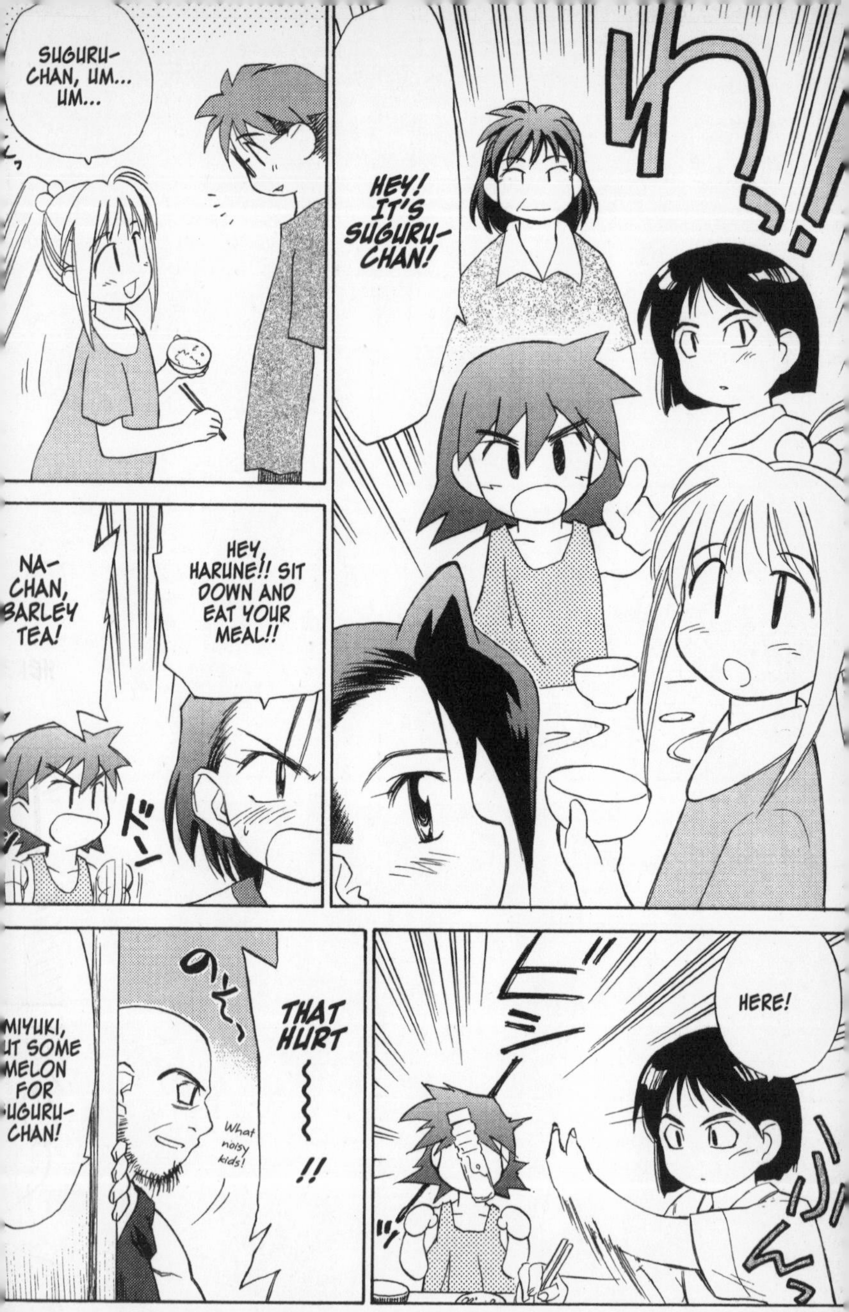
わっ!!
HEY! IT'S SUGURU-CHAN!
SUGURU-CHAN, UM... UM...
HEY, HARUNE!! SIT DOWN AND EAT YOUR MEAL!!
NA-CHAN, BARLEY TEA!
ドン
HERE!
THAT HURT ~~~ !!
のそ、
What noisy kids!
MIYUKI, UT SOME MELON FOR UGURU-CHAN!

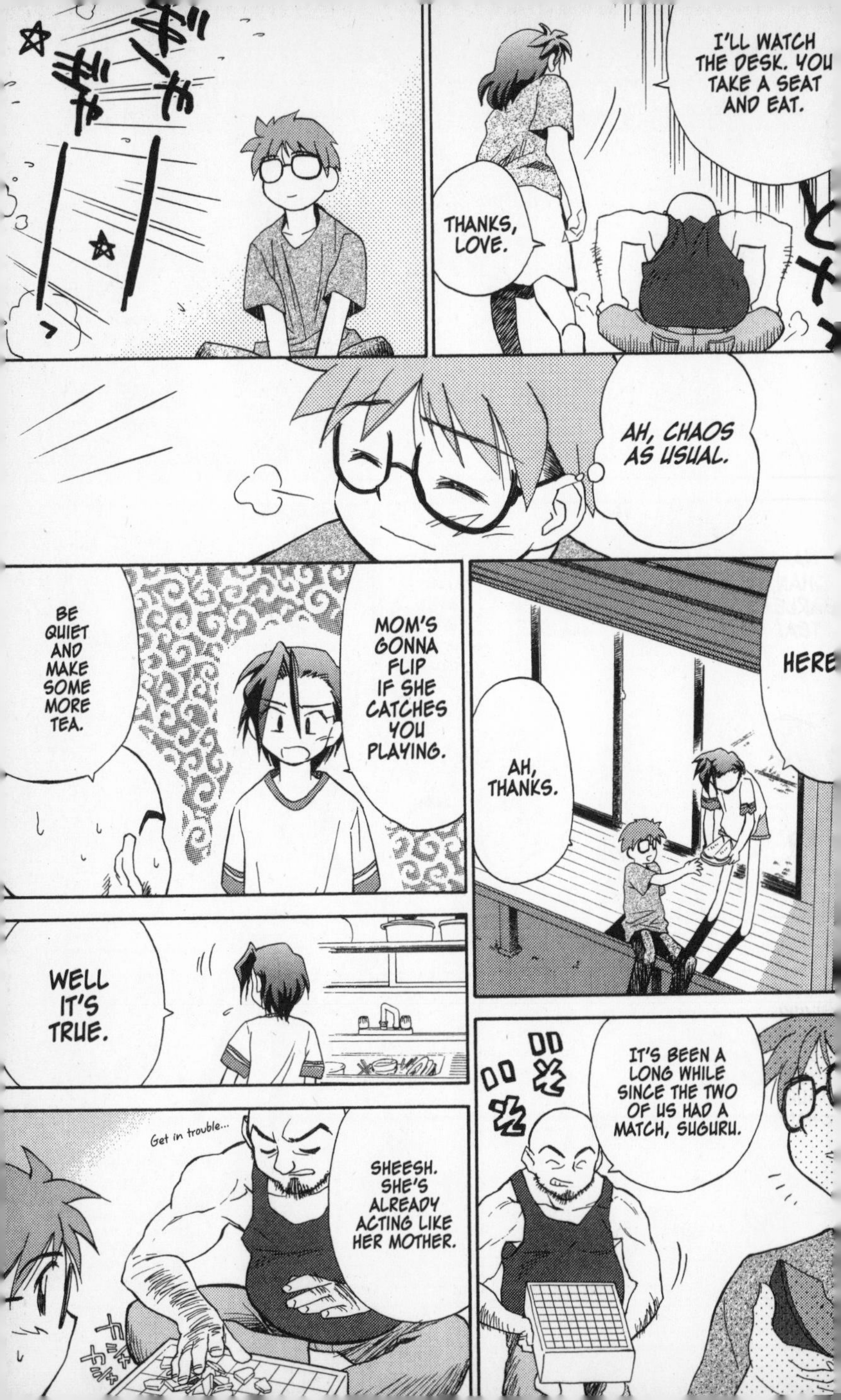
I'LL WATCH THE DESK. YOU TAKE A SEAT AND EAT.
THANKS, LOVE.
AH, CHAOS AS USUAL.
HERE
AH, THANKS.
MOM'S GONNA FLIP IF SHE CATCHES YOU PLAYING.
BE QUIET AND MAKE SOME MORE TEA.
WELL IT'S TRUE.
IT'S BEEN A LONG WHILE SINCE THE TWO OF US HAD A MATCH, SUGURU.
SHEESH. SHE'S ALREADY ACTING LIKE HER MOTHER.
Get in trouble...

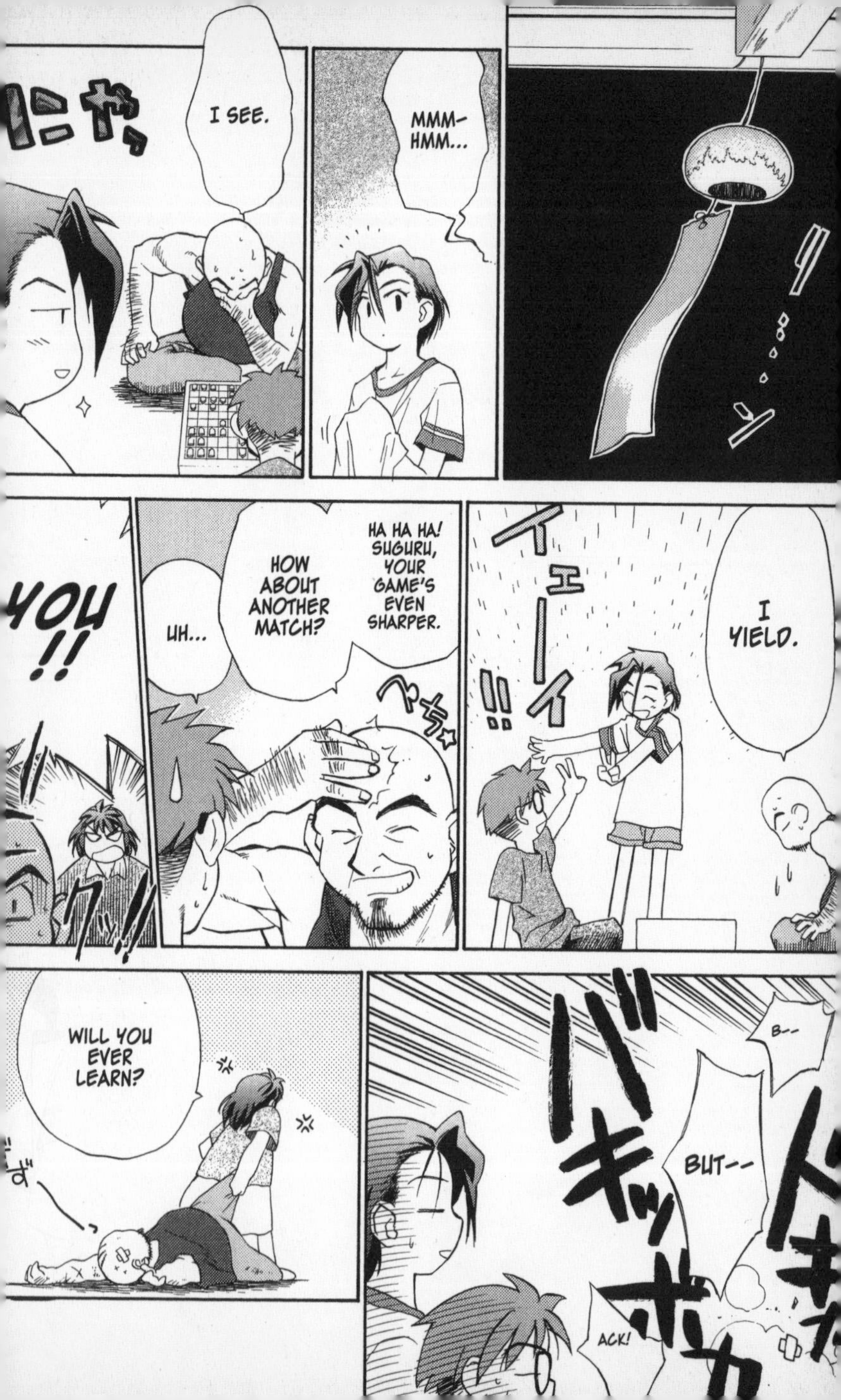
MMM-HMM...
I SEE.
にやっ
I YIELD.
HA HA HA! SUGURU, YOUR GAME'S EVEN SHARPER.
HOW ABOUT ANOTHER MATCH?
UH...
YOU!!
B--
BUT--
ACK!
WILL YOU EVER LEARN?

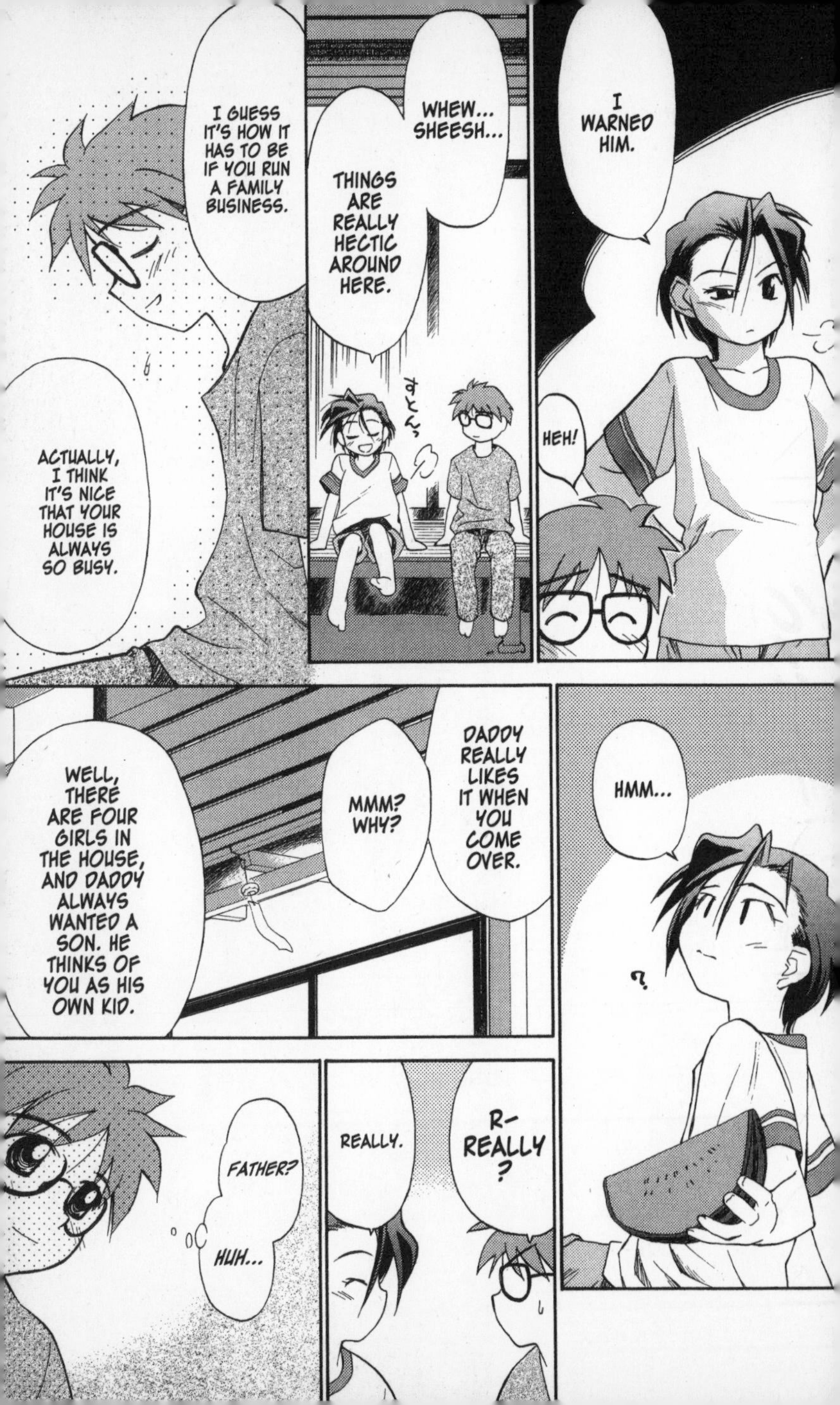
I WARNED HIM.
HEH!
WHEW... SHEESH...
THINGS ARE REALLY HECTIC AROUND HERE.
すとんっ
I GUESS IT'S HOW IT HAS TO BE IF YOU RUN A FAMILY BUSINESS.
ACTUALLY, I THINK IT'S NICE THAT YOUR HOUSE IS ALWAYS SO BUSY.
HMM...
?
DADDY REALLY LIKES IT WHEN YOU COME OVER.
MMM? WHY?
WELL, THERE ARE FOUR GIRLS IN THE HOUSE, AND DADDY ALWAYS WANTED A SON. HE THINKS OF YOU AS HIS OWN KID.
R-REALLY?
REALLY.
FATHER?
HUH...

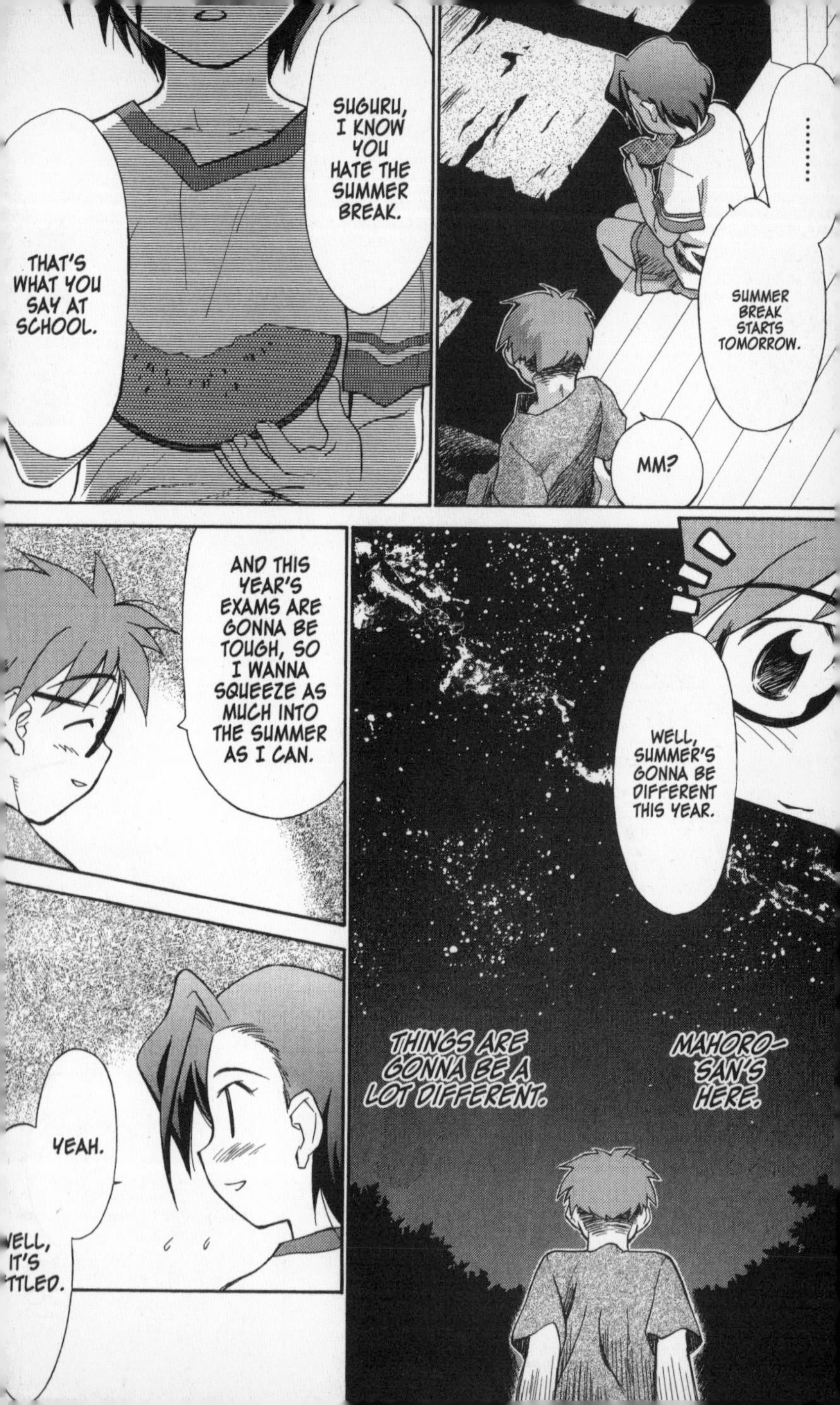
......
SUMMER BREAK STARTS TOMORROW.
MM?
SUGURU, I KNOW YOU HATE THE SUMMER BREAK.
THAT'S WHAT YOU SAY AT SCHOOL.
WELL, SUMMER'S GONNA BE DIFFERENT THIS YEAR.
MAHORO-SAN'S HERE.
THINGS ARE GONNA BE A LOT DIFFERENT.
AND THIS YEAR'S EXAMS ARE GONNA BE TOUGH, SO I WANNA SQUEEZE AS MUCH INTO THE SUMMER AS I CAN.
YEAH.
ELL, IT'S TTLED.

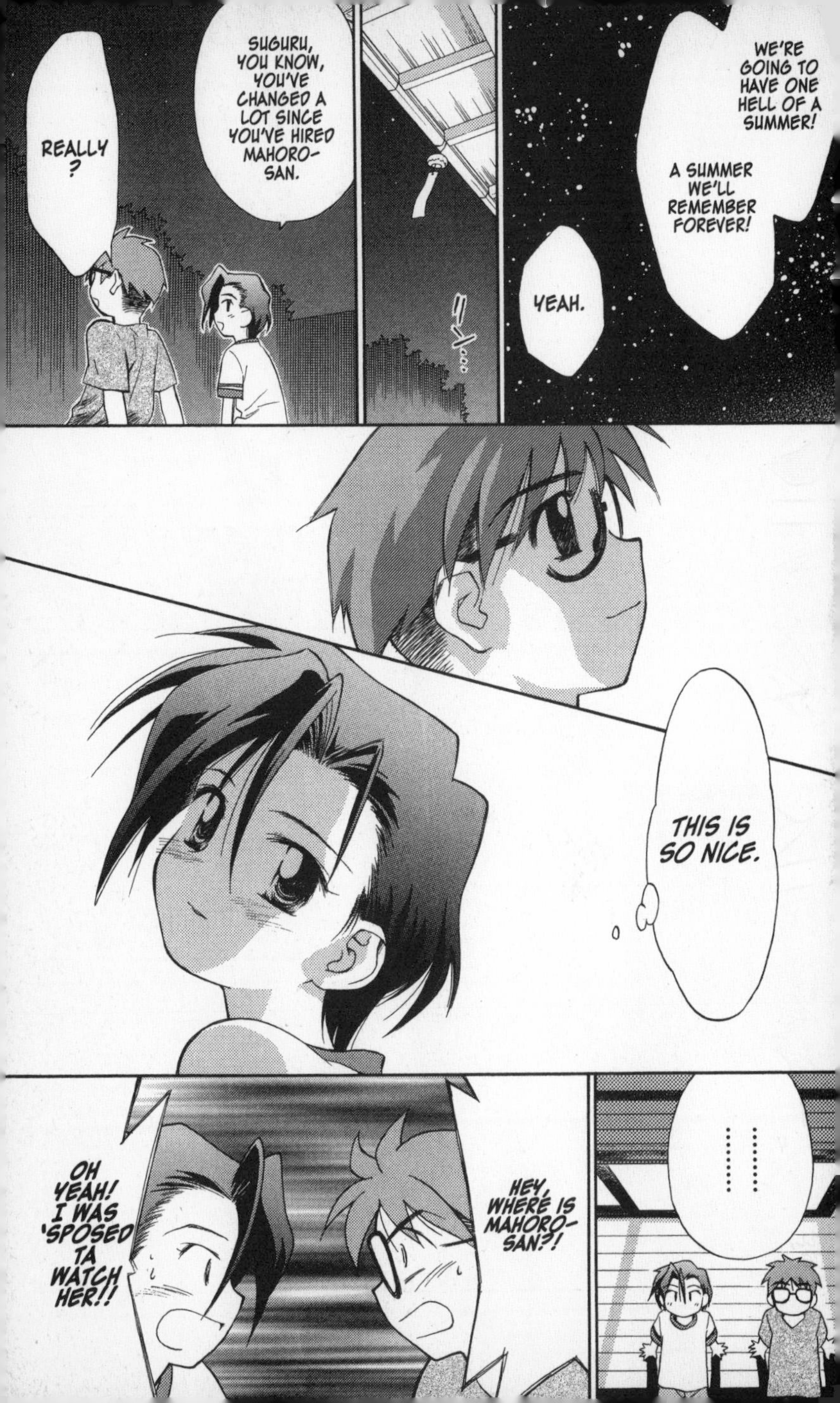
WE'RE GOING TO HAVE ONE HELL OF A SUMMER!
A SUMMER WE'LL REMEMBER FOREVER!
YEAH.
SUGURU, YOU KNOW, YOU'VE CHANGED A LOT SINCE YOU'VE HIRED MAHORO-SAN.
REALLY?
THIS IS SO NICE.
......
......
HEY, WHERE IS MAHORO-SAN?!
OH YEAH! I WAS 'SPOSED TA WATCH HER!!

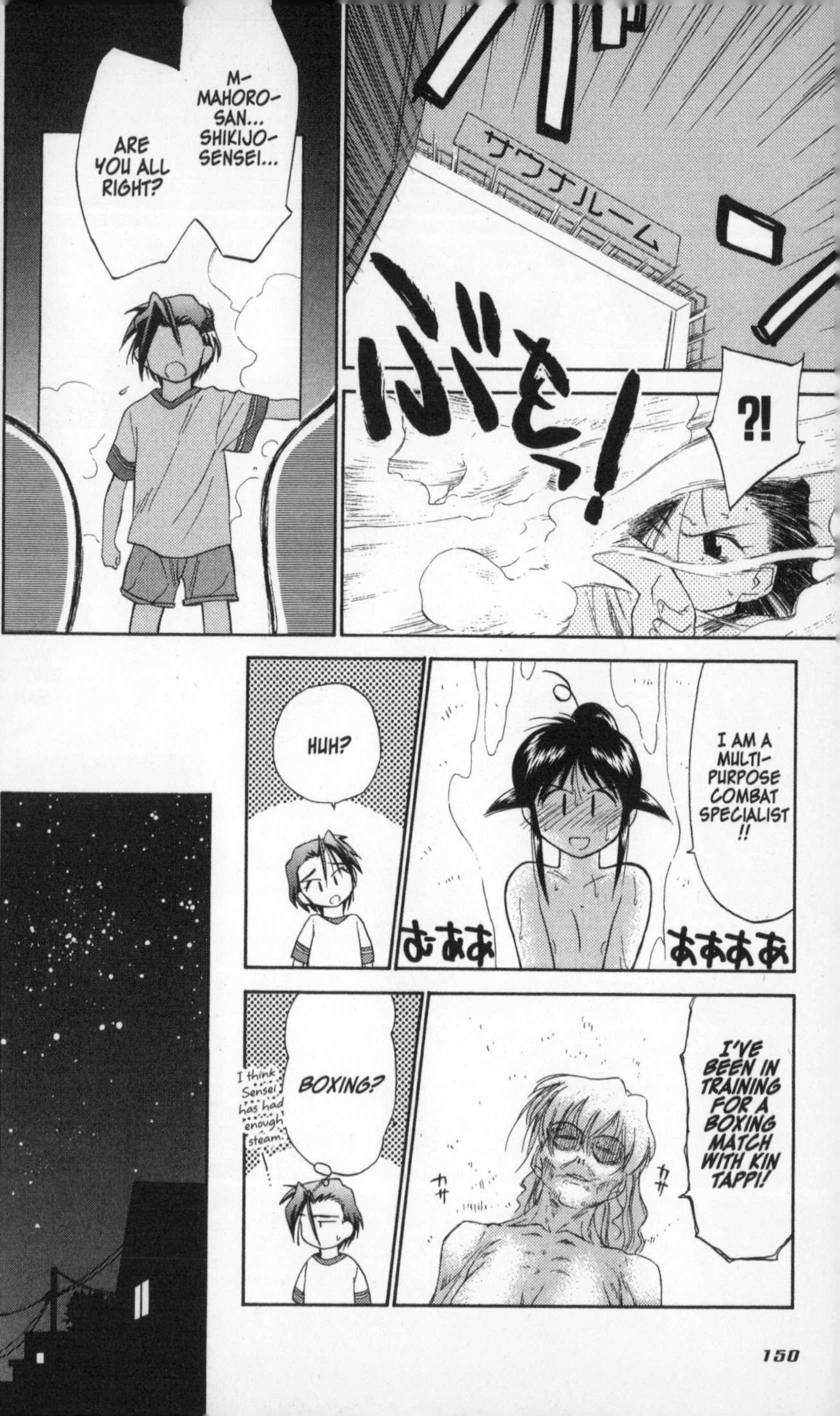
サウナルーム
?!
M-MAHORO-SAN... SHIKIJO-SENSEI...
ARE YOU ALL RIGHT?
I AM A MULTI-PURPOSE COMBAT SPECIALIST !!
HUH?
I'VE BEEN IN TRAINING FOR A BOXING MATCH WITH KIN TAPPI!
カサ
カサ
BOXING?
I think Sensei has had enough steam.

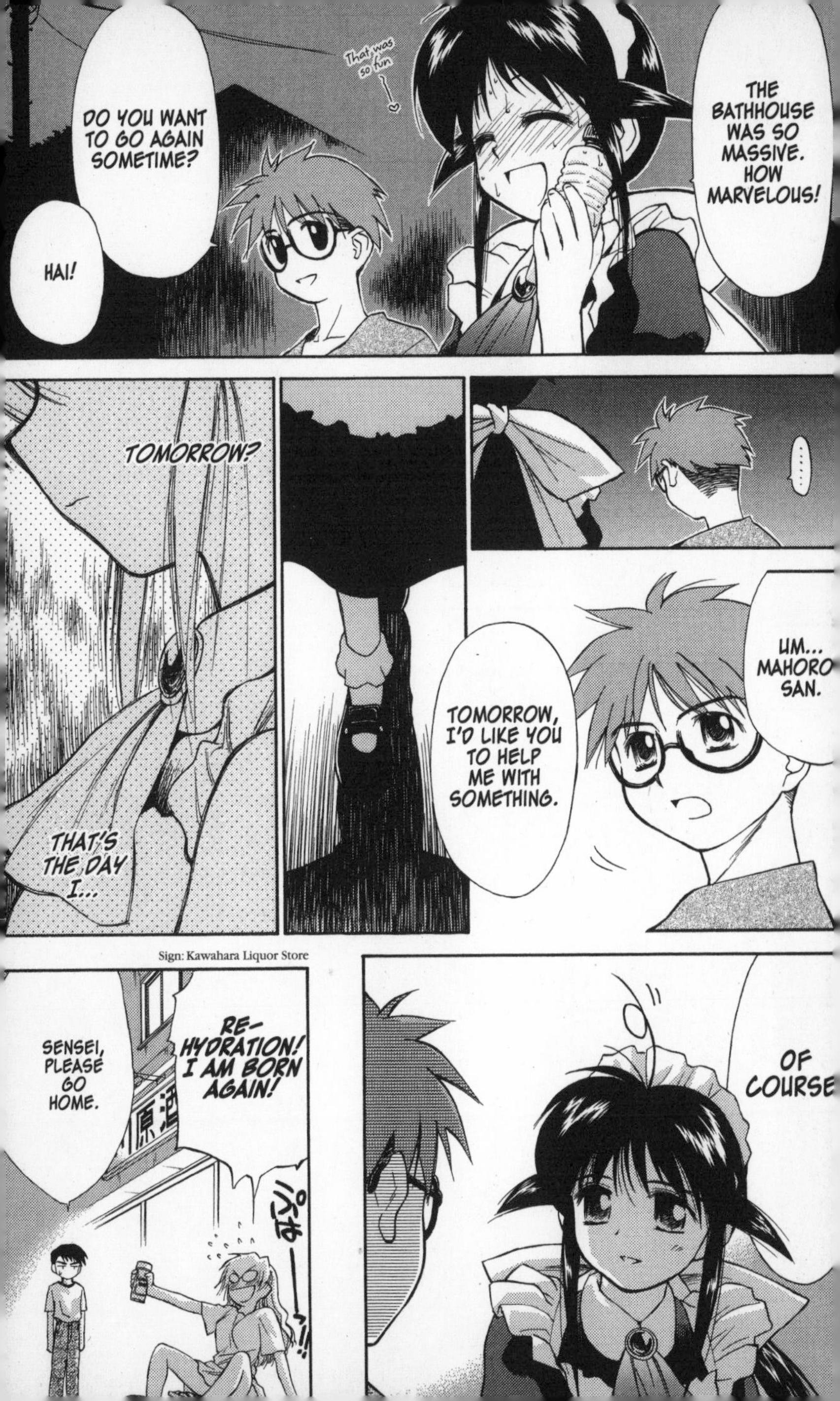
THE BATHHOUSE WAS SO MASSIVE. HOW MARVELOUS!
That was so fun ♡
DO YOU WANT TO GO AGAIN SOMETIME?
HAI!
......
UM... MAHORO SAN.
TOMORROW, I'D LIKE YOU TO HELP ME WITH SOMETHING.
TOMORROW?
THAT'S THE DAY I...
OF COURSE
RE-HYDRATION! I AM BORN AGAIN!
ぷは―――!!
SENSEI, PLEASE GO HOME.

Sign: Kawahara Liquor Store

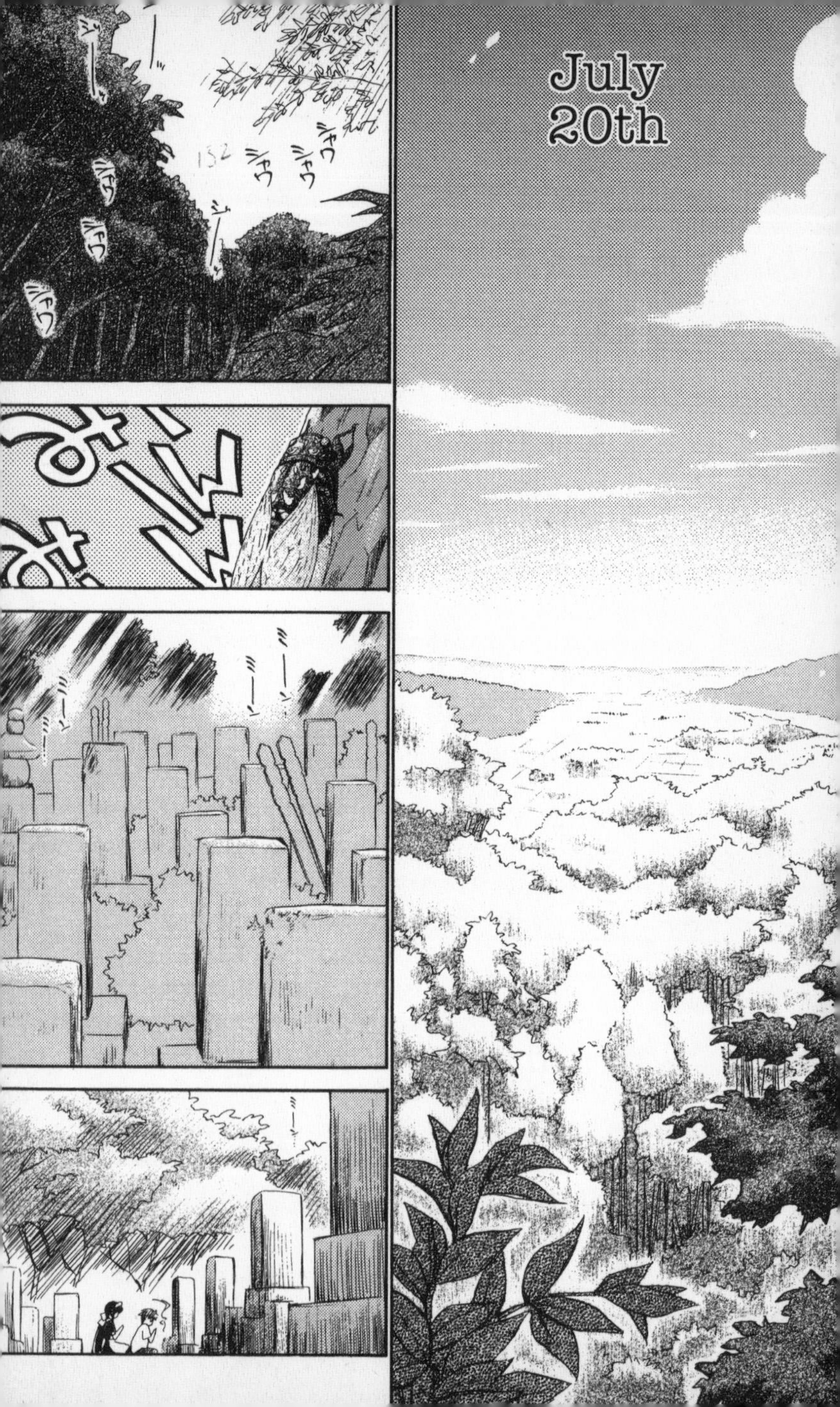
July
20th
ジー…
シャワ
シャワ
シャワ
シャワ
ジー…
ミーン
ミーン
ミーン…
ミー…

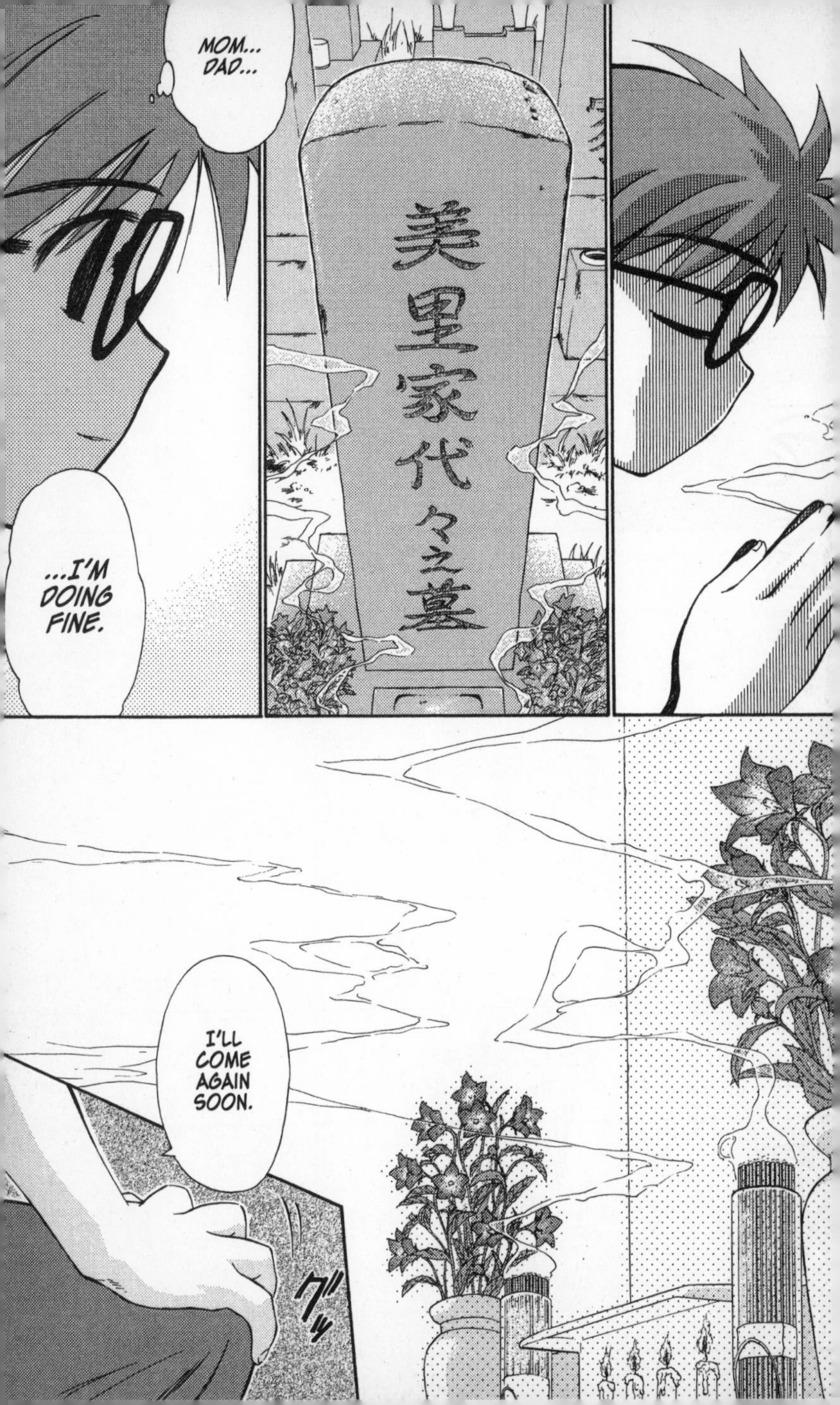

美里家代々之墓
MOM... DAD...
...I'M DOING FINE.
I'LL COME AGAIN SOON.
グッ

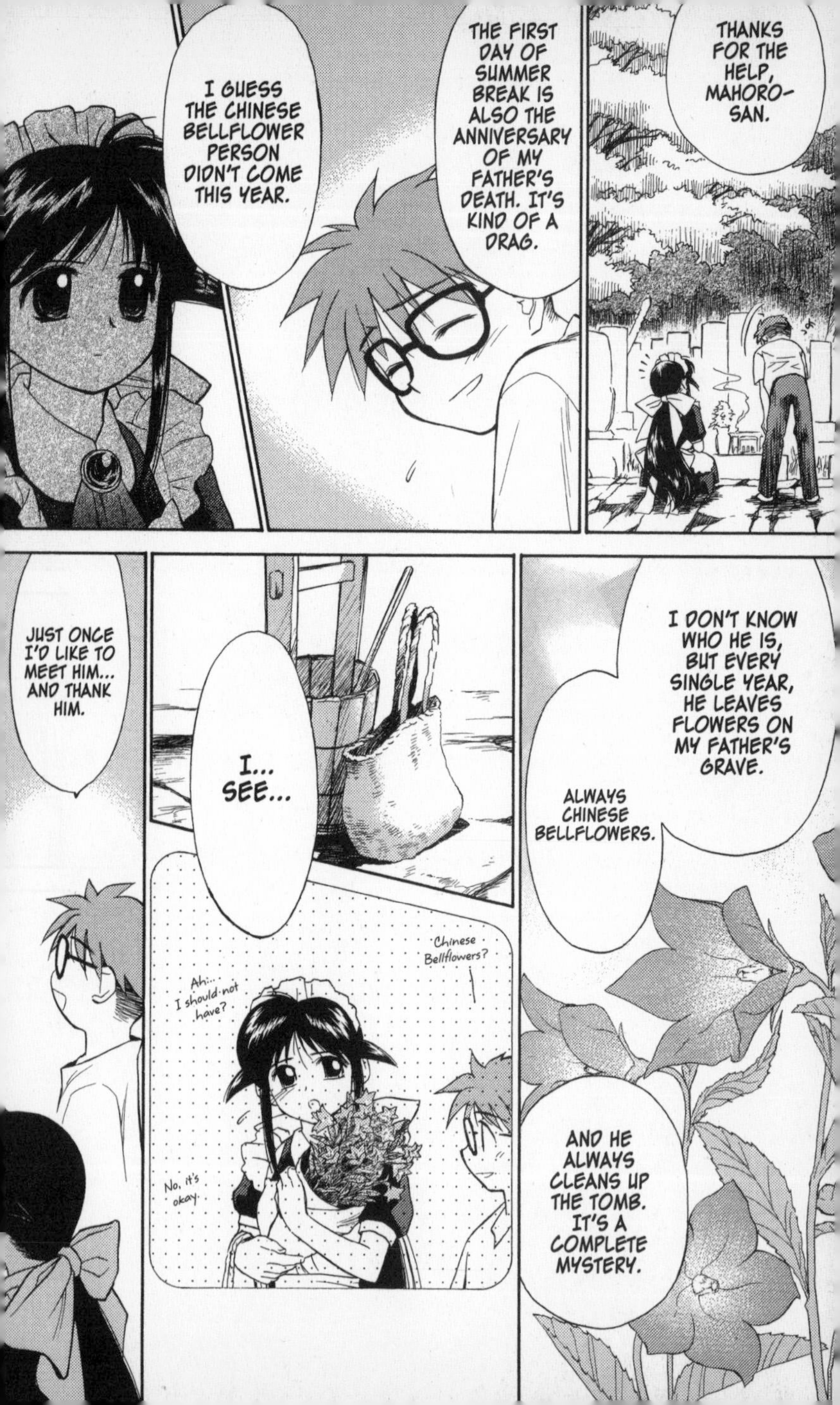
THANKS FOR THE HELP, MAHORO-SAN.
THE FIRST DAY OF SUMMER BREAK IS ALSO THE ANNIVERSARY OF MY FATHER'S DEATH. IT'S KIND OF A DRAG.
I GUESS THE CHINESE BELLFLOWER PERSON DIDN'T COME THIS YEAR.
I DON'T KNOW WHO HE IS, BUT EVERY SINGLE YEAR, HE LEAVES FLOWERS ON MY FATHER'S GRAVE.
ALWAYS CHINESE BELLFLOWERS.
AND HE ALWAYS CLEANS UP THE TOMB. IT'S A COMPLETE MYSTERY.
I... SEE...
Chinese Bellflowers?
Ah... I should not have?
No, it's okay.
JUST ONCE I'D LIKE TO MEET HIM... AND THANK HIM.

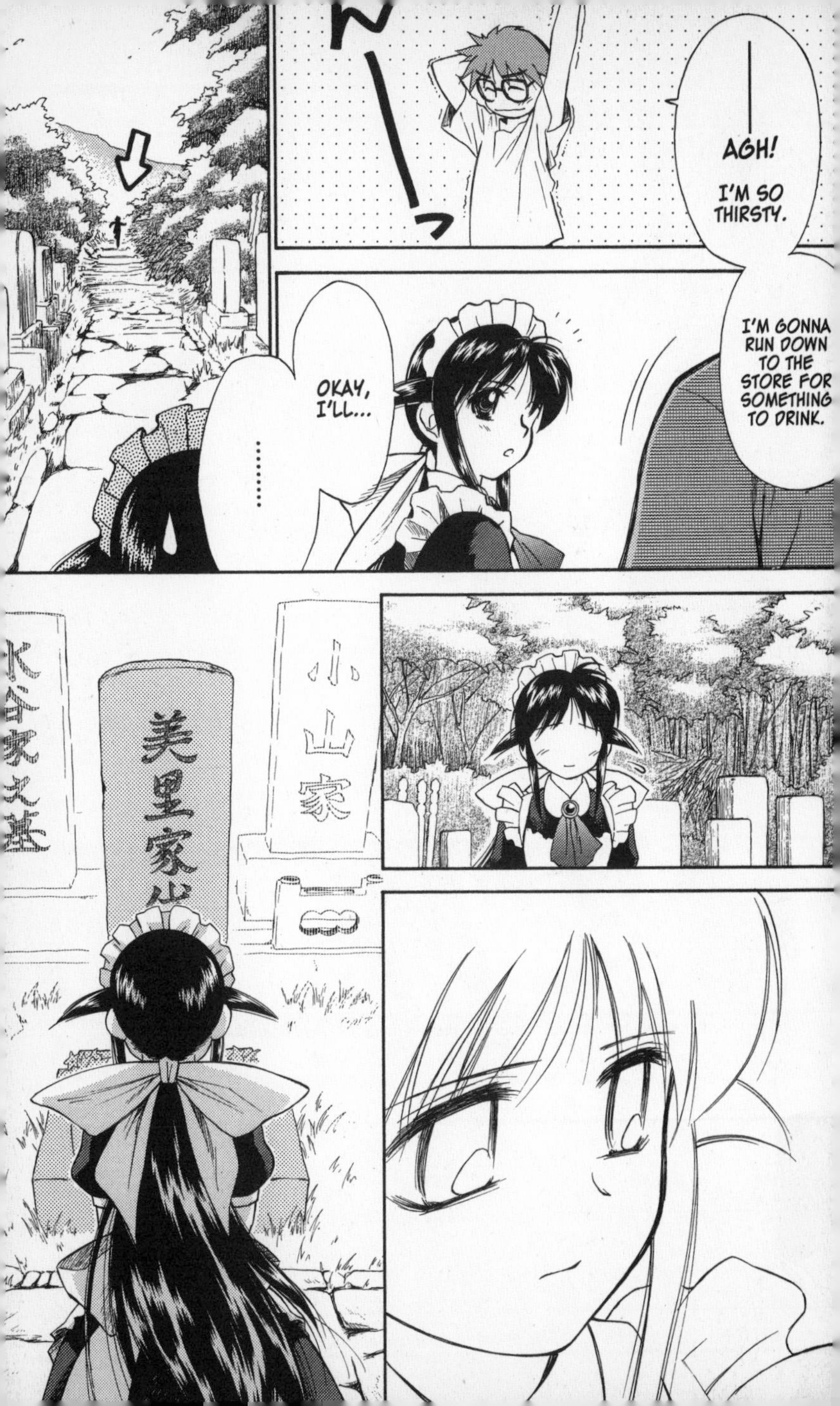
AGH!
I'M SO THIRSTY.
I'M GONNA RUN DOWN TO THE STORE FOR SOMETHING TO DRINK.
OKAY, I'LL...
......
小山家
美星家
谷家之墓

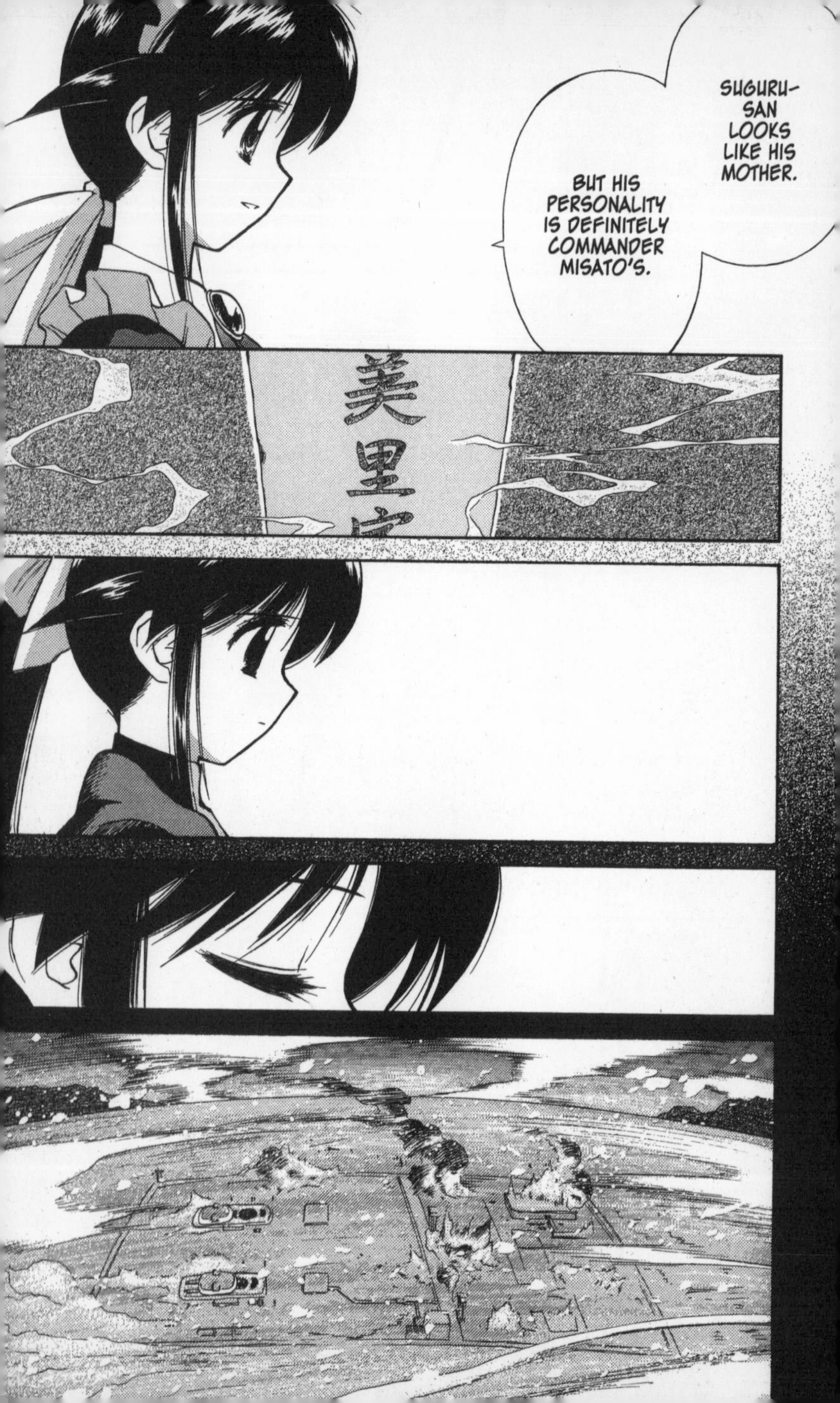
SUGURU-SAN LOOKS LIKE HIS MOTHER.
BUT HIS PERSONALITY IS DEFINITELY COMMANDER MISATO'S.
美里

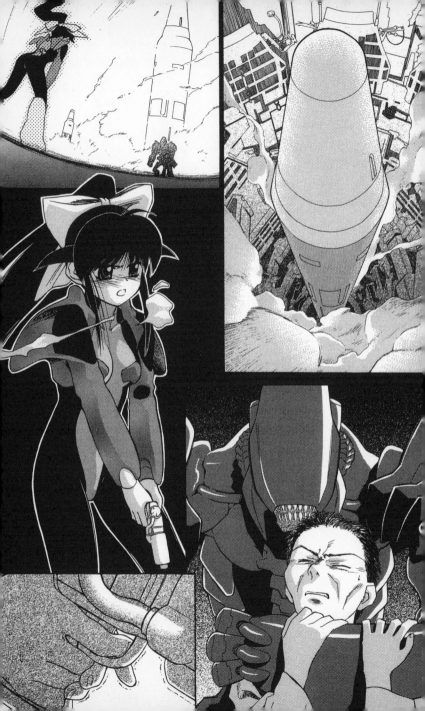

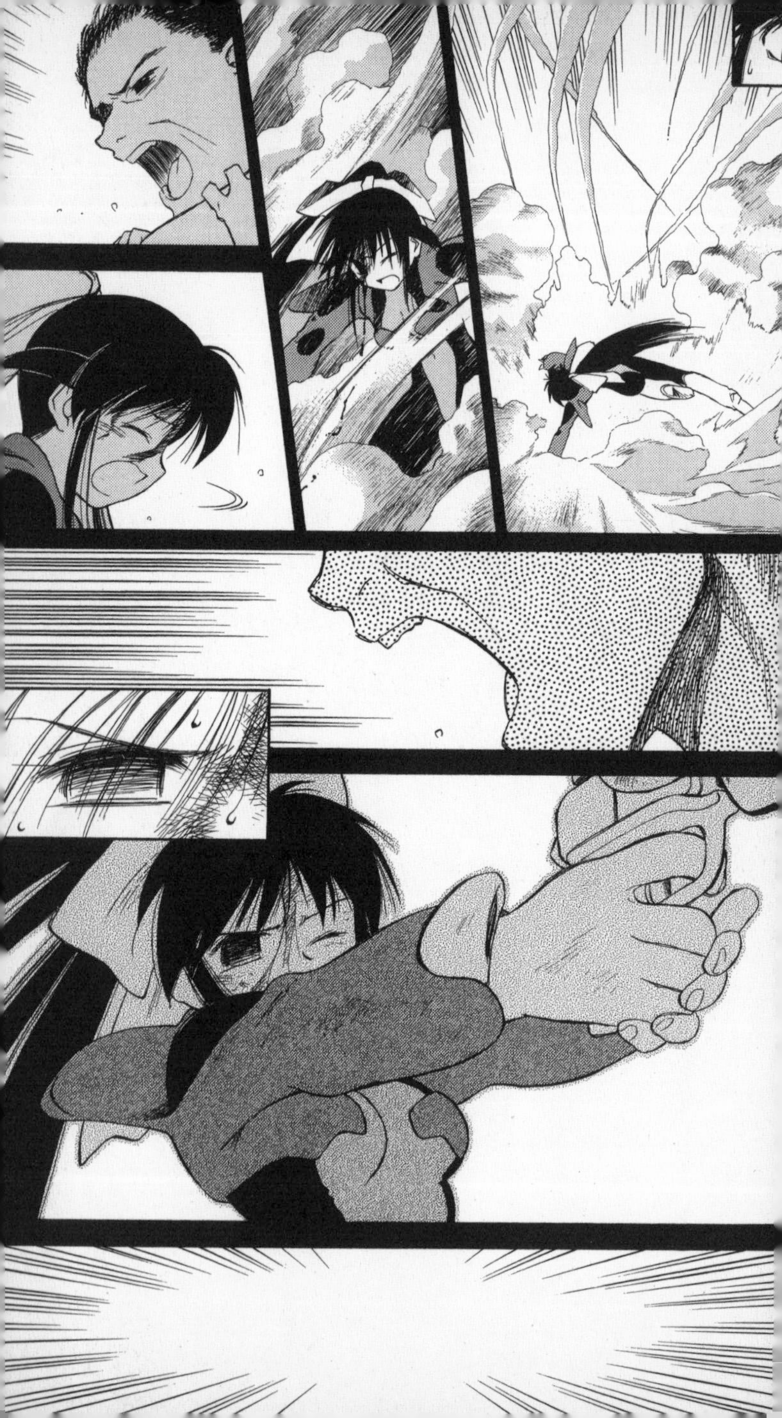

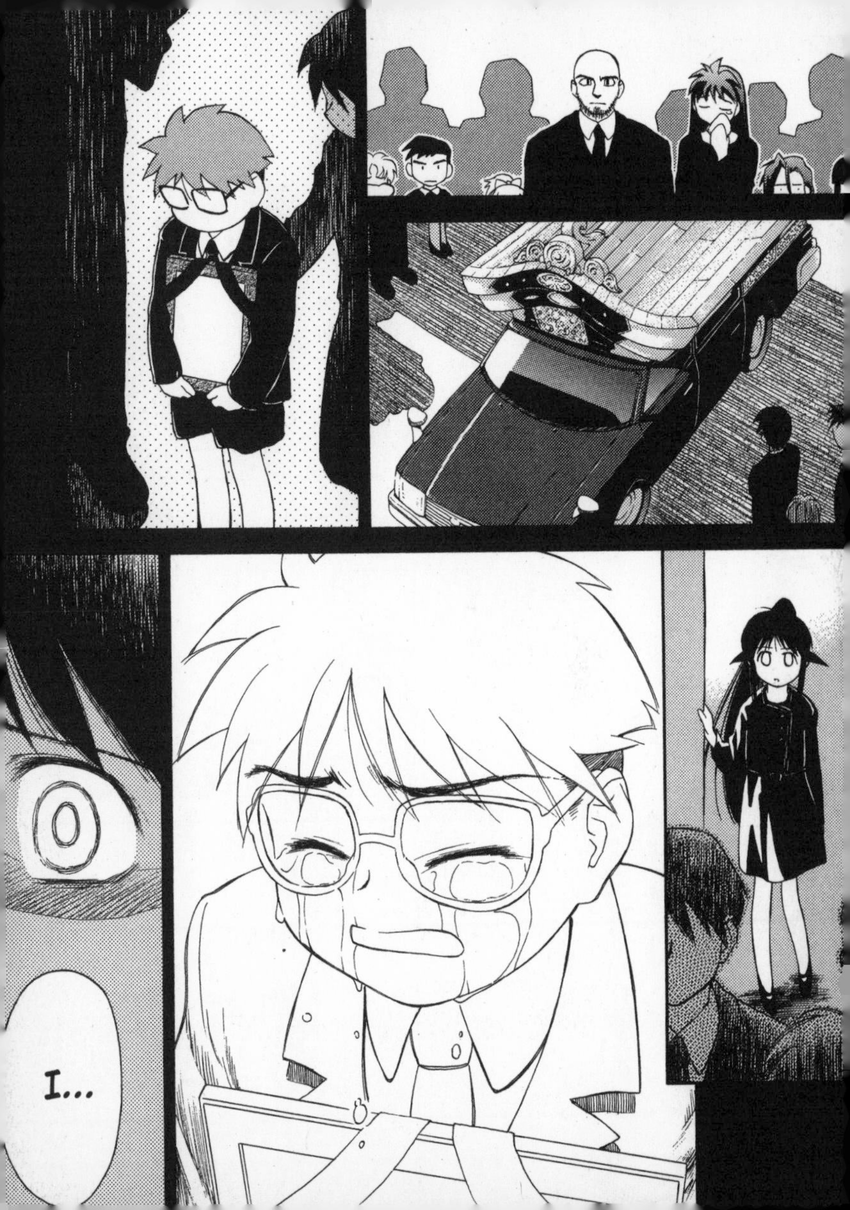
I...

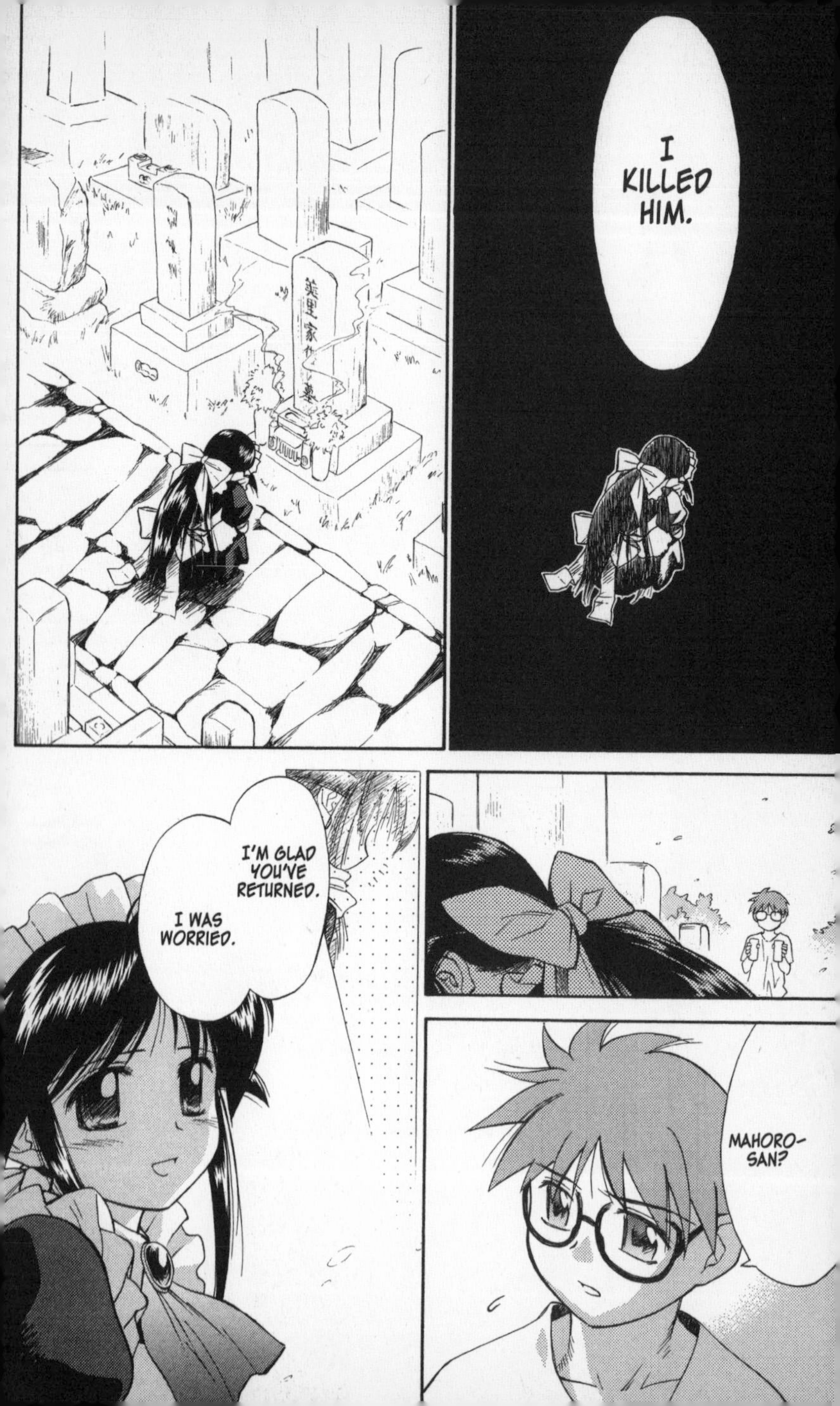
I KILLED HIM.
MAHORO-SAN?
I'M GLAD YOU'VE RETURNED.
I WAS WORRIED.

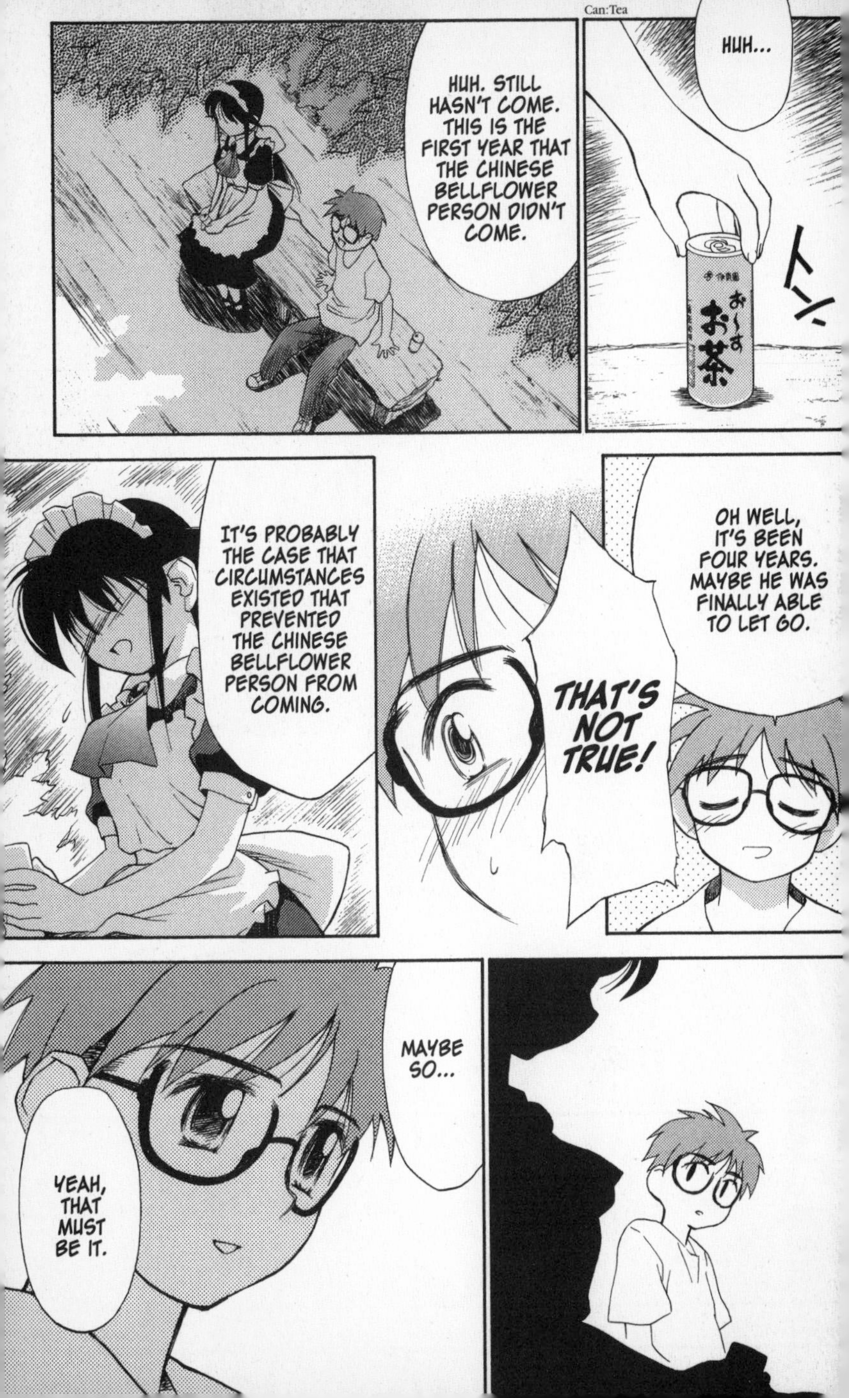
HUH...
トン
お〜い お茶
HUH. STILL HASN'T COME. THIS IS THE FIRST YEAR THAT THE CHINESE BELLFLOWER PERSON DIDN'T COME.
OH WELL, IT'S BEEN FOUR YEARS. MAYBE HE WAS FINALLY ABLE TO LET GO.
THAT'S NOT TRUE!
IT'S PROBABLY THE CASE THAT CIRCUMSTANCES EXISTED THAT PREVENTED THE CHINESE BELLFLOWER PERSON FROM COMING.
MAYBE SO...
YEAH, THAT MUST BE IT.

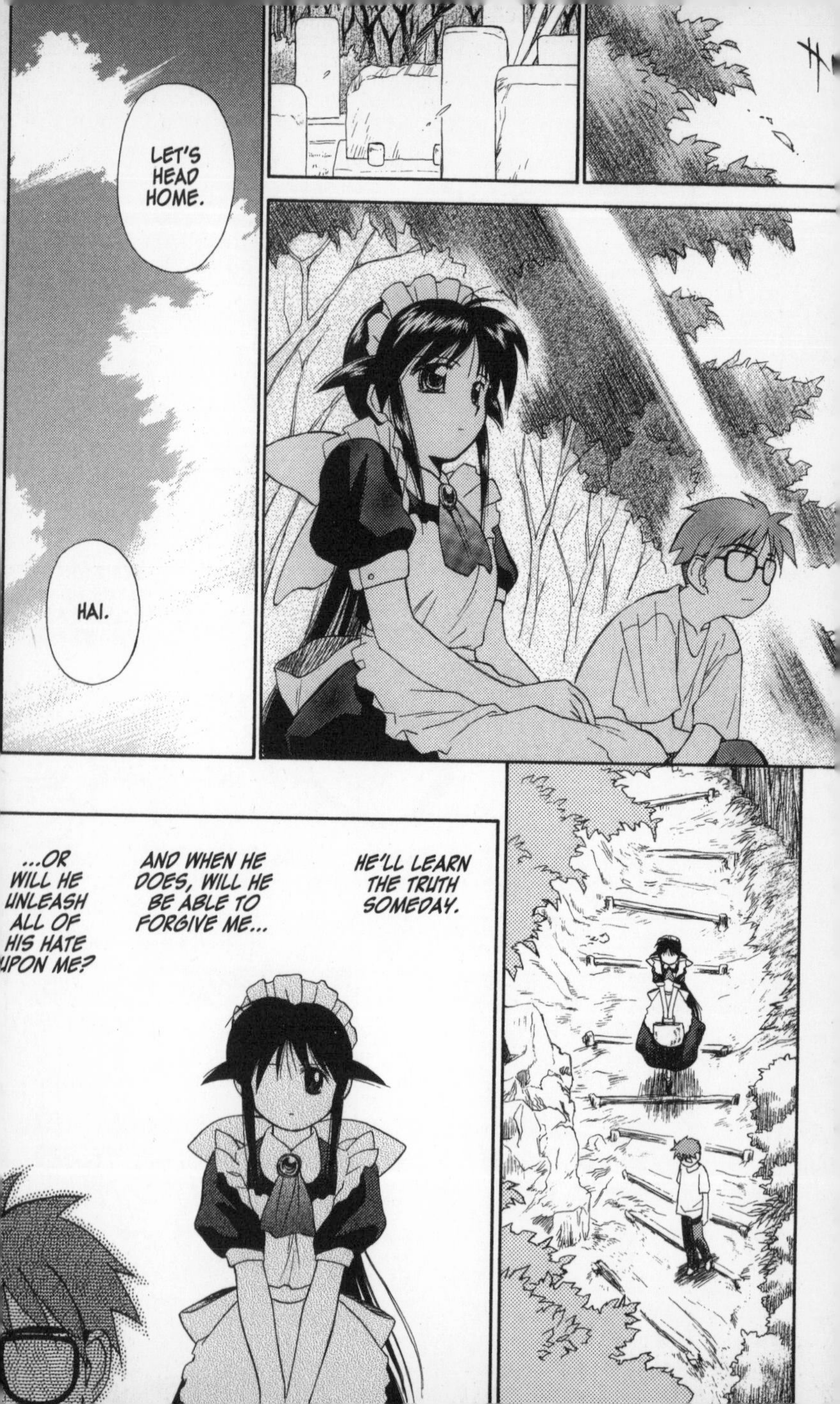
LET'S HEAD HOME.
HAI.
HE'LL LEARN THE TRUTH SOMEDAY.
AND WHEN HE DOES, WILL HE BE ABLE TO FORGIVE ME...
...OR WILL HE UNLEASH ALL OF HIS HATE UPON ME?

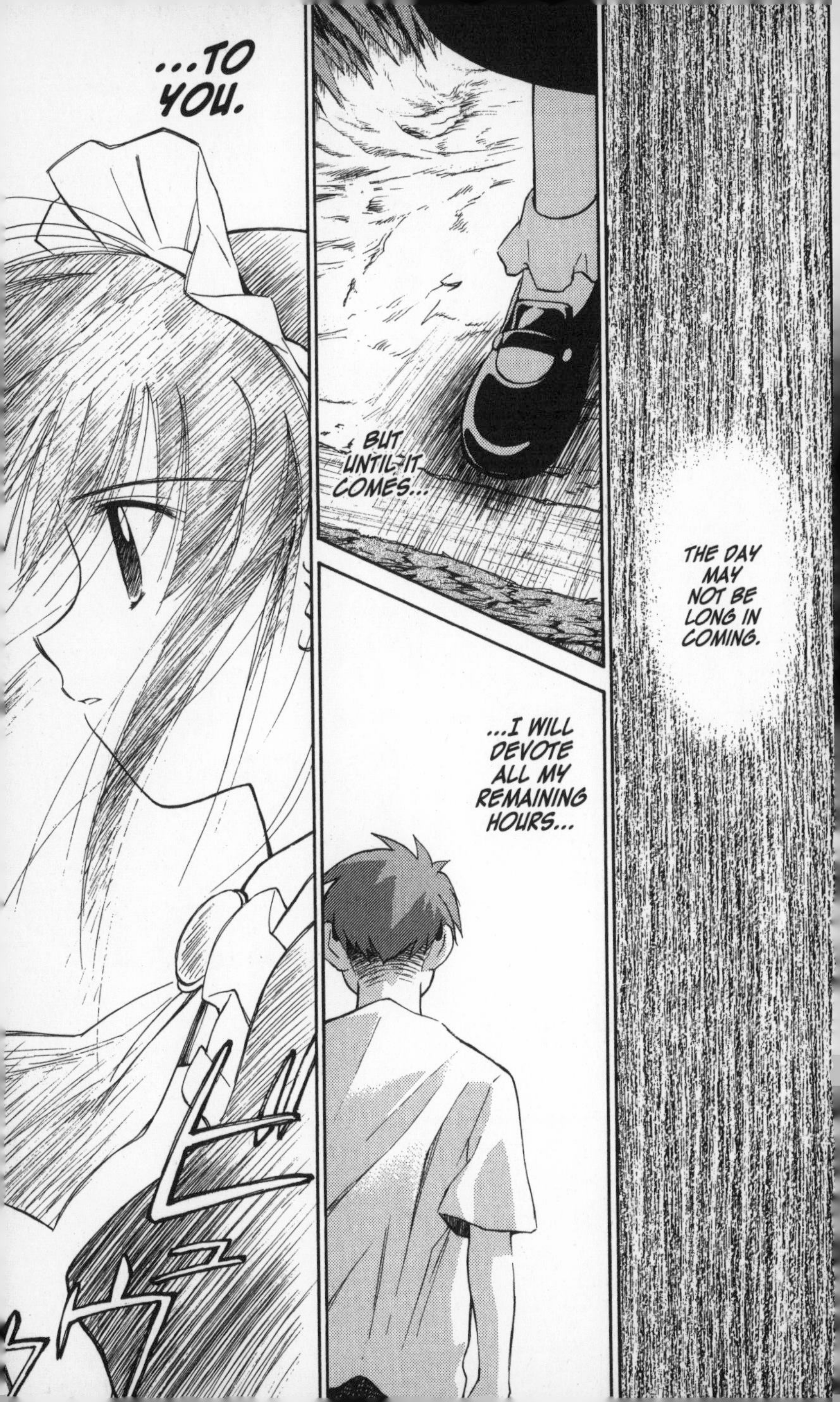
THE DAY MAY NOT BE LONG IN COMING.
BUT UNTIL IT COMES...
...I WILL DEVOTE ALL MY REMAINING HOURS...
...TO YOU.

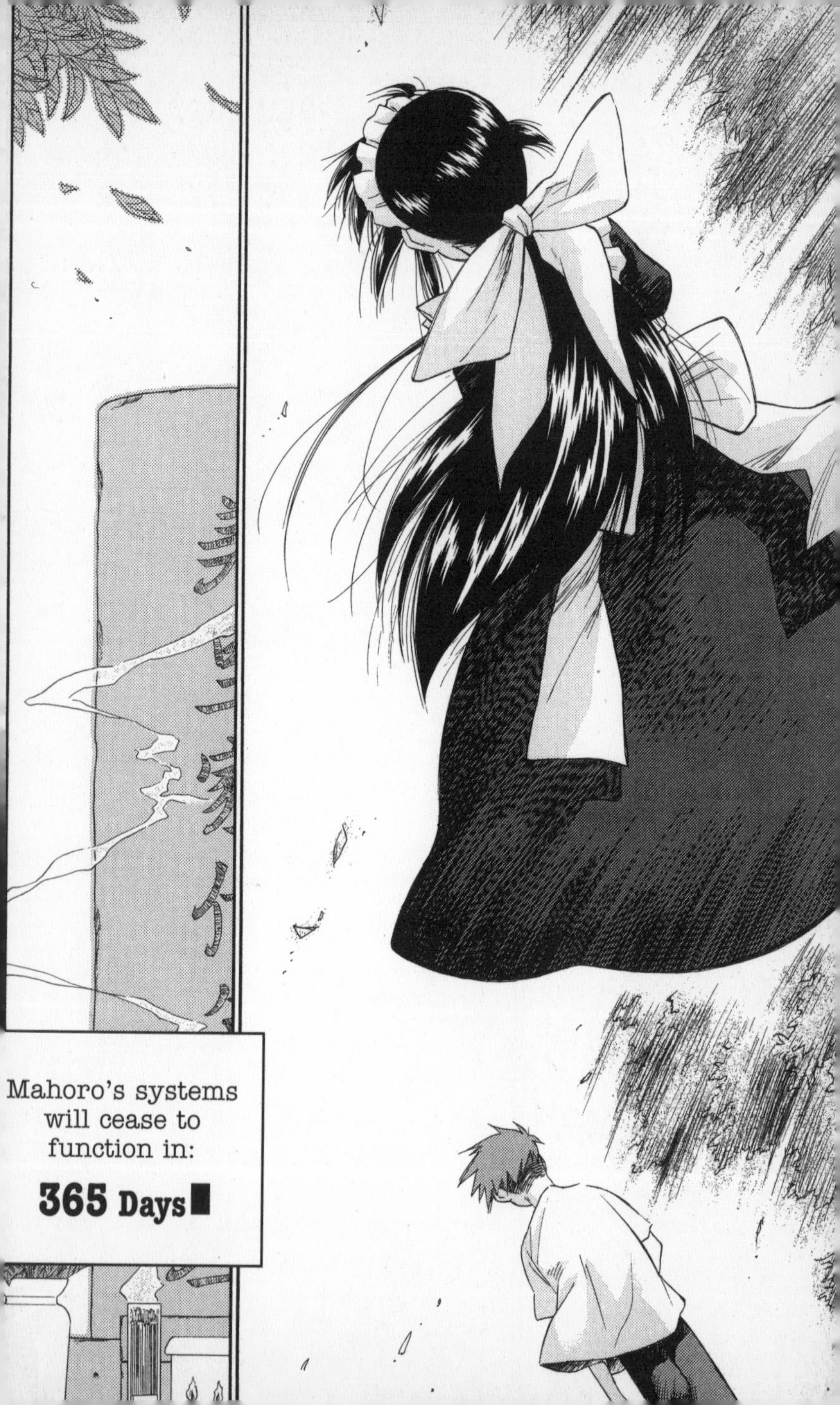
Mahoro's systems will cease to function in:
365 Days

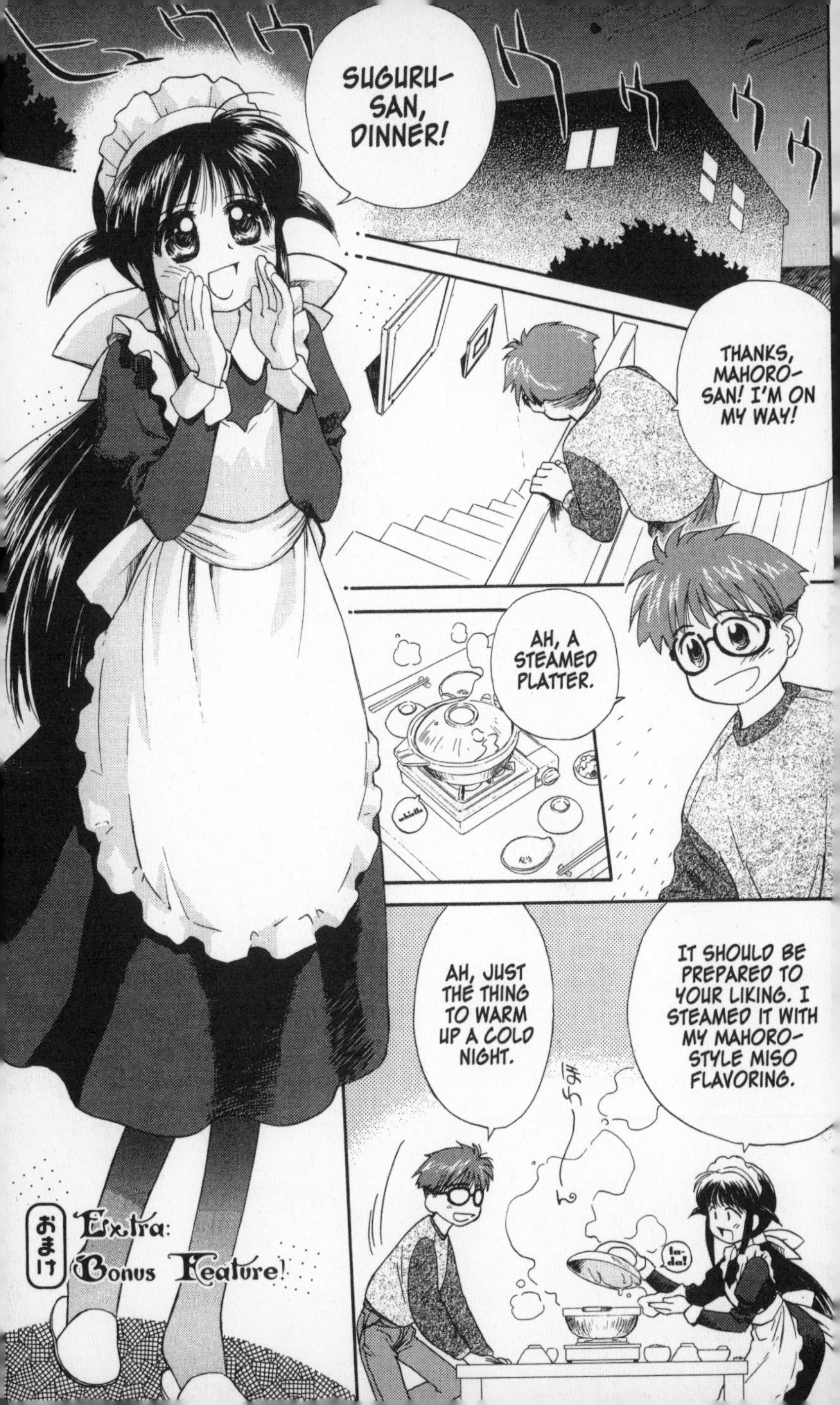
SUGURU-SAN, DINNER!
THANKS, MAHORO-SAN! I'M ON MY WAY!
AH, A STEAMED PLATTER.
whistle
IT SHOULD BE PREPARED TO YOUR LIKING. I STEAMED IT WITH MY MAHORO-STYLE MISO FLAVORING.
AH, JUST THE THING TO WARM UP A COLD NIGHT.
ta-da!
おまけ
Extra: Bonus Feature!

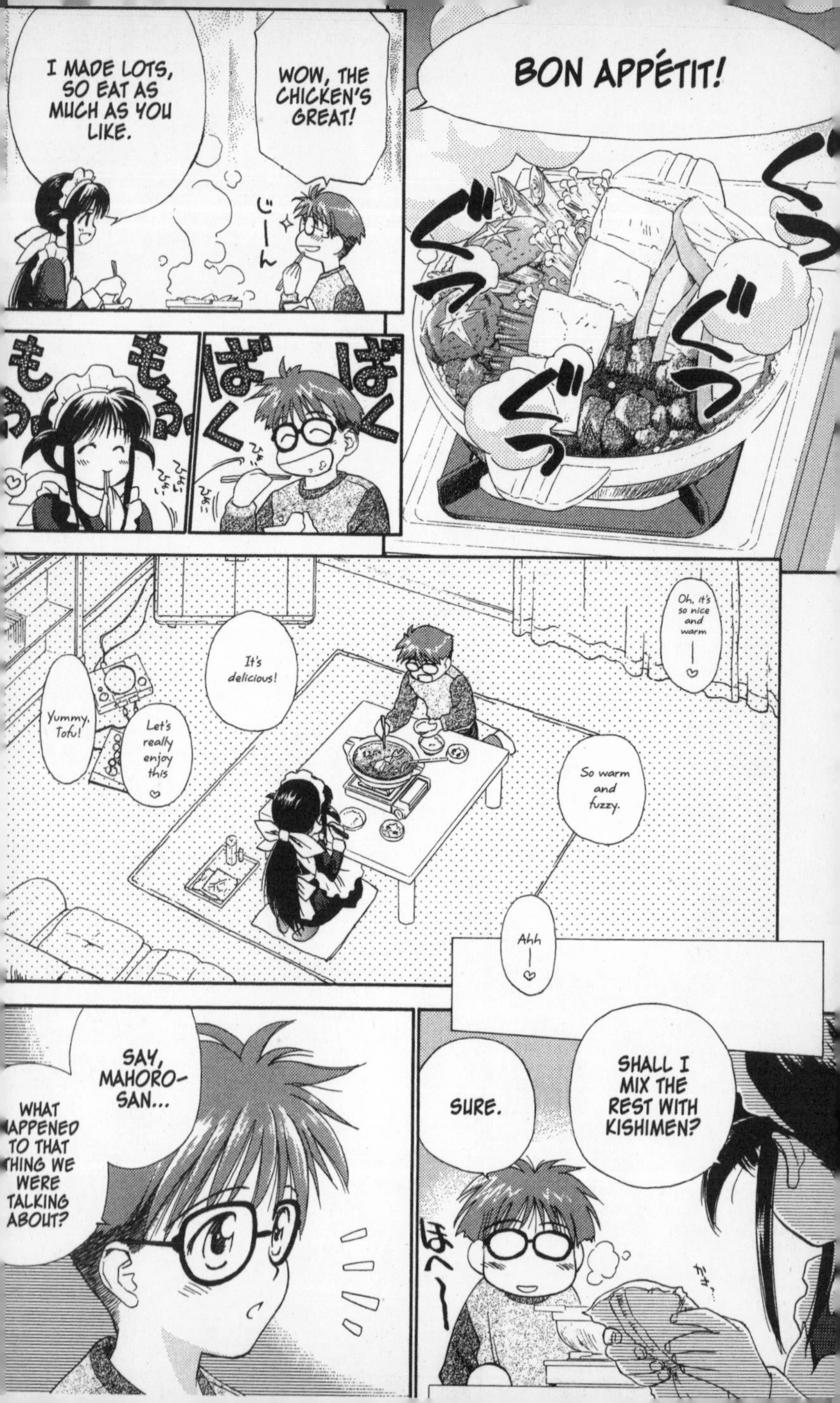
BON APPÉTIT!
ぐつぐつ
ぐつぐつ
ぐつ
WOW, THE CHICKEN'S GREAT!
じーん
I MADE LOTS, SO EAT AS MUCH AS YOU LIKE.
ばくばく
ひょい
Oh, it's so nice and warm ♡
So warm and fuzzy.
It's delicious!
Let's really enjoy this ♡
Yummy, Tofu!
Ahh ♡
SHALL I MIX THE REST WITH KISHIMEN?
SURE.
ほへ〜
SAY, MAHORO-SAN...
WHAT APPENED TO THAT HING WE WERE TALKING ABOUT?

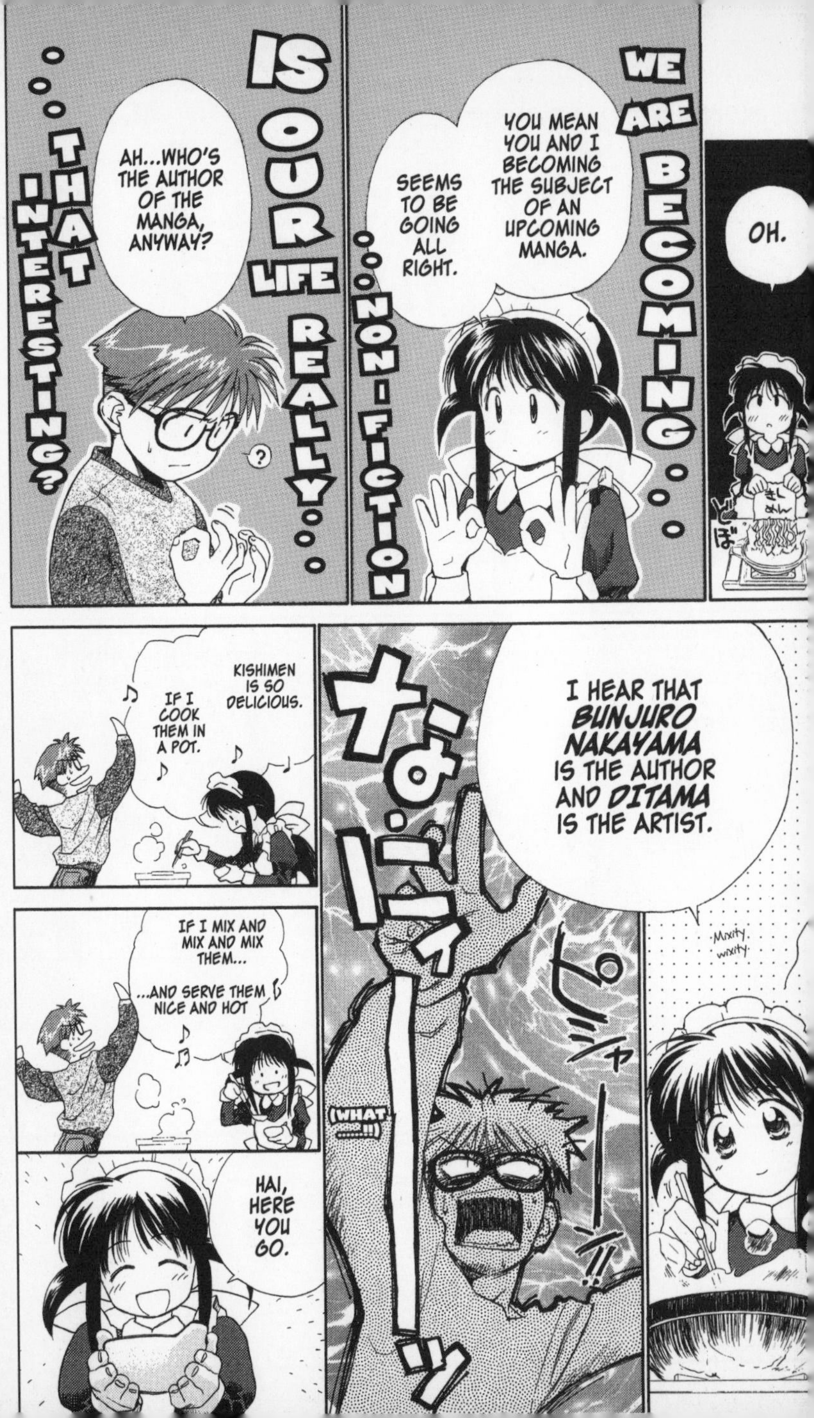
OH.
きしめん
どぼ
WE ARE BECOMING...
YOU MEAN YOU AND I BECOMING THE SUBJECT OF AN UPCOMING MANGA.
SEEMS TO BE GOING ALL RIGHT.
...NON-FICTION
IS OUR LIFE REALLY...
AH...WHO'S THE AUTHOR OF THE MANGA, ANYWAY?
?
...THAT INTERESTING?
I HEAR THAT *BUNJURO NAKAYAMA* IS THE AUTHOR AND *DITAMA* IS THE ARTIST.
Mixity. wixity.
なにィーーッ
ピシャーー!!
(WHAT......!!)
KISHIMEN IS SO DELICIOUS.
IF I COOK THEM IN A POT.
IF I MIX AND MIX AND MIX THEM...
...AND SERVE THEM NICE AND HOT
HAI, HERE YOU GO.

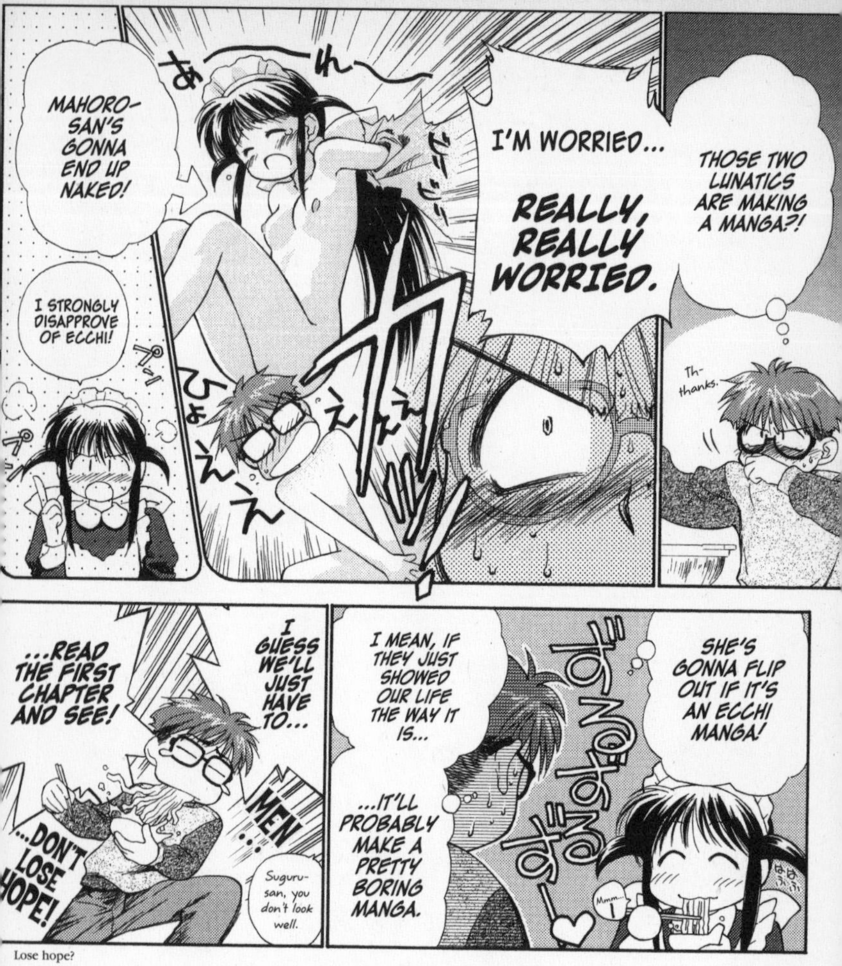
THOSE TWO LUNATICS ARE MAKING A MANGA?!
Th- thanks.
I'M WORRIED...
REALLY, REALLY WORRIED.
MAHORO-SAN'S GONNA END UP NAKED!
I STRONGLY DISAPPROVE OF ECCHI!
SHE'S GONNA FLIP OUT IF IT'S AN ECCHI MANGA!
I MEAN, IF THEY JUST SHOWED OUR LIFE THE WAY IT IS...
...IT'LL PROBABLY MAKE A PRETTY BORING MANGA.
Mmm...
I GUESS WE'LL JUST HAVE TO...
...READ THE FIRST CHAPTER AND SEE!
MEN...
Suguru-san, you don't look well.
...DON'T LOSE HOPE!

Lose hope?

These two may look normal at first glance, but they're not. First of all, who is the maid, Mahoro-san? Will the bond between Mahoro-san and Suguru-san grow? All these questions and more will be answered in the coming volumes of the most amazing manga ever written by man... Mahoromatic, Automatic Maiden.

When Suguru, Mahoro and company set off to the beach for a little hot fun in the sun, they get sand kicked in their faces as a giant crab battle robot emerges from the ocean. The Cloud Crab, originally designed to fight androids, has a screw loose, and now it wants to turn the female sunbathers into a topless—and bottomless—crowd! Well, Mahoro, ever willing to dive into the thick of danger, tightens up the straps of her bikini and vows to make crabmeat out of this robotic creep!

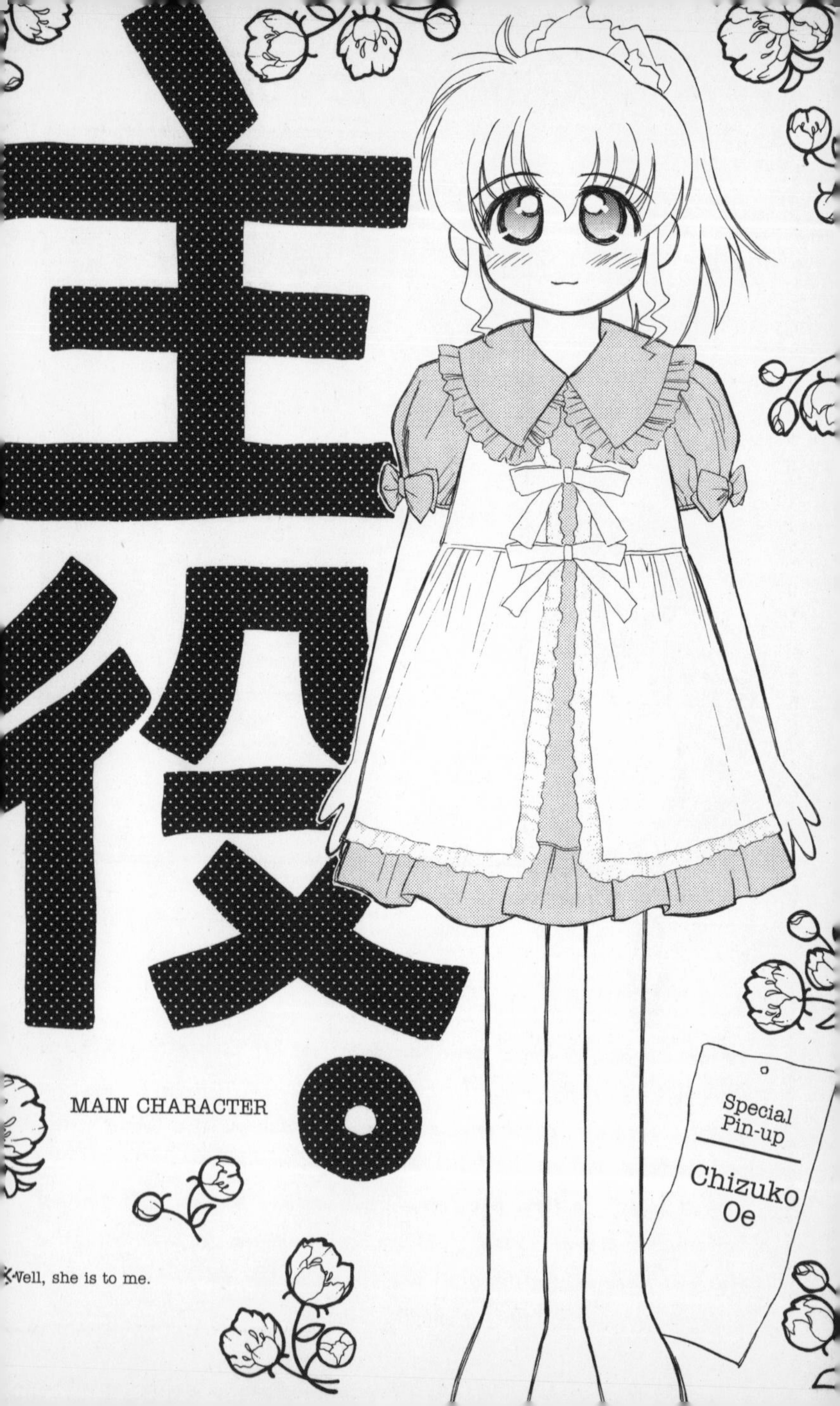
主役。
MAIN CHARACTER
※Well, she is to me.
Special Pin-up
Chizuko Oe

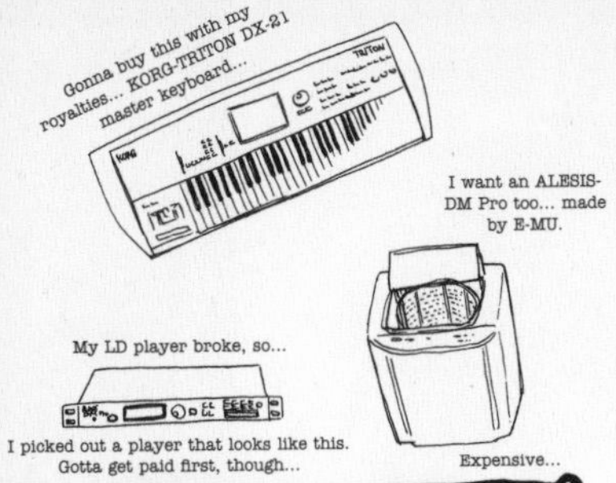
Gonna buy this with my royalties... KORG-TRITON DX-21 master keyboard...
I want an ALESIS-DM Pro too... made by E-MU.
My LD player broke, so...
I picked out a player that looks like this. Gotta get paid first, though...
Expensive...

Afterword

Phew. What to write, what to write... Oh, hello. I am DITAMA, Artist-in-Chief. There are many kinds of maids in this world. Wouldn't it be cool to have your own highly trained, modern maid? I'd just die. I'm one of the authors, so I wanted to say something. Hmm, what was it... this isn't really my thing... I'm supposed to write something down here, but I'm not really sure what. The other author, Nakayama-san, says "So write some poetry." I'm not very good at poetry either :] ....Now, what to do... If I think for a bit, something'll come to me for sure.

Hmm... what do I write......?

Let's see... The author does his work before the manga artists begin. I don't mind that at all. Nakayama-san draws up all the scenarios; I do the other 95% of the work, like page layout, names, presenting characters... all sorts of things :] Lots of stuff, huh? I realize you don't know me very well, but you may have noticed my disorder while reading. Mmm? ... Well if you didn't, my disorder is breast fascination :]. Large breasts, to be precise. People around me say, "That guy in the manga's just like you." I think so, too. I even put big breasts on mecha. Would be super hard to draw if I couldn't throw in stuff like that at all. It's a tough job, but someone has to do it... That's my part of the manga creation process. I always seem to think, "It could be just a little better..." There's only so many pages to work with though [^^;].

Ah, I know! My thoughts about refining the characters. They're not very complicated thoughts, though. Forgive me. I think we were worried about normal things for authors (like if Miyuki should have a younger speaking style)...

Here's some of the names from my original manuscript:

- Sama Tengu
- Kasumi Nakayama
- Osuhi Kenkan

Oh, the shame! We'll never get another job again...!! Er... that's overreacting a little, huh? We'll live somehow.

Phew... done...
August 1999

"Mahoromatic" is another DITAMA production. Wai!

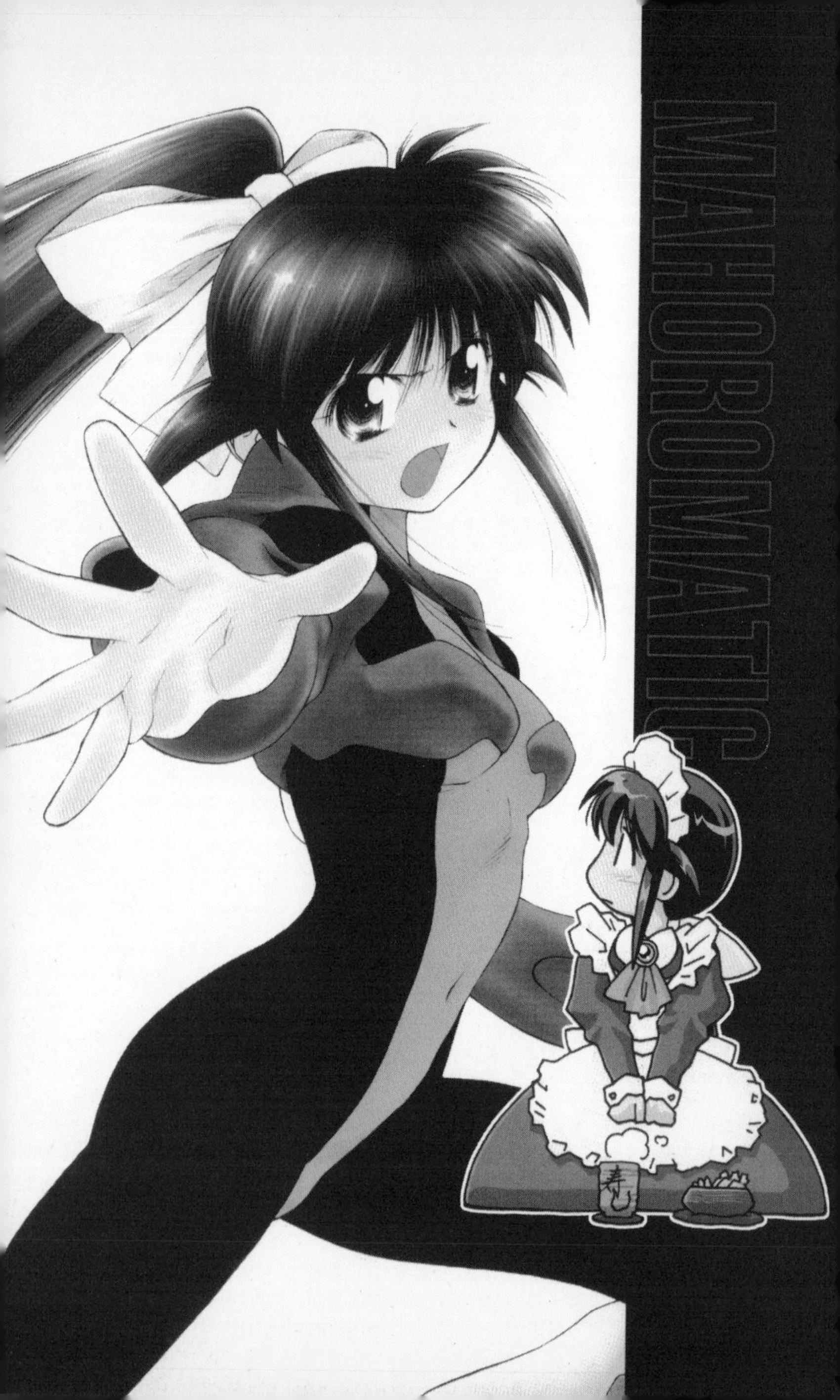
MAHOROMATIC
寿

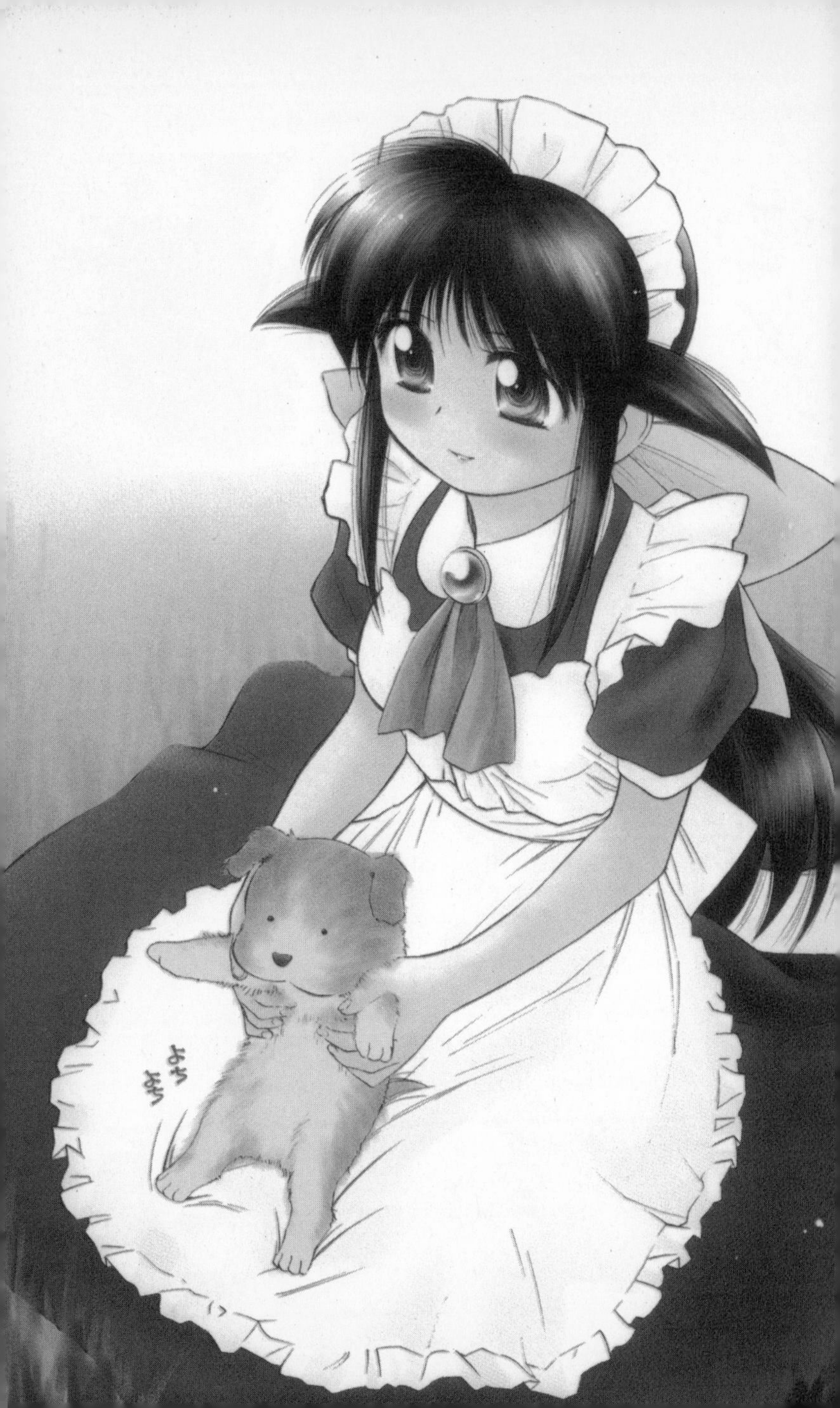
よちよち

Translator - Jeremiah Bourque
English Adaptation - Anna Wenger
Retouch and Lettering - Jose Macasocol, Jr.
Cover Layout - Patrick Hook

Editor - Luis Reyes
Digital Imaging Manager - Chris Buford
Pre-Press Manager - Antonio DePietro
Production Managers - Jennifer Miller, Mutsumi Miyazaki
Art Director - Matt Alford
Managing Editor - Jill Freshney
VP of Production - Ron Klamert
President & C.O.O. - John Parker
Publisher & C.E.O. - Stuart Levy

E-mail: info@TOKYOPOP.com
Come visit us online at www.TOKYOPOP.com

A  Manga

TOKYOPOP Inc.
5900 Wilshire Blvd. Suite 2000
Los Angeles, CA 90036

Mahoromatic: Automatic Maiden Vol. 1

ISBN: 1-59182-729-9

First TOKYOPOP printing: May 2004

10 9 8 7 6 5 4 3 2 1

Printed in the USA

GIRLS WITH HUMAN HEARTS
AND MECHANICAL BODIES
ARE BOUND TO HAVE PROBLEM

100% AUTHENTIC MANGA

Saber Marionette J

STORY BY SATORU AKAHORI
ART BY YUMISUKE KOTOYOSHI

AVAILABLE NOW AT YOUR FAVORITE
BOOK AND COMIC STORES

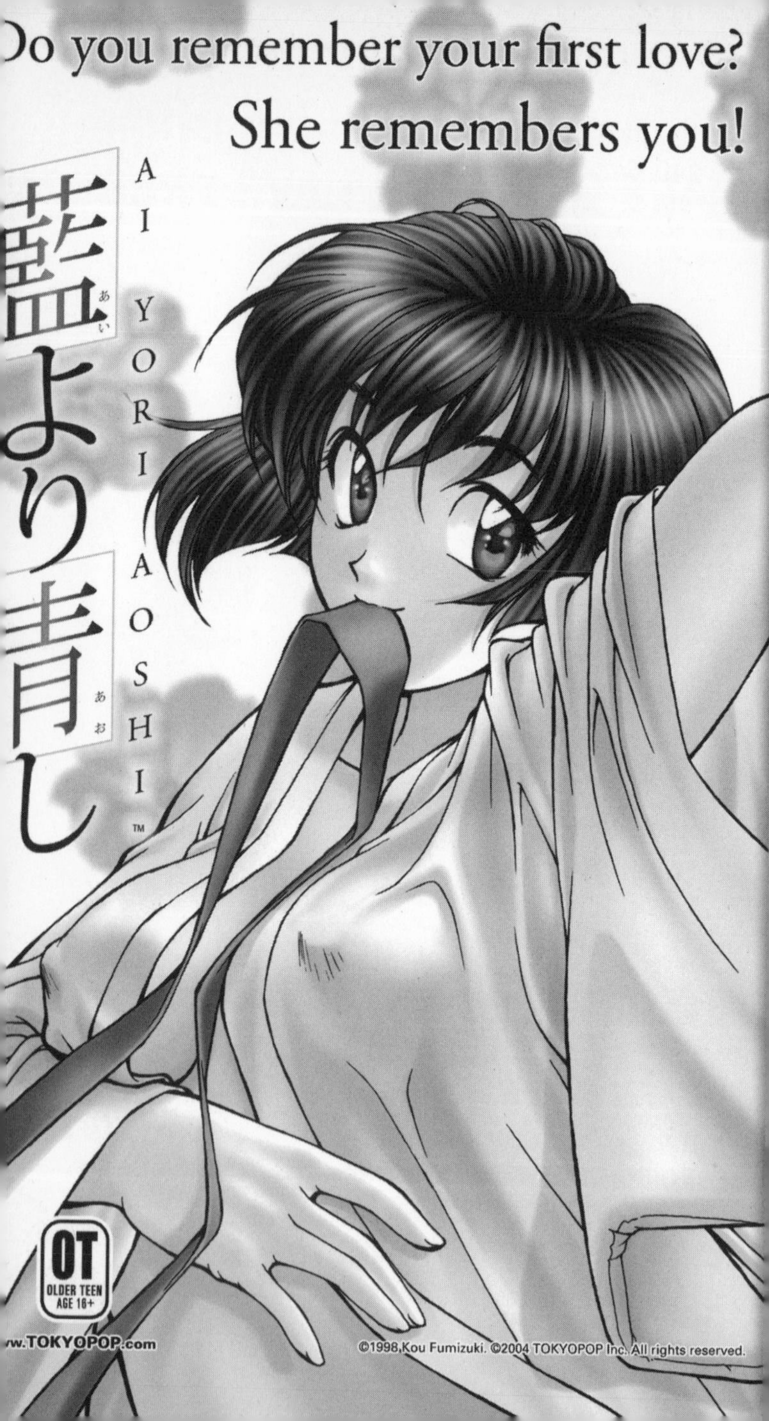
)o you remember your first love?
She remembers you!
藍より青し
AI YORI AOSHI™
あい
あお
OT
OLDER TEEN AGE 16+
w.TOKYOPOP.com
©1998 Kou Fumizuki. ©2004 TOKYOPOP Inc. All rights reserved.

TOKYOPOP
From the creator of the #1 best seller Love Hina
A.I. LOVE YOU™
by Ken Akamatsu
A.I. Program Thirty became a real girl...
Can she turn her creator into a real man?
OT
OLDER TEEN AGE 16+
©1999 Ken Akamatsu. ©2004 TOKYOPOP inc. All Rights Reserved.
www.TOKYOPOP

PSYCHIC ACADEMY™

You don't have to be a great psychic to be a great hero

. . . but it helps.

TOKYOPOP®

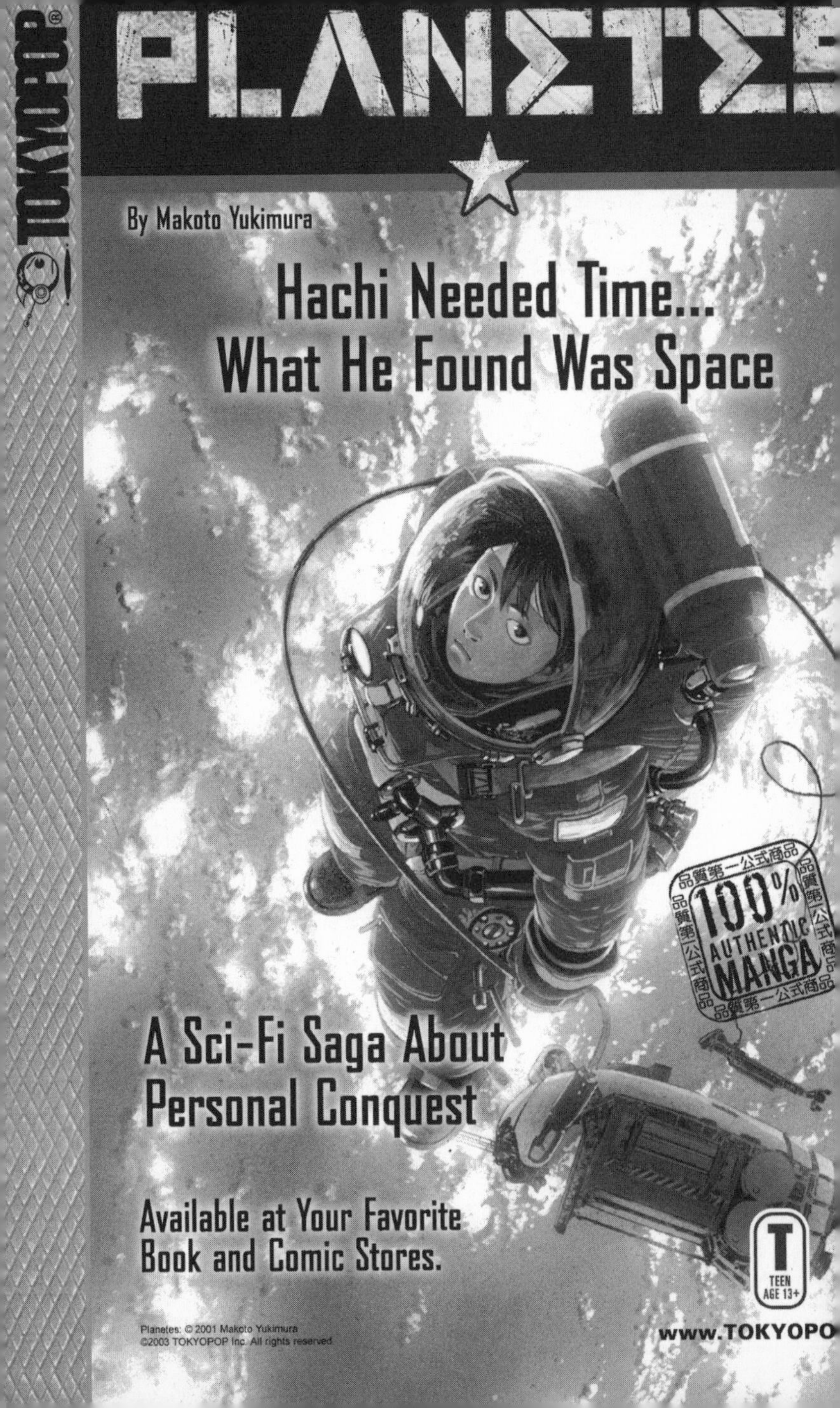
TOKYOPOP
PLANETES
By Makoto Yukimura
Hachi Needed Time...
What He Found Was Space
品質第一公式商品
100% AUTHENTIC MANGA
A Sci-Fi Saga About
Personal Conquest
Available at Your Favorite
Book and Comic Stores.
T
TEEN
AGE 13+
Planetes: © 2001 Makoto Yukimura
©2003 TOKYOPOP Inc. All rights reserved.
www.TOKYOPO

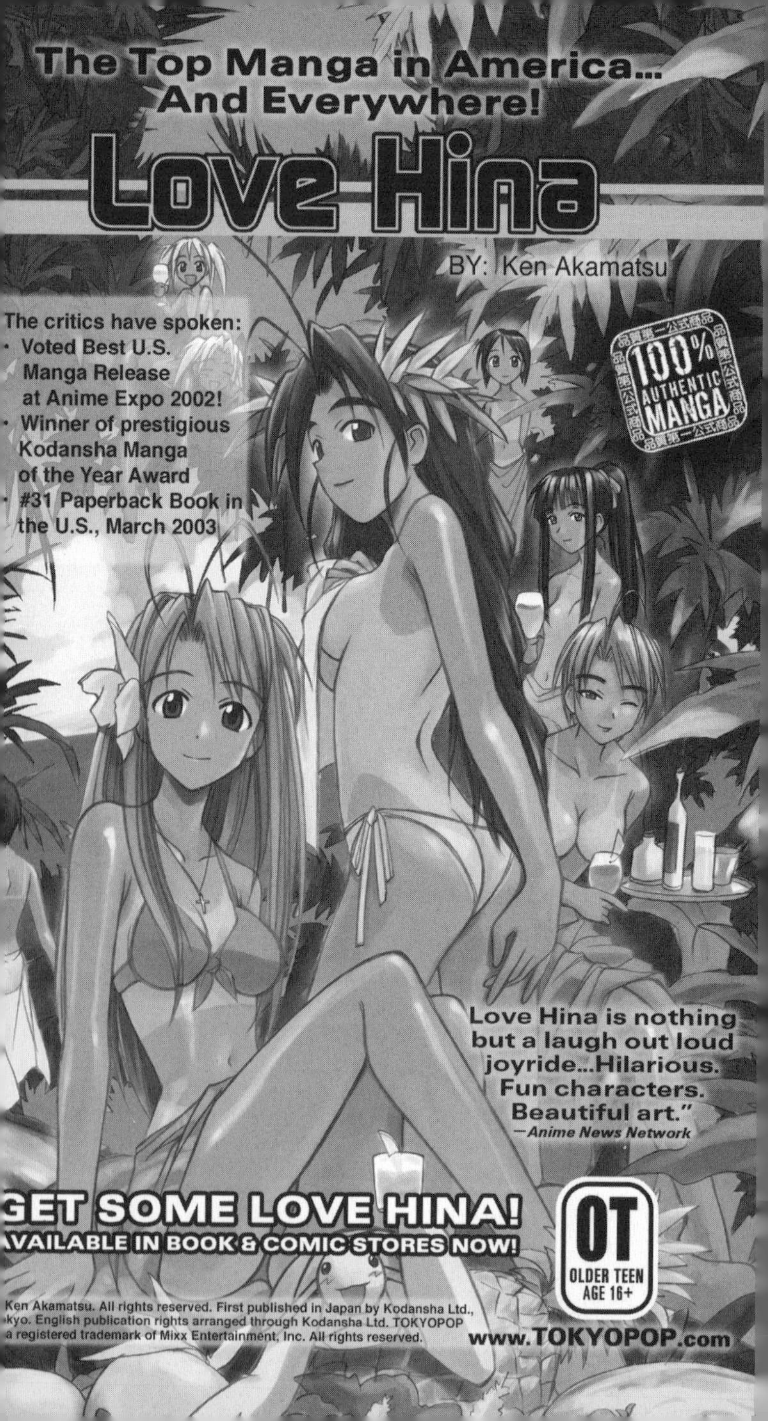

TOKYOPOP
GTO
GREAT TEACHER ONIZUKA
AS SEEN ON SHOWTIME!
DVD VIDEO
NO BIG EYES
NO MAGICAL POWERS
NO GIANT ROBOTS
OT OLDER TEEN AGE 16+
©Tohru Fujisawa – KODANSHA – FUJI TV – SME Visual Works – ST. PIERROT.
©2002 TOKYOPOP Inc. All Rights Reserved.
www.TOKYOPOP

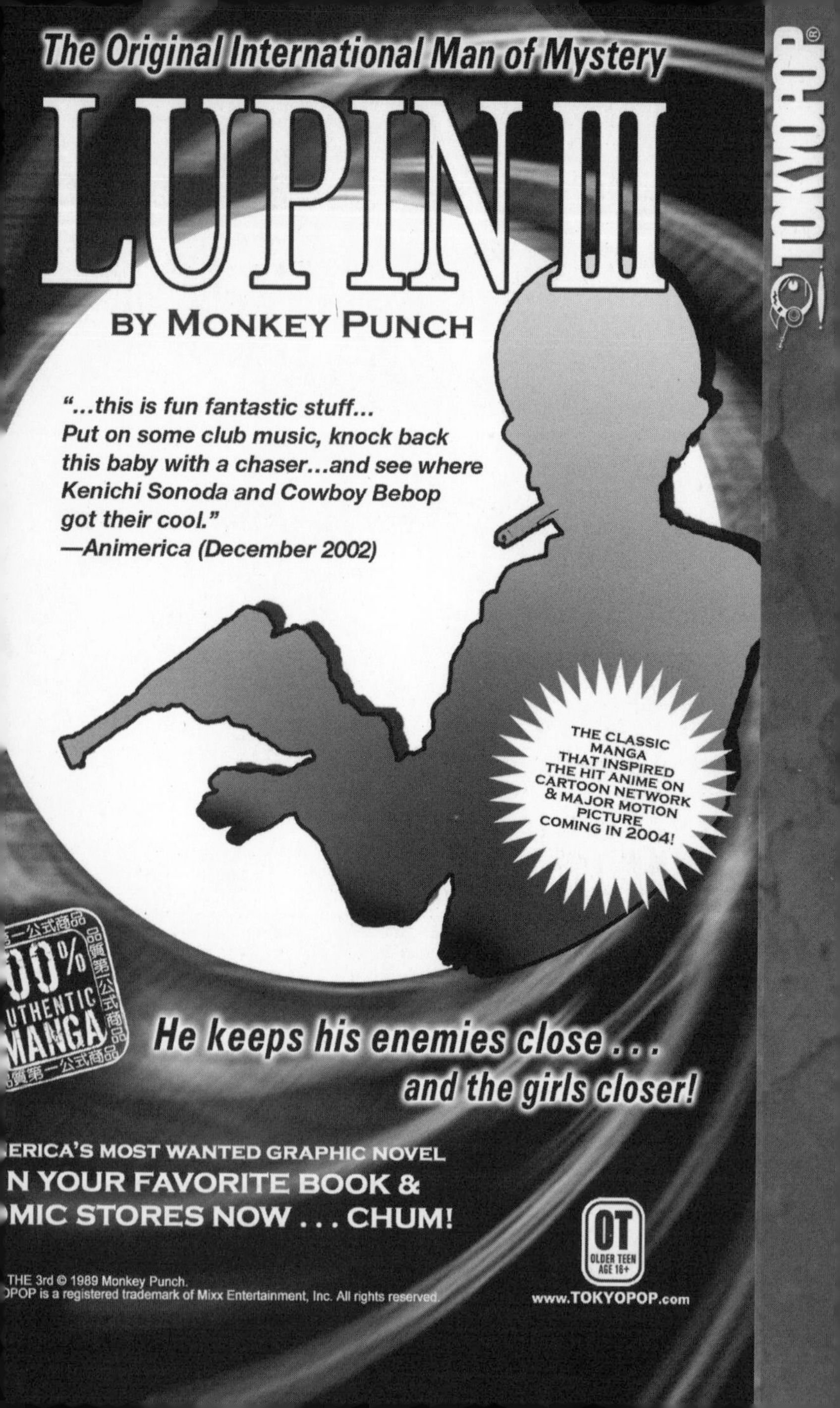
The Original International Man of Mystery
LUPIN III
BY MONKEY PUNCH
"...this is fun fantastic stuff... Put on some club music, knock back this baby with a chaser...and see where Kenichi Sonoda and Cowboy Bebop got their cool."
—Animerica (December 2002)
THE CLASSIC MANGA THAT INSPIRED THE HIT ANIME ON CARTOON NETWORK & MAJOR MOTION PICTURE COMING IN 2004!
00% UTHENTIC MANGA
He keeps his enemies close . . .
. . . and the girls closer!
ERICA'S MOST WANTED GRAPHIC NOVEL
N YOUR FAVORITE BOOK &
MIC STORES NOW . . . CHUM!
OT OLDER TEEN AGE 16+
THE 3rd © 1989 Monkey Punch.
POP is a registered trademark of Mixx Entertainment, Inc. All rights reserved.
www.TOKYOPOP.com
TOKYOPOP®

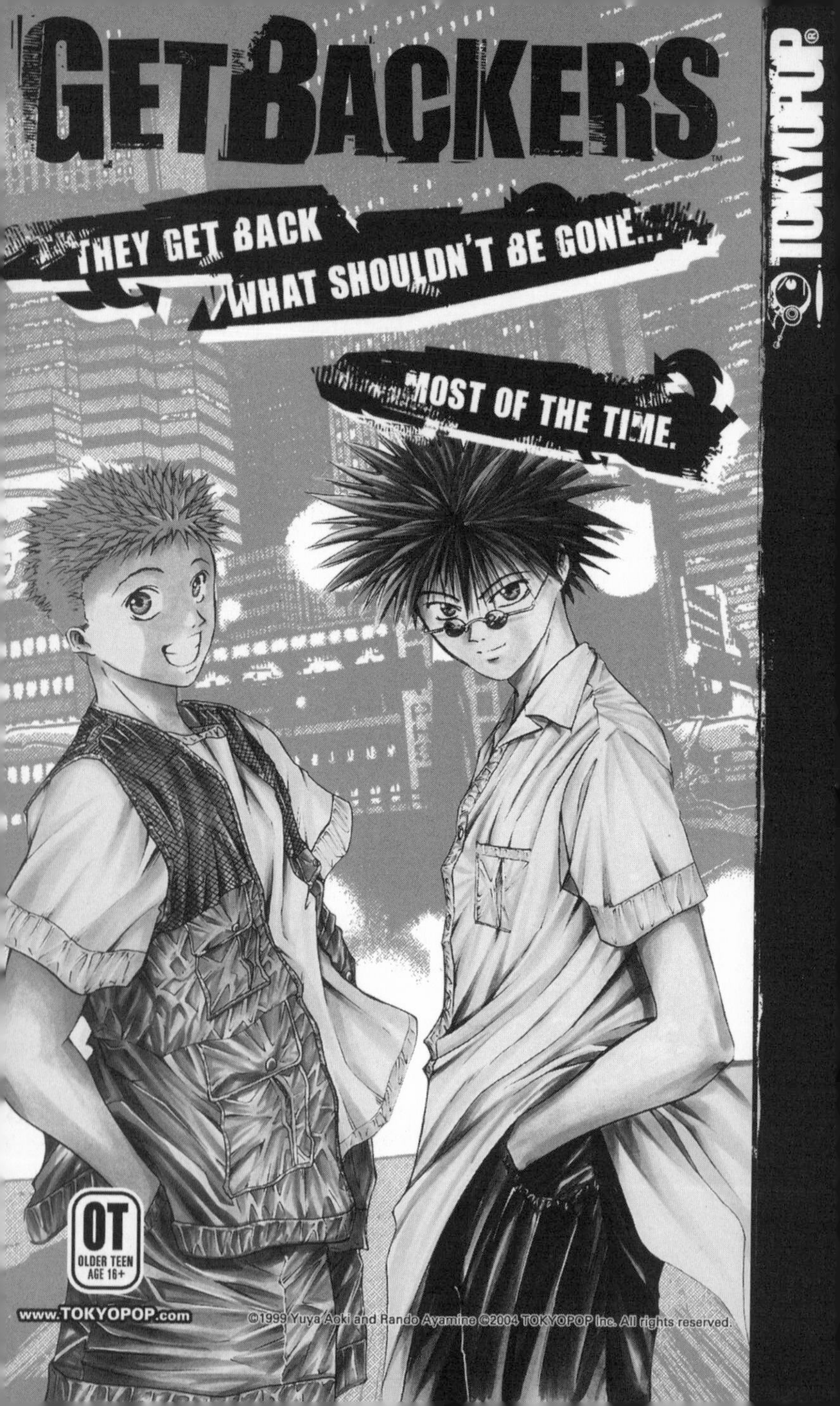
GETBACKERS™
THEY GET BACK WHAT SHOULDN'T BE GONE...
MOST OF THE TIME.
TOKYOPOP®
OT
OLDER TEEN AGE 16+
www.TOKYOPOP.com
©1999 Yuya Aoki and Rando Ayamine ©2004 TOKYOPOP Inc. All rights reserved.

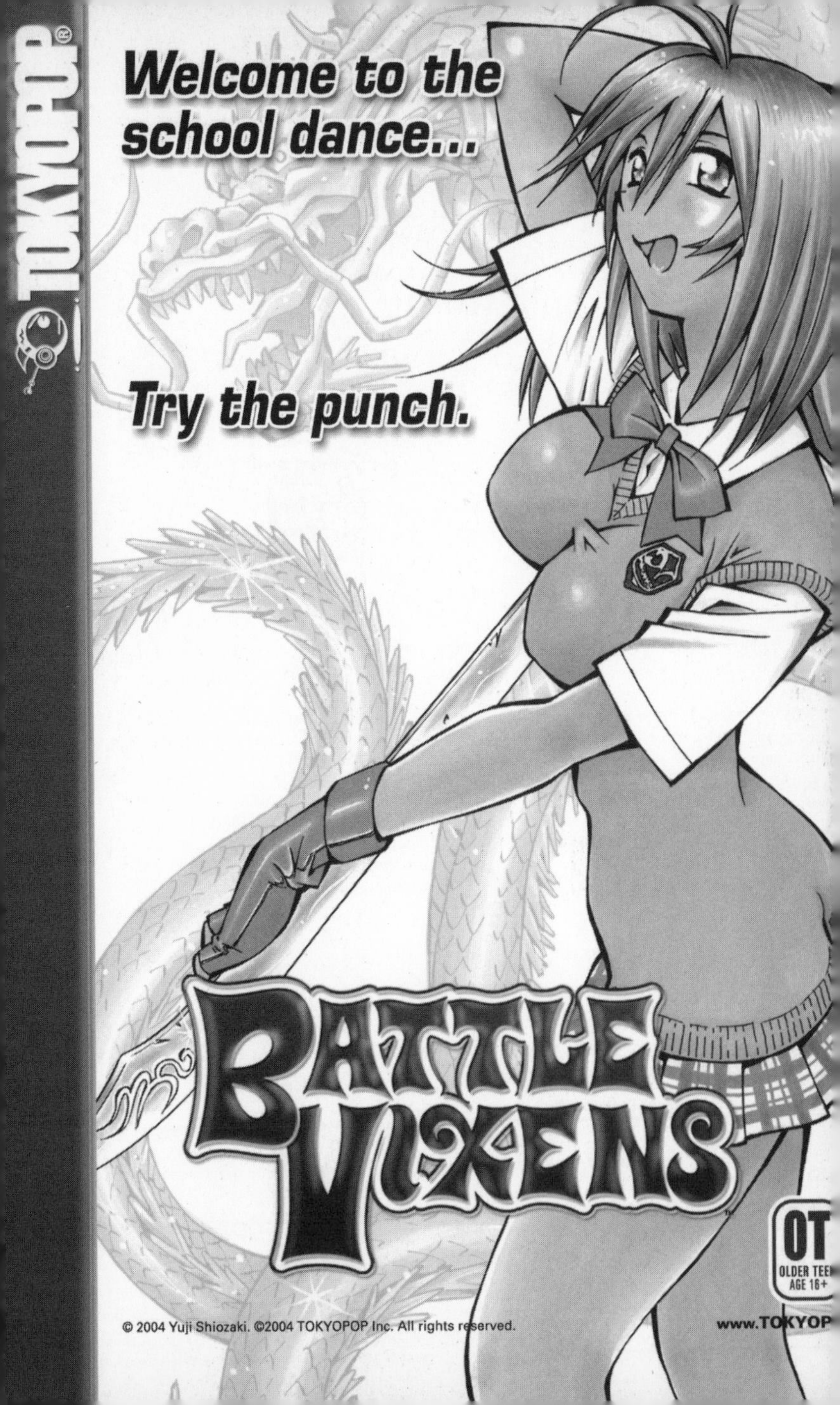
TOKYOPOP
Welcome to the school dance...
Try the punch.
BATTLE VIXENS
OT OLDER TEEN AGE 16+
© 2004 Yuji Shiozaki. ©2004 TOKYOPOP Inc. All rights reserved.
www.TOKYOP

ALSO AVAILABLE FROM TOKYOPOP®

MANGA

.HACK//LEGEND OF THE TWILIGHT
@LARGE
ABENOBASHI: MAGICAL SHOPPING ARCADE
A.I. LOVE YOU
AI YORI AOSHI
ANGELIC LAYER
ARM OF KANNON
BABY BIRTH
BATTLE ROYALE
BATTLE VIXENS
BRAIN POWERED
BRIGADOON
B'TX
CANDIDATE FOR GODDESS, THE
CARDCAPTOR SAKURA
CARDCAPTOR SAKURA - MASTER OF THE CLOW
CHOBITS
CHRONICLES OF THE CURSED SWORD
CLAMP SCHOOL DETECTIVES
CLOVER
COMIC PARTY
CONFIDENTIAL CONFESSIONS
CORRECTOR YUI
COWBOY BEBOP
COWBOY BEBOP: SHOOTING STAR
CRAZY LOVE STORY
CRESCENT MOON
CULDCEPT
CYBORG 009
D•N•ANGEL
DEMON DIARY
DEMON ORORON, THE
DEUS VITAE
DIGIMON
DIGIMON TAMERS
DIGIMON ZERO TWO
DOLL
DRAGON HUNTER
DRAGON KNIGHTS
DRAGON VOICE
DREAM SAGA
DUKLYON: CLAMP SCHOOL DEFENDERS
EERIE QUEERIE!
ERICA SAKURAZAWA: COLLECTED WORKS
ET CETERA
ETERNITY
EVIL'S RETURN
FAERIES' LANDING
FAKE
FLCL
FORBIDDEN DANCE
FRUITS BASKET
G GUNDAM
GATEKEEPERS
GETBACKERS

GIRL GOT GAME
GRAVITATION
GTO
GUNDAM BLUE DESTINY
GUNDAM SEED ASTRAY
GUNDAM WING
GUNDAM WING: BATTLEFIELD OF PACIFISTS
GUNDAM WING: ENDLESS WALTZ
GUNDAM WING: THE LAST OUTPOST (G-UNIT)
HANDS OFF!
HAPPY MANIA
HARLEM BEAT
I.N.V.U.
IMMORTAL RAIN
INITIAL D
INSTANT TEEN: JUST ADD NUTS
ISLAND
JING: KING OF BANDITS
JING: KING OF BANDITS - TWILIGHT TALES
JULINE
KARE KANO
KILL ME, KISS ME
KINDAICHI CASE FILES, THE
KING OF HELL
KODOCHA: SANA'S STAGE
LAMENT OF THE LAMB
LEGAL DRUG
LEGEND OF CHUN HYANG, THE
LES BIJOUX
LOVE HINA
LUPIN III
LUPIN III: WORLD'S MOST WANTED
MAGIC KNIGHT RAYEARTH I
MAGIC KNIGHT RAYEARTH II
MAHOROMATIC: AUTOMATIC MAIDEN
MAN OF MANY FACES
MARMALADE BOY
MARS
MARS: HORSE WITH NO NAME
METROID
MINK
MIRACLE GIRLS
MIYUKI-CHAN IN WONDERLAND
MODEL
ONE
ONE I LOVE, THE
PARADISE KISS
PARASYTE
PASSION FRUIT
PEACH GIRL
PEACH GIRL: CHANGE OF HEART
PET SHOP OF HORRORS
PITA-TEN
PLANET LADDER
PLANETES
PRIEST

02.03.04T

STOP!

This is the back of the book.
You wouldn't want to spoil a great ending!

This book is printed "manga-style," in the authentic Japanese right-to-left format. Since none of the artwork has been flipped or altered, readers get to experience the story just as the creator intended. You've been asking for it, so TOKYOPOP® delivered: authentic, hot-off-the-press, and far more fun!

DIRECTIONS

1
2
3
4
5
6
7
8
9
10

If this is your first time reading manga-style, here's a quick guide to help you understand how it works.

It's easy... just start in the top right panel and follow the numbers. Have fun, and look for more 100% authentic manga from TOKYOPOP®!

100% AUTHENTIC MANGA
品質第一公式商品